MENDELEYEV

". . . Knowing how contented, joyous, and free is life in the realm of science, one fervently wishes that many would enter its portals."

MENDELEYEV

THE STORY OF A GREAT SCIENTIST

by DANIEL Q. POSIN

WHITTLESEY HOUSE

McGRAW-HILL BOOK COMPANY, INC.

NEW YORK : TORONTO

MENDELEYEV

Copyright, *1948*, *by the* McGraw-Hill Book Company, Inc.

All rights reserved. This book, or parts thereof,
may not be reproduced in any form without permission of the publisher.

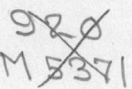

PUBLISHED BY WHITTLESEY HOUSE
A DIVISION OF THE McGraw-Hill Book Company, Inc.

PRINTED IN THE UNITED STATES OF AMERICA

TO THE MEMORY OF MY MOTHER

ANNA

AND MY FATHER

ABRAM

to every Maria and her Mitya
to every Katerina and her Vanya
to every Timofei and his Stepan

this book is dedicated

Preface

DMITRI IVANOVITCH MENDELEYEV was a boy who came out of Siberia, traveled westward to Moscow and St. Petersburg to become one of Russia's greatest scientists. It was he who thought so deeply about the universe that he was able to predict the existence of substances which had never before been seen by man. It was he also who taught his country how to win iron from the Urals, coal from the Donetz Basin, oil from the regions of the Caspian Sea. It was he who exalted the realm of pure science and fervently wished that "many could enter its portals." The Russians finally listened to him, and the country grew industrially, scientifically, and moreover, spiritually, for it was Mendeleyev also who championed the rights of human freedom and protected students from the abuses of the Tsar's regime.

Mendeleyev's chart, evolved into the modern form through the work of Moseley, now hangs in almost every chemistry and physics laboratory in the world. Often, through my years of study I have thought of the Russian scientist, but actually I knew little of him. I halfway expected to probe into his life some day, to uncover the facts behind this obscure genius. One day I read of a contest for books on scientific subjects written for the layman. This was the stimulus I had been waiting for. I entered the contest, I read everything I could get hold of on Mendeleyev and by him—there is no full-length biography in English. Most of this I read in Russian, for I was born in Russia, near the Caspian Sea. And I have lived in Siberia also, and come out of there, it almost seems to me, to tell about the bearded prophet of the snows, the champion of the people. These are the times to tell such a story.

DANIEL Q. POSIN

Acknowledgments

IN WRITING this biography of the Russian scientist Mendeleyev, I have received help from a number of people. The library staff of my college helped by sending for reference books, such as the many volumes of the Journal of the Russian Physico-Chemical Society; my sister Mary looked up original Russian material and sent me notes on it; my brother Jack—head of Stanford University's Russian department—read and criticized a part of the manuscript; my wife Patsy read the original scribbled pages and wrote caustic comments in the margins.

My six-year-old Danny Q. and my four-year-old Kathryn also somehow helped me to write this book. Merely by being so frequently nearby, they seemed to do something to me—and occasionally I to them.

The inspiration to really take hold of the subject and pour the story of Mendeleyev onto paper came to me because of the interest of Miss Beulah Harris, Science Editor of Whittlesey House, who encouraged me in my proposed project and who has now seen it through, to the bitter end.

To all of the people that I mention above, I express my gratitude.

DANIEL Q. POSIN

Contents

Preface vii
Acknowledgments ix

Part I

    I. The Night of 1848 3
   II. Dawn. Maria's Plan 19
  III. The Light in the Window 35
  IV. The Bread on the Window Ledge 40
   V. Timofei, Nadezhda, and the Latin Book . . . 44
  VI. Bassargin's Gift and Mitya's Word for History . . . 52
 VII. To Moscow. And to Nizhny Novgorod 61
VIII. Soldat 75
  IX. Timofei, Nadezhda, and the Strannik 80
   X. Moscow 82
  XI. St. Petersburg 93
 XII. Maria and Elizabeth 101

Part II

 XIII. The Strannik's Story 113
 XIV. The Gold Medal 118
  XV. "Some Spiritual Force" 121
 XVI. Purple Grapes 127
XVII. The Flow of the Tide 133
XVIII. Abroad. And February 19, 1861 138
 XIX. The Road to 1869. The Climb 142
  XX. The Road to 1869. At the Summit 152
 XXI. The Blank Spaces 175
XXII. The Planet Neptune 195
XXIII. Baku, Nizhny Novgorod, America 204
XXIV. Anna Ivanovna Popova 219
 XXV. Mendeleyev and Anna 238
XXVI. To God on a Bubble 255

Contents

XXVII. The Faraday Lecture and Vassya 270
XXVIII. The Petition 283
XXIX. Twilight 289
XXX. The Urals, Tobolsk, Aremziansk 295
XXXI. Shadow 298
XXXII. "Once There Lived and Existed . . ." 310

Appendix I: Principal Published Works of Dmitri Ivanovitch Mendeleyev 321
Appendix II: Bibliography 331
Index 335

MENDELEYEV

PART I

Chapter One

The Night of 1848

THE VILLAGE of Aremziansk, in the area of Tobolsk, slept quietly, unsuspecting. Heavy black night, the cold Siberian night, sat oppressively upon the snow. A frigid breath hovered near the ground. The snow no longer fell from the black space of the sky. It was colder now.

Far out from the Arctic the first penetrating cold air had reached latitude sixty, and unrelenting and tenacious it had rolled in over the unguarded plain. The Ural Mountains to the east sat haughty, snow-bedecked, useless. The mountains, running north and south, stopped nothing but harmless east-west winds and seemed to mock in cruel purposeful jest the cold agony of the peasants of Siberia.

The cold, moving forward over the land, now embraced the Irtysh River. The waters suddenly stiffened, and in a twinkling erected a superficial protective shell—a thin coating of delicate, fragile, nerve-strained ice.

And now the cold air settled around each hut of the village, groped for openings under the doors, stole to the shuttered windows and penetrated the cracks, making convulsive frost designs on the windowpanes. But the windows held firm; the doors were tight. The cold settled, searched, and waited.

In the black of this night, in the heart of this village, a man stood knee-deep in snow. The man was transfixed—as though frozen into a statue of ice; the man was alert, apprehensive, listening. The cold attacked him, but he ignored it. Under his great black coat the cold penetrated his leggings, it bit at the toes of his boots, and in a triumphant shudder it suddenly seemed to reach his flesh everywhere, froze the skeleton of his body, contracted his skull, and pried at his forehead. But the man was indifferent to it. The man was Matvei the Night Watchman, and in his hands lay the fate of the village.

For forty years in the Tobolsk area every *mouzhik*—every peasant—knew that when Matvei was watching the night, all living creatures could sleep in peace. And now Matvei's sharp old eyes narrowed once more as his gaze penetrated the deep black of night, yonder, past the schoolhouse, six versts further east. There, alone, at the foot of a wide snow-smooth hill stood the great successful, productive enterprise—the Glass Factory, on which the livelihood of every being in the village of Aremziansk depended. Matvei had been at the factory only an hour ago, and all had seemed well. But now, as he stood in the heart of the village, he wondered: Was that a rumble? Was it a crash? Or was it a voice out of the night that he had heard? His breath continued to freeze in immediate white tufts, which settled on his beard. He shook the cold out of his body with a tremendous sudden twisting. Then, silently, from a distance, he began to scrutinize the semicircle of huts that stretched before him. His gaze first came to rest on the hut at the left end. . . .

2

In this hut, on the great stone oven that took up nearly one third of the room, slept the gray-bearded Starosta—the Village Elder Ivan Grigorivitch Oblontov—and his old woman Maroosya. Oblontov, president of the village council, was responsible for the collection of taxes and the general policy of village life. His wife assisted him in his work during the wintertime, but during the summer she worked in the fields with the other women of the village in the mornings and at the Glass Factory in the afternoons.

Suddenly she sat up.

"Ivan," she whispered, "my dear Ivan!"

The Starosta stirred in his sleep.

"*Nu chto?*" he mumbled. "What is it?"

"I believe I heard something," said Maroosya. Gazing at the ikon on the wall she crossed herself. "Like a crash, or a great disturbance."

"Sleep," said the Starosta, "Matvei watches the night."

Maroosya lay down. She peered over the edge of the oven, looked for a moment at the two young lambs lying huddled at its base. Her eyes wandered about the dark room and came to rest on the copper samovar.

"Shall I make tea?" she asked. "There are enough glowing coals. We could talk about this noise."

"Sleep," repeated the Starosta. "The noise is in your head. I told you that Matvei watches the night."

The old woman lay down to sleep.

Outside, Matvei shifted his gaze to the second hut. . . .

3

On top of the great oven here slept Timofei Arkadivitch Stepanov, the chief glass blower at the factory. Timofei was a man of great size. As he lay now on the oven his tremendous chest, developed through twenty years of powerful blowing—fashioning bottles of glass—swelled with his deep breathing. The breath, coming in strong blasts out of his mouth, periodically wiggled the ends of his huge brown moustache which was singed near the upper lip. Timofei was a man of great strength. Even at forty he could easily force the shoulders of any man in the village to the ground. But more than a man of strength, Timofei was an artist in his work. The bottles, glassware, and ornaments that his perfectly controlled breath could fashion, and the rolls of glowing cylinders of glass that he could spin on a rod for flattening into windowpanes won the admiration of every artisan in Siberia, all of whom had heard of Timofei of Aremziansk. Timofei, a bachelor, lived for his work, and in every effort sought perfection. He regarded himself as an artist, and with utmost devotion kept his body in excellent health so that his work would be good. Timofei called every man "brother artist," and preached the creed that everything in life, everything in the world, was art. He enjoined his fellow workmen to work harder, think straighter, strive for excellence. And for that he was loved and revered by the village and the entire countryside. Everyone thought of his spirit as unconquerable, of his sincerity as supreme. The Glass Factory was his studio where all his creative instincts found excited, loving expression. Timofei had never married because the woman he once had loved had gradually begun to goad him into seeking another position—a clerical one—which offered greater financial remuneration. He withdrew from her and gave himself more completely to his art.

Next to Timofei on the great oven lay an old man with a white beard and long white locks. The man was a *"strannik,"* a wanderer who had one Sunday appeared at Timofei's door.

"Come in, *dedushka*," said Timofei, extending his hands. "Come in, my little grandfather, and take supper with me."

"Glory to God," replied the strannik, "I have found a true son of Mother Russia."

To Timofei, as to all Russians, a strannik is a relative of all, for he is cast into the world alone, guided by the hand of God. No man turns away a stranger in need. From that day on, the strannik remained with Timofei and filled his house with colorful stories of his pilgrimages and his travels. In the daytime he sat out in the sun and told stories to the village children: of the golden shoes, of the bird of paradise, and the child who went to heaven. At night Timofei would bring his friends to listen to the strannik relate the events in distant parts of Russia—in Nizhny Novgorod, Irkutsk, Moscow.

"From Moscow to Irkutsk is more than five thousand versts," the strannik would say, "and I have traveled that road on foot, and more than once. And many other roads."

Timofei would serve the strannik borsch, and boiled patties, and meat balls dressed in cabbage leaves, and tea from a shining samovar, and a glass dish of cherry jam. The dishes and glassware were those cast and blown by Timofei himself.

"I left my home," said the strannik, "because God came to me one night and told me to go to Jerusalem to pray, and then go out and visit the world, and cheer people, and help them to live. In Jerusalem I got Jordan water. It is here in this tiny bottle. This shirt that I wear bears the official imprint of the Palestine bishop. It is the shirt in which I will be buried, and when I wash it I dry it immediately and put it on again, so when my time comes I shall have it on."

"Tell my friends about Nizhny Novgorod," said Timofei one night.

"Never will I forget," said the strannik. "At every Nizhny fair, the sky is filled with singing birds. There stands a man with a great many cages, and if you give him ten kopeks out fly the birds and sing with the greatest beauty, and then fly back into the cage."

"What else?" encouraged Timofei.

"Whatever you may wish," said the strannik, "you will find there. One Easter morning I knocked on the door of an *izba*, a simple hut. A healthy woman came to the door. 'The Christ is arisen,' I said. 'Indeed he is arisen!' she replied. 'Come on in, little father.' And then we sat down to eat, a meal to make the Tsar wet his whiskers with drooling saliva. A tremendous brown goose filled with all sorts of sweet things, bread of white flour, and a bowl of sour cream, and a pitcher of fermented beet juice, the most delightful *kvahs* that has ever wet my innards. And a cake made of frozen cream, and ice dipped in golden honey."

"You better stop," laughed Timofei, swallowing deliciously. "*Ekh* father, you have seen the world."

"Then at night," said the strannik, "we ate a gorgeous pirog—one of the solidest meat pies I have ever pushed into me. And vermicelli cooked with milk, and sugar squashes. And tea from a shining samovar. Then we went out to see the people at the Nizhny fair. *Ai*, brother, there you have people. And red ones, and yellow ones, and white ones, and blue eyes, and yellow eyes, and round eyes, and squint eyes. And the hair! Golden hair and black hair, Chinese, and Kirghiz, and Turkmen, and Great Russian. There you must go before you die."

"I will," said Timofei.

"Well," said the strannik, "and a peaceful night to you now, dear people. A peaceful night."

The Night of 1848

The strannik breathed softly as he slept. Timofei continued to blow out his breath in great gusts, occasionally snoring. On the walls hung the glass ornaments and bowls that he had made. Over the door were suspended several old gourds and ancient bottles of skins—a part of Timofei's museum of receptacles. The samovar stood silent on the heavy wooden table.

Outside, Matvei turned toward the next izba. . . .

4

On the great oven slept two men and a pig. The pig lay quietly in the arms of the younger man. This man had a pale round face and an abrupt nose. He was Vanka the Fool—the village dolt. Simple of mind, carefree, uninhibited, black-haired Vanka was devoted with all his heart to horses, cows, sheep, hens, pigs, dogs—all animals and birds. He talked to them, and they listened. He fed them and advised them and preached to them. He washed them and combed them, and tended to their bruised feet and all their ills. The horses and cows and pigs and hens and dogs loved Vanka, and followed him everywhere he went, and listened to him intently, soberly, and accepted his advice and recommendations whenever they were not too busy. No one in the village abused Vanka, for the simple people need special help and therefore receive the guidance of God and are holy.

Vanka was twenty-five years old now, and his father, Andrei the Chemist, had long ago given his son completely over to nature and God. Andrei was tired and aged—nearly seventy—and could well have relied on a strong son to help him in his difficult labors at the Glass Factory where he lifted and carried huge sacks of silica sand which he purified through long and difficult processes. But Vanka would die if he were to work indoors away from his animals. Only when Andrei would mix chemicals into the molten glass and create colors of violet and yellow and deep green in the molten mass would Vanka the Fool pop his eyes in childish glee and babble, "*Kraseevo.* [How pretty.] *Ai, kraseevo.*" Then out he would run past rows of glass panes, and shelves stacked with china, out into the village yard to his devoted friends.

On the wooden bed near the oven slept black-haired Katerina, Vanka's mother, Andrei's wife. Katerina, who had married off three daughters, loved Vanka more than she had loved any of her girls.

"He asks nothing," Katerina would often say. "He requires nothing. Some day, somewhere, a person with a heart of stone will abuse my darling Vanya." And here Katerina would burst into tears, and dab her eyes with her rose-colored apron, and blow her nose into it.

"If I can only marry him off to a good solid woman before I die," Katerina would go on, "that is all I ask of the Lord."

From this endeavor to find Vanka a wife, and also from her successful experience in placing her daughters, Katerina had become the village matchmaker, and occasionally earned ten roubles for her efforts. But since this work was sporadic and unreliable as an income, it was on Andrei's work at the Glass Factory that the fortunes of the family depended. But he was old and tired, deeply tired.

Andrei slept quietly. Vanka, in his sleep, talked softly to the pig lying in his arms. Vanka was consoling the pig, and the pig slept well. The night was growing colder. The walls were beginning to creak. . . .

In the snow, in the center of the village, Matvei the Night Watchman shifted and gazed at the next hut—a larger one, the double-roomed izba of the manager of the Glass Factory.

5

The front room was large. At one end stood the great clay oven; on top of the oven two forms were reposing—slight, slender forms, one not fully grown. Through the open door of the second room a wooden bed could be seen. There slept a brown-haired hawk-nosed man and a woman with long yellow hair. In the front room, opposite the oven, stood a narrow wooden bed; it was empty, with the covers thrown back.

In the middle of the room, silent and motionless, stood a woman, clothed in a tightly enveloping blue nightgown that covered her from head to foot, with sleeves to the wrists. She was slight and dark, with full black hair that reached beyond the middle of her back. She was not young; she was fifty-six years old. Her face was tense, her eyes narrow and Oriental, although she did not seem Oriental. Her nose was regular, Caucasian, her face strong, alert, and apprehensive. Her hands were to her heart; she stood rigid, listening, listening to the night.

In the veins of this woman flowed Asian bloods. Hundreds of years ago, out of the Gobi Desert, came a Mongol horde. From the distant ends of Asia and from the regions of Lake Baikal the vast multiplying narrow-eyed race flowed westward across Asia. In a path of blood, these subjects of the warrior Genghis Khan spread wildly, cutting and burning all before them. In an epic struggle during the thirteenth century, the yellow horde mutilated the warriors of Russia. Then suddenly the Mongol onrush abated, the relentless tide turned back, dispersed, thinned out. But during its westward advance portions of the clan intermingled with the west-Asian population and mixed blood with the Turks as the invasion approached the vast southern spaces.

Those that remained developed further the strain of the Turk, settled, found time to exploit the soil, fish in the rivers, follow the flocks. But the love of the wild charge on the back of a flying horse remained, the steel muscles and limitless endurance hardly abated, and the slant of the eyes persisted. These were the Tartars; by Greek mythology: dwellers out of hell. Feared, despised, and despising. The history of Russia was fashioned by their early blood-letting triumphs.

Of such ancestors—descendant of a Kirghiz Tartar beauty and a Russian of the west—was the woman standing in the hut. She was Maria Dmitrievna Korniliev, mother of fourteen children and widow of the west-Russian scholar Ivan Pavlovitch Mendeleyev.

After Ivan's death, only a year ago, Maria's brother Vassili, who lived in Moscow and was owner of the Glass Factory, proposed that Maria, who was manager, be considered essentially the owner. The men at the factory worked harder now, for many of them had once been serfs but Maria had freed them and began to pay them wages. Maria worked. Her mind had a purpose, and for this reason the work went better than ever before. Her purpose went beyond the mere necessity of sustaining her family. The factory, and every pane of glass and every dish and goblet produced, were an investment eventually to be converted to the scientific education of one child, the youngest and dearest to Maria. Somehow, nearly all the others had gone their way. Grown, they overflowed into the city of Tobolsk and beyond—lost in the wide reaches of Russia. For some time there remained near Maria three girls and two boys. There was the yellow-haired Olga—visiting now from near-by Yaloutorovsk—sleeping on the bed with her husband, the political exile Bassargin the Decembrist, one of the men who in December, 1825, took part in a fruitless uprising against Tsar Nicholas the First. Another daughter had been Apollinaria the religious fanatic, who only recently had died of tuberculosis. The third daughter was Elizabeth the gentle, the delicate, and shy, needing Maria's unfailing care, sleeping now on the great oven. Then at the far end of the oven, next to the warm clay wall, slept Mitya, the youngest, aged fourteen, Maria's Mitenka, her treasure, her heart, the final expression of love of her soul. In the city of Tobolsk at the moment was Paul, the blond high-school student.

Standing in the middle of the room, Maria now turned slowly and gazed at her sleeping Mitya.

Mitya's soft blond hair fell down over his broad brow and prominent forehead. His head was large and symmetrical. The pert, precise, well-molded features, the nose which promised one day to be strong and audacious, the soft red lips which seemed to quiver slightly as Mitya slept, all bespoke a healthy organism and a sensitive reflective temperament. Were

Mitya awake now, Maria would see his lively, shining sky-blue eyes and the understanding smile that he unconsciously reserved for her, and that so clearly revealed the rapport between mother and son.

Mitya, from earliest years, was a vivacious, lively boy, gay and carefree, who leaped about in the open fields like an animal, who roamed incessantly in the forests among the larch and cedar trees, picking off the cones and rolling about on the ground, on the long brown needles that strewed the forest floor in the autumn. Frequently, he climbed the sturdiest larch trees, and sitting hidden under a roof of green, looked musingly out past the forest, into the limitless beyond. Often, too, he would lie at the base of a tree, lost in thought, absent-mindedly prying with one hand the thin scaly bark from the fragrant trunk. The love of the deep strong land of Siberia gradually grew in his soul.

From his earliest years Mitya constantly amazed those about him by joining intelligently in the conversation of grownups, by asking mature questions, by remembering without error—for those who forgot—the names, dates, and exact numbers of all sorts of people, events, and things. By the age of seven, he was surprisingly advanced in arithmetical calculations and often performed mentally reckonings for the peasants of the village and planners at the Glass Factory.

In his jaunty walk, in the quick movements of his hands, as well as in the lively play of his reflective face, one sensed a temperament of agility and purposefulness. Mitya, the descendant of the daring and unrelenting Tartar warriors, and Mitya the descendant of the strong western Slavs, seemed to have inherited not only all these qualities but also seemingly something out of the air of Russia, out of its forests and plains, out of the heart of Russia. Maria sensed this before her boy was five years old and solemnly resolved that, come what may, Mitya should be given every love, every opportunity, and every aid to express his life in all its benevolent beauty. Maria took upon herself what she considered a sacred God-given obligation.

Of all the serious activities of men at work, Mitya was attracted most by the bustle and vivid excitement of the making of glass ornaments and windowpanes at the factory. From the time that he could walk he began to comprehend the world of industry, and by the age of seven he could discuss the dexterous glass-handling operations with the men.

It was from Bassargin the Decembrist that Mitya received his special interest in science. Banished to a Siberian prison, Bassargin emerged after nine years to plunge into the intellectual activity of the frozen East, preached that "youth must revolt against traditional authority," that the confusions of the world will come closer to being resolved when mysticism is made to yield to science.

The Night of 1848

"Everything in the world is science," sternly affirmed Bassargin.

"Everything in the world is art," Timofei the Glass Blower frequently told Mitya.

"Everything in the world is love," Maria time and again would whisper to her boy.

Mitya wondered. The tiny wheels of his mind turned.

Tonight he slept. Occasionally, a barely perceptible sigh came from within him.

6

In the center of the village, in the snow, Matvei the Night Watchman, preparing to scrutinize the other huts, suddenly was alerted by another rumble from the left—the direction of the Glass Factory. There was no mistaking it now, and Matvei, lighting his red lantern, began to hurry through the snow toward his home. For an instant, as he passed the chapel on the hill—its snow-laden roof weakly reflecting the red rays of the lantern—Matvei stopped, pulled off his fur hat, and crossed himself. Hurriedly, before the cold had discovered his vulnerability, he replaced his hat and set off once more toward his hut. At his very door a large white hare hopped across Matvei's path and vanished into the dark. He shuddered at this omen of ill fortune, mumbled a curse under his breath, and flinging the heavy door open, burst into his hut.

Marfa, his thin wrinkled wife, with a sudden escape of breath, clasped her heart.

"*Bozhe moi!*" [God of mine!] "What brings you at this moment? What is wrong?"

"I don't know," said Matvei, shaking his head. "There is some sort of noise. From the direction of the factory. The people sleep. They depend on me. Hurry, *baba*, come on, woman, help me with the wagon."

"But first some tea," entreated Marfa. "The samovar is hot."

"No, no!" urged Matvei. "Come on!"

In the barn behind the house, Matvei roused the brown horse, Soldat, and backed him in between two shafts attached to the wagon—the all-wooden telega. The horse was stubborn. Slyly he tried to draw away from the telega. The barn was warm, and the horse knew that outside the Arctic air had come. He whinnied softly and tried to pull away toward his sleeping corner and the warm straw. But Matvei caught him up harshly and backed him in again between the shafts.

"Come on, brother," he threatened softly. "This is no time for fooling. Back up. Back up."

Marfa helped to tie the horse in, and Matvei climbed onto the wagon, took the reins.

"*Davai!*" he shouted. "Give! let 'er go!"

Slowly the telega rattled out of the barn.

Marfa closed the barn door. "*Ai*, mouzhik," she murmured, "how you work!"

In the open blackness, Matvei goaded the horse to more effort.

"Come on, dear little pigeon," he begged. "We've got to see what's going on. Come on, now, a little faster."

The horse paid no attention and continued his comfortable trot.

Matvei fidgeted on his perch. Squinting, he looked hard, eastward. But the night was black; it seemed solid, impenetrable.

Once more Matvei appealed to the horse.

"A little faster, companion," he said. "What does it cost you to go faster?"

The horse pretended not to hear.

And now Matvei was almost beside himself with impatience and anger.

"I'm trying to be good to this creature," he said to himself. "But he's against me. Ah yes. Well, we'll see."

Matvei stood up and took a breath of cold air.

"Hurry up, you *svolatch!*" he roared at the horse. "What are you doing—playing the fool!"

The horse went faster.

Matvei remained standing, occasionally slapping the horse with the reins, as the telega rolled through the snow.

In a few moments the horse made a turn round a hill and ran past an abandoned hut. Once, many years ago, Matvei had lived there with his father, a serf who had run away to become a Cossack.

But Matvei had no time to muse on this now. . . .

The telega rolled past, onward through the snow.

Suddenly, the horse made a turn round another hill. What Matvei now saw froze his heart like no cold of Siberia ever could. The Glass Factory was in flames.

In a moment, turning without a stop, Matvei's horse raced full speed back to the village. Grim, stunned, white-faced, full-bearded Matvei sat rigid on the wagon perch while the brown perspiring horse, with popping eyes and breath that froze at its nostrils, raced madly for the village. . . .

7

Into every izba, into every heart in the village, penetrating all sleep, suddenly came the clanging of a cold steel bell. Startled out of their sleep, the men and the women rose up in their beds or bestirred themselves on the ovens, opened wide their eyes, and listened. The children, puzzled, studied the faces of their parents.

In the first hut, the Village Elder—the Starosta Oblontov—slid off the oven, briskly began to pull his heavy black trousers over his thin legs and white sleeping pants. Maroosya, his old woman, sat upright, her face in tense alarm.

"What do you think?" she whispered. "What do you think, my dear Ivan?"

The Starosta reached for his boots. For a moment he held them in his hands, quietly listening to the bell.

"It's bad," he said. "There is no time to waste."

Only twice before within the Starosta's memory had the bell ever rung out at night. Each time it had been Matvei who had wakened the people; the first time, as a youth in 1812, when Napoleon was in Moscow and the holy city of churches was burning to the ground, he had sounded the alarm in medium tempo. The Starosta knew then that a catastrophe was befalling Mother Russia, but a remote catastrophe, something that the villagers could do nothing about, for the bell had been mournful, casual, weeping.

Then, on a night in December, 1825, Matvei had again stood in the snow and rung the bell. Plainly the Starosta recalled how slowly the bell had rung on that night. Painful, funeral-slow had been the message of the death of Tsar Alexander the First.

The Starosta's eyes met the gaze of his wife.

"This is different," he said. "We must hurry."

In the second hut, Timofei the Glass Blower was almost dressed. His heart was pounding wildly, in unison with the ringing alarm. The strannik, too, was dressing, stuffing his heavy blue pants into his boots.

"This is a summons," he whispered. "Ekh, Timofei, this bell is alive."

In the third hut Old Andrei the Chemist was thrusting his right arm into his overcoat.

"It's calling for an effort," he said hurriedly, his voice trembling. "There's something we can do."

Katerina was rapidly tying a brown ropelike belt about her waist; the heavy green dress now formed itself into two parts—a blouse at the top and a straight skirt below, reaching past her knees to the tops of the high galoshes.

"You stay right up on the oven," she advised her son, Vanka the Fool. "Stay there, my Vanya. It is nothing. Just a bell."

Vanka lay down. He covered the pig with a short red quilt.

"It's nothing," said Vanka to the drowsy animal. "A pretty bell. You sleep."

The door of the fourth hut, the hut of the manager of the Glass Factory, was opening. For a moment Maria stopped for a last word to her yellow-haired daughter, Olga.

"It is too cold," she said. "You stay in. And in the morning prepare Mitya some *kasha*; and two eggs. Some compote. Stay in the hut."

The cold air rolled into the hut past Maria. She slammed the door behind her. Disregarding the cold, Olga scrambled out of bed.

"I'm not staying," she said. "Whatever it is, I'm going to be there."

Bassargin the Decembrist, Olga's husband, was almost ready to go too. Scowling, he was searching for his fur hat.

"The devil take it!" he grumbled. "Where did I put it?"

"I'm going, too," said Mitya, and slid down off the oven.

"Mama wants you to stay here," admonished Olga.

"Listen," said Mitya. The bell was clanging now without pause. "And you want me to stay?"

Over the doors of the huts lanterns were coming to sudden twinkling life, like stars emerging abruptly out of a black sky. The people of the village were in motion. Word had come from Matvei—standing up there in the bell tower of the church—word of the fire.

"The Glass Factory!" wept Katerina. "My poor Andrei's chemicals. *Ai, ai, ai.*"

Horses were being harnessed to telegas, to tarantasses with their tinkling bells, to great blue sleds.

Timofei, in boots, trousers, and heavy red shirt, was shouting orders, organizing the vehicles, directing the pooling of the sleds, forming teams of fire fighters.

Bassargin, bareheaded, was out in a short fur coat.

"Buckets!" he yelled. "This way! All buckets. Hurry, hurry, the devil take it! Hurry!"

Maria, breathless, ran up to him, caught him by the sleeve.

"Mitya says the pumps may be frozen out there. Call for water."

"Water!" shouted Bassargin. "Buckets with the water! And barrels! With water!"

The Starosta Oblontov suddenly appeared out of the dark. He was carrying a tub of water that splashed over his coat and his boots.

"They will be frozen. The pumps out there. I know. Eh, Vasska, take hold. Help me here."

"Get Pavel's horse!" shouted Timofei over the milling crowd. "He's strong."

"I'll go," said the strannik, and disappeared into the night.

Andrei the Old Chemist was bringing extra quantities of chemicals to fight the fire. The seventy-year-old man worked quickly, accurately.

"Katerina!" he shouted. "Bring the yellow can too. *Bozhe moi!* Look at Vanya!"

Vanka the Fool, the beloved simpleton of Andrei and Katerina, was dashing about barefoot in his black overcoat, his night shirt hanging out down to his ankles. He was cheering the horses, throwing blankets on them to keep them warm.

"The pig is inside," he told Katerina. "He's too little to help."

The strannik returned with a great white horse and with Timofei's help began to harness the animal to a sled heavily laden with tubs of water.

The Starosta Oblontov and his wife tugged at an ancient sled in their barn.

"Maybe you better be out with the people," she advised. "You are the Starosta."

"No," said Oblontov. "I am letting Timofei take charge. His head is young. Now let's grab the sled right here. Pull! *Davai!*"

Outside, Bassargin rushed past, caught a rearing horse by the muzzle, began to force him backward between the shafts of a telega.

"Get in there, brother!" he commanded. "This is no time to play the fool."

The ringing bell suddenly ceased its clamor.

Up in the tower of the church, on the hill, Matvei, having given his horse, Soldat, and telega to Old Andrei, now left his post and hurried to his barn. Marfa his wife had already harnessed a second horse.

"*Gotovo*," she said. "It's ready. *Ai*, mouzhik, mouzhik, what is to become of us!"

"Get on," Matvei told her. "We have to get water."

Marfa scrambled onto the wagon and lay down flat on it, mumbling to herself.

"*Davai!*" Matvei ordered the horse, "come on, my little pigeon."

The horse barely stirred. . . .

In front of the Mendeleyev hut, Mitya's sisters Olga and Elizabeth carried piles of empty sacks to a waiting telega. Mitya, with two other boys, had just broken into a locked barn. And now they took hold of an ancient portable pump, for the great wooden tub of water was already tied to a fire-fighting sled.

Maria came rushing to a group piled into a telega, ready to go.

"Be careful," she pleaded. "Please be careful."

The horse suddenly reared. Maria clutched at the reins.

"No, no," she soothed the nervous animal. "What is it, you poor fellow? No harm, no harm."

Suddenly, the entire milling mob of men and animals was ready, and above the jabber came Timofei's voice.

"*Davai!*" he roared. "Give it to them! Let's go!"

The snorting horses rushed out into the night, the telegas, the tarantasses, the sleds, all full of nerve-strained men and women and children. After them came many others, hurrying on foot. The bells of the tarantasses tinkled merrily in the night, as the drivers called to their horses to go faster; first lovingly, with praise, then yipping at them with angry oaths and curses.

At the first great bend around a snow-laden hill, a sudden reddish sky appeared, and columns of dark smoke.

"*Bozhe moi!*" [God of mine!] wept Katerina the village Matchmaker. "*Ai, ai, ai.*"

8

The Glass Factory, a wooden structure almost a block square and surmounted by a giant smokestack, was completely enveloped in orange and red flames. They darted out of the numerous windows, stabbed into the black night, momentarily subsided, then fiercely darted out again. The snow on the roof was melting rapidly and the water descended in a steamlike hiss down the sides of the crackling wooden building.

Scores of men and women were throwing bucketfuls of water at the waving flames springing from the building. Men carried water from the sleds and telegas, and some from a tiny shed where an insulated pump had not frozen. There, the thin Bassargin, stripped to the waist, was pumping savagely, the squeaking noise urging him more desperately. Olga burst into the shed.

"Timofei has just gone into the building!" she announced.

"What are you saying!" exclaimed the perspiring hawk-nosed Bassargin. "He'll be burned alive. Take the pump!"

Bassargin rushed out bare-waisted into the snow. Olga came running after him, carrying his heavy coat. "You'll freeze!" she cried. "Wait! Wait!"

At that moment the fiery door at the left end of the building flew open and Timofei appeared shrouded in flame. He, too, was stripped to the waist, his huge chest glowed from the reflection of the flames, his trousers were on fire. On his back he carried a huge glass-polishing table, loaded with sacks of chemicals. He came slowly out of the fire, lowered the table onto the ground, then rolled in the snow to extinguish the flames about his legs.

Maria Mendeleyev rushed up to him.

"Don't," she begged. "Don't go in there any more. The hot gases may damage your lungs. Don't go!"

The Night of 1848

But Timofei, heedless, rushed back into the burning building.

Then suddenly an upper storeroom inside began to collapse, and tons of glass, spilling over one side, tumbled in a great continuing roar to the floor below. The tinkling crescendo, gaining momentum, sounded like a rushing glassfall.

Men were now throwing water more wildly than before, and sprays descended increasingly upon the snorting horses, in a moment converting their dark coats to white, thin layers of ice.

Matvei the Night Watchman, was casting great buckets of fire-fighting chemicals at the flames, which Andrei the Old Chemist continued to mix on his telega.

An exhausted mouzhik stopping to drink vodka from a green bottle pulled out of his blouse suddenly spilled the invigorating liquid onto the snow.

"Ai, ai, ai," he moaned, and rushed back to help Mitya work the pump on the great water-filled tub.

The fire gained. Maria stood in front of the blazing building.

"Timofei!" she called. "Timofei!"

And suddenly Timofei reappeared, carrying another glass-polishing table on his back. His hair was on fire, and Nadezhda the daughter of Anton the Furnace Man, rushed to him, rubbed his head with snow, kissed him on the lips.

"*Ai, krasaveetz,*" [You handsome creature] she bubbled. "But it's no use."

Then out of the night there appeared a woman in a white robe. This was Avdotya, the religious fanatic to whose cult Mitya's sister, Apollinaria, had belonged to the day of her death. With wild eyes, dark and flowing black hair, she came across the snow toward the fire, a large yellow cross of gold in her uplifted right hand.

"Sinners!" she screamed. "To the chapel! To God. To God's glory. Follow me, sinners! Follow me!"

Timofei's strannik and the Starosta Oblontov, exhausted from carrying buckets of water, leaned against a sled, dazedly throwing handfuls of snow at the fire.

Then suddenly, out of the night, came Vanka the Fool, still barefooted and clad in his black coat, carrying the pig in his arms.

"See," he whispered to the drowsy animal, "*kraseevo.* [Pretty.] Pretty fire."

The fire continued to gain. The yellow and red and orange flames raced each other skyward. A column of white smoke climbed upward from one end of the building. Nothing came out of the silent gigantic furnace chimney.

From under the flaming doors molten glass slowly began to ooze. Then without warning a huge shaft of purple flame reached for the heavens. The color was dazzling. Mitya stopped pumping, entranced.

"Potassium," he whispered. Hurrying over to Andrei the Old Chemist, he asked, "It is potassium, Andrei, am I right?"

"Yes," nodded the exhausted Andrei. And in the next instant a column of bright red leaped at the sky.

"*Bozhe moi!*" wept Andrei. "It has reached my coloring trays. *Ai, ai, ai.*"

In quick succession, yellow, and ruby, and green columns burst from the burning building.

"Copper," whispered Mitya. Absent-mindedly he walked toward the conflagration.

"But this bluish gold," he mused, "what can that be? How strange. Andrei! *Ekh* Andrei! Where are you?"

The fire now ravaged relentlessly. To fight it was hopeless. Men ceased carrying water. For a while they stood dazed, unthinking. Then, the men and the women crawled onto the telegas and tarantasses and into the sleds. Silently they watched the flames reach a mountainous climax. The heat reached the people and warmed them. But the people were sick. They despised the heat. The women wept, and their tears did not freeze now, for their flesh was warm.

The flames exhausted themselves and fell to the ground, melting a great area of snow. In the weakly burning debris great clay crucibles now appeared, undamaged. The crucibles and the tables rescued by Timofei remained.

Bassargin, sneering, stood with his arm around Mitya.

"That was to provide your University education," said Bassargin.

Mitya stood silent. Maria, his mother, stood deep in the snow, watching the hot red shambles.

Vanka the Fool sat in a sled, the pig in his arms. And suddenly, from deep within his heart, from within the soul of him, for he was a man, he began to weep. Somehow, mysteriously, inexplicably, Vanka the Fool understood. Something had gripped his heart, and the tears came in a stream from his little eyes. He wept. He wept like a man. He wept with all his inner self. For the Glass Factory, and the people, and Mitya, and for the little pig in his arms, and for the whole village he wept, and for the serfs, and for all of Russia, the bloody, ages-suffering Russia, for her wept Vanka the Man, Vanka the Heart, for the misery of Russia he wept, and the aimless life and meaningless death. And thus wept Vanka for the world.

Chapter Two

Dawn. Maria's Plan

IN THE east, a faint light softly filtered into the sky. The people had gone back to their huts. Suddenly, without warning, their source of livelihood had vanished. The black bread, the meat, the potatoes, the cabbage—where would a man now do a day's work, to earn the right to keep body and soul together? To the huts went the people—a man had to think. This was a time for thinking. . . .

At the place where the Glass Factory had stood, three men, a boy, and a woman remained. Leaning against their telegas, they gazed silently upon the vast space of glowing embers and smoldering wood. Matvei was there, the strannik too, and Bassargin, and Maria, and Mitya. The strannik's white locks were dirty with soot. His benign ancient face was infinitely more ancient now, after the weary night. The weak light of dawn dimly illuminated his tired face and lusterless deep-set eyes.

"There is too much sadness here in Siberia," said the strannik softly. "Life is too hard to keep together. In all my travels I have never seen life so heavy or so little joy in living. In Nizhny Novgorod, my dear ones, people sing. The gypsies dance. Wonderful, happy gypsies. Costumes of color. And Turks with their turbans, and Tartars in gilded boots. And the hundred races of all Russia in native costume. The people live. There is laughter."

Slowly he shook his head. His tired eyes gazed upon the quietly burning wood before him.

"And there is fire," said the strannik. "*Akh*, yes, there is fire, but fire of happiness. On some holidays the people near the Caspian Sea bring great barrels of oil to the waters. There is oil in the ground there, my dear people. Uncounted quantities of oil. Great barrels of it are thrown onto the waters, and at night a lighted taper is thrown on the sea. *Akh*, yes, there is fire. But no one weeps at the fire. It is a fire of joy. The entire sea bursts into flames of blue. That is a sight to behold. But here, all is cold, cruel, barren. And now your fire has burned out your lives. Why does God do this? Why did God invent Siberia?"

2

Matvei thought of the words of the strannik. Yes, life here was a burden. Life here was a struggle. But never had Matvei known life of any other sort. True, his father, who had escaped from serfdom to join a Cossack tribe, had seen adventure. With other escaped serfs, turned Cossacks, he joined the romantic men on horseback and sold his services to the military Chieftain Grigory. There were enough wars everywhere, continuously, both in and out of Siberia and Russia, to provide employment for great numbers of such gay mounted killers. On the western front alone, before, during, and after the reign of Ivan the Terrible, in the course of ninety years, forty-five had passed in an active state of war. In the south of Russia, too, there was occupation for the Cossacks, who charged to battle against the remaining Tartars caught besieging villages and kidnaping young Russian girls. Matvei's father, roaming the expanse of Russia with his Cossack band, had had his share of near-mortal combat, and clearly could Matvei remember the scars of battle on his father's face and arms and chest. There were stories for Matvei too, told by his father, of great migrations on horseback with the Cossack clan, to the Altai Mountains where the westward-spreading rich black soil begins—a heritage of the glacial crushing of rocks and trees.

On a day when the Chieftain Grigory fell in battle, Matvei's father assumed command and, seeking new fields of combat, led his men to the south, to the Caspian Sea where great winds and barren earth and lakes of salt water stretched everywhere before them.

Thus through the long years Matvei's father galloped with his men over these vast steppes, from the treeless regions of the black-soil plains to the treeless expanse of the salty south.

But one day he returned to the estate from which he had fled. In the dead of night, disguised as a soldier, he quietly stole his family away on a sled drawn by his warrior horse. He settled in a hut in the little village of Aremziansk, hundreds of miles away, adopted a pseudonym, and contrived to live a life of quiet freedom. There Matvei grew up and at the age of twenty he married and moved to his own izba with his bride Marfa.

But life in Siberia had not been easy. A man fought constantly for existence. Was there another way to live? The strannik affirmed that there was. But now had come this fire. Matvei was the Night Watchman. Was he responsible? And still how could one man be everywhere? Who was responsible?

Matvei gazed hypnotized at the glowing embers. How could one live another way? his mind repeated. Where should one go? Perhaps the strannik could tell him. But there was Marfa—she would not leave the village. Already Marfa had picked out her burial spot and had saved twenty roubles for her funeral. Perhaps a man should remain where he was born, live as he could, then die. In the same village. Perhaps on the same spot.

3

The glowing embers held the fascinated gaze of Maria Mendeleyev too. Confused, dazed by the struggle against the fire, she was nevertheless acutely conscious of the double loss—the means of livelihood for the village and the money for Mitya's university education. But Maria was a woman who rejected defeat.

The family Korniliev, in whose line of ancestry once lived a Kirghiz Tartar beauty, had settled in central Siberia, in Tobolsk, early in the seventeenth century. The family was shrewd, energetic, able to appraise the great undeveloped, wooded spaces, the empty, snow-covered, limitless distances. They turned with purpose to the development of the land long regarded by the Tsars as suitable only for banished criminals and exiled political dreamers who advocated the emancipation of Russian serfs and clamored for a constitutional republic. In these wild, thinly populated areas, the Korniliev family built the first plants for the manufacture of paper and glass. Here, later, in 1787, the merchant Korniliev, father of Maria, established the first Siberian printing press, simultaneously with Benjamin Franklin in America, and two years later brought forth an amazing product in this benighted land—a newspaper. It was called the "Irtysh," for the river that flowed past Tobolsk, bringing communion by boat between neighboring villages.

But the merchant Korniliev, after the death of his young wife, began to suffer in health, and with the failing of his hearing and accompanying mental confusion and loss of memory the family enterprises lost vigor and direction. Soon only the Glass Factory remained as a means of sustenance, in the village of Aremziansk, seventeen miles outside of "metropolitan" Tobolsk.

The care of the home and her ailing father prevented Maria from attending school. Besides, she was a woman, and this was Russia, moreover—Siberia; so fate had prepared for her not intellectual enlightenment, but serfdom at home. But Maria was one of those women who have a way of circumventing fate. Her narrow eyes narrowed further, her heart beat with firm challenge, and she set about educating herself. Night after night, year after year, she studied the lessons that her brother Vassili learned at school and carefully read every book he brought to the house.

Inevitably Maria grew strong-willed and self-reliant, confident, enlightened, and sympathetic. Then it was that, grown to dark lovely womanhood, one day she encountered in Tobolsk a sturdy-shouldered, blond, blue-eyed

Slav. This was a man of the ancient peasant peoples, the cultivators of the soil who originated in the regions between Lithuania and the Carpathian Mountains, and settled along the rivers Vistula and Dnieper and the Dniester. Many of these Slavs found their way to the Baltic, where they built great open boats, sailed the seas, and survived on the fish of the waters. These were the "Rus," originating in the word "Rothsmen"—Men of the Sea. The land that these Rus came to inhabit as they spread inland from the Baltic coasts came to be known as "Russia."

It was such a Slav, a western Russian, who won the heart of Maria. He was a scholar from St. Petersburg, and his knowledge and intellect opened the wellsprings of Maria's heart. He had an irresistible attraction which found a sympathetic reaction in her spirit. He had started life at a handicap, a menial trader in horses. This man, Ivan, was the son of Pavel Maximovitch Sokolov of the Province of Tver, a member of the lower clergy in the Greek Church. Pavel could marry inasmuch as celibacy is not obligatory for the lower clergy of this church, and he eventually became the father of four sons.

Of these four brothers Ivan early became fond of horses and became a dealer, specializing in exchanges. As so readily happens in Russia, Ivan's business gave him a new surname—for "menyat" means "to change," and "delo" means "business"; so that presently Ivan came to be known as "Mendeleyev." And this surname replaced Sokolov.

But a spirit stirred within Ivan and one day, forsaking his trade and selling his horses, he made his way to St. Peterburg. There, in the city built by Peter the Great, Ivan Pavlovitch Mendeleyev entered the Chief Pedagogical Institute, and plunged into a world of words instead of horses. He studied philosophy and the fine arts, political economy, logic, and Russian literature.

Time passed, the snows fell, the mind of Ivan grew keener, the frame of Ivan filled out to a happy solidity—and then the day came when Ivan was considered the man for a difficult job: a teaching position which might lead to the directorship of the secondary school—or Gymnasium—at Tobolsk, Siberia, and government school director. Ivan went to Tobolsk.

This was the man, the Slav scholar, who in Tobolsk captivated Maria Dmitrievna Korniliev.

Ivan's scholarly mind longed for the associations and academic facilities of the more advanced cities of Russia, and it was with happy anticipations that he was transferred—after seven years at Tobolsk—to a school directorship at Tambov, and later at Saratov. Children were born. But Maria could not forget her home in Siberia and not too long afterward Ivan took her back to Tobolsk, where he became director of the college. Ivan and Maria now settled down permanently in the Tobolsk area. More children were born, the last one, Mitya, in 1834 when Maria was forty-two years old.

Dawn. Maria's Plan

Their home drew the foremost intellectuals of Tobolsk. The spirit of the mother was always buoyant, the quiet devotion of the father to knowledge and learning was a subtle inspiration, and they attracted high government educators and authorities, aspiring artists and students. Also the banished revolutionaries, the Men of December, gathered there.

Gradually, after 1834, Ivan began to suffer impairment of vision and in a few years became completely blind. He was forced to resign his position and the family prepared to live on the pension of one thousand roubles a year—about five hundred dollars.

In addition to the burdens of rearing her brood of children, Maria now contended with the calamity that befell her Ivan. Furthermore, she worked at the Glass Factory, but her spirit remained unbroken. In 1837 Ivan was taken to Moscow where a successful operation was performed on his eyes, but his body yielded to further ills, and in 1847, after years of ravage by tuberculosis, Ivan Pavlovitch Mendeleyev, né Sokolov, died.

There was no time for the luxury of long mourning and grief. Maria had to work. Maria had to care for her family. Maria had to provide for the education of as many of her children as possible. Above all, the house of the late Ivan Pavlovitch Mendeleyev must remain a center of intellectual advancement and enlightenment so that the children would have every opportunity to learn about life and the world.

Maria, drudging at home, still found time to manage the Glass Factory owned by her brother, who lived far away. The profits from the factory were to serve, above all other considerations, as the means for providing the higher education, university study at Moscow, for the gifted Mitya.

Maria looked up from the red coals. The bleak Siberian sun was there ahead, barely perceptible through the cold frosty air. Into her eyes there gradually came a light. An idea had grown in her mind. An idea which no calamity, no obstacle, no catastrophe on earth could root out. The fire at the Glass Factory had burned the idea into her brain. The idea was simple; it activated her whole being, poured life into her, possessed her to her very depths: Mitya would still go to the University of Moscow. What is money when a heart beats in a mother's breast; what is distance when a child must be carried over it; and what are the Ural Mountains to a mother whose son lives, and needs help to grow?

Maria turned to her son.

"Mitenka," she said, "when you get through looking at these coals, come home, my darling. I want to talk to you about some plans. Don't be too long, my dear, and come to me soon if you feel that you are getting cold."

"I will," said Mitya. "I won't be long. I just want to look at that colored fused glass."

In a telega, Maria drove away with Matvei and the strannik, Matvei gently urging his brown horse Soldat homeward.

Mitya and Bassargin remained at the dying fire.

4

For Mitya, the Glass Factory had been a source of constant mystery and adventure. Accompanying his mother on tours of inspection and consultation with workers, he had gazed with fascination upon the exciting work of the skilled craftsmen. Andrei the Old Chemist, though officially assigned only to the task of mixing coloring ingredients and other chemicals, also worked at purifying the silica sand brought in from the distant hillsides.

"It's the iron impurities in this that bother me, Mitya," he would say as the boy watched him shake great sieves piled with sand.

"Maybe some day you'll find a hill that gives purer sand," Mitya consoled.

"Maybe we will," Andrei the Chemist would sigh. "Then I will make really fine glass. What I like to have in my glass, when I can manage it, Mitya, is 75 per cent silica, 13 per cent sodium oxide, and 12 per cent lime. But it's not easy to get things just so. Especially when Mikhail keeps bringing me so much iron in those mounds of his sand."

"Last time you told me that you like the potash glass," reminded Mitya. "That had something else in it. Isn't it true?"

"Yes, that is correct," agreed Andrei. "The best kind is the Bohemian kind, like that from which those crystal goblets in your house are made. That was a nice job that Timofei did. From fifty parts of potassium carbonate, fifteen parts of lime, and one hundred parts of quartz."

From Andrei, Mitya learned that borax is sometimes added to the glass to make it more fusible. But always Andrei complained about the iron impurities.

"That's why, the devil take it, the glass comes out greenish," Andrei would say, shaking his gray head. But one day, after a number of little experiments, Andrei discovered that if he added a certain chemical to the molten glass the green blemish was destroyed, and the glass came out glistening white. The whole factory was jubilant, and old Andrei, in his patent-leather boots, did a little hop of exultation.

"What is that chemical?" Mitya asked. "That one, that makes the glass so nice and clear?"

"Manganese peroxide," said Andrei. "Wonderful, magical manganese peroxide."

"And why does it banish the green color?" asked Mitya.

Andrei shook his head sadly. "*Ai*, Mitya," he said, "if I only knew the reason why, I would be truly happy. Just to know. But maybe you can think about it, eh Mitya?"

"Yes," agreed Mitya musingly. "I will think about it."

Mitya loved also to stop in front of the huge furnaces. Inside of these, large stone and clay crucibles were being heated by roaring flames, and inside the crucibles the final glass-forming mixture was slowly melting. More fuel was being added to the firebox below, and the temperature of the molten mass in the crucibles was slowly rising.

"It's about two thousand degrees now," Anton the Furnace Man told Mitya.

Mitya nodded and watched the mass in the crucible nearest the furnace entrance. After the first stage of the operation, the stage in which the mass intermixed and began to react, Mitya now was watching the fusion, the escape of the carbonic acid gas, and the formation of the molten substance. Presently, at the highest temperature, the mass became homogeneous and liquid. Anton the Furnace Man began to lower the temperature by diminishing the fuel and deflecting a portion of the flame.

"It's ready for Timofei," he said and turned toward a door. Behind this door the glass blower, stripped to the waist, was flexing his arms and whistling.

"Timofei!" called Anton. "*Gotova!*" [She's ready!]

"*Khorosho*," replied Timofei, and opened the door.

"Hello, Mitya," he said. "How are you living?"

"Fine," said Mitya. "I came to watch you."

Timofei waited until another workman came up. This was Pavel the Gatherer. Pavel thrust the end of an iron blowpipe into the white-hot glass and in a moment had gathered a mass of about forty pounds on the end of the pipe. Withdrawing the mass from the crucible, Pavel, still wielding the iron pipe, pressed the end with the glass mass into an iron mold until the glass blob had assumed a pear shape. He passed the pipe with the glowing pear-glass to Timofei. Timofei's huge chest swelled to barrel proportions as he filled his lungs with air. He pressed the pipe to his lips and began to blow. The glowing glass inflated; then suddenly Timofei stopped, and rapidly began an intricate maneuver of swinging and revolving the pipe with the glass; then he blew again, then swung again, rapidly, precisely, with perfect concentration. Mitya followed the operation carefully. The glass had pulled away from the end of the blowpipe and assumed the form of a cylinder six feet in length. It seemed to be perfectly symmetrical. Timofei allowed the cylinder to cool a little, then rapidly placed the end of the cylinder in the furnace, blew into the iron pipe and covered the opening with his thumb. At once, the enclosed air, being heated, began to expand and in a moment had forced the glowing, heated end of the cylinder to pop open. Timofei made this opening larger, as large as the cylinder's cross section, by swinging the end vigorously in the furnace. Then he allowed the glass to cool to a red-orange heat.

On a long clay table he detached the glass from the pipe and with a red-hot iron rod split the cylinder along its length. The clay table was pushed by Anton the Furnace Man into an oven where the table was made to spin on a platform. In a few moments the heat and the spinning had flattened the split cylinder into an irregular pancake mass. The glass was next flattened smooth by regular wooden blocks, then placed to one side, in a cooler part of the furnace, finally removed to a huge slab of stone, upon which it was placed to cool, in the open air. This work was being done by other men, while Timofei, Pavel, and Anton rested for a moment preparatory to beginning over again. Old Andrei the Chemist withdrew to the chemical room.

When the flattened glass on the cooling stone had cooled to rigidity, three men carried it to the annealing chamber where it was slowly heated until it approached melting temperature, and then once more permitted to cool.

"This is the part that puzzles me a little," once said Timofei to Mitya. "This annealing. Just what happens?"

Mitya pondered. "I guess it goes through a regular gentle contraction all through it, while it cools," said Mitya. "But exactly what happens inside, I'm not sure."

"No," laughed Timofei, "and neither am I."

He gathered up a small blob of glass on the end of a pipe and, walking to a pail, allowed drops of the molten glass to splash into the water. Mitya put his hand into the water and picked up six little glass spheres.

"I know what you mean," said Mitya. "It is very interesting." He dropped one of these rapidly cooled glass spheres onto the floor; it shattered into a fine white powder. Then he chipped a small section off another sphere, but this sphere too shattered into powder in his hand.

"Well," said Timofei, "I have to do the next cylinder."

"It's very interesting," Mitya mused, rubbing the powdered glass between his thumb and fingers. "It's all so interesting," he repeated, then walked slowly toward the room where Andrei the Chemist was preparing coloring powders for making stained-glass windows.

In the chemical room he showed Mitya the huge metal trays that had just arrived with the new coloring materials for the special glasses.

"For green glasses we're going to use these oxides of chromium and copper," he said, "and for the blue we'll use the cobalt oxide, as before."

"And what is this?" asked Mitya stirring a little glass rod in a darkish powder.

"That is for violet," explained Old Andrei, "and the powder is manganese oxide. We can also get a pink color with it, or amethyst. It depends on how much we use. The red colors will come from adding cuprous oxide as before, and also I will try out this purple of Cassius; that's made of gold and tin, they say. For the yellow glass we still will use iron oxide or maybe silver oxide. Timofei would like me to mix carbon for the nice brown tints for his bottles."

"What if you use gold?" asked Mitya.

Andrei laughed softly. "Yes, if we can get gold to buy gold, we'll have a pleasant color in our glass. Like a ruby."

"And the tin will give white. I remember," said Mitya.

"That's true," the old man agreed. "By the way, there is a large order that has just come in for red glass. Another church is going up in Tobolsk. Did you know that?"

"No," said Mitya, "I didn't." He sat down on a wooden bench, and drummed his slender fingers on it.

"If you can spare a moment," said Mitya, "would you please burn some of these new powders in a flame. I would like very much to see the new colors."

Then for an hour both Mitya and Andrei burned tiny samples of the coloring materials and thrilled to the sight of vivid living reds, and blues, and violet colors, and green, and purple, and yellow, and cherry red, and silken corn yellow.

Mitya made penciled entries in a little notebook.

"Thank you, Andrei," he said when the experiments came to an end, "thank you very much. I will think about this."

Then Mitya walked jauntily, with shining exhilarated eyes, past the workmen in the furnace rooms, past the rooms where molds were made for casting glass into various shapes, past the sand rooms piled high with newly arrived silica sand, past rooms with sieves, clay bricks, fire-clay crucibles, tables for rolling glass, hoisting mechanisms, rooms with tremendous supplies of glass panes ready to ship, rooms with long rows of shimmering glass goblets and glass saucers, rooms with colored panes of glass assembled into mosaic combinations. He walked out to the yard in back where his mother Maria was giving instructions to a foreman.

Later, when they rode home in their telega, Mitya recounted to his mother his experiments with Andrei.

Maria's narrow eyes smiled, as she lightly tapped the horse with the reins.

Unfortunately, Mitya had rarely made such visits to the Glass Factory since the age of seven, for, since that time—when he already knew how to read and write very well—he was a resident student at the Gymnasium at

Tobolsk. But whenever he came back to the village of Aremziansk, he invariably sought opportunity to visit the practical laboratory of flowing glass and luminous flame.

When Mitya was first carted away from the village to Tobolsk, from the carefree life in the forests and the antics of Vanka the Fool, he found it difficult to make the initial adjustment to the city life and the regimen of the secondary school, the Gymnasium. But soon, when he found that what was required of him was merely an exertion of the intellect, he began to accept the demands and found interest in mathematics; then in history, where his memory, unequaled in his class, made it possible for him to recall all sequences of events and dates after only a little study. He seemed to do well also in the physics course, where the demands for sustained logical thought found in him an agreeable response. But in the courses in the classics, in languages, and especially the study of Latin, Mitya was an abysmal failure. Bitterly he complained to his mother.

"If they admit that Latin is a dead language, then why don't they keep it buried? Everything in me rebels against that nonsense," he would say. "I want to live for the future, not for the past."

"But Mitya," his mother would say, "to live intelligently in the future, a man should know the past."

"Even Latin?" Mitya asked, looking up at his mother with pleading and incredulous eyes.

"Well," said Maria, "you are my little heart and how can I tell you anything but what I truly believe? I don't think you need to know Latin to grow up to be a splendid man." Maria sighed. "But it is required in your school, and you will have to be successful in it to be admitted to the University. Why don't you just use your wonderful memory, Mitya? It would be so easy."

"My memory is not for that," said Mitya sadly. "God of mine, I do not know what is to become of me."

"Well, fail it, then," said Maria with tears in her eyes. "If that will make you happy. I want you to be happy."

"No," said Mitya, "that won't make me happy. I'll try to pass it. But you may be certain that I will not be foremost in it. I want you to be prepared."

"All right," said Maria softly. "All right. All my life I have been prepared for everything. Let us go now to the picture exhibition."

To Mitya, from the age of seven to fourteen, his periodic return to the home village with his entire family was more than an opportunity to visit the Glass Factory or to lose himself once again in the fragrance of the cedar forests; it was also an opportunity to lie once more on the warm oven at night, listening to the conversation of his mother and father and visiting intellectuals, and especially the caustic and iconoclastic Bassargin. At such times, Maria knew that Mitya was not sleeping, but listening, and invariably at some point in the evening she would softly reach up to his place on the oven to hand him a glass of tea and some cake with raisins, or a cup of warm milk. After that, Mitya would gradually relax and presently be asleep.

All, all except Latin, was wonderful, thrilling, challenging. True, great sadness had come to the family with the death of Ivan in October, 1847, and the death of Apollinaria three months later. But now Mitya was fourteen, and in another year would graduate from the Gymnasium. But here now— here had come this fire. . . . What would that do? Well, never mind.

For the moment Mitya thought of only one thing. Before him, in the dying flames of the former Glass Factory, there among the orange coals, lay purple and gold and green-red pools of solidifying glass.

"Beautiful," whispered Mitya. "Just beautiful. Look, Bassargin, the strangest combinations!"

"Yes," said Bassargin, "beautiful and painful." He stepped back a little and looked up at the rising sun. The dim white rays explored his weary face and the tired blue eyes. Only the hawklike nose seemed strong. Off into space he gazed, and in a moment his distracted mind wandered out into the distances, westward, over the Urals, to St. Petersburg, from where he came.

5

There, in the capital of Russia, twenty-three years ago, on December 27, 1825, the twenty-six year-old Bassargin had stood shoulder to shoulder with two thousand university comrades and some intellectual palace guards.

"*Constitootsiya!*" they screamed. [Give us a Constitution!] "Give us a Republic!"

Tsar Nicholas the First, ordering cannon brought up, gave them grape-shot.

The plan for the uprising was the final expression of long-brewing discontent among students, educators, and some staff officers, at the condition of the Russian peasants. Most of these were serfs on the estates of the nobility. The demonstration was also a protest against censorship and the stifling of free thought.

In 1820, Magnitsky, a favorite sycophant of Alexander the First, after inspecting Kazan University, proposed that it be abolished, because it encouraged original thought. Tsar Alexander was more liberal than his henchman and magnanimously decided not to abolish the university but merely to reconstruct it along different lines. History and philosophy were to be based on the Bible and the prophets; physics and medicine were to be made compatible with the "Biblical viewpoint"; geometry was to give immediate recognition to the conception that the triangle was a symbol of the Father, the Son, and the Holy Ghost. Any deviation from these teachings by a professor was to be followed immediately by punishment and dismissal.

As one of several groups, which agitated for reform, an organization under the leadership of the Staff Officer Paul Pestel appeared to be most effective. Pestel advocated the establishment of a republic. He proposed that as a preliminary step of an exploratory nature, the Tsar and his family be murdered. Next, the peasant-serfs were to be freed; after that, all class distinctions were to be abolished. Finally, Pestel held that half of the land should be divided among the entire population and the other half be placed at the disposal of private enterprise.

But Pestel's plan was inadequate and the final Decembrist uprising accomplished only the assassination of the Governor-General Miloradovitch. However, the Men of December inspired future reformers.

After the cannonading of the rebels, there followed the hanging of five of their leaders, the sentencing to life service in the army of many others, and the banishment to Siberia of still others of these conspirators, suspects, near-suspects, and friends of near-subjects.

In 1826, after the Decembrist uprising, Nicholas, the new Tsar, at the instigation of Admiral Shishkov, a new royal sycophant, decided to "make printing harmless." It was decreed, therefore, that all works on logic and philosophy were to be banished except those issued as textbooks after government censorship; authors were forbidden to imply subversive meaning by the stratagem of leaving spaces marked with dots; books on physiology and anatomy were to be rendered "decent," so that nothing in them could offend the genteel human sensibilities. Authors were also asked to review their works and expunge from them all material which might tend to unbalance the *status quo*. Tsar Nicholas himself asked the famous poet Pushkin to prepare a new version of *Boris Godunov* which would eliminate "all unnecessary material, and issue the work as a novel in the spirit of Walter Scott." To applaud the works of desirable authors, Nicholas publicly commended the writer Bulgarin, who was despised by liberal writers and university students. In Bulgarin's creations the point of view of the Tsar was most accurately mirrored.

Of the Decembrists, Pestel was among those executed. Others escaped death by turning state's evidence and divulging the names of all their associates, even those who once had seemed to be their bosom comrades and deathless compatriots. Many others wrote letters to the Tsar from their places of banishment, explaining in detail the reason for their revolt, begging the sovereign to institute measures of reform. On occasion, Nicholas replied to these communications, promising to take the matter under advisement at the nearest opportunity, which seemed uncannily elusive. Still others wrote letters of servility and self-abasement, and begged for release from confinement in the cold wastes of Siberia. But most of these *Dekabreestui* [Decembrists] preserved their character and self-esteem. Prominent among these was the poet Ryleyev who, though regretting the uprising, remained unbroken to the very hour of his execution. Another who did not bend or break was the thin, mop-haired, hawk-nosed Bassargin. Banished to Siberia, he served his prison sentence; then, in Tobolsk, he fell in love with Olga, married her, and took her to Yaloutorovsk. Occasionally they returned for visits to the Mendeleyev household.

Pacing to and fro in the confines of the Aremziansk family hut or in the house in the parish of the Church of Archangel Mikhail where the Mendeleyevs resided when in Tobolsk, the restless, brilliant Bassargin incessantly castigated the government, quoted reams of Pushkin's poetry, and planned sleepless nights for a whole series of future Tsars. In his spare time he taught Mitya snatches of chemistry and astronomy, Newtonian mechanics, and the theory of the circulation of the blood. Bassargin and Mitya became close friends. The fire, seemingly consuming Mitya's future, stirred a well of pity within the heart of the unbending Bassargin. And yet he wondered whether it was not for the best that Mitya remain safely in a forgotten village, away from the cruel perturbations of the civilized centers of western Russia. . . .

Bassargin came closer to the crumbling red ruins and watched Mitya poke about in the multicolored glass slag.

"It might be just as well," he said quietly, "for you to remain here. Life is so uncertain at Moscow. What do you think?"

Mitya looked up from the embers and gazed out into the distance where the village lay in snow.

"I know my mother," he said, a barely perceptible smile playing about his eyes. "I'm going to the University, you may be certain."

"Did she tell you?" asked Bassargin. "After the fire?"

"No," said Mitya. "I just know her. She makes me feel so good. Confident. I'll go all right." He picked up a piece of splintered wood and began to explore in the embers. "But exactly how she will manage it, I don't know."

"Well," said Bassargin. "Let's go and find out."

Mitya sat in the driver's seat. Slowly the telega rolled through the snow toward Aremziansk. The horse, barely trotting, occasionally turned his head to blink at the pale white sun.

6

Alone in the izba, Maria sat silently on her bed. In her hand was a pair of scissors, and as though of their own accord the dull black blades sheared through the rough green mattress cover. She placed her hand within the opening and withdrew the rose-colored paper money. The handsome theatrical face of Tsar Nicholas gazed beyond Maria—somewhere out into space.

"Twenty," she whispered, her fingers carefully spreading the banknotes, "forty; sixty; sixty-three." Once more she made the count, now silently.

"Sixty-three." Again her hand reached into the opening but Maria knew there would be no more.

From her black purse she drew twelve roubles, and now, working more quickly, placed all the money into the mattress, then reached for the spool of black thread, and the needle. . . . Her narrow eyes slowly inspected the contents of the izba, appraising the value of each article, and of the hut itself.

Suddenly Maria rose.

"I am going to talk to the people of the village," she said to Elizabeth. "Yes, what will they do now, for their livelihood?"

In the izba of the Village Elder, Maria sat down on a round wooden stool of heavy cedar. Near by, the two lambs were dozing at the base of the oven.

Maria looked up at the Starosta Oblontov.

"What will the people do?" she asked.

Old Maroosya came from the ikon corner, a red kerchief tied loosely about her gray hair.

"What will you do, Maria Dmitrievna?" she said. "About the little Mitya's future, I mean?"

"Yes," nodded Oblontov. "One must think of the future. We ourselves are merely fragments of the past."

Maria sat pensive. "About Mitya it will be all right," she said. "There will be more than a hundred roubles. Next year when he finishes the Gymnasium at Tobolsk I will take him to Moscow, to the University."

Oblontov shook his head. "One hundred roubles will pay for nothing," he said. "Only the journey, and a little more. It will take about three weeks to travel, you know."

"I know," said Maria. "There might be more money from the sale of the izba, and some things we have in Tobolsk. And Timofei saved two good tables, which may be sold. And I still get something on the pension. In any case, I am only counting on money for the journey, and for living a little time there."

"Then?" said Oblontov. "Your brother is there, isn't he? Will he help?" Maria shook her head.

"I do not take that into serious consideration," she said. "I believe that he wants Mitya to go into government business. But Mitya will not think of it. His heart is in science. Mitya must try for a scholarship, through an examination."

"That's a possibility," agreed Oblontov. "But with regard to the Latin language. I understand Mitya suffers a weakness."

"That is my nightmare," sighed Maria. "Well, and if he fails the scholarship examination, then I will work. I will wash floors someplace. I will only be fifty-seven."

Oblontov's old woman Maroosya began to weep. She put her arms about Maria.

"That's all right, Mamasha," said Maria, consoling both herself and the weeping old woman. "They say there is a God. I believe it."

The old woman blew her nose in her apron; then taking her red kerchief off her gray head, she dabbed at her eyes.

"There is a God," she affirmed. "But my old stupid head cannot understand the things he does. Stupid I am. Stupid. Always have been."

She turned quietly and walked to the ikon corner.

"What will the people do?" asked Maria. "The little summer work here in the fields is not enough."

"No," agreed Oblontov. "That is true. It is possible to go to the village of the landowner Podolsky, and work for him."

Maria was astounded. "You mean work with his serfs, and perhaps become one?"

Oblontov evaded her glance. "What is a man to do?" he replied.

Maria could not answer.

"I myself will not do it," said Oblontov. "It is time for me to die. In my case it will be simple. My old woman will die too. But the younger . . ."

Maria went to the door.

"Wait," said Oblontov.

From under a pile of wood lying near the great oven he pulled out a red cedar box. From this box he withdrew a thin rose packet. He unfolded the bills bearing the portraits of Nicholas.

"It would be possible to spare a twenty," he said. "I have fifty."

Maria stood by the door.

"This cannot be," she said.

"But wait, Maria Dmitrievna," insisted Oblontov, "this is not a case of charity. It is a loan for Mitya's education. An investment. He can help Russia. Perhaps he will remember us."

The old woman Maroosya came forward, and taking the banknote from her husband's wrinkled hand, she walked toward Maria.

"My man knows best," she said softly. "He is not the Village Elder for nothing. This is for Mitya. And for Russia."

"I will take it," said Maria. A few tears rolled down her tired cheeks. Facing the heavy log door, and leaning against it, she wept.

The old woman Maroosya reached out her hand to Maria.

"Leave her," said Oblontov gently. "If the heart weeps it will not die. There is sorrow in this world which is beyond tears. But this is a sorrow for tears. Let her weep."

He blew his nose into a large blue rag, turned, and, looking at the ikon on the wall, slowly shook his head.

Chapter Three

The Light in the Window

IN THE izba of Matvei the Night Watchman the wrinkled Marfa sat at the heavy table, gazing intently at the pink paper roubles and the large silver coins, and the smaller ones, and the many pennies—the brown kopeks.

Full-bearded Matvei sat on the oven, his flat bare feet hanging over the side. "How much?" he asked. "How much will it take to bury you, *baba?*"

Marfa pushed the coins nervously. "The devil take it," she said. "It would seem to be twenty-one roubles and sixty-seven kopeks. But the first time I counted, the kopeks were eighty-three. What do you make of it?"

"Try again," advised Matvei. Intently he watched as Marfa began anew to push the coins into rows on the table.

For a long time Marfa continued. "Add the two," she advised herself, "and make it ten. Bring in the silver ones, and now the half. We're up to sixteen, now gather the singles. We reach the seventeen, now borrow a half. Replace the kopeks, now round out nineteen. Unfold the paper, that carries two. We're up to nineteen, bring in the quarters. We call it twenty. Now these extra kopeks."

"How much?" asked Matvei.

Marfa shook her head crossly. "Don't interrupt," she said. "There's a kopek on the floor. There you have it—the reason why I am confused."

"That cannot be," said Matvei. "A kopek is merely a kopek. Your confusion is larger."

Marfa nodded her head. "Strange how one kopek could cause such confusion. Could it be a question of when the kopek is counted? Or perhaps it is missing from an important column."

"How much was it this time?" Matvei demanded.

Marfa considered. "It would seem like thirty-one roubles. Not counting the kopek either way. To be fair."

Matvei slid down from the oven. "*Ekh baba,*" [old woman, old woman] he said. "You're as stupid as a cork. Here, let me."

Matvei began the counting. "First the Nicholas faces," he said. "The paper. Seven. Then the silver lads. What handsome creatures! We're up to twelve. Push in the halves and reach for the quarters. We flow at eighteen, now grab for the trash. We squeeze a nineteen. Now roll the kopeks." Matvei stopped for the final crushing calculations.

"How much?" asked Marfa.

"Twenty-five roubles and sixteen kopeks," said Matvei. "You have a head like a cabbage. Only you can't make borsch out of it."

"The question is," began Marfa, "the question is whether you counted this kopek." She stretched out her wrinkled palm with the small copper coin lying in it.

"I wish it would perish," replied Matvei, "that kopek of yours."

Matvei climbed back onto the oven.

"Perhaps I had better recount," he suggested to himself, and once more slid down the oven and began to manipulate the money.

"Twenty-three roubles and fifty-six kopeks," he announced, and leaned back against the oven, amazed. "The devil take it! There is an evil thing in this house!"

"Take tea," advised Marfa. "Then after our heads are clear we will count together."

Matvei alternately sipped the tea from the glass and made small crunching bites on a cube of white sugar.

After the tea they counted together and decided that the money came to exactly twenty-four roubles. Matvei spat on the extra kopek and threw it in the corner.

"Now," he said. "As to the coffin. That would be fifteen. And the priest five. That is twenty. And Stepka at least four for digging the hole and throwing the dirt. The money would be all gone."

Marfa sighed deeply, then rose from her stool, and stepped close to Matvei. Gently she took hold of his beard, and tugged on it.

"Listen to me, you old goat," she said. "Maria needs money for her Mitya, for that school in Moscow."

"University," said Matvei.

"Well whatever it is," said Marfa. "And I want you yourself to make me a coffin. Why pay for it?"

Matvei was dubious. "It would not be good," he said. "I am not expert in such things. It might come out too narrow."

"I'll lie on my side," said Marfa.

"Well, but maybe it would not be square. One foot might have more room."

"I am not going to dance in it," explained Marfa.

Matvei considered. "Well, but if it's too short. . . ."

"I'll double my knees. It won't be my first time."

"Don't joke, *baba*. This is no joking business," chided Matvei gently.

"No, this is no joking business," agreed Marfa. "Will you make the coffin?"

"If you wish," assented Matvei. "It is your funeral."

"All right," said Marfa. "Agreed. Now measure me. Get things under way. Because when my time comes I want it to be ready. No confusion."

"All right," agreed Matvei. "Lie on the floor, old woman, I'll make a measure."

Marfa stretched out on the floor.

With a daggerlike knife Matvei made scratches on the floor, below Marfa's feet and above her head and at her sides.

"Allow a little more in case I should grow," suggested Marfa.

"Stupid as a cork. You're not going to grow in that box. What ideas!"

"One does not know about the other world," said Marfa.

"All right," said Matvei, making new scratches on the floor. "Four inches for the head and four inches for the feet. Go ahead and grow."

Marfa stood up.

"All right," said Matvei, "let us see how thick you are. And a little to grow. Some for your belly, and some for your tail. All right. I'll remember."

Marfa was happy. "Work on it soon," she said. "Now another thing. There is the money for the priest. Can a cheaper priest be found?"

"He is a good one," said Matvei. "He's worth the five roubles. Let it be."

"All right," agreed Marfa. "Then the question of four roubles to Stepka for digging the hole and throwing the dirt. You do it. You dig and throw. We will save four roubles."

" I can dig the hole," agreed Matvei, "but I can't throw dirt in your face when you're dead. I can beat you when you are alive, old woman, but I can't throw dirt in your face when you're dead."

"Well then, just dig. And let Stepka throw the dirt. Pay him one rouble. Save three."

"All right," agreed Matvei. "Now we have fifteen saved on the coffin, and three on the digging. That's eighteen. Shall I take it over?"

"Yes," said Marfa. "Take it over to Maria. Tell her it's for Mitya. Tell her you found it. Before God you can tell this lie."

"I will do it," said Matvei.

He wound the long cloths around his feet, and pulled on his boots, then his fur cap and the great black coat.

"I will do it," repeated Matvei, and left the hut.

2

By evening of the day after the fire, Mitya's frail sister Elizabeth had gone to Tobolsk to prepare the household in the parish of the Church of Archangel Mikhail. Her brother Paul was already there. And there they would all live presently when the school work at the Gymnasium recommenced after the vacation period.

In the Mendeleyev izba Olga sat on the bed beside Bassargin. Bassargin was writing furious letters full of catastrophic anti-Tsarist schemes. Maria and Mitya sat at the heavy log table. Mitya studied his mother's face.

"You are certain," said Mitya, "that you do not want me to quit the Gymnasium and go to work . . . I am fourteen."

Maria waved her hand in front of her face.

"Don't say such a thing," she ordered. "Your duty is to pass your Gymnasium course and in Moscow try for a scholarship."

Maria's face was a tired face, a face of pain, of pity, a face near frustration. The fire of the previous night still flamed in her mind. She was on the verge of breaking. But the final break would not occur. Maria knew that Mitya must never see her broken. She knew that as yet he needed desperately to see that someone had unbreakable courage, self-confidence, strength. She knew that as yet he could not walk alone. Not in Moscow.

Slowly Maria interlaced the fingers of her hands, bent them back, and cracked the joints. She spoke to Mitya. "Let me consider your studies," she said. "History is going well. Am I right?"

"Yes. Everything. Except . . ."

"Latin," said Maria. "I know. Well, can you conjugate 'to be'?"

"If necessary," said Mitya. "If absolutely necessary."

"Must you be driven to it?"

Mitya was embarrassed. "Well, mama, I don't want to cause you pain. But it is so repugnant to me. So ancient and mystical and unnecessary. . . ."

"Who knows?" said Maria. "Perhaps it is not all bad. Will you learn it if I drive you a little? Just a little. Drill you in it?"

"You don't know it," said Mitya.

Maria stood up. "Where is your book?" she asked. "Give me your Latin grammar."

Mitya brought the book. Bassargin, seated in his room on his bed, suddenly stopped writing, and looked up at Maria. Mitya too watched his mother. She held the book in her hands.

"Mitya," she said. "I am going to know this Latin. This I am telling you. You will see, and I will drill you. I am fifty-six, my darling, and I want you always to remember that I learned this material at my age. And I want

The Light in the Window

you always to remember that no task in life is too hard for you. When you are a man, remember this. Will you remember?"

Mitya stood watching his mother. "You make me believe in God," he said softly.

"Go," said Maria, "study physiology with Bassargin. Will you help him, Kolya? I want to be left with this book."

Bassargin nodded his head. He ran his hand through his brown curly hair.

"Come in here, Mitya," he said. "I will tell you about Harvey's work."

At eleven o'clock, twenty-four hours after the fire, in the izba of the Mendeleyev family all slept. All except Maria. Seated at the heavy table, she gazed fixedly at the open book before her, the yellow light of the oil lamp falling revealingly on the lines and furrows of her brow, on the intent narrow eyes. The window near her was unshuttered, and occasionally she looked up from her study to gaze onto the open blackness before her.

At two o'clock in the morning Maria still sat at her work.

And at three o'clock, if a stranger had wandered through the village of Aremziansk, or if a convict fleeing from his Siberian prison should have chanced through this village, the heart within him might have gained some warmth from the lone burning light in the window of the snow-covered hut. Or if a child lost in the dark had seen that light, or a woman thrown onto the mercy of the snows—all might have felt a glow within them, and a lifting of the spirit. For the light in the window burned with the warmth of a slow but undying flame, and the essence of that flame was love.

Chapter Four

The Bread on the Window Ledge

THE MENDELEYEV family soon went back to live in near-by Tobolsk. In addition to Maria there were Mitya, his older brother Paul, and his sister Elizabeth. Olga and Bassargin had gone to live in Omsk, where many of the banished revolutionaries—the Decembrists—had settled. Mitya and Paul were uniformed students in the high school, the Gymnasium of Tobolsk. In about a year both would graduate. Both, that is, if Mitya passed Latin and the other classical studies. Mitya's excellence in history and the sciences was now clearly recognized. Then would come the journey to Moscow, to the university.

In the evenings Maria and Mitya had their lessons in the Latin language.

"There must be in my life," said Maria to herself, "one—at least one—success."

"Come, Mitya," she would say, "sit down. Give me the future tense of 'to be.' "

"*Ero*," said Mitya, "*eris, erit, erimus, eritis, erunt.*"

Maria dabbed her eyes with a small white handkerchief. "That's fine," she said. "Now, how do you say, 'I was loving'?"

"*Amabam*," said Mitya.

"And 'they were loving'?"

"*Amabunt*," replied Mitya.

Maria shook her head. "It's *amabatunt*," she said.

"*Akh* yes, I suppose so," admitted Mitya frowning, and snapping the buckle on the belt of his uniform. "I guess it's '*amabatunt*.' But I cannot imagine how they could love in Latin."

Maria, rising in her long black dress, left the room. She returned shortly, bringing Mitya a cup of hot milk. "Take it," she said. "It is good."

Mitya sipped the milk.

"This, too, is in your lesson," said Maria. "How do you say 'I cough'?"

"*Tuss*," said Mitya.

Maria frowned.

"No," she said. "No, no."

The Bread on the Window Ledge

"*Akh*, mama," protested Mitya, setting the cup down with a bang so that some milk bounced out. "I don't know how to say it. If I have to cough, I just cough. It's the same in all languages. *Bozhe moi, bozhe moi,*" [God of mine.] he sighed.

Maria sat watching her son.

"And do you cough much?" she asked. "I heard you last night."

"That was Elizabeth," said Mitya.

"Yes," said Maria, "but I also heard you. Do you have any pain?"

"No," said Mitya, "let's go on with the Latin torture. Maybe I will know something."

Maria turned to the book. She looked at it intently. "Guard against colds, Mitya," she whispered. "Please. And eat well, and sleep well. Please. My first child, the first daughter, Maria, died in Saratov, of consumption. Before you were born. Your father died of consumption last year." Maria wept softly, and a tear splashed down upon the page of the Latin grammar. "And Polya died of it."

For a while they both sat silently. Maria mastered her tears.

"Elizabeth has a very bad cough," she said absent-mindedly. "That's enough. Shall we say 'That's enough for this family,' Mitya? Shall we say we have had our share of coughing in this family? Shall we, Mitya? Tell me."

Mitya rose and placed his arm about his mother's shoulders. "Yes," he said. "Enough. My cough is trivial. I will get rid of it at once."

He sat down again, and drank the rest of the milk.

Maria turned to the book before her.

"How do you say 'my father'?"

"*Pater meus,*" said Mitya. "The vocabulary is not too awfully stupid. I'll learn it, and pass the examination. Don't worry, mama."

2

Later in the year, Bassargin and Olga arrived in Tobolsk for a short visit. Bassargin seemed haggard and exhausted. His hawk-nosed face with the burning blue eyes and drawn mouth told of sleepless nights or of illness. The brown curly hair seemed a wild tangled mass. Olga seemed well but was concerned about her husband. She constantly hovered near him.

Mitya met his sister alone in the dining room.

"What's the matter with Kolya?" he asked, alarmed.

"Someone died," said Olga. "Belinsky. Do you know about him?"

Mitya shook his head. "Well, maybe," he said hesitantly. "A writer. Vissarion Grigorivitch? Is that the man?"

"Yes," said Olga. "Vissarion Grigorivitch Belinsky, a liberal writer—a fighter. The most important thing in Kolya's life. More important than I am," she added softly.

In the evening Bassargin and Mitya were alone in the front room.

"Be careful of secret police," said Bassargin, "when you go to Moscow. They would be your drivers on the carriage, your waiters in the restaurants, your booksellers. And, my boy, your best friends."

"*Bozhe moi,*" [God of mine] exclaimed Mitya. "Is everybody followed by police?"

"*Akh* no," consoled Bassargin. "Just people like me. Well, let me tell you. Belinsky escaped arrest by going abroad, and from there he wrote 'The Letter to Gogol,' upbraiding him for turning reactionary." Suddenly Bassargin began to weep.

Mitya was astounded. For the first time in his life he saw the furious, unbending Bassargin in tears. But Bassargin quickly regained composure, blew his tremendous nose with an equally tremendous blast into the inadequate white handkerchief. He opened a window near the yellow couch and threw the handkerchief out into the street.

The dining-room door opened. Maria, standing there, held a cup of hot milk toward Mitya.

"Come," she whispered, "in here."

Mitya went.

"Keep your mind on science," whispered Maria. "In the name of God, do not stray, Mitenka."

Mitya drank the hot milk.

Later, when the samovar began to sing, from the corner of the hallway Bassargin brought forth a bulging, battered portfolio. Mitya came into the room.

"I brought you documents to study," Bassargin said to him. "They will help you in your Moscow examinations. Read the material and use your mind. That's all you have to do."

He shook the papers and cards and pamphlets out of the portfolio onto the wooden floor. Mitya, dropping down on his knees, gazed questioningly at the mound of material.

"That's quite a bit," he commented.

Maria and Olga stood silently watching.

"There is no scientific material here," explained Bassargin. "I am assuming you will know all that. By and large it is literature and history. They expect a man to know his country thoroughly, though they do not expect him to draw radical conclusions. Understand?"

Mitya nodded his head. "I can't guarantee anything about my conclusions," he said. "What I feel I understand, I will say. Whenever I can prove it."

Maria bit her lip.

"What do you think, mama?" asked Olga, in alarm.

Maria sighed deeply. "Anything he can prove, let him say," she said softly. "I will not betray my boy. But he must be able to prove it."

Bassargin shrugged his shoulders. "Well," he said, "these are all just facts. I give you my word on it, Maria Dmitrievna. Not a single opinion of my own. It was hard to do, but I did it. For you. And for him, and for Olga. It's up to Mitya now. Let him study."

Mitya began to gather up the papers and cards and pamphlets.

"Put them into the portfolio," said Bassargin. "You can have it, too. My school days are long since over."

The next day Bassargin and Olga left for Omsk.

But before he left, Bassargin placed a loaf of bread on the outside ledge of the back window—sustenance for some fleeing criminal or political rebel escaping from one of the Siberian camps of doom.

Late in the night Mitya got up out of bed. In the dining room he took the remaining loaf of bread and placed it on the same outside ledge of the back window. Bassargin's loaf had already disappeared.

Maria, in her nightgown, was standing in the hallway, watching her son. He was surprised.

"That's all right, Mitenka," she said. "That's all right. But keep your mind on science. I beg you, my darling. Don't let Kolya upset your plans."

Mitya shook his head slowly. "There is suffering," he said. "How much suffering and turmoil there is. But I will study, *mamachka*. I promise. I will study science. Maybe they will leave me alone. Maybe with science I can help. I promise."

In the dark, outside, a hand slowly reached up to the window and closed around the bread.

Mitya watched.

Chapter Five

◇◇◇

Timofei, Nadezhda, and the Latin Book

KATERINA THE Matchmaker came to see Timofei on the first day of spring. Timofei's heart beat with a secret excitement when he saw her.

"How is Vanka?" he asked, assuming a casual attitude.

Katerina sat down at the heavy cedar table and drew off her bright kerchief.

"Vanya is not well," she said gravely. "But that is another story. Do you know why I have come?"

Timofei shrugged his shoulders. He wore a heavy blue shirt, with rolled-up sleeves. The brown trousers were stuffed into patent-leather boots. Timofei bent over and pulled one boot off. He sat down opposite Katerina and began to polish the boot with a black felt cloth.

"Why do you suppose I have come?" repeated Katerina.

"If I knew a woman's mind," said Timofei, still absorbed in his boot, "I could become a rich man."

"Or a happy one," added Katerina, a gleam coming into her eye.

Timofei stopped polishing his boot. He laid it gently on the table, stroked his moustache once, then gazed serenely at Katerina.

"Go ahead, woman," he said. "Talk. Enough of us both playing the fool."

"What happened the night of the fire?" asked Katerina in a preliminary way.

"The factory burned down," said Timofei.

"*Ekh*, Timofei," said Katerina soothingly. "How you dread this subject. Did a certain maiden of exceptional beauty kiss you on the lips?"

Timofei flushed suddenly, then frowned. He bent down and pulled off his other boot.

"Things happen during fires," he said. "During a time of stress . . ."

"A woman speaks her heart," finished Katerina. "I have spoken to Nadezhda."

Timofei jumped up with excitement. The dirty boot fell out of his lap. Katerina picked it up, and the felt cloth.

"You need a woman to polish your boots," she said. "To make borsch, *goloubtsee, pirog,* roast goose. You need a woman to smoothe your brow, and to sleep on the oven."

Timofei was confused. "That's too much to say," he muttered. "Just because of one kiss."

"One kiss buys another," said Katerina. "I have spoken to her."

"I do not understand," said Timofei. "In what sense have you spoken to her?"

Katerina maintained a painful silence. Slowly, deliberately, she finished polishing Timofei's boot, then set it on the table next to the other boot.

"Which one is better?" asked Katerina. "Tell."

Timofei marched barefoot about the izba.

"Boots! boots!" he finally exclaimed. "Yours is better. The question is in what sense did you speak to that innocent lady?"

"*Akh* yes, she is innocent," said Katerina. "No question about that."

"But what did you say to her?" Timofei's enormous chest rippled under the heavy blue shirt. "Well, what?"

Katerina set the samovar on the table.

"The glasses," said Katerina, bringing three glasses out of a wall cupboard, "the lemon, and sugar cubes. Where do you keep the spoons? *Akh,* here."

Katerina stood on the cedar stool and peering over the oven reached for the sleeping strannik.

"Let him rest," said Timofei.

"Sleep is for the young," said Katerina. "*Dedushka!* Strannik! Wake up. It's a fine afternoon. It's not night."

The strannik awoke, and slid down the oven. His white locks rested on his thin shoulders.

"Tea!" he said. "That's the life. And how is Vanka?"

Katerina led the strannik to the table, then motioned to Timofei to sit down too.

"What's the boots on the table?" asked the strannik. "Where are they going?"

Katerina laughed. "They might go to church," she said.

The strannik was puzzled. "Now how's this?" he asked. "What is being prepared here?"

"Strannik," said Katerina. "Which boot shines better?"

The strannik picked up Katerina's boot.

Katerina stood up and poured the tea.

"There is a discussion here," said Katerina, "about Timofei and Nadezhda."

"The maiden at the fire?" asked the strannik.

"That one," agreed Katerina. "I have spoken to her about Timofei."

"The devil take it!" burst in Timofei. "What did she say?"

"She said, 'No,'" answered Katerina. "What did you think she would say?"

Timofei was confused. "Then what is this business all about?" he asked. "What more is there to do? She said 'No'!"

The strannik and Katerina laughed gently.

"Between a woman's 'no' and 'yes' there's no room for a needle to pass," said the strannik.

Timofei took his boots off the table and put them on.

All three drank the hot tea in silence broken only by the crunching of the sugar cubes between sips.

"Well, perhaps," said Timofei, stroking his brown moustache. "Perhaps, if I had land, a good house, two hundred roubles. . . ."

"If grandmother were not grandmother, she'd be grandfather," said Katerina. "A man lives on what he has. The maiden loves you."

"Is she kind?" asked the strannik.

"Kindness itself," said Katerina. "Very often I have seen her put bread on the windowsill for the wandering unfortunates."

"Is that true?" asked Timofei.

"My tongue should fall away if I lie."

Katerina stood up and poured tea again for each one.

"I have spoken to her father," continued Katerina, "to Anton the Furnace Man. He is your friend."

"Excellent workman," said Timofei. "An artist."

"He could afford a dowry of forty roubles. . . ."

"*Akh*, but this is preposterous!" exclaimed Timofei. "If I should be so fortunate as to be loved, let us say, by this delightful creature, I do not need to be paid. *Akh*, but this is upsetting!"

Katerina laughed. "You are like gold," she said. "I knew you would refuse, and I told him so."

Timofei was amazed.

"This woman was not born yesterday, Timofei," said the strannik. "How many marriages have you made, Katerina?"

"This will be the sixtieth," said Katerina, glancing mischievously at the now placid Timofei. "And my charge is only fifteen roubles."

"How did you know I would refuse the dowry?" asked Timofei.

"Why do you suppose your chest is so large?" replied Katerina. "It's that tremendous heart of yours. What else!"

Timofei laughed. "You're a shrewd one," he said. "You have a way about you, woman."

"I was thinking of autumn as the time," said Katerina matter-of-factly. "After the harvest. With a great choral festival the day before—a *khorovod* that would always be remembered in Aremziansk."

"Autumn is happy for weddings," agreed the strannik. "Delicious autumn."

"Are you agreed on autumn?" asked Katerina. "There would be plenty of time before then for you to build a larger izba for you and the maiden. . . ."

"What about the strannik?" asked Timofei.

"I will be going," said the strannik. "It is time to move on. Perhaps you and the maiden could go with me. Weren't you planning to see Nizhny Novgorod with me?"

Timofei's eyes were shining. "Why not!" he exclaimed. "Maybe she would go!"

"She will go anywhere," said Katerina, "if she marries you for love."

"You could sell the izba," suggested the strannik.

Timofei was growing more excited. "Or maybe I could build a larger izba and live there till next year. And you could live in this one, *dedushka*. Then, when Maria takes Mitya to Moscow, we three could also set out on a journey."

"That could be," said the strannik. "But of course we would go on foot."

Katerina stood up. "Go to see her in ten days," she said. "I must have time to talk to her a little more. After all, she has not yet said 'Yes.' "

Timofei was now alarmed. "Go see her now, Katerina. Can you go now?"

The strannik laughed.

"*Ekh*, Timofei," he said. "What a bouncing lamb you are. *Davai chai*, [pour out the tea] Katerina."

Katerina poured a third glass of tea for each and drinking hers quickly, arose to go.

"Go to see her in ten days," she repeated. "And, Timofei—do you wish one word of advice?"

"*Akh*, yes," said Timofei. "Tell. By all means."

"Well," said Katerina, opening the door, and tying the red kerchief about her head, "there is one thing only for a marrying man to remember. It's this: a wife is no balalaika; you can't put her on the shelf after playing."

When autumn came, Timofei and Nadezhda were married and went to live in a new izba in the forest.

2

Vanka, thin and haggard and with a look of bewilderment in his eyes, lay on a rough wooden bed outside the izba of his mother Katerina and Old

Andrei the Chemist. No longer the Fool, Vanka, from whose mind the veil of imbecility had suddenly lifted on the night of the great fire, lay inert on his bed, in the sunshine. The dogs that surrounded him sat silently, only occasionally darting their long red tongues in and out of their mouths as the sun poured its warmth about them. Near the foot of his bed, a pig snouted in the ground, grunting contentedly, and a few steps beyond stood one of the brown indolent horses belonging to Matvei.

Katerina came out of the izba with a bowl of soup in her hands and sat on the edge of Vanka's bed.

"How old am I?" asked Vanka quietly.

"Twenty-five," said Katerina. "Eat."

Vanka opened his mouth indifferently, and took part of the soup on the spoon.

"How old are you?" he asked.

"Fifty-two," said Katerina. "Eat some more."

Vanka ate a little more.

"Tell me everything," said Vanka gently. "How old is Mitya?"

"About fifteen," said Katerina. "Why?"

Vanka watched the pig groveling in the dirt.

"Why do we live?" he asked.

Katerina frowned. "Take some more soup."

"Answer," said Vanka.

"We live because we are alive," said Katerina. "Now eat. You are alive, so live."

Vanka took a spoonful, but it was clear now that he did this only to prolong Katerina's stay—so that she might answer his questions. Katerina, instinctively understanding this, considered the bargain worth while.

"Why were we created?" asked Vanka.

"Because God wanted it," Katerina explained. "It is His will."

"I can't understand," said Vanka softly. "Don't fool me, *mamachka*. Maybe I can live, if there are answers. Tell me the answers."

Katerina's eyes filled with tears. She crossed herself.

"I will never fool you," she said softly. "There is a God who wants us to live."

"Why?" asked Vanka.

"We do not know God's way," said Katerina.

"Is He kind?" asked Vanka.

"Kind and wise," replied Katerina. "Kinder than any man."

"I do not understand," said Vanka. "Is He powerful? Can He do anything?"

"Yes," said Katerina, "Anything."

"Then why is there illness? Why am I a fool? Why do we suffer?"

"You are not a fool," said Katerina. "*Akh*, no, Vanyachka my heart. You were once a little bit dull. But not now. See, you talk to me!"

"Why do we suffer?" asked Vanka. "If God is wise and can do anything, why didn't He make us strong?"

"We are strong if we want to be," said Katerina gently. "Make your heart say it, Vanya. Make it say, 'I am strong' and you will be strong."

"I can do it," said Vanka; "that's true."

"Then do it!" exclaimed Katerina jumping up in excitement. The soup spilled on her dress. "Do it!" she repeated.

Vanka watched his mother's face. Katerina placed the wooden soup bowl on the ground. The pig came over and put his snout into it. Two dogs came over and sniffed. The pig scolded them and the dogs retreated. Matvei's horse, Soldat, now approached and lay down in the shade of a tall larch tree.

"Sit down," said Vanka to his mother. "Answer everything."

Katerina sat down. "All right," she said.

Vanka began anew. "Why didn't God make everything just right? No suffering, no hungering, no pain, no lying, no fear, no death?"

"It would be dull," said Katerina.

Vanka thought this over for a moment. He shook his head. "Doesn't sound right," he said. "Will your life be less dull if I die?"

Katerina began to weep. "There are more answers," she said.

"Tell," said Vanka.

"There are people who believe that God gave man a chance to live the kind of life you ask me about. But man made a sin. . . ."

"Why didn't God make man so he could not sin?" asked Vanka.

"It is His way," said Katerina. "Men cannot understand His way."

"But I must," said Vanka. "Or I cannot live. Can you answer?"

"No," said Katerina softly.

Vanka put his hand over the edge of the bed.

"Boris," he said, "come here."

The eyes of the heavy dog lighted up. He came closer and buried his nose in Vanka's hand.

"The animals need you," said Katerina. "Think of them." Suddenly her eyes brightened. "Yes!" she exclaimed. "That's right. We are made to live for each other. That's the reason. You see, Vanya?"

Vanka shook his head. "But why with suffering? Maybe God is not able to do better?"

"No, no," said Katerina. "He can do everything."

Into Vanka's eyes came a look of hopelessness.

"Maybe there is no God," he said, rising on one elbow. "It would all be clearer. Miserable. Terrible. But clearer. Tell me, *mamachka*. Tell me."

"There is a God," said Katerina. "Pray to Him."

"Impossible," said Vanka.

Katerina went into the hut. Inside she broke down in the arms of her tired Old Andrei.

"You go to him," wept Katerina. "Answer his questions."

"I can't," said Old Andrei. "I can't answer them."

They sat down on the heavy wooden bench. Old Andrei was reflecting.

"It seems this way," he finally said. "If you tell him there is a God, then you can't answer his questions, and he will die. But if you tell him there is no God, he will suffer but live. Can you tell him there is no God?" A look of fear stole into Katerina's eyes.

"I cannot say that," she said. "Can you tell him that?"

"No," he said softly. "I cannot say that."

Then Old Andrei had an idea, and rose from the bench.

"I will go and say, 'Vanya, I do not know about God. Perhaps there is or perhaps there isn't, but it is for you to live and find out. And tell us all.' This I will say to him." He started for the door.

Katerina too arose. "But he will ask you what you really believe," she said. "What will you say?"

Old Andrei bowed his head. "I am a believer," he said. "I will say that I believe."

"Do not go," said Katerina.

They stood in the middle of the room, considering the problem.

"We must send to him a person who does not believe," said Katerina. "Then, as you say, he may want to live, in a meaningless world without a hereafter. Can we send him such a person?"

"No," said Old Andrei. "And I do not know any such person. Except one."

"Bassargin?" asked Katerina.

"Yes," nodded Old Andrei. "But he is not here. And I would not send him, in any case."

Katerina considered further. "Is there a person who is not sure about God? Then Vanya may want to live, to find out."

"Timofei is such a person," said Old Andrei.

"Shall we send him to our son?"

"No," said Old Andrei. "If you believe in God, and if I do, what is there to make tricks about? What is there to fear? Come."

Old Andrei led Katerina to the ikon corner and kneeling before the Mother of God and Her Son, they prayed.

The next week Vanka died.

3

In the early summer of the following year, 1849, Mitya took his final examinations. The night before he had spent without sleep, studying the Latin grammar.

Late in the day, after the examinations, Mitya came home exhausted. Maria, standing on the steps, awaited him eagerly.

"Well?" she whispered.

"Passed," said Mitya.

Maria almost collapsed. Mitya helped her inside, and she lay down on the old yellow couch.

"That is, everything?" asked Maria to make certain. "The Latin?"

"Yes," said Mitya listlessly.

"And the other classics?"

"Yes," Mitya said again. "Everything, everything. Let's go to Moscow."

Wearily Maria stood up and left the room. In a moment she returned with a cup of hot milk.

"Take it," she said.

Mitya silently sipped the hot milk. Occasionally he coughed.

At each cough Maria glanced up in alarm.

"Never mind," he said. "It's nothing. Where is my book?"

"Which book?" asked Maria puzzled.

"The Latin book," said Mitya.

Maria looked closely now at Mitya. Her eyes narrowed in perplexity.

"You're not going to study some more?" she said. "Isn't it over?"

"It is over," said Mitya. "Where is the book?"

Maria brought him the battered brown book.

"*Davai*," [Give it] said Mitya quietly.

He took the book, and left the house.

At the corner of the street Mitya met school comrades, also in uniform. There were Orlov and Pertinsky and Brakhman and others. Each carried one book or more in his arms.

At the next corner more boys joined the group, and at the next still more.

Night was beginning to fall now, and the crowd of high-school boys who had just graduated climbed over dark rocks and ascended the hill overlooking the city of Tobolsk.

There they gathered shrubs and branches and short heavy logs. When the fire was lit and crackling, the boys tossed into it those books which had brought them pain during their high-school years.

When Mitya tossed in his *Principles of Latin Grammar,* he stepped back for a moment, and calmly thumbed his nose.

Chapter Six

Bassargin's Gift and Mitya's Word for History

MITYA WAS ready for Moscow.
It was bright midsummer of 1849, and there remained little for Maria to do: to sell the few possessions in Tobolsk, the izba in the village of Aremziansk, then to hitch the horse to the telega and roll away across the fields toward the Urals. Maria would go, and Mitya, and the frail Elizabeth, his sister, needing Maria's care. The older boy Paul was leaving to take a clerical position in Omsk.

But besides the problem of selling the possessions, there also remained one more matter to take care of—Bassargin's portfolio.

The battered portfolio that Bassargin had given Mitya contained many documents dealing with Russia's history. This material, prepared by Bassargin, was considered by him to be of the greatest importance in readying Mitya for the entrance examinations at the University of Moscow.

Mitya had spent three months studying the documents, and now a certain decision had been reached by him, Bassargin, and Maria: Bassargin would come once more from Omsk, and cross-examine Mitya on Russian history and literature. This would be a dress rehearsal for the Moscow examinations.

"I can stay only a few days," Bassargin wrote. "With some trepidation, my dear Maria Dmitrievna, I must tell you that I am bringing Mitya a certain parting gift. It is painful for me to do this, but it is my duty. Please do not mention the matter. With a bow to all my friends, Nikolai Bassargin."

Maria disposed of her Tobolsk belongings and with Elizabeth and Mitya returned to their village izba for the last sojourn in Aremziansk.

To the Mendeleyev izba, for the first evening session of questions, came Timofei, the strannik, and Old Andrei the Chemist. But Katerina his wife, the weeping mother of the departed Vanka, did not come. Alone, still bewildered, she chose to remain in her house of mourning.

"Go," she had said to Old Andrei. "You go. I want to stay here. There are thoughts to think."

Bassargin's Gift and Mitya's Word for History 53

Mitya helped Maria serve tea to their friends, whom they would be leaving in a few days—perhaps forever.

"Drink," said Mitya smilingly to Timofei, who had set his glass down for a moment. "It's only water. And the river is full of it."

Suddenly Old Andrei stood up. "A vehicle is coming," he said. "I hear the horse. Is that Bassargin?"

He opened the door of the izba.

Maria hurried to the door. Outside, in the dark night, a horse, and a smoothly rolling telega were rapidly approaching the hut. In a moment the telega drew up before the door, and Bassargin hopped off the driver's seat.

Maria embraced him. "How is Olga?" she asked.

"Better," said Bassargin. "Sends her highest regards. She may come tomorrow. I'll be right in," he added hastily. "The horse is starving."

Bassargin hung a bag of oats over the horse's head, and the animal promptly began to eat.

"That is a remarkable telega," said Old Andrei, stooping to look at the wheels of Bassargin's wagon. "It was rolling like a tarantass."

Bassargin nodded. "It was made from a tarantass," he said. "The wheels and the axles and all that lower part. It cost me heavily."

Bassargin took a flat package wrapped in brown paper from the wagon. "All right," he said. "Is Mitya prepared?"

"I think so," said Maria. "He has lived with your portfolio. Come on. There is hot tea."

Bassargin greeted Mitya and his other friends quietly and placed the flat package at his feet on the floor. And now in the lamplight it was clear that Bassargin, as usual, had bad news to impart.

"What is the trouble?" asked Maria.

Bassargin drank of the hot tea, then set down the glass.

"Dostoyevsky has been arrested," he said.

"What is the reason?" asked Timofei.

Bassargin's tired face now slowly developed a scowl.

"There does not need to be a reason," he said. "I received a letter today. There was a group meeting at Petrashevsky's house. They were apparently reading Belinsky's letter to Gogol, and as usual bewailing the plight of our Russia. The secret police raided at five o'clock in the morning and brutally dragged away Petrashevsky, and Dostoyevsky, and his brother Mikhail, as well as about thirty others. It is said they are to be shot."

"When will life be a little easier?" asked Elizabeth, rising on her elbow, on the oven.

Bassargin shrugged his shoulders. He turned to Mitya. "All right, Mitya, what have you learned? Can you tell us Russian history in two words?"

"I can do it in one," said Mitya, lifting Bassargin's portfolio and placing it on the table among the glasses of tea.

Maria was puzzled. Timofei held his glass of tea in mid-air. Old Andrei and Timofei exchanged glances. Even the strannik roused himself from his reverie and sat up in his chair.

Bassargin's face seemed to play with a fleeting and suddenly recurring grin—an ironical grin.

"What do you mean, Mitya?" he asked. "What is the word that summarizes Russian history?"

Mitya poured the contents of Bassargin's portfolio out onto the table.

"What is the word?" Bassargin repeated.

Mitya's eyes were fixed on the documents—the pamphlets, the summaries, the charts before him.

"Blood," he said softly. "The word is 'blood.' "

Maria stood up. Her eyes were narrowed. Slowly she walked out of the izba into the village night. Bassargin could sense that she expected him to follow. He rose.

Standing in the roadway in front of the hut Maria contemplated Bassargin's face. The yellow moonlight made him look ill and old.

"Kolya," said Maria, "I trusted you."

Bassargin seemed puzzled.

"I do not understand," he said. "What have I done?"

"What have you done?" echoed Maria.

"I completely do not understand," said Bassargin sternly. "I labored for weeks writing out the historical material. . . ."

"He calls it 'blood,' " said Maria quietly. "He is a boy. Fifteen years old. I did not expect his mind to be poisoned, his life to be soured. Not at the age of fifteen."

Bassargin's voice rose. "I did nothing evil," he said carefully. "I did my best."

"I have tried to protect him," went on Maria, heedless of Bassargin's reply. "I had always counted on you—to help in difficult times."

"You may continue to count on me," said Bassargin, now gently. "But please try to understand. I wrote out facts for him. The conclusion that he has drawn is startling, I would say. But it is his own. Have you read the material?"

"No," said Maria, sighing.

"Then come, listen."

"But how will it be in Moscow?" wondered Maria, looking out into space, seemingly addressing the western stars. "What if they question him on Russia's history?"

Bassargin's Gift and Mitya's Word for History

Bassargin smiled. "They will only ask single facts," he said. "Who was Ivan the Great? When was Catherine born? Believe me, Maria Dmitrievna, they do not dare to ask a man to summarize or draw conclusions. . . ."

"But how will he reply now?"

"To facts," said Bassargin, "he will match facts. His mind is good. Ah, but he has a good mind. Come on. Just listen."

In the yellow moonlight Maria's eyes glistened.

"Wait," she said. "I believe you. But wait. Tell me something."

Bassargin stood waiting.

"Tell me this," said Maria. "Is it true that tuberculosis is hereditary?"

"Has he been coughing?" asked Bassargin.

"Somewhat," said Maria. "Mitya's father died of it; and two of his sisters. Elizabeth too has it, I know. And now he is coughing—somewhat. Is it hereditary? Tell me, Kolyachka." Maria wept, softly, barely audibly.

"It is not hereditary," said Bassargin.

Maria watched his face.

"Tell me the truth," she said.

"For you," said Bassargin, "for you, because you are a good woman, I cross myself and call unto God to witness—though I do not believe in such things. I say the disease is not hereditary. He will be well."

Maria embraced him.

"How can you be sure?" she asked.

"His character," said Bassargin. "He is strong. His will is unbreakable. And it is you who made him that way. Don't give in now. Don't," and he started for the izba.

"Wait," said Maria putting out her hand. "Just one moment."

Bassargin stopped.

"Kolya," said Maria, "what is this present of yours, lying on the floor, in the izba?"

Bassargin winced. "A present," he said, "for Mitya. But I cannot give it now. It would be impossible to give it before we finish our practice examination. Let us go."

Silently they walked into the hut.

2

Mitya stood near the samovar, and Timofei was asking him questions about Siberia.

"When was Tobolsk founded?" asked Timofei.

"In 1587," said Mitya.

"How many days with snow?" asked Timofei. "In Tobolsk—per year?"

"About fifty," said Mitya. "Do you want the rain?"

Timofei lifted his great arm and waved away the rain.

"Strannik," said Timofei, "it's your turn. Or, Bassargin, maybe you want to start."

Bassargin shook his head.

"Let the strannik," he said.

"*Khorosho*," said the strannik. "All right. Mitenka, my little dove, where does a man buy the best felt boots in the world and the best karakul hats, *ekh?*"

"In Nizhny," smiled Mitya. "In Nizhny Novgorod. Where else!"

The strannik stood up. "A head on his shoulders," he said. "No cabbage there."

The strannik walked to the cupboard and took down a jar of raspberry jam.

"Why is this hiding?" he said, looking at Maria. "Is it spoiled?"

"I was confused by everything," said Maria. "Come, *dedushka,* open it up."

The strannik sat down.

"Mitya," he said, "tell me some more about my beloved Nizhny."

"It is a very important trading post," said Mitya, "and was especially so in the thirteenth century when it connected Moscow with Persia, central Asia, and the rest of the East. Trade goods from the East used to come to the Caspian Sea, then they would go up the Volga in boats, and much was unloaded near Nizhny, so it became a center of trade and of world importance."

"*Ekh,*" sighed the strannik nostalgically. "We must go there, Timofei. I am going in five or ten days. Will you come?"

Timofei nodded.

"It is agreed," he said. "Nadezhda and I will go with you. Now ask him your questions," he said to Bassargin.

"*Khorosho,*" [All right] agreed Bassargin. "My questions are not hard. Does the name 'Nevsky' mean anything to you?"

"Alexander Nevsky," said Mitya, "crushed the Germans on April 5, 1242, on the ice of the frozen Lake Ilmen. It was considered an important victory."

"Aha," said Bassargin. "Aha. Now this. The struggle against the Tartars was about when?"

"Well, it really all dragged on for centuries," replied Mitya.

"Did they do us any good whatever?"

Mitya glanced at Maria. He smiled. "They gave us my mother," he said. "That compensates for everything."

"I asked that on purpose," said Bassargin. "That's the only good that ever came from them. Well, let's go on. Oh, by the way. What does 'Tartar' mean?"

Mitya shook his head. "Something in the classics," he said, "about which I know nothing and never expect to."

Bassargin explained. " 'Tartarus' means 'Hell' in mythology. And 'Tartar' —the word we use mostly around here is a Manchu word, and means 'Nomad.' "

"I'm not interested," said Mitya.

"But you ought to be," said Maria gently.

"Well, maybe, mama. But I'm not." Mitya scowled.

Bassargin lowered his gaze to the flat brown package at his feet.

"Who finally drove the Tartars away?" he asked quietly.

"Dmitri of the Don," said Mitya. "He was the son of the Moscow Prince Ivan the Second. Dmitri built a great stone wall around the heart of Moscow —around the Kreml and after great bloodshed, the Tartars finally retreated."

"When?"

"About 1380, I think—something like that."

"Who first used the title of 'Tsar'? And what does the word mean?"

"I think that officially it was Ivan the Terrible. I'm not sure. He took the word 'Caesar' and made 'Tsar' out of it, for the Russians."

"I notice that you call him 'the Terrible,' " said Bassargin. "Some call him 'the Great.' "

"It means the same thing. Just a lot of bloodshed."

Bassargin glanced at Maria.

"Go ahead," she said. "Go on."

"Well, Ivan was born in 1530, crowned in 1547, and died in 1584. Shall I tell a little?"

Bassargin nodded his head.

"Ivan tried to unify Russia, and he was ruthless about it, with many beheadings, and so on. He even struck his own son and killed him."

"A veritable devil," said the strannik. "What a creature!"

"He married a very beautiful woman," went on Mitya. "Her name was Anastasia Romanov. She had a brother, boyar Nikita Romanov. That's the same Romanov name that the present Tsar line belongs to. It was a happy marriage. But Anastasia was poisoned."

"I didn't know that," said Maria.

"*Akh da,*" said Mitya. "Some plotters. Now for the strannik. I think it was Ivan who suspected Novgorod—the old city, not Nizhny the Lower. He suspected the people of the city of planning with Poland to rise up against his rule. So he marched on Novgorod in 1570. And the blood that he spilled I think probably could make a river. For five weeks, fathers, mothers, children, everybody was slaughtered." Mitya stopped for a moment. "That's what it says here," he went on, "in the papers of Kolya's portfolio."

"Those are simple facts," said Bassargin glancing at Maria. "Tell your mother, Mitya. Did I give personal opinion in any of that material?"

Mitya shook his head.

"No," he said slowly. "It's factual, all right. Murders, wars, executions! *Bozhe moi.*"

Bassargin picked up his package.

"That's enough for tonight," he said.

3

At the practice examination held the next night Mitya told of Stenka Razin, the Russian Robin Hood, who in 1667 organized fugitive serfs and Cossacks to fight government troops and to plunder the rich. In 1670 Stenka sailed up the Volga and called for recruits to wage war against the faction in power. He raided Nizhny, but in June, 1671, he was captured and executed.

Maria was excited. "Near Saratov," she said, "there stands a hill with Stenka Razin's name carved on it. *Akh,* how often I used to see it."

"I have seen it too," said the strannik.

"And I," said Bassargin.

"Someday I suppose I will have to see it," said Mitya. He then told of Peter the Great, Catherine, Alexander, and the war with Napoleon. "More blood," said Mitya.

"That's about enough, isn't it?" said Bassargin, rising suddenly and upsetting his glass which fell to the floor and shattered, the spilled tea wetting the brown package.

The strannik, who had just begun to drowse, was startled out of his sleep by the crashing glass.

"*Noo!*" he shouted. "*Akh da.*" He looked at Mitya perplexed. "Tell about Nizhny Novgorod," he said and, sitting down again, fell asleep at once.

"I'll take him to his izba," said Bassargin, picking up the package and drying it. "Come on, *dedushka.* And Mitya, wait up for me—there's something I must give you. I'll be right back."

Mitya and Maria exchanged glances.

"Something peculiar," said Mitya. "I can tell."

Bassargin and the strannik left.

Mitya stood waiting in the middle of the hut.

4

When Bassargin returned, the brown package was in his hands. He began to unwrap it, and for a moment stopped. With a pained look in his eyes, he turned to Mitya.

"I hate to do this to you," he said. "I love you, Mitya. Believe me."

Mitya and Maria stood speechless, waiting. Bassargin finished unwrapping the gift—a brown book. He stretched out his hand with the book. Mitya took the volume and read the title, *Advanced Latin Grammar and Composition.*

"A very difficult examination has been announced in this at the university," Bassargin said. "Very difficult. Far, far harder than the one you managed to pass at the Gymnasium."

Mitya, with the book in his hands, sank onto a stool.

Tears began to roll down his cheeks. He sat stupefied, gazing at the brown book on which a few tears had already fallen.

Maria, watching Mitya, also began to weep.

"I don't know what to say," said Bassargin.

Maria put her hand on Mitya's shoulder.

"We cannot do this to you, Mitenka," she said. "When I see you this way, the University isn't worth it. Nothing is worth it. Let us not go. . . . If it breaks your heart."

Mitya stood up. He picked up a matchbox from the table, and with Bassargin's gift under his arm walked out of the izba.

Bassargin and Maria stood in the middle of the hut, silently following him with their eyes.

5

On top of the hill with the church that Maria had built for the village, Mitya stood for a moment quietly. Then, drawing a match out of the box, he struck a light. Suddenly from the other side of the hill, at its base—in the cemetery—a loud bark sounded. The match died out; Mitya struck another, and again the bark of a dog sounded.

Mitya descended the hill toward the black cemetery below.

Carefully he walked among the crosses, straining his eyes in the darkness. He struck another match. It burned in silence. To the left Mitya became aware of a soft breathing. Striking another match he saw the grave of Vanka and at the head of the grave, silently mourning, lay Boris, Vanka's shaggy brown dog, the most devoted of his friends.

"Boris," said Mitya.

The dog watched Mitya quietly, not stirring from his place.

Mitya drew closer to the grave, watching the mound and the dog.

Once more he struck a match and, peering at the cross, read the inscription:

HERE LIES OUR VANYA
WHO COULD NOT LIVE IN THIS WORLD

"He could not live," whispered Mitya. "No heart can pity that much." He thought of the sacrifices and sufferings of his mother, and of all the villagers and of the bleakness of their lives.

"I must help them," Mitya whispered. "Somehow."

And now suddenly in a flash he saw the history of Russia rush past him with its incessant killings, and the word "blood" came to his lips again.

"What can a man do?" wondered Mitya. "What can a man do for people—for all people, to appease the misery and to stop the blood?"

Once more his eyes returned to Vanka's grave.

"No, Vanyachka," he said. "A man cannot die. Of what avail is that, Vanyachka?"

Boris stood up and shuffled over to Mitya, touching his snout to Mitya's hand.

"No, Vanyachka," Mitya repeated. "I will not die. I will live."

He dropped to his knees. "*Akh* God," he said, "give me a chance. Let me find a way to help. They couldn't stop the rivers of blood with wars; they couldn't stop them with governments and politics—*akh* God, let me try with science. Give me a chance. Just one."

Mitya glanced down at the book in his hand, the *Advanced Latin Grammar and Composition.*

"All right," he said. "All right, come on. Now."

He hurried through the dark lonely cemetery and, increasing his pace, came presently to his izba and flung the door open.

Maria and Bassargin stopped talking.

"Pack!" said Mitya. "We're going."

"Pack?" said Maria.

"Yes," said Mitya. "Pack. We're going now. Immediately. To Moscow."

Maria glanced in alarm at Bassargin.

Bassargin was looking carefully at Mitya.

"Yes," he whispered to Maria. "Yes, you have to go now. You'd better pack. At once."

Chapter Seven

To Moscow. And to Nizhny Novgorod

THE SKY in the east was coming to life with the pale blue dawn.
Maria, Mitya, and Elizabeth returned from the cemetery, from the last visit to the grave of Ivan.

Somberly Mitya collected his books, tied them together, and placed them on the telega that Bassargin had given them—the smoothly rolling telega with the under portions taken from a tarantass.

Maria spread a sheet on the floor of the hut, and onto it began to pile the possessions of the family: galoshes, an extra pair of shoes for Elizabeth, a brown skirt and a green one, a black fur cap, kerchiefs of several colors, pictures, Bassargin's portfolio, a leather jacket, a Tartar costume, a wire frame for making hats, a belt. . . .

Elizabeth helped her tie up the bundle and Mitya carried it out to the telega.

Then she made smaller bundles of wooden bowls, and a pot for cooking on the way, a clay salt shaker and spoons, knives, forks, jars of raspberry preserves. Still another bundle contained food to be used in the immediate future—loaves of rye bread, goose fat, a cabbage, a bag of potatoes, black prunes, and slices of dried reindeer meat.

Elizabeth stood over the oven boiling eggs; and when they were hard she wrapped them in a white cloth and put it into a bag. Mitya brought the bag out to the telega, and he also brought out a foot-length of bologna and a bag with village-made white cheese. Meanwhile, Maria ripped open her mattress and extracting the pink banknotes placed them with the money given her for the hut by the Village Elder—and with the money from Matvei, and from several others. She sewed the entire packet, 253 roubles, into the lining of her brown coat.

Mitya brought out the teakettle and a large bag of loose black tea and four lemons. The lemons he dropped into the empty teakettle.

Bassargin and his Olga, who had come during the night, had not yet returned from the strannik's izba where they had gone to discuss the route that the travelers should follow.

Presently, Matvei appeared leading Soldat, his horse, a horse far superior to the one which had drawn Bassargin's smooth telega. Matvei now proposed that this horse, Soldat, be taken to carry the voyagers.

"Let me hitch this one to the telega," said Matvei to Maria. "The horse that you have will die in three days. He can hardly stand."

Without waiting for her protesting reply at his intended sacrifice, he unhitched Bassargin's horse and replaced it with his own. Mitya helped to tie the horse in, pulling tightly on the long black belts. The horse turned to Mitya and blinked.

"Too tight," said Matvei. "Remember, when he blinks, loosen him someplace. And always feed him as soon as you make a stop for the night. Then he'll behave. And also, never hit him to make him go faster. Just swear."

"All right," said Mitya. "He's strong, this partner—isn't he? Look at the muscles."

"I feed him good," said Matvei. "And he works hard. But slow. If you don't go fast, and rest him often, he can take you all the way to Moscow, without any fresh horses."

"I'm in a hurry," said Mitya.

"Well, if you're in a hurry," said Matvei, "you'll have to change horses once or twice. If you don't miss the post stations."

"I'll watch carefully," said Mitya.

Matvei made the final adjustment of the duga—the bow-shaped wooden harness above the horse's head.

"Never beat him," Matvei repeated, "just swear. Better first to appeal to him with friendship, give him a chance. Usually, he likes you to swear, so give it to him good, Mitya. Burn his hair up with a fiery tongue. *Ekh*, he likes it. He's a queer one."

"I'll do everything," said Mitya.

Matvei kissed the horse on the nose.

"I'll be back," he said, and driving Bassargin's horse before him, he started toward his own izba.

In the middle of the dusty road Matvei stopped and turned around.

"Tell Bassargin he can have this one any time," he called. "I'm just going to feed him, and then I'll let him sleep. I'll be back."

Mitya nodded his head and went back into the izba. The horse turned to look after the retreating Matvei, then slowly started to draw the telega after him.

Apparently Matvei heard the wagon begin to roll, for he suddenly turned.

"*Ish ti!*" [Hey you!] roared Matvei. "Go back, Soldat! Go back!"

The horse considered a moment, then, having decided to obey, reluctantly turned back.

As the light extended further across the sky, the villagers began to emerge from their izbas. One glance at the horse and loaded wagon was enough to make clear that the Mendeleyev family was leaving.

"Maria's going," the word went round. "They're taking Mitya. Right now. Imagine. *Ai, ai, ai.* To Moscow!"

Gradually a crowd gathered round the stolid horse and his burden. The faces of the mouzhiks and their babas were pale and grave, the faces of people who live in great cold and snow and in meager sunlight.

"A good horse," said a young clean-shaven mouzhik. "Matvei's Soldat. Lazy, lazy, strong horse."

Several women brought black bread and small jars of jam from their izbas and quietly placed them on the telega.

An old man emptied the pockets of his blue trousers and poured a handful of kopeks onto the wagon, under the driver's seat.

"For luck," he said. "And maybe a pencil. A big green pencil."

"To Moscow!" said a fat woman in a green kerchief. "Imagine that to yourself!"

Then Timofei arrived with Nadezhda, having heard of the sudden news. Breathless they burst into the izba.

"Is it true?" exclaimed Timofei.

Maria explained Mitya's sudden decision.

"There's no stopping him," she said. "His mind is made up. We have to go now."

Mitya was examining the izba, to see if anything vital were being left behind.

"Why don't you go to Nizhny now?" asked Mitya.

Timofei pulled Nadezhda to the door. "I just wanted to make sure you were going," he said. "Come on, Nadenka, let's tell the strannik."

"He knows," said Elizabeth. "Bassargin and Olga are over there."

"We're going to Nizhny," called out Timofei, and disappeared through the door with his breathless Nadezhda.

2

Maria, Elizabeth, and Mitya mounted the telega.

About them were gathered their casual village friends and their dear friends too—Matvei and Marfa, Oblontov and Maroosya, Katerina and Andrei, Bassargin and Olga. Timofei, Nadezhda, and the strannik had not yet come to bid them farewell. More villagers were arriving, the mouzhiks wearing their caps against the crisp early morning, the women wearing their kerchiefs or shawls.

Maria was weeping. Elizabeth, too, wept, occasionally stopping to cough. Mitya, grim, sat in the driver's seat, holding the reins in his slender hands. He knew that the moment had not yet come. There would yet be good-bys to say . . . sudden, unplanned words. And now they began.

"I'll keep a flame under the ikon for you," said an old wizened woman.

Maria, tearful, nodded. "God bless you, Varvara," she said.

"Do not let anyone admire the horse or praise your son," said an old feeble mouzhik. "The devil will hear, and in his envy, will do you harm. The horse will die, and the son will fall ill."

Maria nodded her head.

Matvei moved forward through the crowd.

"Give the horse a drink," he said to Mitya. "When he pops up his ears like that, he's thirsty."

Mitya glanced at the popping ears of the horse.

"*Tse*," said Mitya, and lightly tapped the reins. "*Voda*, [water] Soldat."

The horse stirred and slowly pulled the telega through the crowd, which at once followed.

At the trough, Soldat began his last drink in the village. Occasionally, he shrugged his shoulders. Now he stopped for a moment, and lifting his head, looked up wonderingly at the blue sky. The villagers followed the glance of the horse.

"Wheeeeeeeeeeeeen!" said the horse, and once more lowered his head to drink. Again he whinnied at the blue sky.

"He won't drink any more," said Matvei. "When he does that twice—that's all he wants."

Mitya smiled. "What else should I know about him?" he asked.

"Don't forget to curse," said Matvei. "For speed."

Bassargin urged them on.

"It's about time, I guess," he said. "Study hard. Be careful at the University. You are independent in your ways, but you must not talk too much or they will expel you."

Mitya's eyes filled with tears.

"I will always remember you," he said. "I appreciate everything. I will write."

Bassargin's cheeks were suddenly wet with tears.

"That's all right," he mumbled.

"Good-by, dearest Kolya," said Maria to him.

"Good-by," said the frail, tearful Elizabeth to Bassargin and Olga. "Farewell, everybody. I love you."

The mouzhiks and their women bowed their heads. Many wept silently.

"Take care of yourself, mama," said Olga, distraught.

"This is no time to start," Maria answered gently.

Katerina came forward.

"In Vanya's name, Mitya, I give you the blessing. Stay strong, Mitya."

Then the Starosta Oblontov spoke firmly from the crowd.

"If you do not pass the examinations, Mitya, it is possible to present a petition of mercy to the Tsar himself. Write to me. I will secure a special form and send it to you."

And the Starosta's wife spoke.

"Just always be honest, Mitya," she said. "Like you are. That's all. And will you be able to cross the Urals, Maria Dmitrievna?"

Maria wiped her eyes with her hands.

"Let God grant that the Urals be our worst obstacle," she said.

Again Matvei spoke.

"If things do not go well, little boy, you come back to us. We'll always take care of you. I'm getting old now. They'll be needing a new night watchman soon. Remember, Mitya."

Then, suddenly, through the crowd came Timofei, with Nadezhda and the strannik.

"We are going today, too!" Timofei said excitedly. "Later. In the afternoon."

Nadezhda's eyes were sparkling.

"We are going to Nizhny," she addressed Maria. "With the strannik. On foot. Akh, how delightful, how delightful."

"They wouldn't wait longer," said the strannik, "these lambs. And some day we will find you in Moscow, and bring you to Nizhny."

"Yes," said Mitya. "Be sure and find us. We will always be waiting."

Timofei withdrew a paper bundle from a large pocket of his trousers.

"Here, Mitya," he said. "I made this long ago. It is the best I have."

Mitya took the paper packet and unwrapped it.

"Akh, what a beauty!" exclaimed Maria at the sight of a tiny sky-blue vase.

"That's to remind you, Mitya," said Timofei, "that everything in the world is art."

A heavy-set peasant with red hair moved closer.

"We have nothing, little boy," he said. "Most of us here have nothing. But if you succeed, we will all be rich. Will you remember?"

Mitya stood up.

"You are all in my heart," he said. "I will never forget you, I promise."

Nervously he sat down.

"Don't upset the boy," said a voice from the crowd. "Let it be."

An old woman with a cane moved toward the telega.

"It's about my son," she said. "He went away thirty-two years ago, March sixth. He was tall, honest, and strong. His name is Stepan and he went to Moscow. I cannot die. My soul is twisting within me, until I find him. Will you seek?"

"What is the patronymic, and the family name?" asked Mitya.

"Stepan Andreyevitch Yusulov," said the old woman. "Blue eyes he had. Like yours."

"I will seek," said Mitya. "*Yei Bogu,* [Honest to God] I will seek."

"I will pray," said the old woman, and slowly retreated through the crowd.

And now Old Andrei the Chemist stepped forth.

"If I ever obtain more coloring chemicals," he said, "I will send them to you, Mitya. They may help with the knowledge you'll need."

"Will you ever come back?" called a voice. "When you are famous?"

Maria stood up.

"I think I shall never come back," she said. "It is God's way. Mitya may some day come back."

Matvei was urging his old woman Marfa to say something.

"Your heart is full," said Matvei. "I know. Say it."

"I do not know what to say," replied Marfa. "What do I know? What can I say?" She began to weep.

"Let it be," said Maria. "Let things be."

"Well," said Mitya. "It is time. *Praschaitee* [farewell]. Or, *da svidaneeye. Au revoir.*"

"*Da svidaneeye,*" said the voices.

Mitya started the horse.

"Come on, Soldat," he said.

The horse stirred, and the specially constructed telega began to roll smoothly.

3

In the village, before noon, Timofei, Nadezhda, and the strannik were ready to start on their travels. Timofei sold his village izba to the Elder, Oblontov, for the community's disposal.

"The hut in the forest," Timofei said, "is a gift, for the next man and woman who wed."

Nadezhda's excitement at the prospect of leaving was so great that she could do nothing about final arrangements, such as making up bundles of clothing or food.

"*Ekh* you," Timofei chided. "Flying like a bird. With no cares."

"We'll find something on the way," Nadezhda bubbled. "Food and everything. Come, Timofeyushka, come—do hurry!"

The strannik had no preparations whatever to make. When Timofei and Nadezhda were ready, he picked up his sturdy walking stick with the green bundle containing half a loaf of black bread, a few prunes, a pat of cheese, and a small bottle of holy water from the Jordan. Out into the sun he strolled in his blue trousers that were stuffed into old leather boots. The brown shirt hung outside his trousers, and a rope was tied about his waist.

"Time to go," he sang. "Time to go. Time to leave Siberia. Farewell, people, farewell."

A small group of villagers watched the travelers walk away, toward the road over the hill.

"Why is everyone leaving?" wondered an old mouzhik. "Will they ever come back?"

But suddenly the strannik was surrounded by a group of tiny barefoot children who had learned that "the old man of the stories" was about to forsake them.

"*Dedushka!*" they implored, "Little grandfather! A last story. About paradise or the boy with blue hair. Tell, *dedushka*, tell."

"Tell," encouraged Nadezhda. "Tell them, strannik. But walk too—*akh* we must walk—out to the world."

Timofei carried two white bundles over his back and with wonder gazed upon his exuberant mate.

"Like a creature," he mumbled.

At the top of the hill upon which stood the church built by Maria, the strannik paused to tell his story to the barefoot children.

"Sit down, *dedushka*," they begged. "Then the story will grow longer, and you need rest, too."

The strannik lowered himself upon a gray boulder, and the children swarmed about him, some running their tiny fingers through his long locks, others tugging gently at his soft white beard.

"Once there lived and existed a boy," began the strannik.

"*Akh*," said the children with pleasure. "Tell."

"This little boy had blue hair and strong brown shoes, because the little boy was rich, and lived far far away in a distant city."

"Tell," interrupted a little girl, "tell, *dedushka*."

Nadezhda stood on the crest of the hill, waving her red kerchief to the people in the village below. Timofei lay on his back on the grass, his face drinking in the sunshine, his long brown moustache stirring faintly in the soft summer breeze.

"This little boy of blue hair," continued the strannik, "once put on his strong brown shoes and went out for a walk in the deep green forest. Night came and the boy of the blue hair was lost."

"Oo," said a little barefoot girl.

"But soon the little boy came to an old poor hut, and he knocked on the door."

"No, first the wolf," interrupted the children.

"*Akh* yes," said the strannik.

"A black wolf with green eyes came to eat the little boy. But the little boy prayed, and suddenly fear came into the wolf's heart, and he turned and ran deep into the forest. Then in a short while the little blue-haired boy with the strong brown shoes came to an old izba and he knocked on the door. 'Come in,' said a voice, and when the boy walked in he saw an old woman with white hair sitting near a tiny bed and on this bed lay a sick little boy with brown hair and no shoes. The old woman gave the little blue-haired boy black bread and a lump of sugar. 'Why is he sick?' asked the little blue-haired boy pointing to the bed. 'The evil cold has come,' said the old woman. 'The freezing wind has blown for forty days and the little boy has chilled, for he has no shoes. And his mother is dead, and I am his babushka. He has nothing in the world except me, his old granny.'"

The little boys and girls in the strannik's arms and those standing near listened attentively.

"Tell," said a little barefoot girl. "Tell."

"So the blue-haired boy took off his strong brown shoes and put them on the chilled feet of the sick little boy, and the sick little boy stood up and was well."

"*Akh*," said the little children and embraced the strannik.

"*Akh*, how kind he was. Tell."

Nadezhda bent down and kissed the strannik too.

"Tell," she whispered.

"Then the blue-haired boy started to go home. And when he stepped outside of the izba, there on the ground stood a pair of shining golden shoes, and he put them on. And these golden shoes made his feet go the right way and took him quickly over the highest mountains and through the darkest forests straight to the heart of his mother. And his mother was gay and his father sang and the little blue-haired boy with the golden shoes was happy all his life. And when he grew up he married a beautiful princess and I was present at the festive wedding supper and mead poured down my beard."

The strannik stood up.

"Good-by, my dear ones," he said. The children arose and looked at their bare feet.

"When will we have golden shoes?" asked a little girl.

"Someday," said the strannik.

"Good-by, *dedushka*," said the children softly. "Someday, come back. And bring the little golden shoes."

Nadezhda kissed the strannik's hand, and her eyes glistened with tears. Timofei arose.

"You're a good old man," he said quietly.

Nadezhda, Timofei, and the strannik began to descend on the other side of the hill. At the sight of the stretching yellow fields, the undulating blue of the hills, and the dark shadows of the distant blue-green forest, Nadezhda's eyes once more began to glow. The land stretched endlessly beyond.

"Look," she whispered. "Look. There lies the world. Come, let's hurry. It needs us."

The summer wind swirled her flowing blue dress and her long hair.

On the hill above, the children stood silent, then slowly turned about and descended to the village. Their eyes were cast down, observing the movements of their bare feet.

4

Summer night had fallen over Siberia. The gloom of the dark pine forests grew heavy under the veil of blackness.

In the black open, vast marshes and sudden bogs reposed under the weightless blanket cast by the moonless night.

The Irtysh and the Tobol rivers silently flowed along their unseeing courses. The hushed meadows stood as breathless guardians over them.

To the north of Tobolsk the low plain stretched toward the Arctic. In this sloping plain grew the wild cone-bearing forests and the endless treacherous marshes, now camouflaged by the deep of night.

To the south of Tobolsk, the silhouetted triangular pines, and the spruce, the cedar, the fir, and the great larch trees yielded in grudging measure to the stands of birch and aspen. There the trees were sparser, and the forest embroidered with tall grasses and ferns and juniper and raspberry growth. There in the morning sun the open spaces gave promise of more happiness. But now, at night, they, too, wore a shroud, standing silent watch over the sleeping animals within.

To the west of Tobolsk stretched the dense forests, their carpet of eternally sunless mosses weighted with fallen needles and cones.

Westward, on this moonless night in the summer of 1849, Soldat pulled the telega with its cargo.

Maria, enveloped in her dark coat, sat firmly in the driver's seat, the jogging reins in her hands. In the back of the wagon, amidst the bundles and the pots, lay the sleeping Mitya and the fitfully slumbering Elizabeth.

Maria's eyes searched the darkness before her for the light of a post station where a tiring horse and ten roubles might be exchanged for a fresh horse. But nowhere was there a light.

She brought the horse to a halt.

At once, Mitya awoke and came forward, carefully stepping over the reclining Elizabeth.

"Mama," he whispered. "Where are we?"

"In the forest," whispered Maria. "We must have missed the post station."

Mitya descended from the telega and groped forward toward the horse. He patted the animal on the flank, then approached his head, and talked to him softly. Soldat sighed, and in the dark his ears seemed to pop up and down spasmodically.

Mitya came back to Maria.

"We shouldn't have gone this long," he said. "The horse is thirsty, and exhausted."

"*Akh*, what a pity," whispered Maria. "I was hoping to reach a post station."

"We must sleep here," said Mitya. "I will look for a stream."

Maria was alarmed. "You may get lost," she said.

"No. I have matches. Wait here."

Maria sat breathless, watching the sudden flashes of light.

In a few minutes Mitya returned.

"Yes," he whispered. "This way. I will lead him. Come on, you poor creature."

At the stream, the thirsting horse drank twice, then began to shuffle uncomfortably.

Mitya unhitched him.

Maria took two blankets from the back of the wagon.

"You sleep in the wagon," she whispered. "I don't want you to be on the ground. It's damp. I'll sleep here, under this tree."

Mitya brought out the box of feed for the horse, then climbed onto the wagon and curled up under the driver's seat. Maria came and covered him, and tucked the blanket around Elizabeth.

"Peaceful night," whispered Maria. "Sleep well."

There was no reply.

Maria lay down under the tree.

In a moment the horse, too, had found a resting place.

Presently Maria arose and walked softly to the wagon. She took Mitya by the arm.

"Mitenka," she whispered, "Mitenka. Awake."

"What?" said Mitya barely audibly.

"The money. It is sewed in the lining of my coat. And on the other side are your graduation credentials. Remember. If anything should happen."

Mitya sat up.

"What do you mean? Robbers?"

"No," said Maria. "It is nothing. But my heart is beating a little badly. I do not feel as well as I should. You sleep now."

Mitya descended from the telega. He took Maria's hands.

"You are cold, *mamachka*," he whispered. "Shall I make a fire?"

"No, no, no, I just need rest."

Mitya helped Maria onto the wagon, and covered her.

"You'll be all right," he whispered.

"Of course," whispered Maria. "Cover Liza. Don't worry, I shall always be with you. I feel better."

"All right, *mamachka*."

Mitya spread a blanket and sat down near a rear wheel of the telega.

"Three weeks of this," he said to himself. "We must stop the hurrying. We must sleep in some hut every night and travel only in the daytime."

He arose now, and groping silently found his book on the telega. He carefully cleared a spot of ground and built a small fire. Then, opening Bassargin's parting gift, fixed his attention on the page.

With the breaking dawn the fire had gone out, and the sleeping Mitya sat with head leaning against the wheel of the telega, the open book sprawling in his lap.

Soldat, refreshed, stood by, watching.

5

On the afternoon of the next day, though they had reached a post station where eight fresh horses browsed about in the yellow meadow on the edge of a placid stream, Mitya, Maria, and Elizabeth jointly decided not to give up Soldat, who somehow had gradually become a link with their vanished Aremziansk and their lifelong friends. He seemed to understand their decision and whinnied repeatedly at the blue sky and the drifting, tuftlike clouds. The post horses in the meadow pricked up their ears and exchanged puzzled glances each time that Soldat whinnied triumphantly into the sky.

In the post-station hut, a stocky pale-faced mouzhik served tea and sugar cubes and Maria brought in the white Aremziansk cheese to supplement the midday refreshment. She drew her handkerchief from her coat pocket and untied the corner containing the loose change reserved for incidental expenses.

"Two kopeks per glass," said the heavy-set mouzhik. "And one kopek for each sugar cube."

Maria paid, and gave the man an extra five-kopek coin.

"For tea," she laughed, speaking the expression meaning "a tip."

The mouzhik dropped the money down his right boot and went out to look at Soldat.

In a moment Mitya followed him out of the post-station hut, and waited for him to speak.

"Your horse will die," said the mouzhik. "He can't run for three weeks."

"He doesn't run," said Mitya.

The mouzhik considered.

"All the same he will die," he concluded.

Mitya shook his head.

"We all sleep at night. We're not driving without stop. And the horse understands life. When it's difficult, he stops. We all get down, and everybody rests. When he's ready he walks to the wagon."

"The horse is a fool," said the mouzhik. "He should run away."

Mitya shrugged his shoulders.

Maria and Elizabeth came out and climbed into the wagon. Mitya mounted the driver's seat and took up the reins.

"I will give you my best fresh one for your horse," said the mouzhik, "if you throw in even only five roubles, not ten." Maria looked at Mitya.

"No," he said. "The horse belongs with us."

He started Soldat gently.

"Wait," said the mouzhik, stepping onto the roadway. "I'll give you my best fresh one for this one. And no money from you. *Ekh?*"

Elizabeth looked down at the mouzhik.

"The horse belongs," she said softly. "He's from Aremziansk, from our home."

The heavy mouzhik stepped out of the roadway.

"Akh," he said, scratching his nose. "I see now how it is. *Bog svamee* [may God be with you]. *Tse.*"

Soldat waited for Mitya's order.

"*Tse,*" said Mitya.

The horse stepped forward and the telega began to roll, westward, toward the stretching forest, over the lowlands leading toward the Urals.

6

Night. In the distance a lone light burned. Mitya encouraged Soldat toward the beckoning glow.

When the telega rolled up to the izba the door opened and an old mouzhik came out. In his outstretched hands he carried bread and salt. Maria and Elizabeth smiled with tired eyes, and Mitya tasted of the food of hospitality.

"*Dedushka*," [Little grandfather] he said, "is there space in the izba? Just for my mother and my sister. I can sleep out here."

"Come in, *strannikee*," said the smiling old man, "little wanderers sent by the Lord God. Come in, there is space and food for twenty more."

In the izba the old lone mouzhik brought forward a greening samovar, and glowing embers from the stove to kindle the charcoal and the splinters of wood in the fire-pan of the samovar.

Maria and Elizabeth untied two bundles of food, and putting their provisions with the old man's prepared to cook a great pot of borsch.

"It's from Tula, this samovarchik," said the old man. "My *baba* brought it, and the children grew up and the *baba* died. I look for gold sand in the rivers, and I find enough to live on."

Mitya explained that they were on the way to Moscow, and then he went out to unhitch Soldat, and feed him.

Maria and Elizabeth slept on the oven, Mitya and the mouzhik on the floor.

In a corner of the room a small lamp burned dimly under the holy image.

7

The next day they came upon the Tavda River, and from atop the wagon watched peasant men and women panning for gold. A lean mouzhik took them to his hut.

It was very large. Built of timber and plastered over, it stood on a small rise overlooking the flashing stream below. Inside, in the middle of the room stood the great oven, and on top of it now brown hens were setting. At one end of the room was a trough for calves to feed from, but now, during the summer, the calves were out grazing in the sun. A maiden wearing a yellow kerchief, and a young mouzhik, her man, carried the trough outdoors, where Soldat immediately began to eat out of it.

Mitya sat on the grass near the horse and contemplated a difficult passage in the Latin book. The others busied themselves clearing up the hut so more people could sleep in it that night. Then the young mouzhik walked away, down the slope of the hill.

Presently, from the plain down below came the heavy thud of an axe assaulting a tree. Elizabeth came forward to gaze below.

"That's my Fedka," said the smiling maiden with the yellow kerchief. "He's building a hut. We will marry next week."

"That's good," said Elizabeth. "I am glad. Very very glad. I am awfully happy for you. How old are you?"

"Eighteen. And you?"

"I am twenty-six," said Elizabeth.

A spell of coughing took possession of her as she stood on the rise of the hill gazing down below. The blows of the axe against the firm tree continued to resound without pause.

8

The Toura River lay behind them now. Mitya held the reins as Soldat pulled the telega at his comfortable pace. Though Maria sat with the Latin grammar book on her lap and conjugated the verbs for Mitya, his mind continually escaped from the irregular endings. He was excited and nervous, for soon now an obscuring forest section would end, and the Ural Mountains would loom clearly ahead. So he had been told only an hour ago at the gray post station.

And indeed the forest was ending; for there stood the Urals.

Soldat stopped of his own accord and seemed to gaze meditatively at the vast stretch of green mountains before him. Mitya, Maria, and Elizabeth all sighed at the same moment as their gaze froze to the vast shapes ahead.

"Urals," said Maria.

"Dark," said Elizabeth. "How dark they are!"

Almost covered with a blanket of deep green pine growth, the mountains were enveloped at their peaks in a dark sky of frowning black clouds. Only an occasional brown patch where the mountains had eroded broke through the seemingly endless green barrier. Some of these patches had been cleared by mountain laborers who had struggled to extract from the earth its mineral riches, for here was the greatest concentration of wealth in the world. Within this belt were buried violet amethyst beds, pale platinum, heavy black coal, summery brown coal, gleaming multifarious stones, sturdy blocks of black iron, veins of copper, yellow chrome, nuggets of gold, purpling deposits of potassium, colored phosphates, gray somber aluminium, red topaz, and exhilarating green emeralds.

Mitya gazed open-eyed upon the great range.

Chapter Eight

Soldat

NIGHT HAD fallen upon the roadway, and upon the great mass of mountains looming overhead.

And now a strange phenomenon took place. Mitya, trying to unhitch the horse for a night's rest before attempting to cross the mountains, found that Soldat resisted all attempt at unharnessing. Maria, and even Elizabeth, came forward to reason with the animal, but nothing could be accomplished. Soldat persisted in remaining with the telega, and made clear that he meant to draw it without awaiting the dawn.

"Perhaps he will be content if we go a little further," suggested Elizabeth.

Mitya shrugged his shoulders.

"Get back on," he said. "We'll have to go. I don't want to argue with him. He's doing the work."

Soon the actual ascent began. Soldat moved along at little better than a walking pace, but uniformly and without hesitation.

Elizabeth curled up on the wagon, and after a short coughing spell fell asleep, the pale moonlight casting a green shadow upon her haggard face.

Mitya handed the reins to Maria and lighting the small oil lamp purchased at the last post station, he sat on the perch next to his mother and opened the Latin grammar book.

"Let it be," said Maria. "This is night. Go rest, in the back."

Mitya began to study the dimly lit page.

"If he's going to work at night," he said, "I will too."

An hour later when a side clearing appeared on the mountain face, where a wagon could find rest, Maria tried to persuade Soldat to draw into the space. But her effort was unavailing, and the stubborn animal kept to the road.

Again and again thunderous roars shook over the mountains, and now a stab of flashing light could be seen preceding each sounding spasm.

At midnight a tarantass came dashing down the road, and at the moment of meeting, a burst of flaming jagged light spread over the mountain, and the face of the wildly driving *yemshcheek* [the professional driver] lit up in raucous audacity as he sang a volley of oaths unto the three horses dashing his tarantass down the steep incline. Soldat unerringly drew to the right edge of the road overhanging the black valley below, and the wheels of the two vehicles scraped as they passed each other by. Maria mumbled a prayer. Mitya turned a page of the book.

Shortly after midnight, a summit was reached, but this only revealed that beyond the slight valley ahead another greater summit loomed.

Once more Maria and Mitya made offer to Soldat to rest for the night, but again he spurned their proposal and started more rapidly across the valley toward the new obstacle ahead.

And now the sky unfolded its watery ways and a streaming rain descended upon them. The road began to flow with gravel and the feet of the horse slipped perilously as he plodded relentlessly forward.

Mitya's lantern was suddenly extinguished by the descending torrent. Hurriedly he thrust the book into his bosom.

Then he covered Elizabeth. Maria's hair was streaming water.

"Get under the blankets," she told her son.

"It's my turn to drive," protested Mitya.

"No," said Maria. "Mitenka, I order you. Quick! Keep dry!"

Mitya plunged under the cover of the blankets.

The horse ignored the rain and continued his upward way along the narrow slippery road.

With the next spasm of lightning Mitya awoke. He sat upright and was amazed that Maria was not on the driver's perch. Peering ahead through the night he saw his mother in the pouring rain, out on the inclined road, leading the slipping Soldat through a stretch of mud without firm footing. He jumped off the wagon and joined in dragging the sliding animal over the treacherous path.

But soon the muddy stretch was passed and Soldat again took command. Onward he plodded, up the mountainside.

Maria and Mitya climbed into the wagon as it moved, and sat silent in the inundating rain. The lightning flashes grew longer, more brilliant, more frequent. And the deafening accompaniment of the roaring heavens clattered about them. The horse was again oblivious to all, now that the footing was sure.

A cooling wind began to blow.

"We must cover," Maria said in alarm. "Come, Mitya, under the blankets. Do what you can—keep the wind off."

"The blankets are soaking," said Mitya.

"Come," said Maria again. "It is better than this."

Maria tied the reins to the wooden arm on the driver's perch, and both she and Mitya huddled under the dark wet blankets, while the chill wind blew over them.

Soldat was alone with the cargo. Turning back once to look, he increased his pace.

On, and up, rolled the wagon, through the dark pouring night.

It was ten in the morning when it came to a stop and Maria peered from under the blankets.

"Mitya!" she exclaimed. "Mitenka! Liza! There is a hut."

They awoke and peered about them. The rain had ceased. Soldat stood on the top of the last barrier. Far below him, forgotten, stretched the dark valley, the immense black distances of western Siberia. Soldat raised his head to the blue sky and whinnied.

2

A middle-aged peasant woman in a gray skirt, with a linen kerchief on her head, came out of the izba carrying bread and salt.

"*Ai, ai, ai,*" she sympathized. "Look at you. Like drowning fish. But come, we're related. You and I dried our rags in the same sun."

Elizabeth gazed in wonder about her.

"Did I sleep?" she said. "*Akh*, how wet you are, *mamachka*. And look at Mitya."

"*Nitchevo,*" said Maria. "If only Mitya has not taken cold."

Mitya shook his head.

"No," he said. "But the book is soaked." He withdrew the Latin grammar from his bosom and followed the peasant woman to the warmth of the great oven in the hut, and to dry clothing for all.

In the morning sunshine everyone gathered about the huge pot of mush cooking over a soft fire.

"The best *kasha* I have ever eaten," said Maria, and then told of Aremziansk and the Glass Factory, and later spoke of Moscow, somewhere to the level west.

Near the fire sat a small boy named Kolya and a tiny girl named Fenya and the father, a tall brawny, smooth-shaven mouzhik. He was interested in Mitya's story of how Soldat had behaved.

"That happens," he said. "But it is not often. An animal, like a man, sometimes feels he wants to meet a challenge."

"I never knew that," said Mitya.

"Yes," said the mouzhik. "A man can become discouraged when he feels the challenge—but an animal never does. He goes until he dies, if necessary."

Mitya walked over to his reclining horse. In a moment he was back.

"He's all right," said Mitya. "But why did he do it?"

The mouzhik shrugged his shoulders.

"He understands, I think. He wanted to cheer you up, so you'll never surrender to anything."

Mitya looked over the huge expanse stretching below.

"When we came to one summit after another," he said, "I began to think, 'Is all life like that? A continuous series of struggles? Doesn't it ever end?'"

"When you go back to the warm ground," said the mouzhik, "for the real rest, in the arms of Mother Russia. But first you must earn it. You must live."

The woman of the izba served more *kasha*, then led Maria aside, to a spot near the house.

"You are ill," she said. "Your eyes are swollen, and I think your legs, too. Go to bed, rest today."

"We must go to Moscow," said Maria. "We must not be late for the University."

"Time enough," said the woman. "The slower you go the further you get. Go to bed, and I will manage everything."

Maria obeyed.

3

The next morning Maria felt better, and Elizabeth seemed to cough less. Mitya harnessed Soldat to the telega. Now everyone sat down for a last chat.

"In the spring we can get wheat here," said the clean-shaven mouzhik, "and oats grow well, and barley. And also potatoes, and some green things. But no sunflowers. *Akh*, how I love the seeds. There is nothing just like a pocketful of *semochkee* to keep you going. Now—is there?"

Maria laughed.

"In Saratov," she said, "we used to have great quantities."

"It is possible to have sunflowers in the Urals," said the pleasant woman of the hut. "But farther south."

"I just love *semochkee*," said the little girl, lifting her pudgy hands in small exultation. "The way they crack under my teeth is simply clever."

"That's true," said Kolya. "There's something about them."

The woman asked about the Aremziansk fire.

"Did anyone admire or praise the Glass Factory?" she asked. "Did anyone give it the Evil Eye, do you suppose?"

"I am not a great believer in that," said the mouzhik. "Except occasionally, in delicate questions. I never praise a child's health in front of the mother. Here too much is at stake if the devil is listening."

"*Akh!*" exclaimed Maria. "I forgot to fill the teakettle. Or is there good water all the way down?"

"It is good," said the mouzhik. "And soon you will come to the rivers all around Perm, and then the Vyatka, and the Volga."

"*Akh*," said Maria with pleasure. "The Volga. How long it must be! In Saratov, where my first little daughter died, I knew the great mother Volga."

"It is a good river," said the mouzhik. "Beyond that will be Moscow. *Bog svamee* [May God be with you]."

"*Praschaitee*," [Farewell] said the woman.

"*Da svidaneeye*," [Until we meet again] said Kolya.

Mitya nodded as Soldat moved forward.

Chapter Nine

Timofei, Nadezhda, and the Strannik

IN AN open boat, under a clear blue sky, the strannik, with Nadezhda and Timofei, floated down the Tobol River. The blunt-nosed craft and the long guiding pole had cost Timofei twelve roubles, but once the excitable Nadezhda had spied the "ship" in the water near Tobolsk, the purchase could not be denied.

Timofei, standing in the stern, wielded the huge guiding pole as they drifted casually with the flowing river.

Occasionally, Timofei forced his boat to the shore, and the three travelers walked to a small village to talk with the peasants, help them with their farm chores, eat hot cabbage soup, and meat too, at night. Sometimes they spent the night in a peasant's hut, sometimes in the cool, open fields, and occasionally in the boat, allowing it to drift wherever the river's summer fancy chose to take it.

The towns of Tourinsk, Tumen, Yaloutorovsk, Eeshim, Kourgan—all were lazily passed; some at night, while the boat slept, some during the bright orange day, when Nadezhda's voice poured across the river in a trilling chain of songs.

At some distance below Kourgan, where the shallowing waters forced them to abandon the river journey, Timofei sold the boat for half its cost, and the three sat on the green shore, watching the idling water wallow softly onward.

"This is southwest," explained the strannik. "And I admit it is direct west to Nizhny. But the Caspian should be seen first. You must see the sight of burning oil on the Caspian Sea, when the holidays come and the people rejoice in blue flame."

"How far does this river go, *dedushka?*" asked Nadezhda, pulling the soft green grass from the mellow earth.

"Near Orsk, the Tobol is altogether gone. It becomes a streamlet, then a creek, then dies."

Timofei stood up and started for the village. Nadezhda followed, and then the strannik picked up his cane and bundle and started after them, across the wide yellow meadow.

In the village the strannik learned of a family where sickness had disabled a mouzhik's three boys and the mouzhik himself.

"This started last night," recounted an old woman in a white kerchief. "They say the mother is working furiously. Someone must soon help. . . ."

"Now," said the strannik. "We will go."

For three days Nadezhda nursed the boys, while the woman Aniuta built up the strength of her mouzhik with constant care, and hot borsch and vegetables, and tea. Timofei milked the cow, and worked in the field, and cut wood for the oven. His huge bare chest glistened in the sun, and his brown moustache shone with perspiration.

The strannik cooked most of the meals, and sat in the sun with the boys, telling them of the rich little boy who had blue hair and strong brown shoes.

At the end of three days, the family was well, and the travelers prepared to leave.

"The Lord sent you," said the grateful woman with tears in her eyes. "Take jam with you."

"This could be done," said the strannik accepting the red jar. "*Nu, praschaitee*" [Farewell].

Timofei gave the pale, bearded mouzhik two roubles, and embraced him warmly.

"Stay strong," he said. "And don't beat your woman. Her character is good."

The mouzhik wiped away a tear.

"I shall never beat her again," he said, "unless it is absolutely necessary."

In the village, children and dogs followed the strannik, for it was clear that here was a wise pilgrim who knew much, and had seen the world, and could tell many stories, each more stirring and tearful than the previous.

"Let us hurry," whispered Nadezhda, "to St. Petersburg. Perhaps—perhaps, I am tired of being a peasant girl."

"First to the Caspian," said Timofei, "to see the blue fires on the water."

"Then to Nizhny," added the strannik.

"*Akh* you both," sighed Nadezhda. "Well then, hurry. Hurry, hurry."

"*Dedushka*," said Timofei after a pause, "I have been thinking much. We wander about and help people, with work and advice. And Mitya has gone to Moscow to learn science and help people with his knowledge. He told me, and I know. Which is the better way, *dedushka*—which is the way to help?"

"*Ekh*," sighed the strannik, "there are things I do not know. But the world is great and the misery is large. And the love that the world needs is greater than the water needed by the largest desert."

Chapter Ten

Moscow

Moscow lay ahead. Behind the plodding Soldat lay a succession of winding refreshing rivers—the Chousovaya, the Kama, the Vyatka, and now here was the Volga.

Maria, Elizabeth, and Mitya sat fascinated by the view of this legendary river, the Volga, that flows as the lifeblood through the body of Mother Russia. They watched the boats and barges laden with cargo, plying their way to the northern terminus Rybinsk, there to be transported along the upper stretches of the coursing river.

Maria sat in the driver's perch on the telega, one hand holding the reins, the other resting on the small of her back, seeking to alleviate somehow the dull incessant pain that had come upon her so suddenly during the journey. Her eyes were swollen, her ankles too, and even—she fancied—her legs had begun to swell.

"Mama," said the frail Elizabeth, "let me take the reins. You go rest in the wagon."

Mitya sat in the wagon, his eyes unswerving from the open Latin grammar.

But Maria continued to guide Soldat, for she knew that Elizabeth had only small reserves of strength. Elizabeth's eyes wandered to the scenery about her, to the open spaces spotted with the exciting leafy trees—the spreading oaks, the elms, and beeches. These were the trees that could find sufficient moisture in the soil and which lived in winters of sufficient moderation to permit them by centuries of evolution to luxuriate, and, unlike the Siberian pines, to grow lush, broad-leafed, and expansive in their more moderate climate.

Around them stretched fields of fading flax and crops of hay and farmyards with busy white pigs, occasional thatched cottages with open gardens, and fruit trees. Here, in a garden, grew a profusion of multicolored flowers; there the rectangular stretches were dedicated to the potato plant. Everywhere the soil seemed airy, full of life, eager to give birth to living things.

In the distance to the right, dairy cattle were browsing in groups of two and three, and beyond them lay a stern wall of dark forest.

TOBOLSK

The church at Aremziansk, with its bell tower, where—in the story—Matvei the Night Watchman stood on The Night of 1848. (Church was built by Maria Mendeleyev.)

Maria

At the next turn in the open roadway a wooden mansion came in view, and beyond it a huge expanse of small bedraggled cottages, then fields, barns, cattle, and vast numbers of peasant men, women, and children, laboring in the fields and vegetable gardens.

"Serfs," said Maria.

Mitya looked up.

In silence they watched as the telega rolled on along the stretching estate. The men and the women in the fields occasionally glanced up and nodded at the passing wagon.

"There are about a thousand," said Mitya pensively. "That's a large estate, isn't it?"

"I have seen them with fifteen thousand souls," said Maria.

Elizabeth too watched the scenes in the fields. Occasionally she coughed, her frail body tottering on the wagon perch.

"Mitya," said Maria, "you know that we ourselves had a serf."

"Yes," said Mitya. "You've told me."

"It always grips my heart to think of her," continued Maria. "It was not my fault. I inherited her from my family. Do you remember her, Liza? She nursed you—Praskovya Ferafontovna."

"I remember," said Elizabeth. "A very old woman. A very kind woman. Tall and quiet."

"When I first married," said Maria, "I wanted to free her. I said to her one day, 'Praskovya, go into the world. I release you, I will fill out the papers.'"

Maria stopped for a moment.

"What she replied almost broke my heart. She said to me, 'Where will I go now? I am sixty years old. Where is there a place in the world for me? What is "free" to me? Free to die? If only I had been freed forty years ago, my madam—then it might have meant something. Once there was a man. A young mouzhik, with a heart of gold.'"

"Why didn't they marry?" Elizabeth asked.

"Ah," said Maria, "it's according to the fancy of the masters. His master was a vicious one, and worked him like a beast, and gave him no life of his own."

"Why didn't he run away?" asked Mitya. "With her."

"That's what he once told her, but she was a very timid soul. You remember, Liza? Even when she was an old woman."

"I think I remember," said Elizabeth.

"So she just stayed with us, and nursed the girls, and soon she died. In Saratov. And in all my life I never saw her smile. She carried the thought of that young mouzhik in her heart until the day of her death."

Elizabeth dried her eyes with a small blue handkerchief.

"Mitya," said Maria softly, "don't ever let anyone break you down, my darling. Never let them break your spirit."

Mitya rose in the slowly rolling telega, and gazed toward the approaching city of Moscow.

"Me?" said Mitya. "*Akh, mamachka,* let them try."

2

Moscow. On a green hillock on the outskirts of the city the weary Soldat paused with his Siberian cargo.

Maria and Mitya got off the telega and standing on the top of the incline gazed into the new world stretching before them.

Elizabeth, worn and dull-eyed, silently studied the scene.

In every direction rose bulging golden cupolas, surmounted with crosses glistening in the late afternoon sun. Spires with crosses reaching to the sky seemed to puncture the vault of the heavens. Ahead lay wooden houses and expansive buildings of stone, a towering monument, arched bridges, and the silent strong river. There, too, was the bustle of carriages drawn by galloping horses, and in the distant center an array of gleaming white edifices—the Kreml. In the Kreml—called "Le Kremlin" by the French—the buildings were of stone; and there, from within, rose many shining cupolas, and a stone tower of Ivan the Great. A stone steeple standing in this inner castle of Moscow rose to a height of more than three hundred feet. Its thirty-four bells were ringing out the vesper call, and the great booming bell of more than sixty tons struck ominously into the slowly falling twilight. And now all the bells of the church-besprinkled city joined in the chiming chorus calling the people to devotions. Strong heavy bells, and soft mellow ones, and clearly ringing bells, and booming ones swelled into a compelling chorus. Holy Moscow, it was called, this city of religion, this city of a veritable population of houses of prayer. Mother Moscow, it was called, this city which had taken upon herself the evolution of the Russian state, this city which gave birth and guidance to the Russian people—for better or for worse. Although Peter the Great had moved the Russian capital from Moscow to the city of his own name, Holy Moscow and Mother Moscow still remained the heart of the pulsing body of Russia. And yet, somehow, though it was Russian to the core, the city of Moscow had many aspects of an Asiatic settlement. The bulging green cupolas, and the fantastic unrestrained architecture, as well as the bustling bazaars, all tended to orientalize Moscow, and so it was that this Mother of Russia, like the mother of Mitya, had the slanting-eye aspect of distant Asia.

Mitya, from atop the green-hill vantage point, intently studied the structure of the central Kreml, the city's history flooding his mind. Moscow, on the elevated bank of her river, found protection from Tartar hordes behind this waterway, with its forest screen and vast marshlands stretching on all sides. But this had not been enough, and hence an inner citadel—the Kreml —was built of stone, the ultimate rampart of defense. Although the inner citadel was in fact a fort, it was well populated with palaces and churches. Around this Kreml strong walls were built in the fourteenth century by the ruling Prince Dmitri, for the Tartars had previously been able to breach the meager defenses of the city, and burning it to the ground left twenty thousand Russian dead before retreating. Outside these walls a village of wooden buildings had grown up. These settlements in turn had found some security through the construction of another encircling stone defense erected in the sixteenth century. As the city continued to grow, the new population had to find homes outside the second rampart, and thereafter a third defense was built, the "White Wall." Still another bulwark of defense—of wood and earth—was erected at the end of the sixteenth century after a recurring attack by the Tartars.

Between wars, the Muscovites found a chance to welcome the exotic cargoes of tea and incense and Oriental rugs flowing up to the Baltic area from the distant East, via the Caspian Sea and the Volga. Taking advantage of the growing trade the Moscow princes increased their levies on the spices, the tea, and the silks constantly flowing from Asia.

By the eighteenth century textile factories had sprung up in the focal Moscow city, and articles of cotton, wool, linen, and silk were manufactured in great quantity. But in large measure these products were for the growing export trade, to England, and to the continental western states.

Slowly, the vesper bells ceased their imploring clamor.

Mitya's mind returned from the city and its painful growth. He turned to his mother.

"Shall we drive in?" he asked. "I want to go right in, but maybe you should rest here?"

"No use stopping now," said Maria. "We will try to find my brother's house. Vassili will help us. And tomorrow morning we will put on our best and seek the University."

For a long time the telega wound its way about the dynamic city, with Soldat the village horse trotting villagewise in the center of the streets in the face of calumnies cast upon him by city drivers of rolling carriages.

"*Akh ti!*" screamed the driver of a handsome black one, "Hey you—over to the side!"

Maria dismounted the telega to soothe the perplexed Soldat, and led him gently from the middle of the roadway. But in a moment he had once more eased into the center of the street and was again startled by the oaths of headlong-rushing city drivers.

Over the Moscow River Bridge they rolled, past the turreted, dreamlike Cathedral of Saint Basil, erected by Ivan the Terrible. To the "Red" Place—meaning "Beautiful"—rode Maria with her children to gaze upon the wide space separating the Kreml from the region of bazaars. Eventually they reached the top of Poklonnaya Hill. There Napoleon had stood on September 14, 1812, as he prepared to enter the city he most wished to conquer.

As Maria stood upon the Poklonnaya Hill seeing a vision of the Napoleonic fire, her mind inevitably turned to another conflagration—the burning of the Glass Factory in Aremziansk.

"Mitenka," she said, "this city burned. It burned to the very ground. But the hearts of the people were not burned. The people built again upon their own ruins."

Mitya was silent. Elizabeth stood by the side of Soldat's head, one arm resting upon his neck.

"I was thinking of the Glass Factory," said Maria. "Really a small calamity, wasn't it?"

"I guess so," said Mitya. "It didn't look small at the time. But we're here."

"Let us rest," said Elizabeth. "Let us find a lodging or the house of Vassili, and rest. For, tomorrow is your day, little brother."

"Yes," said Mitya. "Tomorrow is my day."

3

Late in the night they found the house of Maria's brother Vassili. Vassili was rich and kind, and lived in a mansion. He was of medium height and had shrewd dark eyes.

"I will obtain a position for you at once," said Vassili, welcoming Mitya. "You can start as a clerk in the office of the Governor of Moscow. He is my friend."

Mitya, Maria, and Elizabeth exchanged glances. Elizabeth, exhausted, sat down on the resplendent green couch.

"I came to study science," said Mitya.

Vassili frowned.

"If you start in the Governor's office, you will have a great government career before you."

Maria shook her head.

"You are wasting your time, Vassya," she said. "Mitya's mind is made up. He thinks he can help Russia best through science."

"Ridiculous," said Vassili. "Childish notions. Do you wish to starve on a teacher's pittance?"

Mitya shrugged his shoulders.

"That is irrelevant," he said. "I came to study science. I ask you, Uncle, to consider that statement as absolutely final."

Vassili turned and started to walk out of the room. At the door he stopped.

"As you wish," he said. "I will make your stay in my home completely comfortable."

"Tomorrow is my day," said Mitya, "regardless of who helps me or doesn't help me."

4

"Impossible," said the man of the dark eyes and the clipped brown beard. "Quite impossible."

Mitya, in a white shirt that hung outside his blue trousers, stood by the large arched window, his thumbs resting in the belt about his slender waist. For a moment he turned his eyes to the view outside. At the curb stood Soldat, with the telega. In the driver's seat Elizabeth sat patiently, holding the reins, her eyes fixed on the university building.

Maria, in the office, sitting opposite the man at the desk, was cast in stony silence.

For an hour that morning Maria had placed cold towels upon her puffed eyes to reduce the swelling. Carefully, too, she had tended to her face—darkened her narrow eyebrows with burned match sticks, and faintly applied powder.

Her freshly washed hair was wound in black coils about her head. The blouse of light blue, embroidered in colorful Tartar design, was Maria's best, and the long dark-blue skirt hung gracefully about her, reaching almost to the black low-heeled slippers on her swollen feet. Her back had ached incessantly that morning, but her eyes had carried a smile for Mitya.

Now she sat, frozen within, shocked into speechlessness.

The man glanced again at Mitya's credentials.

"In the first place you did not graduate from a high school in the Moscow district," he said. "You belong to the Kazan University district."

Mitya turned from the window. His blue eyes seemed to have absorbed the mellowing sunlight pouring in from the world outside. The long yellow hair seemed silky after the washing and combing of the previous night but his broad forehead was pale.

He spoke to the man in the chair.

"Your regulations do not exclude high-school graduates outside the Moscow area."

The man nodded. For a moment he closed his dark eyes.

"No," he said. "What I meant is this. With your unimpressive record of classics in Tobolsk, you have no chance. However, had you graduated from a school here we would not have regarded this classics record in so severe a manner."

"You mean," said Mitya, "that you consider your standards here superior to those in Tobolsk."

The man nodded.

"Without offense," he said.

"My father introduced the St. Petersburg system to Tobolsk," said Mitya.

Now Maria spoke softly.

"His father," she said, "was a scholar, graduate of the Pedagogical Institute at St. Petersburg. For many years director of high schools in several cities. In Tambov, Penza, Saratov, Tobolsk. He gave his life to Russian education, to Russian youth."

The man of the dark eyes and clipped brown beard bowed low.

"I respect this," he said. "But my duty forces me to say that it is irrelevant."

"He was Ivan Pavlovitch Mendeleyev," said Maria, holding back the tears in her narrow eyes.

"I regret," said the man, "at never having had the pleasure."

Mitya came forward.

"I stand ready for all examinations," he said.

"Akh, but my boy," replied the man behind the desk. "We go by the record. You are not eligible for examination."

"But I insist," said Mitya coldly, a spark flashing in his blue eyes. "I insist that you test my knowledge. In all the classics and in all other studies."

"You are not eligible," said the man.

Maria, sensing something, put her hand out to Mitya, in a gesture of gentle restraint.

Mitya ignored his mother's hand. He stepped forward.

"We have come far," he said in measured tones. "I have come to study science. I wish to compete for a government scholarship. If my classics record, which is a passing one, precludes this, then I wish to enter as a simple nonscholarship student. If an examination is necessary for this too, then I am ready in all subjects, to be examined."

The man behind the desk now rose. His face was tense. Out of his vest pocket he removed a tiny silver box, and taking a pinch of snuff said, "Kindly leave this office. You are utterly ineligible for consideration on any basis whatever."

"I dare you to examine me against your best!" exclaimed Mitya. "Come, bring them in!"

For an instant Maria was about to rise, but suddenly, intuitively, something flashed within her mind. She looked upon her defiant son, her eyes smiling.

"Go ahead, Mitenka," she said softly. "Tell him. Tell him everything, my darling."

Mitya stepped closer still to the desk, and his blue eyes shone with a burning penetration.

"I came to study science!" he roared. "By God! you take me in! Do you hear, you mass of regulations, you—do you hear me! In the Urals lie treasures for the people of Russia, to lighten their burdens. In the south lie seas of oil under the earth. Everywhere, everywhere, our land cries for men with skill to come and take from her the treasures and secrets to help men live less dreary lives. I am to be one of these men. Do you hear me, old man? Do you hear me, I say?"

The man behind the desk stood silent with a scowling face.

Maria stood up and embraced her son.

"That's all I wanted to hear," she whispered, her narrow eyes shining with tears. "That's all I wanted to hear. Come, my darling, we will try again. Somewhere. Anywhere. Everywhere."

5

Aimlessly the telega rolled through the bustling streets of Moscow. Soldat himself seemed to sense a lack of sharp purpose, and turned into whatever streets the slightest whim might take him. Elizabeth, silent with pity for her brother, sat watching his face as he looked ahead, lost to the world. Maria's head ached with dull pain, and a similar pain enveloped the small of her back.

Suddenly, Mitya recalled his promise to the old woman in Aremziansk, to seek her long-lost son. He drew the telega to a halt near a street corner and dismounted to talk with a stalwart blue-uniformed gendarme.

"Good morning," said Mitya.

"Good morning," replied the officer. "Are you visiting?"

Mitya nodded his head.

"We are new," he said. "How would one seek a man here, with no address?"

"What is the name?"

"Stepan Andreyevitch Yusulov. From Siberia."

"Wait," said the gendarme.

He disappeared into a confectioner's shop, and presently returned with a large yellow book. For several minutes the gendarme searched through the book. Finally he looked up, shaking his head.

"Not here," he said. "Not registered in Moscow. Are you sure he was here?"

Mitya shook his head.

"No," he said. "An old woman seeks him. First he went to Moscow. He's been gone many years, from a village in Siberia. The woman is his mother."

"How pitiful," said the officer. "Poor woman."

Mitya climbed back onto the wagon.

"This is a big land," said the gendarme, raising his hands to the Moscow air.

"Yes," said Elizabeth. "This is a big land."

The telega moved forward.

That night at the house of her uncle, Vassili, Elizabeth fell violently ill. The coughing fits that shook her frail body brought blood to her lips. Maria, hardly able to stand because of the incessant pain in her back, hovered about her daughter, calming her. At midnight Mitya arrived with a sleepy round-faced doctor.

"She'll be all right," he said after examining the thin Elizabeth lying on the wooden bed. "Fill this prescription and feed her much milk, eggs, clear soup. She must remain in bed, without any exertion. At least six months."

Maria stood dazed in the middle of the room. Elizabeth called Mitya to her bedside.

"I'm sorry for you," she said weakly. "I know that mama has been thinking of taking you to St. Petersburg."

Mitya sat on the edge of the bed.

"Rest," he said. "Don't talk, Lizachka!"

"To St. Petersburg," repeated Elizabeth. "To try at the University there."

"*Nu, nitchevo,*" said Mitya. "We'll go in the spring. You'll be all well."

"Yes," whispered Elizabeth. "I will be. For you."

At the door the round-faced doctor gave final instructions.

"If it's warm and sunny outside," he said, "the window may be opened. I'll be back every Friday night. Don't worry."

Maria took three roubles out of her black purse and offered them to the doctor.

"Two's enough," he said. "A peaceful night. Don't worry."

Late that night Elizabeth finally fell asleep. Mitya and Maria sat at the small table and talked.

"Vassili wants to help us with money," said Maria.

"Shall I go to work somewhere until Liza is well?" asked Mitya. "I would rather not take money from my uncle. It is not fair to him. After all, I am not going to follow his advice about my future."

Maria emptied the black purse of its money, and from the secret lining of her overcoat took out a packet of pink banknotes.

"If we are careful," she said, "this will last quite a while, until spring or perhaps a little longer. When Liza is well enough to be left alone I will work."

"I can work now," said Mitya.

"No," said Maria. "You must study, not work. Somewhere, some University will give you the examinations. I am counting on this. I have nothing else. And I want you to be ready when the time comes."

For months Mitya spent long hours at the libraries of Moscow, reviewing history, the sciences, and the classics. Maria gave him money for lunches somewhere near his libraries, but often Mitya saved this money to buy a needed book of science or mathematics.

"Think of it," he would say to himself as he fondled a college treatise on physics, "just for the price of two meals."

He pursued his studies on foot, for Soldat had been rented to a baker.

During his walks he hardly became acquainted with Moscow, for he nearly always read as he made his way along the streets. At home, Maria maintained an atmosphere of cheer as she nursed Elizabeth. And always Mitya's health, too, was in her mind.

As soon as he entered the door in the evening, arms laden with books, Maria would hurry to the stove to heat the milk for him, and then serve him a steaming supper.

Elizabeth was seemingly getting well. As the months passed the cough diminished and she ate better.

"*Mamachka*," Elizabeth once said, holding her mother's hand. "You are everything in the world to Mitya and me. You are our guardian angel."

Maria kissed her cheek.

"That's all right," she said. "Just get well."

In August the temperature stayed around 63 degrees, and in the well-built home of her uncle, Elizabeth was comfortable. In September it was 10 degrees colder; and in October the thermometer stood at 28. Mitya still went almost daily to the libraries, even in December when the heavy snows fell, and the thermometer hovered near 17. In January it dropped to 12.

At home Elizabeth lay quietly watching the snow falling past her window and seemed steadily to improve in health.

In February the temperature began to rise, and on March 18 came the first thaw, followed next day by the cheering sight and sound of the return of the migrating rooks. In April the wholesale thaw set in, and in ten days nearly all of the snow was gone from the city and the surrounding area. The Moscow River freed itself of ice and once more began to flow. Everywhere, spring flowers began to pop smilingly into view.

Elizabeth felt well. It was spring of 1850.

"To St. Petersburg," said Maria. "Good-by, Vassili."

Mitya went out for the horse and the telega.

"*Akh*, it's got to be now," he said, "it's just got to be now."

Chapter Eleven

St. Petersburg

AFTER THE long cold trip on the winding road from Moscow to St. Petersburg both Maria and Elizabeth were trembling from exhaustion. Silently they sat in the back of the wagon, the sweeping Petersburg wind whining about them.

Mitya, holding the reins, guided Soldat over the last stretches of the wet roadway. The great spring thaw, softening the earth, had made the land here alive with deep and slippery mud which overflowed onto the paved road.

They had come, through Klin and Tver, and other towns, and across several rivers, to the Russian capital—the City of Peter.

It was at the mouth of the Gulf of Finland that Tsar Peter the Great had built his new capital in 1703. Peter wanted a port leading to the Baltic Sea and the open northern waters for developing his sea trade with the English, and commerce in general with the West. Tsar Peter dreamed, too, of Westernizing his Russian land industrially and socially as well. And all of this was principally for evolving a powerful military force. Under his personal knowledge of Western techniques industry began to grow. Ships were built which carried wool and cotton to England and returned with iron and coal for the Russian factories. Manners and social conduct, too, turned somewhat to the better, for the Tsar himself prepared a treatise on the fine art of personal relationships: be amiable, he taught, be modern, learn languages, look people in the eye, refrain from spitting on the floor. . . . In certain strata of society Peter, by force, made his new culture acceptable, but the millions of mouzhiks and serfs, seeking their precarious daily bread, failed to comprehend the significance of the Tsar's social amenities.

In a gloomy building of the city itself Mitya found the home of the Skerletov family, acquaintances of Vassili. Nikolai Pavlovitch Skerletov, the son of the family, helped Mitya, Maria, and Elizabeth to carry in the bundles from the wagon. There in a brown-papered room, Elizabeth, exhausted, lay down on the creaking wooden bed.

Maria and Mitya set out at once in search of the Medico-Surgical Institute.

"My heart is really not in being a doctor," Mitya said softly as the telega rolled on the cobbled street.

"I know," said Maria, "but it is a work of service. You could help a great many people."

"A man could do more with pure science," said Mitya, "if he would use it to take the wealth from the land."

"Perhaps," said Maria sighing deeply and holding her hands to her back. "Perhaps. But we have little choice. We must try all the institutions. One of them must take you in. And if two of them should be willing to take you, then we will choose. But one of them must."

In front of the Medico-Surgical Institute a great crowd of serious students was milling excitedly about.

Maria and Mitya dismounted from the telega and tied Soldat to a wooden post.

"What is happening?" asked Maria addressing a dark slim student wearing pince-nez.

"It's about Dostoyevsky," the student replied. "A meeting about him." He started into the crowd.

"If you please," said Mitya. "Wait a moment. What sort of a meeting?"

The hurrying student stopped and turned. He took his pince-nez off and gazed closely at Mitya.

"Are you new?" he said.

Mitya nodded his head. "We're from Siberia," he explained.

"Siberia!" exclaimed the young man replacing his pince-nez. "Siberia! That's where they took him. That's where he is!"

"Dostoyevsky?" asked Maria.

"Yes. You haven't heard?"

"We have heard," Mitya explained, "that he was arrested on suspicion, together with others, and taken to jail. That's all."

"Aha!" said the young man with pleasure, sensing an opportunity to tell a detailed story. "*Akh,* but that was last April, in forty-nine. And now we are in April fifty. *Bozhe moi,* [God of mine] how lost this Siberia must be, where no news reaches."

Maria took Mitya by the arm.

"We'd better go in," she said.

"Wait," said the student, feeling suddenly that the story might be lost. He turned to Mitya.

"In December of last year the police took him out to Semyonovsky Square to be shot with twenty-six others. In freezing weather they were stripped of their overcoats. The sentence was read to them for almost half an hour. Then the police put the long white death shirt on them, tied them in groups, and the officers waved swords in the air for the soldiers to aim. And this, my dear people," the slim student whispered as he put his hand on Mitya's arm, "this was pure inhumanity and torture. Because, believe me, the sentence of the men had really been commuted to imprisonment in Siberia. This was all a hoax. Believe me. One officer suddenly explained the joke. Among the prisoners Grigoriev went raving mad!"

Maria shook her head.

"So they were sent to Siberia," the student concluded. "And now we're trying to get them out. Excuse me, I must see Lozovsky. *Akh,* there is a mind!" And he pushed his way through the crowd, his gold pince-nez jiggling precariously on his sharp nose.

"Come on," said Maria. "Come on, Mitenka."

In the waiting room of the Medico-Surgical Institute, Mitya and Maria stood facing a round excited man with prancing eyebrows.

"Impossible!" the man was saying. "Impossible! Impossible! Do you see that crowd outside? We have enough trouble with our own, without taking in strangers. And from Siberia!"

"But my son has come merely to study," said Maria imploringly.

"Impossible!" exclaimed the round man, his dark eyebrows almost leaping off his face.

"I want to apply for admission," said Mitya. "Here are my credentials."

"You must be out of your mind!" exclaimed the round man. "The enrollment is closed. No strangers! Please go at once! I am sending for the police to break the mob!"

He turned abruptly and hurrying along a blue strip of carpet entered an office and slammed the door.

Maria and Mitya pushed through the crowd outside. Mitya untied the horse and they mounted the telega.

But Mitya would not give up the possibility of entering the Medico-Surgical Institute quite so easily. At the Skerletov home, young Nikolai had a plan.

"Before you make a determined effort," he said, "why not find out if you are cut out to be a doctor. Let me take you to a class there which dissects corpses. Now."

Mitya, worn, shrugged his shoulders.

"*Khorosho,*" he said. "Let's go."

The class was dissecting the corpse of an old woman who had drowned. The odor was overwhelming and the sight of the partially dismembered corpse was shocking to Mitya. He fell into a faint. Nikolai Skerletov brought him home.

Maria wept.

"You were denied admission anyway, Mitenka," she sobbed. "You shouldn't have gone."

The next morning Mitya and Maria set out again.

"To the University of St. Petersburg," Maria said as though from a far-off dream. "That is the last chance. Drive, Mitenka."

2

"Mendeleyev?" the tall gray-haired man, was saying as he turned in his chair. "Mendeleyev? Not the son of Ivan Pavlovitch?"

"Yes!" exclaimed Maria, her heart beating wildly and tears suddenly pouring out of her narrow, swollen eyes. "Yes! His son! Did you know him!"

The gray-haired man stood up and took Maria's hand.

"Is he dead?" he said. "How long ago?"

"Three years," said Maria, as the tears flowed down her worn cheeks.

"Please do not upset yourself," said the man. "Yes, I knew him. I was as close to him as a brother. My name is Pletnov."

"Pletnov!" exclaimed Maria. "*Akh*, how often he spoke of you."

Mitya watched silently as Maria recounted the story of her life with Ivan in Saratov, Penza, Tambov, Aremziansk, and Tobolsk. She told, too, the story of the great fire and of the journey from Siberia with Mitya and Elizabeth.

"*Tse, tse, tse,*" said Pletnov. "How hard life is. *Da, da,* Ivan was my best friend in this very school. A great mind he was, and gentle."

"They told us to go into this office," said Maria drying her tears. "And to think that you are the Director!"

"Has there been unrest among students here," asked Mitya, "like at the Medico-Surgical Institute?"

Pletnov sighed in despair.

"Hardly a month passes," he said, "without some sort of trouble. The students are so politically conscious—it is amazing."

"They seek more freedom of expression, I suppose," said Maria.

The gray-haired Pletnov nodded.

"And not only that," he said. "Some are wild nationalists. Of course, some are mild. They love our Russia desperately and talk about helping the mouzhiks. They think that the plain people are our salvation. Of course no one would object to that, except that the mouzhiks find out how bad off they are."

Pletnov laughed nervously, and glanced about him.

"I must be a little careful," he said shyly. "One never knows when a government agent may be passing by."

Mitya frowned.

"*Da*," said Pletnov. "That's right, son. All student groups are under scrutiny. By the way, Madame Mendeleyev, your Ivan always thought of the people—a great Liberal."

Maria sighed.

"Yes," she said, "in Saratov, when he was director of the high school, he fed the resident students too well, and the government reprimanded him."

"That is the way it goes," said Pletnov. "But we, too, feed them well here."

A silence suddenly fell upon the group. Each was conscious of the same thought in the other.

Then Pletnov said, "These student disturbances have forced the government to cut off enrollment."

Maria felt faint and quickly inclined her head to prevent falling into unconsciousness. Now once again the oppressive backache clamored for recognition, and Maria's heart began to palpitate. With an effort she maintained her poise and straightening up in her chair, sat silently, waiting.

"It's mostly the West-minded students here who demand liberal reforms like those the French introduce. And of course every liberal event in the West brings more repression at home. I don't know how it will end. You see now what the government policy is? To keep intellectual development low, and guard against strangers."

"Would we be called 'strangers'?" asked Mitya.

"Not by me. But you know—Siberia, with so many political exiles living there, perhaps influencing the population. You see how it is."

Mitya and Maria exchanged glances.

"Well then, is there any chance?" Mitya asked, taking his mother's hand.

For a moment, Pletnov looked at Mitya silently, studying his broad white forehead, the shining yellow hair, the direct blue eyes, and full sensitive mouth, then his eyes dropped to Mitya's hand, holding Maria's.

"Because of my friendship for the late Ivan Pavlovitch, your good father," said Pletnov, looking pensively at Mitya, "I will do the utmost to obtain permission for you to take government examinations for a scholarship, for the Pedagogical Institute where teachers are trained. Then I will take you to meet the Rector Davidov."

Maria, leaning on Pletnov's desk, laid her head on her arms.

"Mama!" said Mitya in alarm. "*Mamachka!*"

"*Nitchevo*," Maria whispered through barely audible sobs. "I'm just resting."

Pletnov brought her a glass of water.

"I understand," he said.

In a moment he resumed.

"It will be necessary to do many things," he said, "to obtain permission for eligibility—that is, to take the examinations. First, you will have to see many people, Madame Mendeleyev, to establish character and fill out applications and petitions and answer questions in this department and that. Perhaps for several months."

Maria was nodding her head eagerly. "That is nothing," she repeated over and over. "All we want is a chance. Just a chance to do something."

"Meanwhile," continued Pletnov, "I will work from the top. I will go to the Minister of Education directly, and tell of your late husband's splendid scholarship and government service."

"*Akh*, Ivan," said Maria softly. "If only you knew how much you have helped."

Mitya shook hands with Pletnov.

"You'll never regret anything," said Mitya. "That's all I can say."

"What shall I do first?" asked Maria.

Pletnov looked at her carefully.

"Please excuse me," he said, "if I say that you do not seem well. I think that you should have medical care and rest. And then begin to worry about your son's eligibility for the examinations."

"No," said Maria softly. "No, no, please. I must begin at once—immediately."

Pletnov gazed into her face. He read her eyes. For an instant he glanced at Mitya who was intently reading the titles of the books in a towering glass case, then looked back to Maria.

"*Khorosho*," [all right] he said. "You may begin at once. Go across the corridor to the other office and begin to fill out the papers, and then you might seek the help of the mathematician Chizhov, who knew your husband very well."

Mitya was now listening.

"If God grants that all goes well," Maria said, "then he would live at the Pedagogical Institute and be given all food and clothing and books, at government expense. Is that right?"

Pletnov nodded.

"Until he graduates," he said. "Also, God forbid, but if necessary, he would have all medical care. Everything. In return he would have to serve eight years as a teacher, to repay his country in that way. You would do that, wouldn't you, Dmitri Ivanovitch?"

"I am ready to serve all my life," said Mitya.

Pletnov stood up and embraced Mitya.

"You remind me of your father," said the gray-haired Pletnov. "He always spoke the same way."

Maria dried her eyes.

"Perhaps we had better go now," she said. "I wish to start on the papers. And to see Professor Chizhov."

"Yes," said Pletnov. "Then the young lady in that office will send you to see some other important people. . . ."

"*Akh*, yes," said Maria; "that is good."

She gave her hand to Pletnov, unable to speak further.

"*Nitchevo*," said Pletnov. "I will be here always when you need advice, and I will go to see the Minister. Remember, I am your friend."

"Friend," repeated Maria. "What a wonderful word! The most wonderful word in the world."

Mitya smiled and followed his mother.

3

"A friend?" said Elizabeth. "Did he say that himself?"

"Yes," Maria assured her. "Yes, it is true."

Elizabeth's tired eyes gleamed for a moment.

"How different it makes things," she said. "Tomorrow I will go with you to help see all those people and fill out the papers."

Maria shook her head.

"No," she said. "Your duty is to get well. Mitya's duty is to study and be ready for examinations—whenever they come. And my duty is to arrange for everything. Is that clear, Lizachka?"

Elizabeth nodded.

"Also, we must move presently," said Maria. "The Skerletovs have been good to us, but we must find a room of our own."

"All right," said Elizabeth. "Where is Mitya?"

"At the University Library. The teacher-training school—the Pedagogical Institute—is located within the University buildings, and many of the professors teach both the ordinary University students and the future teacher groups, too. You may go visit in a few weeks, when you are stronger."

The next morning they found a room and moved into it. Maria prepared breakfast, and also set aside a midday meal for Mitya and Elizabeth. Then, dressing in her best, she left on her round of errands to government officials.

It was late in the evening when she returned, exhausted and dazed, but all she said was, "It's going fine. Only a few days of this."

But it was for weeks that she rushed through the maze of Petersburg streets, through the endless corridors of government buildings.

Then, one evening, late, she burst into their new room where Mitya and Elizabeth sat awaiting her. Panting, she stood in the doorway.

"Study, Mitya!" she gasped holding her hands to her heart. "Study, my darling! You are eligible! The examinations are tomorrow. In the morning!"

Elizabeth glanced apprehensively at Mitya.

Quietly he arose, in his hands a new book.

"I bought this just today," he said. "The best Latin grammar there is. I wanted to go through it."

Maria stood in the doorway, her hands pressed to her back.

"I must study it through," said Mitya. "Tonight."

Morning light was beginning to creep in through the folds of the green curtain over the window.

Mitya stood up. Suddenly swinging his arm vigorously he threw the Latin book across the room. With a crash it struck against the back rest of a chair, then dropped onto the seat. Maria and Elizabeth sat up in bed startled.

Mitya hurried to the door.

Chapter Twelve

Maria and Elizabeth

THE EXAMINATION room was crowded. Scores of desperate students were competing for the all-inclusive government scholarship. Only a handful would be picked. Sixteen- and seventeen-year-old boys, with white faces and trembling hands, bent over their papers. Some were writing furiously, some wrote reflectively, carefully moving their heads from side to side as though to punctuate their thoughts. Still others were not writing at all. Some of these sat quietly, thinking intensely, and others sat as though paralyzed, a look of fear frozen on their faces, their eyes like those of hopeless condemned criminals.

The huge clock resting on the table at the front of the room ticked loudly, relentlessly beating out the fateful seconds. Throughout the room, first here, then there, then in the middle, a head occasionally looked up at the clock, and discovering the passage of precious minutes, suddenly bent down again. At the front of the room sat the examination master, motionless, his cold green eyes unfeelingly observing the struggling students before him.

At the end of the first row, at the back of the room, sat Mitya.

He had rapidly scanned the examination pages on literature, history, geography, physics, mathematics, chemistry, and biology, and laid them aside. He chose to work first on the Latin.

Now the clock stood at ten minutes before noon. Mitya was working on the Latin verbs. His blond head was motionless, the large pale forehead crossed with a deep frown.

At one o'clock several students began to eat lunches at their desks, still continuing, however, to work on their questions. Near the front of the room a door opened and a number of women appeared with lunches for their sons. One of these women was Maria. The women spoke softly with ushers, gave them the lunches, and pointed out their sons.

A tall dark man brought Mitya his lunch and opened it to see that all was in order—no books or notes.

At three o'clock Mitya was eating a little with his left hand, and with his right he wrote his version in Latin of Caesar chasing an elusive adversary who wrote ballads in his spare time.

An hour later he was writing of Hannibal crossing the Alps while his father's late brother diverted a Roman child from the path of a chariot whose leading horse snorted eloquently as it pranced past the bubbling fountain. He wrung his hands trying to recall the Latin for "fountain," in desperation wrote "sea," and attacked the next sentence.

At five o'clock the Latin was done. He plunged into history and in short concise sentences wrote that Empress Elizabeth founded the University of Moscow in 1755, the peasant Lomonosov became the first Russian poet of note, and historian, philologist, and scientist too; by 1371 the Mongol conqueror Tamerlane the Great had vanquished all between the Caspian and Manchuria; Alexander Nevsky defeated the Germans on the ice of Lake Ilmen on April 5, 1242; in 1760 a Russian force of Cossacks and Kalmucks raided Berlin and terrorized Frederick the Great and his population. . . .

In geography Mitya dashed off curt replies stating that Lake Ladoga in the St. Petersburg area was the largest European lake, and Lake Onega, also in the same general area, was the second largest. . . . Mitya wrote furiously, and finally came to physics, chemistry, and mathematics.

"*Slava Bogu,*" [Glory to God] said Mitya, and performing all the calculations in his head dashed off the answers as fast as he could write.

It was ten minutes to six. The room was still almost full as Mitya hurried down the aisle. He thrust his paper at the examination master and turned toward the door.

"*Akh!*" he exclaimed, turning back for an instant. "I forgot to write my name—it's 'Mendeleyev.'"

Mitya passed everything. In the Latin he did fairly well, although he left Hannibal stranded on top of an Alp during a blizzard. In the sciences his grade was high.

He gained admission to the "Physico-Mathematical Faculty," to study the sciences as a prospective teacher.

There remained only certain arrangements to make—to meet the professors, discuss his study program, and move to the Pedagogical Institute as a resident scholar.

Late at night Maria washed out shirts and underwear for Mitya, mended his clothes, went with him day after day to meet Professor Lenz of physics, Ruprecht of botany, Brandt of zoology, Savitch the astronomer, Ostragradsky the mathematician, Zinin and Voskresensky the chemists.

Finally, one day, they harnessed the faithful Soldat, drove to the Pedagogical Institute, and Mitya moved in as a resident scholar. This was the fall of 1850. To save money, Maria and Elizabeth moved to an attic.

Maria went soon after to see the gray-haired Pletnov, the director, to thank him for helping make Mitya eligible for the examinations.

Pletnov stared at Maria's swollen face.

"You are ill," he said in a soft voice. "You are very ill. *Bozhe moi,* go at once to a doctor. Why didn't you go before?"

"There was no time," said Maria. "I have come to thank you with all my heart. And also, I wish to know something definitely. Will he now be taken care of completely? Is that right? Food, books, lodging, hospital care—till he graduates?"

"*Da, da,*" said Pletnov. "Everything is done. You've done it all. Now go; please go to a doctor."

Maria stood up. "All right," she said. "Now I can go."

But Maria did not go to a doctor. On her way home, in front of the building in which she lived, she collapsed.

2

At the University of St. Petersburg, in the Pedagogical Institute section where he now lived and had just begun his training for the career of teacher of science, Mitya was amazed to see his sister Elizabeth suddenly appear in the doorway of the dining hall. Here, about a hundred uniformed men students were eating their evening meal when a sudden commotion focused everyone's attention on the doorway. There stood the thin, distraught Elizabeth.

Mitya sprang from his seat and hurried to his sister.

"Quick!" she said. "Come! Mama is sick!"

Out in the dark street in front of the university, Mitya climbed to the driver's seat and excitedly urged Soldat to make haste. The brown horse had never heard Mitya employ such a tone, and immediately responded with his full speed.

"The doctor is there," Elizabeth explained, weeping softly. "I don't know yet what is wrong."

"Hurry, Soldatik," Mitya implored. "Come on, Little Soldier. My *mamachka* is sick."

Soldat strained to his utmost as the telega rolled along the cobbled street.

In the room, at Maria's bedside, the doctor had finished his examination. Maria, with face swollen, was lying listless on the bed.

Mitya rushed to her.

"*Mamachka,*" he whispered, "*chto takoye?*" [what is it?]

Maria tried to smile. She glanced at Mitya's uniform.

"*Moi studentik,*" she whispered.

The doctor and Elizabeth approached the bed.

"It is dropsy," said the doctor in a hearty tone, addressing himself to Maria. "You may have to go to the hospital."

Maria nodded her head slightly.

Outside in the hallway, speaking to Mitya alone, the doctor assumed a different tone.

"It is very bad, my son," he said, placing one hand on Mitya's shoulder. "She may not live."

Mitya stared, uncomprehending.

"I didn't want to tell your sister," said the doctor. "I know that she is older, but she herself seems unwell. Perhaps you had better not tell her. It will be bad enough later."

"Is my mother going to die?" asked Mitya incredulously, in a whisper.

The doctor looked at him seriously.

"She is very ill," he said.

Mitya studied the doctor's face, seeking somewhere to find a great monstrous mistake. The doctor's eyes were kind, gray, and intelligent. Mitya understood that there was no mistake.

"Why?" he asked quietly, "why exactly is she dying?"

"There is the dropsy, for one thing," said the doctor. "Long ago, apparently, her kidneys began to function badly, and her body started to absorb fluid. Sometimes fluid appears only in the abdomen, and it is possible to puncture with a needle and withdraw the liquid. Of course some more usually comes. Then in some cases the entire body tissue begins to absorb the fluid. This is very bad. This is so in her case."

Mitya was shaking his head from side to side.

"Her body is now all swollen with this fluid," the doctor resumed. "In addition, her heart is not strong. Quite the opposite. She must have had a heart ailment for years. How many children were there?"

"Fourteen," said Mitya.

"*Tse tse*," said the doctor. "That did not help anything. And I imagine she worked like a slave all her life."

"*Da*," said Mitya quietly. "She shouldn't have done it."

The doctor stood silent.

"She was a mother," he said.

Mitya stood wringing his hands.

"You might say," said the doctor, "that she is dying of an occupational disease—being a mother."

Mitya's chest was now heaving.

"How old is your mother?"

"Fifty-seven."

Maria and Elizabeth

"I am amazed," said the doctor. "Utterly amazed how she has lived this long in her condition. There must have been some unbreakable incentive."

"There was," said Mitya. He placed his arm against the wall and leaned his head on his uniformed sleeve.

"Shhhh," whispered the doctor. "For your sister's sake. . . ."

"How long?" Mitya asked.

The doctor shrugged his shoulders.

"Perhaps a week. Or two."

Mitya stood silent.

"We could take her to a hospital," said the doctor. "But it wouldn't help any. Let's wait awhile and see."

Mitya took three roubles out of his pocket, but the doctor shook his head, patted Mitya on the shoulder, and hurried down the dark hallway.

Maria's condition remained apparently unchanged for a few days. She weakly urged Mitya to attend to his college work, and to come to see her only at night.

In a few days, on September 15, Maria found strength to be propped up in bed. She asked Elizabeth to bring paper and pen and ink and for a long time she wrote slowly, laboriously.

"Lizachka," said Maria weakly, "this letter is to be read by all my children, wherever they are, and finally to be sent to your older sister Ekaterina in Omsk. Write that on the back, darling."

Elizabeth wrote on the back of the letter.

Then Maria asked for an envelope and placing the letter within it gave the envelope to Elizabeth.

"Put it into the bureau, Lizachka," she said. "Read it later."

After that, she called for her personal ikon, the large wooden cross with the figure of the Mother of God. On the back of it she began to write.

When the writing was finished, Maria placed the ikon under her pillow.

One afternoon a few days later Mitya left his classes and came to see his mother.

"I felt like coming now," he said.

Maria nodded her head.

"I want to speak with you. But first with Lizachka."

Mitya stood up.

"Mama wants you," he said to his sister.

Then Mitya went out into the hallway and knocked on the door of the landlady's rooms. A boy appeared.

"Kostya," said Mitya. "Go get our doctor again. Tell him to come immediately. Hurry—and here are thirty kopeks for you."

Kostya shook his head.

"I won't take the money," he said. "But I'll hurry—I'll fly, Mitya."

Maria held Elizabeth's hand.

"*Dorogaya*," she whispered, "my dear one—if anything should happen, be brave."

Elizabeth was frightened. Thin, worn, exhausted of her reserves of strength, she wept easily, without restraint.

"No, no, no," soothed Maria. "I have lived a great long life."

"You are our guardian angel," wept Elizabeth. "Do not leave us."

"I will never leave you," whispered Maria. "Somehow, I will always be near."

"You are our guardian angel," Elizabeth repeated.

"Be brave," Maria said softly.

"Someday," said Elizabeth, "I want to be a mother. Like you."

Maria nodded.

"You will be," she whispered.

"I am twenty-seven," said Elizabeth, "and a little ill. . . ."

"Come closer," said Maria.

Elizabeth moved closer.

Maria raised her hand and made the sign of the cross over Elizabeth's head.

"With this I thee bless," said Maria, "and give thee unto God. Forever and ever, my darling, my daughter."

Elizabeth pressed close to Maria and wept.

"Call Mitya," whispered Maria.

Mitya came to his mother's side, and waited silently.

"Mitenka," said Maria. "I loved you more than all the others—because you are the baby."

Mitya intently watched his mother's lips, striving with his supreme memory to remember every word.

"The Glass Factory," whispered Maria. "I managed it—for you. . . . Work, Mitenka, refrain from words. Always search patiently for divine truth—and scientific truth."

Mitya held his mother's hands firmly.

"Tell more," he whispered. "Tell, my *mamachka*. Tell all I must know. I will need this, *mamachka*—now, and later, when I am a man."

"You are a man," whispered Maria, and with her remaining strength drew the large ikon from under her pillow and raised it over Mitya's head.

"I bless you, Mitenka," she said. "On you were centered the hopes of my old age." Maria stopped. "Mitya," she resumed, "later, read what I have written here, on the ikon that I give to you. I am too weak to say the words."

Mitya nodded and took the ikon into his hands.

"Mitenka," whispered Maria, "light the candle."

From the top of the bureau Mitya took a long wax candle and lighting it, placed it in her hands.

He gazed intently into his mother's eyes, and in them he saw her last act of strength, her last possible use of self, and it was for him. And he knew that for the rest of his life the strength of that last glance would be with him.

Maria's eyes continued to look upon his and then into them came the ultimate gleam of light, the last message of love. She lost consciousness, and a few hours later she died.

Then a new gesture spontaneously came into Mitya's life. His hands stole to his head, and his head rocked slowly to and fro.

Elizabeth was kneeling before the ikon in the corner. The flame of the candle burned on, and its light fell softly upon them casting a shadow on the wall.

3

Maria was buried at Volkovo Cemetery in St. Petersburg.

After the funeral Mitya drove the wagon back to their attic room where Elizabeth would now live alone.

"Do you want to move somewhere else?" Mitya asked.

"No," whispered Elizabeth. "She'll be closer to me here."

For a long time the brother and sister talked of their lives. Then, in the late afternoon Mitya prepared to leave.

"I'll sell Soldat and the telega," he said. "It will be money for you. There is also some left in—her coat. And I'll bring you my allowance from the college."

"No," said Elizabeth, "you'll need that."

"They provide for me completely," said Mitya. "Well, I'll come back tomorrow morning."

Mitya sold the telega and Soldat.

The horse understood that he was being sold. The manner of the man in examining him before purchase left no doubt. Soldat stood silently, watching Mitya walk away.

Mitya stopped for a moment and spoke to the horse.

"For myself, I wouldn't do it," he said. "But it's for my sister."

Mitya returned now to the deserted cemetery and gazed upon the fresh mound of earth, and the small bunch of roses. Then, walking away to a parked carriage for hire, he was about to enter, to be driven to the institute. Suddenly, he thought the flowers on the grave were too meager, and hurried away from the puzzled driver. The *izvoschik* watched him walk down the street and stop at a flower shop.

"For one rouble," said Mitya to the woman. Then, thinking of Elizabeth, he changed the order.

"Make it only for fifty kopeks," he said.

She fixed the flowers—red and white roses and ferns.

"That's too much," said Mitya. "I can only spare fifty kopeks."

"I saw you go by this morning," said the woman. "It was your mother, wasn't it?"

Mitya nodded his head.

"And the driver later told me that you have no father."

Mitya nodded his head again.

"Here," she said. *"Bednyazhka"* [you poor little thing].

The woman would not take the fifty kopeks.

"Not from an orphan," she said. "Some day, when my own little Volodya is an orphan, I know somewhere a woman will give him flowers. May God guard you. Come back every month—as long as I live."

Mitya took the flowers and returned to the grave.

When he left the cemetery again, he walked slowly down the street, toward the institute.

4

In his classes Mitya tried desperately to put his mind to work. The first few days were difficult ones, but as time passed he joined more and more in the intensive exchange between the students and teachers. The strict systematic training began to fashion new habits of study for him, and his thirst for knowledge became greater than ever. The work in the laboratory grew more entrancing daily. The books were often inadequate, and Mitya was compelled to invent his own explanations, and his own experiments.

Then, one day, three months after Maria's death, the routine was again suddenly broken—Elizabeth collapsed in the hallway of her lodging place.

Mitya, summoned by the landlady's boy, immediately had his sister taken to the Maryinskoy Hospital. There she lay, coughing out her life's blood onto the white pillow.

Mitya abandoned his classes and spent all his time with her. But at ten o'clock each night he was forced to leave the hospital.

One night Mitya felt an even greater reluctance to leave.

"You must," said the gray-haired nurse with the white cap.

"She seems very bad tonight," said Mitya aside to the nurse. "Let me stay."

The nurse shook her head. "I'm sorry," she said. "It is the hospital rule."

So Mitya left and in the hospital Elizabeth coughed for a long time, the blood flowing from her.

"*Mamachka*," she called. "*Mamachka*. Mitenka, Mitenka, little brother."
In his bed at the Institute Mitya turned restlessly.
"Mitenka," again called Elizabeth, and died, alone, in a strange city.

5

Elizabeth, too, was buried in Volkovo Cemetery, near Maria.

Then Mitya went to the attic where Maria and Elizabeth had lived. For a while he did not know why he had come. As he moved about the room he fancied that people were walking about him. Matvei was there, and the strannik, Timofei, and the old woman of Aremziansk whose son had gone away so many years ago. Then suddenly the faces of Bassargin and Olga, and Katerina and her Vanka appeared. And always, always among these faces moved Maria and Elizabeth.

Mitya packed the clothing that remained, some books and a picture, two towels, a comb. From the empty bureau drawer he took the letter that Maria had written a few months before, on September 15. He and Elizabeth had read it the afternoon of Maria's funeral.

Now he sat down on a chair and read it again. It was addressed to all the family then remaining—to Elizabeth, to Mitya, to the married daughter Ekaterina in Omsk, to sons Ivan and Paul residing also in Omsk, to Olga, and to another daughter also named Maria. To all of them the dying mother in a feeble script had sent her blessing, gave advice and instructions, and to all of them she wrote, "Farewell, my dear and kind children. . . . There is not much time now left for me to breathe on this earth and apparently no longer to see you again. . . . Love one another. . . . Remember that your mother lived on this earth for you. . . . God is assigning a new role to me. . . . Pray for me. . . . It is difficult for a mother of a family to part with her children. I loved you, love you now, and will love you beyond the grave. . . . The kind Lizanka has been with me continually and has softened my last moments of life. Mitya is an orphan, he too needs help, don't forget that he is your brother. . . . Let God's will prevail."

On the back was written by Elizabeth, "Our dear little mother asks you that this letter be finally sent to Omsk, to Kitty. Pray, my dear, my own people, for our dear little mother, she is very weak."

From his pocket Mitya took the ikon of the Virgin Mary and once again read the inscription. "I bless you, Mitenka. On you were centered the hopes of my old age. I forgive all your wandering mistakes and entreat you to turn to God. Be kind, revere God, honor the Tsar, and the Fatherland, and do not forget that you will have to answer for everything at the Judgment. Farewell, remember your mother who loved you more than she loved anyone else. Maria Mendeleyev."

Mitya walked to the window and pushed it open.

Outside in the growing afternoon, the City of Peter moved on its way.

"What do I want in life?" whispered Mitya.

"Work and not words," he recalled his mother's words.

With the white bundle of clothes Mitya left the lodging house.

At the institute the classes were still on.

Mitya walked through the hallway with his bundle. At the end of the corridor he stopped. "Laboratory of Chemical Studies" read the inscription.

Mitya put his hand before him, and opened the door.

PART II

Chapter Thirteen

The Strannik's Story

THE BLUE flames on the Caspian had burned and gone out. The people in holiday spirit had poured endless bucketfuls of oil—seeping from the ground near by—onto the dark Caspian waters, and the night sky glowed from the soft blue flames of the sea.

But now this was gone. And somehow it had been an empty experience for Timofei. Even now, weeks after the great sea fires, the emptiness of the festivity dwelled in his heart. There was a time—a year ago in Aremziansk—when he could think of nothing more exhilarating than the prospect of viewing the Caspian flames and then journeying to Nizhny. True, Nadezhda had been excited by the spectacle of the flames, and Nadezhda still dreamed of one day reaching St. Petersburg, to see a life other than that of a lost village in a forgotten wilderness of snow. But even Nadezhda's enthusiasm was not so great as before.

All this the strannik understood.

"*Ekh*, Timofei," he said, as they labored together in the vast field of sunflowers, near the village of Anzhan, north of the Caspian Sea, "you've seen too much sorrow. That is your trouble."

Timofei thought of the strannik's words. Yes, there had been endless families with sorrow—illness or poverty—whom the three travelers had aided since leaving Aremziansk. Even now they labored in the field of "the cultivator" Andreyev who with his wife Anna lay ill of typhoid fever in the house. Nadezhda was there now, caring for the man and his wife, and attending the needs of their four children.

"You've grown older," said the strannik as he cut a dried sunflower and began to scrape the seeds—the *semochkee* beloved throughout Russia—into a wooden bucket with a screen across the top. "There is work to do in the land," he continued. "Noble work. Do you regret what you have seen?"

Timofei breathed deeply of the mellow southern air. Then a sigh escaped from his great chest.

"I don't regret," he said. "But neither do I rejoice."

"All through the land there is work to do," said the strannik, spreading his thin, sunburned hands, pointing beyond the field of sunflowers. "And all a man needs is love in his heart."

Timofei wiped his perspiring brow on his sleeve.

"I think you fooled me, *dedushka*," he said. "I think you wanted me to see the great need. I think you lured me with your fires on the waters."

The strannik nodded.

"It is true," he said. "I cannot lie to you." He put his hand on Timofei's shoulder.

"You are strong," he said. "Give your strength where it is needed and you will grow stronger."

Timofei's two buckets of *semochkee* were now full. He picked them up and started for the white house. The strannik, with his cane in one hand and the wooden bucket in the other, followed the strong figure marching ahead.

In the house, Nadezhda was sitting at the table, giving the children their supper. The oldest was fourteen, a boy named Yasha, home on vacation from school. Next was Dousya, a boy of nine, who sat at the table silently eating the rice and lamb that Nadezhda had prepared. The third, a girl, Manya, was seven, and she sat with her eyes not on the food but on the window through which she could see the brown camels undulating along the country road. The last child was the five-year-old boy Danya, now utterly devoted to the heaping bowl of pilav before him.

When the strannik and Timofei came in, Nadezhda silently set bowls of food before them, then went back to the children.

"How's the mother?" asked Timofei.

Nadezhda nodded.

"She's much better. Might be up tomorrow."

"And the father?"

"Perhaps tomorrow. Or in another day," said Nadezhda, spooning more pilav into Danya's bowl.

The next day both the mother and father were up. They were worn from the fever, but thanks to Nadezhda's care had recovered a part of their strength. The man, Andreyev, was of medium height, and had smiling blue eyes, now dulled by the illness. The woman was thin, but gay despite her weakness. Her eyes smiled upon her children, and she frequently embraced Nadezhda.

"You're a good woman," she said over and over. "A good woman."

"The crop is all picked," said Timofei, "and you have lost nothing. Now we must leave. Am I right, *dedushka?*"

The strannik agreed.

"There's nothing for us to do now. We would only eat their food."

"It is the function of science to discover the existence of a general reign of order in nature and to find the causes governing this order. And this refers in equal measure to the relations of man—social and political—and to the entire universe as a whole."

"There exists everywhere a medium in things, determined by equilibrium. The Russian proverb says, 'Too much salt or too little salt is alike an evil.' It is the same in political and social relations."

Andreyev and his wife entreated the travelers to remain longer—as non-working guests.

"Impossible," said Timofei, and at once collected his few possessions.

The strannik and Nadezhda were ready to go.

Outside, in the field, the youngest boy, Danya, suddenly began to cry. Everyone hurried out.

In Danya's palm a long quill was sticking.

Anna, the woman of the house, almost fainted.

"*Chto takoye*, Danya?" she cried, embracing the boy, and carefully pulling the quill out of his hand.

"He tried to pick up a porcupine," said Yasha, the oldest boy, sympathetically. "He doesn't understand, he's so young. *Akh*, how young he is."

Danya howled incessantly.

"Last year," said Manya, the seven-year-old girl, "he took a stick and poked it into the eye of the little Semenov girl. He doesn't seem to understand."

Danya howled more.

"And six months ago," interposed the nine-year-old Dousya, "he took a little kitten and poured a bucket of mud on it."

"It scratched me," yowled the tearful Danya.

"He's so young," Yasha repeated, and strode off toward the camels.

The strannik began a story, and at once Danya stopped crying and listened with his mouth open.

"Once there lived and existed a rich boy with blue hair and strong shoes. . . ."

Andreyev and his wife watched silently as their children drew closer to the strannik. In the distance, Yasha, the oldest, had already mounted a camel.

Timofei and Nadezhda were waiting for the strannik.

The warm southern sun was now setting behind the distant hills.

"Good-by," said the strannik. "Good-by, my darlings," and he set off through the sunflower field with Nadezhda and Timofei.

At the white house the children stood watching. Tears were flowing from the soft blue eyes of the woman Anna.

"Good people," she said. "But the big strong man is sad."

2

The year was 1850.

On the shore of the Volga River, near the city of Tsaritsin, the strannik lay dying.

"Sing," whispered the strannik, his sunken eyes fixed on Nadezhda. Softly Nadezhda sang, the tears slowly making their way down her cheeks.

"Volga, Volga,
Native Mother . . ."

"*Dedushka*," said Timofei, holding the old man's hands. "Little grandfather, soon I will make a cross for you. A sturdy cross. But I cannot write 'Strannik' on it. What name shall I write on the cross, *dedushka?*"

The strannik nodded.

"You speak true," he said barely audibly. "My name is Stepan Stepanovitch Baltinsky. I am seventy-four years old. I was born in the Crimea, but I wished to die on the Volga."

Nadezhda glanced up at the great river in front of them.

"I sinned when I was young," whispered the strannik. "My woman was a good woman, but I beat her once with a stick."

Nadezhda suddenly placed her hands on the strannik's mouth. Nadezhda's dark eyes were alarmed and compassionate.

"Don't tell, *dedushka*," she begged, "don't tell."

Timofei drew Nadezhda's hands away from the strannik's mouth.

"He needs to tell," said Timofei.

The strannik went on.

"My woman looked at me with eyes that gripped my heart. She loved me, and I could never forget the look in her eyes. She forgave, but the eyes haunted me, and one night the Lord came and told me to go over the face of Russia and do good unto the people, and lighten the hearts of the children. And the Lord himself told me the story of the little boy with the blue hair and the golden shoes."

"Rest, *dedushka*," begged Nadezhda. "Rest now."

"The time has come to rest," whispered the strannik. "Lift my hand."

Timofei lifted the strannik's right hand.

"I bless you, Timofei," said the old man, "and you, Nadezhda, his mate. And all your future progeny."

The strannik turned his head toward the river, and lay without speaking until twilight. Then he merely said,

"*Praschaitee*, my children. Farewell," and died.

Timofei dug the grave and buried the strannik. In the dark he made a strong cross of two wide branches and carved the old man's name on the wood, and added his age.

The next morning Nadezhda placed wildflowers on the grave.

Timofei took up the strannik's cane.

"How will it be, Nadezhda," said Timofei, "will you go to St. Petersburg?"

"I am going with you," said Nadezhda, "to the people who need us, wherever that may be."

But Nadezhda could go little farther, and they settled in a near-by village to wait for their child to be born. And in this birth Nadezhda died.

Timofei named the boy Stepan for the memory of the strannik.

"We will wait, my Stepan," said Timofei, "till your legs are strong and then go into the world. It needs us."

When Stepan was four years old, Timofei took up the strannik's cane and set out once more.

"All roads lead to Nizhny," he said. "Sooner or later we will get there."

At the first village, a group of children ran out into the road.

"Here comes a strannik!" called a little girl. "And a boy with him."

Timofei and his tiny son were surrounded by the children.

"Strannik," said the little girl. "Tell a story. Tell."

Timofei knelt and drew the children to his heart.

"Once," he began, "there lived and existed a little rich boy with blue hair and strong shoes. . . ."

Chapter Fourteen

The Gold Medal

THE SIBERIAN student Dmitri Ivanovitch Mendeleyev entered the Teacher Training Institute of the University of St. Petersburg in the fall of 1850. He was enrolled in the Physio-Mathematical section, and at first his work was not very good. This was because freshman courses started not every year, but every second year, and 1850 was not a freshman year. So the "young Mendeleyev" had been obliged to take the sophomore course. But even so, soon his performance improved, and by the end of the second year he was doing well in all courses, both theory and laboratory, and especially in chemistry. By the end of the third year no student could compare with him.

Many wondered what there was about the youthful Mendeleyev that gave him such superiority. Some of his colleagues, who had known of the death of his mother and sister, thought that these events were largely responsible for his academic zeal, to win success as though in memorial payment to his departed dear ones.

The student Petrov once remarked in a group, "I would say it's pure brilliance."

Young Nikolayev was of a different opinion.

"There is some purpose in him," he said. "But he does not speak of it."

Ostrovsky had his theory, too.

"He seems like a person who does not expect to live long, and does everything correctly the first time. As though there were no time to waste."

Ostragradsky, the professor of mathematics, wondered about the student Mendeleyev, too, but could not quite fathom him. And Zinin, the chemistry teacher also marveled.

"He's like some sort of an elusive compound," he said. "Something rare, defying analysis."

In young Mendeleyev's room, on the shelf above his study table, reposed a book on the natural sciences. This book was a clue to him. It was one of those given to him by Bassargin. The book itself was of small consequence—it was obsolete. But the memory of Bassargin, and the seeds of science that he had sowed within the heart of the blond student bent over his desk there were of consequence. Bassargin had taught well. More, by his intelligence and forthrightness, he had inspired. The seeds of science had taken root.

Next to Bassargin's book on science stood a small blue vase. This was the vase that the glass blower Timofei had made and had given to his young friend. It was a work of perfection, an epitaph to art. The tiny vase, the art of the vase, was also a clue to the student Mendeleyev.

Next to the vase, on the wall, hung the ikon with its message from Maria. "I loved you more than anyone else. . . ."

The ikon, too, was a clue to the boy Mendeleyev.

Thus the elements of his success became Bassargin's message, "Everything in the world is science."

And Timofei's, "Everything in the world is art."

And Maria's, "Everything in the world is love."

Mendeleyev himself was quite unaware of the fusion within him. He worked, and before him eternally hovered the vision of the Russian people whom he knew he could aid through science.

2

At the end of the first exciting and challenging year, the spirit of young Mendeleyev had become integrated, but his body began to shatter.

Through constant colds and attacks of pneumonia—his lungs apparently already affected in Siberia—he began to cough blood.

By the end of his third year, he was so ill that the institute doctors feared for his life. Though he had spent more than half of his time in the institute's hospital, his work went on. Attacks of pneumonia came more frequently. In bed, feverish, he studied his lessons and worked at his problems.

The students brought him books and told him of the assignments, then came back later to take his finished work to the professors. The professors themselves often came to young Mendeleyev's bedside, and the chemist Voskresensky, his special advisor, frequently gave him private chemistry lectures at his bedside.

Students and professors knew that logically Mendeleyev should be made to give up his career and be sent to a drier, warmer climate. But logic was not applicable in this case. For anyone, glancing merely once at the lean blond youth with the large forehead, the sunken cheeks, and the burning blue eyes focused on a tome of chemistry, knew that it would be criminal to tear him away from his life's work—short though that life might be. None dared to suggest to him that he desist from his studies. And so he studied, and in the examinations stood a brilliant first.

At the graduation exercises, when the gold medal for excellence was awarded to him, the entire student body and the professors rose in a great ovation. The youth from the village of Aremziansk in the area of Tobolsk, grown taller, thinner, more broad-shouldered, marched coughing to the center of the stage, accepted the award, and bowed.

At this graduation his principal chemistry professor, Voskresensky, received superlative praise from the renowned Academician Fritzsche. Mendeleyev shook hands with many men of fame from St. Petersburg and Moscow.

Then, as soon as he found a free moment, he put on his *polushubok*—the half-length sheepskin coat—and the fur cap, and walked out of the building.

At the graves of Elizabeth and Maria in Volkovo Cemetery he dropped to one knee and, opening his hand, gazed silently at his palm on which lay the gold medal.

Chapter Fifteen

"Some Spiritual Force"

DMITRI MENDELEYEV was now desperately ill. He had tasted of the sweet fruits of scientific knowledge, but the price had been high.

It was 1855, and he wanted to go on with further studies at the institute, but the decision of the Physician Professor Zdekauer made this impossible. Mendeleyev was ordered to leave and seek health. The High Council of the institute would petition the Minister of Education to transfer him to some southern university.

He suffered at the thought of leaving the institute, which had become a second home to him. Everything here was readily available—books, library facilities, lectures, friends, seclusion in a private room, and alas, a hospital. Here one could study through all sorts of weather, in the most violent Petersburg storms, without leaving to walk to and fro, without loss of time. Here the influence of the fellow students of other departments—economists, historians, philologists—was like the yeast in the bread of his life.

Here at the institute, too, besides his formal lessons, he had launched successfully a number of original chemical investigations. To do worth-while work it was first necessary to become acquainted with the works of foreign authors, and young Mendeleyev—who disliked aimless language learning—now learned French and German with a will, for there was science to know in those languages, great amounts of it superior to inadequately supported Russian science.

His original laboratory work was principally on the structure of crystals, and especially a study of the similar crystal structures that are left in two containers by two analogous chemical substances whose liquid parts are allowed to evaporate. He was intrigued by the dependence between the crystalline form and the chemical constitution of such analogous compounds, and wrote a dissertation of 234 pages on the subject, covering his experiments and his theories. On the surface of his mind floated the image of the crystal glass forms he once saw at the bottom of the molten debris that had been the Glass Factory.

At the institute too Mendeleyev further cultivated the habit of setting down his fresh ideas in a notebook, and often his half-musing mind turned to the thought that he felt must have a compelling answer: iron, copper, zinc, aluminium, carbon, potassium, nitrogen, oxygen, sodium, hydrogen . . . are they and their interminable numbers of compounds all unrelated, without rhyme and reason and sense, or are there certain illuminating relations between all of them? Twenty-one-year-old Dmitri, the almost mature scientist, understood that the essence of science is simplicity, and the eternal goal is the explanation of much in terms of little, and less.

The love of the institute, where a world of new ideas came flooding through his mind made him grieve at the prospect of leaving. For a while he took a room outside of the institute, with his friend Vishnegradsky. Here he expected to rest and then continue with the work at the institute.

But the decision of the exacting doctor Zdekauer was irrevocable and ominous.

"Dmitri Ivanovitch," said the stern Zdekauer one morning at the institute, "your body is clamoring for help. You must give it all the aid you can."

Zdekauer then stepped outside of his office and conferred for a moment with the chemist Voskresensky.

"Shall we withhold the true judgment?" Zdekauer asked. "With most people in this condition it is better not to tell."

Voskresensky shook his head.

"This boy I know," he said. "*Akh*, what a brilliance—that it should be so mercilessly attacked."

Zdekauer waited.

"Tell him everything," said Voskresensky. "Mendeleyev fears nothing. He is a scientist."

Zdekauer went back into the consultation room.

Mendeleyev, stripped to the waist, gaunt, skeletal in appearance, stood with his tired blue eyes fixed on Zdekauer.

Zdekauer nodded.

"Voskresensky says you can be told everything."

"Naturally," said Mendeleyev, placing his hand to his hollow chest, as he coughed. "Tell."

2

"How shall I tell you . . . ," began Zdekauer. "The illness is a serious one."

"Tuberculosis of both lungs," said Mendeleyev. "I know."

"You know!" exclaimed Zdekauer.

Mendeleyev spread his hands, palms turned out.

"Why of course I know. What else could it be? What I want you to tell me is how long I have."

Zdekauer ran his hand over his head. He looked at Mendeleyev's quiet waiting eyes.

"Eight months," said Zdekauer.

In the small consultation room a silence began to grow. Zdekauer stood watching his patient, who still was standing stripped to the waist. Mendeleyev turned aside to cough into a dark cloth. He rolled the cloth up and opening the door of the black iron stove tossed it into the flames.

Now he picked up his shirt and took his notebook out of the pocket. He turned its pages, then with his eyes fixed walked through the side door into the adjacent empty classroom. Zdekauer picked up Mendeleyev's shirt and followed.

Mendeleyev walked to the small blackboard, and after consulting his notebook once more, picked up the chalk and began to write.

Zdekauer, with Mendeleyev's brown shirt still in his hands, watched intently.

In a moment, Voskresensky came into the room, and after him other professors, and then a number of curious students. Standing, their eyes on the tall blond youth writing on the blackboard, they waited. Frequently Mendeleyev coughed and placed his left hand on his chest.

He had now covered the blackboard with his long-range scientific plans. Completely oblivious of the watching men, utterly alone with his thoughts, he now studied the blackboard.

"It would be necessary first to get all available data," he spoke audibly, though to himself. "From Germany and France, and England, and from Amerika—and Prague. From everywhere. I would then need to do not more than ten, or perhaps fifteen, years of experiments. It is possible—yes, it is inevitable that the connection would be found—a plan of unity among the elements."

Mendeleyev paused, and looked at the section on the blackboard showing another of his projects. There were the words "Urals, Baku, Caspian. . . ."

He turned to Zdekauer now and seeing only him, said softly,

"But this part, the development of the resources, could be done while the other problem went on. I would not need any more time for that."

Zdekauer stood speechless.

Mendeleyev's friend, the graduate student Petrov, took the shirt from Zdekauer's hands and placed it over the boy's shoulders.

Mendeleyev spoke to Zdekauer.

"I need ten years," he said.

Zdekauer still did not speak.

Mendeleyev watched the tired doctor.

"Five years," he said softly.

Zdekauer, hardly breathing, gazed at his patient's eyes.

"Two years," said Mendeleyev.

Zdekauer slowly lowered his head. There was no reply.

Voskresensky gently led his protégé back into the consultation room. The people in the classroom remained hushed, motionless.

Voskresensky found his undershirt and gave it to him.

"Mitya," he said, "the director thinks you should spend your remaining months in the Crimea. Here, in Petersburg, you won't live even several months. There is something you can do down there, Mitya. The Gymnasium at Simferopol needs a science master. They want a good program to get started. Or would you rather just live there—the months?"

Mendeleyev went to the door. He paused.

"I'll start that work for them," he said.

Suddenly through the door he was listening to the voice of Zdekauer.

"Some spiritual force is needed," Zdekauer was saying. "What am I? I am only a man. When I said he had eight months it was from generosity. Perhaps four months is closer. No. I am only a man. To cure him would take more than a doctor."

Mendeleyev stood at the door transfixed.

An infinitesimal trace of a smile slowly appeared about his tired eyes.

3

In his *polushubok* [the fur-lined half-coat] and fur cap he wandered through the windy Petersburg streets. These were the streets of the eternally turbulent Petersburg—the streets of restless Russia.

The period 1850–1855 was a period of suffocation under Tsar Nicholas. Every expression of political and intellectual freedom was stifled in the cradle. At the university, philosophy and divinity were merged into one; moral philosophy was withdrawn; discussion of these changes was forbidden under threat of reprisal. All groups capable of original thought were placed under police surveillance. Published works of music were scrutinized by government agents for suspected radical innuendos concealed in song. Within the written notes themselves was sought in code the crescendo conspiracy of the composer, contemplating countermeasure against the bloody harmony of the song of the sycophants of the Tsar.

The youthful Dostoyevsky spent shattering epileptic years in a Siberian prison at Omsk, from 1850 to 1854.

In 1852, the talented new writer Turgenev, a large man, whose squeaky voice reflected the twisted torment of his soul, was hushed into silence—isolated upon his estate—for daring to write in a Moscow newspaper a heartfelt obituary on Gogol's death. For though Gogol had made a pilgrimage to Jerusalem and resigned himself to preaching obeisance to the *status quo*, still, none could forget his earlier work in the defense of the dignity of man.

In 1855 a new Tsar came to the throne—Alexander II. In the windy capital streets of St. Petersburg the people wondered about the future.

Mendeleyev was now walking along these streets.

He stopped at the small flower shop.

"*Akh*, there you are," said the round woman. "It has been more than three months. Where have you been?"

"A little bit unwell. And much study."

"*Bednyazhka*," [you poor little fellow] said the woman, shaking her head.

Rapidly she fixed the regular bouquet of roses and ferns. He took the flowers. The woman beamed.

"I was afraid," she said, "that you had begun to buy them somewhere. You would not do that, would you? This is between you and me and God."

"No," he said, "I would not get them any place else."

"*Bog stoboy*," [God be with thee] said the woman.

He took a step, then stopped.

"I will be gone," he said, "for a while. I must go away."

"How is that, go away?" asked the woman puzzled.

"To the South. To the Crimea."

"The lungs?" asked the woman.

Mendeleyev nodded.

"*Tse, tse, tse*," said the woman, shaking her head. "*Akh, bednyazhka.*"

"Good-by," said Mendeleyev.

"I'll pray," said the woman. "There will be a light burning under the ikon."

At Volkovo Cemetery evening had come. Mendeleyev sat on the ground, on some dry branches near Maria's grave, and coughed for a long time. Then a calm descended upon him.

As he gazed upon the mound before him his mind turned about. Before him were visions of Aremziansk and the destitute men and women of the village, and of all Russia. Before him, too, rose the native potential riches of the land crying for scientific usage. There stretched the mineraled Urals, the inefficiently used harvest lands, the wasted oil lands of Baku and the Caspian shore. In his thinking the chemistry laboratory came to life and the test tubes bearing colored liquids yielding secrets from the heart of nature.

And as he continued to gaze upon the grave before him, there appeared Maria on her deathbed giving unto him her last look of strength.

He rose, walked erectly from the cemetery, and left for the Crimea.

It was August, 1855.

Chapter Sixteen

Purple Grapes

THE CRIMEAN peninsula hangs like a trembling heart in the body of the blue Black Sea. The mountains shield the lands of the coast from the chill winter winds sweeping across the great open spaces offshore. In the north, during winter, cold dry winds blow over the plains and a thin snow falls to the ground. But in the southern Crimea in summer the climate verges on the subtropical, and the vegetation grows lush and mellow from the warm damp soil and the benevolent sun. And as if to return the sun-smile from the sky, vast fields of sunflowers turn their round faces upward, to the warmth of the light above.

And even as all multifarious wealth dwells in the bosom of the Urals, so do all living varieties of plant grow in the warm heart of the Crimea.

In the central valleys are the oaks and the white hornbeam trees, on the hillsides the forest of beech, and higher still the verdant pines. Far in the south evergreens, cypress, Lebanon cedar, laurel, and olive trees grow. Here, too, vast areas are devoted to wheat and barley and tobacco. On both left and right lie orchards of apple and apricot trees and, most bewitching of all, opulent vineyards of long purple grapes.

Mendeleyev stood in a vineyard of crowded bunches of these grapes. It was his first day at Simferopol, and he looked tired and worn.

He was coughing, his lips tinged with the red fluid rising from within him. The sun was beating down from a cloudless blue sky, and the subtle aroma of the ripe grapes filled the air. Slowly, laboriously, he took off his gray jacket, his blouse, and cotton undershirt. Gaunt and stooped, he stood in the sun and gazed upon a luscious purple grape, half the length of a finger. Within the purple grape throbbed life. Within the body of Mendeleyev life struggled to endure. His eyes were fixed on the grape. How purple it was, how rich, how gleaming in the sun, how bursting in its velvet silkiness. Fascinated, almost entranced, he drew nearer to it. Here lay the test. Here was a crucial experiment for a scientist. With all his tired body and mind he gazed upon the grape and waited.

The minutes passed. Unswerving in his glance he looked upon the exuberant fruit before him. Not yet. He waited. His cough returned once more, and once again blood seeped between his lips. But the experiment had to be done. The warm sun slowly relaxed the drawn lines of his haggard face. His eyes were still dull—but they waited for the body to respond.

Now it began. Slowly, subtly, his mouth began to water. Slowly first, then more, then deliciously, undeniably more. There was no mistaking it—he was hungry for the first time in months. *Akh,* how his mouth watered as his eyes devoured the grape! He drew his mouth close to the vine and bit the purple grape off the stem. His teeth closed over it, his body trembled with life, and he hungrily seized the whole bunch.

2

The next day he returned to the vineyard. Once more he stood before the throbbing fruit and gazed upon its color and contour. Again the time was long, but he waited, and at last his body hungered and the juices flowed within him—deep, somewhere within, and provocatively under his tongue. Before no other food could his body thus react. All other foods he merely forced with half a will into his mouth and past his throat. Once more he pressed his mouth to the grapes and ate them off the vine.

The days passed. And each day, after his work at the Simferopol High School, where he was preparing to teach several branches of science, he regularly made his way to the purple vineyard where life still had a chance. Stripping to the waist, coughing but absorbing the light of the sun, he stood face to face with the purple grapes and waited till his body cried for food.

There came at last the most delicious day of all, and then it was that he knew that he would live.

It was Sunday morning. At nine o'clock he stood in the long dark vineyard. And suddenly, as soon as his eyes fell upon a heavy mass of purple grapes, he hungered. The juices stirred within his entire body. In every cell life seemed to sing. His mouth threatened to overflow with saliva. He reached out his hand, plucked a bunch, and ate without restraint. His long-starved thirsting body drank the wine, and his heart began to beat with renewed life. His hands and face dripped with the purple juice. He sat upon the fragrant ground and ate, his sunken chest dripping with streaks of blue and his eyes gradually beginning to shine.

Mendeleyev stood up and removed all his clothes and standing naked in the vineyard turned his face to the sun. Then, breaking off another bunch he lay stretched full upon the ground, the grapes before his face, no longer to eat, but only to seek the delicious aroma.

He fell into a deep sleep under the Crimean sun.

3

The high school at Simferopol was soon closed because of the Crimean War raging in the extreme south and threatening to spread northward. Mendeleyev could not afford a room—which cost thirty roubles per month, his salary being thirty-three roubles—and therefore took shelter in the high school itself—in a small chamber adjoining the archives department. Actually, he lived almost completely outdoors. He allowed his yellow hair and blond moustache and youthful beard to grow. At table he ate with an almost normal zest, and in the vineyards he took the fruit exultingly and slept under the sun without a dream.

As his cough grew less, he wandered over the countryside, breathing the mellow air, and laughing at the hills and streams. Not since he had left the Siberian cedar forests had he been so stirred. But here, even more, he gave himself unto nature, climbed the hills, splashed in the brooks, swam in the rivers, and slept in the vineyards. Life returned. Glowing, flowing, throbbing life.

Frequently he came across galloping Cossacks, with muskets hanging over their backs. Frequently he met the narrow-eyed descendants of the Tartars in multicolored jackets trimmed with silver.

And everywhere people marched about cracking *semochkee* (sunflower seeds) between their teeth, each carrying a pocketful. Often, they sat outside their white cottages and drank tea in the sun. Many times, in his wanderings, Mendeleyev sat with the people to drink their tea, and though often neither could understand the language of the other, there was an ineffable communion of the spirit.

His frame was losing its gauntness; his face grew tan.

4

But the war which England and France had declared on Russia and which brought them to the Crimea on September 14, 1854, soon devastated Sevastopol at the tip of the Crimea where a great siege was in progress. The rivers of blood seemed ready to overflow onto the rest of the peninsula. Every day Cossack reenforcements passed through Simferopol, galloping toward battle with obscene abandon. Tall Cossack hats sat at jaunty angle, white robes flapped in the stir of the created breeze, and diagonal leather belts crossing sturdy chests confined the muskets slung over the backs, while the tips of bronze bullets in the upper pockets shimmered in the sun. At their sides these galloping warriors carried cutlasses and heavy pistols.

Foot soldiers, too, came marching over the Crimea, heading for Sevastopol. Raucously they marched along, shouting at the mellow air, threatening to throw the enemy out of the Crimea into the Black Sea.

As far back as central Simferopol came the wounded—in telegas, dragged by camels—and the dead, overflowing the Simferopol Hospital, the private homes, the open countryside. But still reenforcements came and among them great hordes of mouzhik serfs who had begged to purchase their freedom on the field of battle. Many of the serfs were runaways, who wanted to die fighting for someone's freedom rather than die slaving in their own bondage. Many of these, too, were brought back shattered by the cannon, and many were placed into the warm damp earth forever. Over the great plains ambled the hordes of harnessed camels eating away the grass.

The blood flowed but the war went on.

Mendeleyev had his own plans for Russia, and he prepared to leave the Crimea to pursue once more the elusive goddess of science.

One day, as he made ready to depart, he strolled into Simferopol and there saw a sturdy man in uniform, chatting with the soldiers and peasants about him, and making entries furiously in a notebook.

"Who is it?" Mendeleyev asked.

A tall dark-haired soldier, cap in hand, replied.

"Our officer, Tolstoy. He writes things, too."

Mendeleyev had heard stories of this man. He had been born of noble heritage in Yasnaya Polyana—Bright Meadows—on the estate of his father, in the province of Tula. He had studied at the University of Kazan but had left before completing the course. In 1851 he had sought adventure in the Caucasus, joining the Cossack forces as a yunker—a youth of noble birth attached to the army as a noncommissioned officer.

In the Caucasus he had galloped against the Chechen tribesmen in pure physical exultation. But his mind was alive with the thought of the world, and at every spare moment he poured his contemplations onto paper. In 1852 the story *Childhood*, appeared and was received by the critics as the work of a man of promise. In 1854 he fought against the Turks and then was sent to the Crimea to fight the English and the French. There he served with a field battery till May, 1855, was promoted to the rank of divisional commander, and took part in the Battle of Chernaya and the storming of Sevastopol. He had fought bravely, remembered much, and made penciled notes of the mutilation of men.

Tolstoy had already written his *Sevastopol*, and the soldiers and sailors in the barricades and hospitals had begun to know him as an intrepid human spirit, who wrote of the things in their hearts.

The tall dark soldier took Mendeleyev by the sleeve.

"What do you think?" he asked. "Will we beat the English? Do you think we'll win?"

Mendeleyev thought of Tolstoy striving to reach the conscience of men.

"Whether *we* win is irrelevant," he said. He looked at the energetic writer in the midst of the group. "The question is, will *he* win?"

Walking along the dusty road Mendeleyev was lost in his thoughts. He had gone too far and now he turned about and followed the road to the hospital.

In a private consultation room he stood face to face with Dr. Nikolai Ivanovitch Pirogov—one of the medical men who had been attached to the Pedagogical Institute. Pirogov remembered how ill the student Mendeleyev had been, and he also knew that Zdekauer had given him only a few months of life. Now Pirogov stood staring at this tall sturdy man with the sun in his cheeks, eyes full of light, blond whiskers, moustache, and yellow hair glistening with life.

"Impossible," he said. "Simply impossible. How did you do it!"

Mendeleyev laughed and his laughter was deep and hearty.

"So Zdekauer gave you eight months," said Pirogov.

Mendeleyev shrugged his shoulders.

Pirogov examined him, listening carefully to his chest.

"You do not have tuberculosis," he said, "and I am quite certain now that you never had it. Yes, I know you coughed blood, and very likely you will in the future. But it is a functional condition of the heart. Valvular defect, and it is possible to live with that to a great age."

"Good!" said Mendeleyev. "I need the time. But how strange! How surprising!"

"Of course, one must take care," said Pirogov. "Not too much violent activity. *Akh*, but this horrible war."

Pirogov had come to the front where medical men were in appalling demand.

"Blood runs in the streets," he said.

Mendeleyev stood at the window. Outside, more telegas were arriving, bearing more wounded.

"Sometimes," he said, "I wonder why I live. And yet I know I must and I know I will."

"That's pretty obvious," said Pirogov. "You'll outlive both me and Zdekauer. Wait till I write him. *Akh!* but I would like to see his face when I tell him you have mastered death."

Outside, the wagons continued to roll.

"It is life that must be mastered," said Mendeleyev.

Pirogov sat down and began to write a letter.

"This is for you," he said. "It is the letter permitting your return to our frozen north. Someone will want to be sure that you are well again before you will receive employment there."

Mendeleyev nodded.

"First I am going to Odessa," he said. "They want me to teach physics and mathematics at the Richelieu High School. I'll be there just a short while—until I am sure I am really well enough to go north, back to St. Petersburg."

Pirogov finished writing the letter.

"You will like Odessa," he said.

Mendeleyev nodded.

"Yes. I like it already. They write that I will have enough spare time to work on my thesis for a master's degree."

"What will it be about?" asked Pirogov.

"On the chemical elements. How much some of them expand when they are heated. It's something I need to know for a certain idea."

"*Akh da*," said Pirogov.

They shook hands and Mendeleyev left.

In the morning he gave money to the woman at whose home he took some of his meals, left her some special instructions, and then departed for Odessa. This was the winter of 1855.

In Odessa he plunged into work with a new zest, teaching and writing his master's thesis. In the spring of 1856 he left for St. Petersburg, but before he left, a box came from the woman in the Crimea. Mendeleyev knew. He opened the box and carefully took out the bunches of long purple grapes.

With the suitcase—bearing his clothes and his master's thesis—in one hand, and the purple grapes in the other, he walked out into the night, whistling.

Chapter Seventeen

The Flow of the Tide

IT WAS spring of 1856. Mendeleyev, twenty-two years old, tanned and bewhiskered, arrived in St. Petersburg.

At the university he at once presented his master's thesis of 224 pages dealing with research and theories on the expansion of substances due to heat. The thesis was accepted and he passed the master's examination.

Afterward, he went to the flower shop. A boy was standing inside, arranging a mass of red roses. Mendeleyev watched him. "Where is your mother?" he asked.

The boy looked up from the flowers. "She died."

Mendeleyev stood studying the boy. "And your father is not living, is he?"

The boy shook his head. "No. He died long ago."

The boy was twelve, but his face looked much older and he seemed tired. He sat down on a low stool, and fingered the buttons on his jacket.

"I live with a friend now," he said. "The woman next door. The woman came one day before my mother died. They talked."

"Yes?"

"She cooks and fixes my clothes. I work here."

"Does she have a family?"

"Yes. A large family. I stay in my own room, but I eat with them, and I can go to their rooms any time."

Mendeleyev casually examined the flowers in the shop. He turned back to the boy.

"What about school?"

The boy shrugged his shoulders.

"Perhaps later," he said.

Mendeleyev took a drawstring purse out of the inside pocket of his jacket. "You know how to take care of money?" he asked.

The boy nodded.

"Yes. I buy the flowers and I save the profits. The woman takes nothing from me. I just pay my rent to the landlady. But the woman who feeds me takes nothing."

Mendeleyev took a packet of pink banknotes from his purse.

"Take this," he said. "Your mother gave me flowers for years."

"That was free," said the boy. "I know about you."

Mendeleyev put the money into the boy's hand.

"It was free," he said, "I know. But now I am paying. Have it."

The boy put the money in his pocket.

"Fix three bouquets," said Mendeleyev.

The boy prepared the roses and ferns.

At the cemetery he pointed out his mother's grave. It had flowers on it. Mendeleyev added his bouquet. Then they walked over to the graves of Elizabeth and Maria. Here, too, there were flowers.

Mendeleyev turned to the boy.

"How is this then?" he asked.

"They're small bouquets," said the boy. "My mother told me always to tend to them. She said you would be back."

Mendeleyev placed his flowers on the graves.

"From now on I'll take care of this," he said.

The boy nodded.

"*Khorosho*," he said. "I have to go back to my shop now. Someone might come."

They walked out of the cemetery.

"Your name's Volodya," said Mendeleyev. "Isn't it?"

"Yes."

"Well, think a little about learning things, Volodya. Just think about it. About school and the world and what you can do."

"I think about it," said the boy. "My mother talked to me."

"That's good. Perhaps some day I may be able to help."

The boy nodded. "That is a possibility," he said and walked down the street.

Mendeleyev fell in love. The girl was Sophia Markovna Kash, sixteen years old. He met her at a resort where his sister Olga was resting during the summer. Years before, at a dance in Tobolsk, Mendeleyev had met Sophia—endearingly called "Sonetchka." He was at that time fourteen years old and she was eight. Even then he was attracted to her—she seemed so round-eyed and dainty and fragile. She had wanted to dance with him, but he merely shook his head. He didn't know how to do "that European ballroom dancing."

Now he was attracted to her deeply, and after a shy but unrelenting courtship he proposed to her. Sophia consulted her parents and together they decided to accept the offer.

Then Mendeleyev really found out about his Sonetchka. The most wonderful thing in the world to her were her canaries.

"Next, I love my darling dolls. . . ."

"And next?" wondered Mendeleyev.

"Next I love my pink room—I would never dream of giving up my canaries, my dolls, and my pink room."

"I know, but when we're married?"

Sonetchka frowned. "You'll have to live here. And help with the canaries and you'll learn to be interested in my dolls, really."

Mendeleyev frowned. "No, no," he said. "That's not me."

He went home slightly disturbed.

The next evening, in the front room of Sonetchka's home Mendeleyev talked about books.

"Do you read many romances?" he asked.

Sonetchka blushed deeply. She lifted her hands in astonishment.

"*Okh,*" she said. "*Okh,* how could you?"

"Romances," he said. "What's wrong? I mean novels of men and women. Romances."

"*Okh!*" exclaimed Sonetchka. "And we're not even married."

She told her mother. The next night Sonetchka's father explained to Mendeleyev, man to man, that the engagement had been a mistake.

"You apparently are quite a man. And she is young. . . ."

Mendeleyev plunged back into his studies.

"Never again," he muttered for days. "Never again."

2

In the next two years Mendeleyev worked endless hours in the laboratory, repeating experiments over and over, to be absolutely certain of the results. His manipulative technique with chemicals, balances, pipettes, and all sorts of glass equipment was a wonder to behold. Older staff members came to watch him. He worked quickly, with agility and accuracy, and always with a demand upon himself to think only of the work as his hands handled the apparatus. Concentration was his intellectual key. Artistic perfection was his manipulative aim. In the realm of creation, science was his medium.

He was appointed Private Instructor, a post without definite compensation but with the official recognition that he was considered able to give private lessons. The students came. But day and night he experimented in the laboratory and studied theory. He also wrote articles for popular and technical journals.

In these two years, between 1856 and 1858, he published fifteen or more papers and articles. His master's thesis on expansion was one. "New Events in Science" was a series for the government journal addressed to the people. There followed soon a commentary on the book by E. Hofman, *The Northern Urals;* a critique of the work of A. Strecker; analysis of the newest metallurgical researches; the burning of explosives, liquid glass—like that which flowed in Aremziansk in 1848. An original contribution was "The Connection between Certain Physical Properties of Substances and Their Chemical Reactions." This investigation had been growing in his mind for some time, and although not of lasting importance, still it was a seed of the fruit to come. There were others, too. Some published, some in process of publication, and some merely dormant in his mind.

At the same time he studied more and more the works of advanced foreign writers—men preoccupied with the atomic and molecular constitution of matter.

Early in 1859 the Minister of Public Instruction decided that the graduate student Mendeleyev should go abroad at government expense to see foreign advances in science, to work with the Germans and the French, and bring back to Russia his conception of needed scientific and technical innovations for the land. Would Mendeleyev go abroad?

Within him, the slowly waking sea of advanced science was stirring. He packed his suitcase.

His tide was in flow.

3

Over the land of Russia, too, a tide was beginning to flow—the ominous tide of the stirring serfs. Riots and clamor for freedom were in evidence on every hand. Tsar Alexander II understood the nature of the great rumbling which was gathering momentum with each passing day. On March 30, 1856, addressing a gathering of Moscow nobility he said, "It is better to abolish serfdom from the top than to wait until it begins to be abolished from the bottom."

In the same year the Tsar gave the banished Decembrists permission to return to western Russia. From Siberia at once they came, white-faced and haggard. With them were their wives, the women who had followed them into the Siberian exile. And with many, too, came children, gazing in awe at the great cities of the West.

Out of Siberia there came Bassargin and Olga. . . .

He was now fifty-eight and seemed exhausted and ill. Olga at forty-two was well preserved and handsome. Mendeleyev was overjoyed to see his sister and the tired but unbroken Bassargin.

In 1857 there were serious police attacks made on students who were printing circulars calling for emancipation of the serfs and for freedom of thought.

Bassargin shook his head.

"This will all have to stop," he said. "Freedom must come. And soon."

But Mendeleyev was on his way abroad to bring Western science to his Russian homeland.

Chapter Eighteen

Abroad. And February 19, 1861

IN PARIS Mendeleyev began to work at once with the outstanding scientist Henri Regnault. In his university laboratory Regnault was occupied with such problems as the determination of the weight of air. Regnault had already found that 1000 cubic centimeters of air weigh very nearly 1.29397 grams, 1000 cubic centimeters of water weighing at a certain temperature 1000 grams. He was interested in making such determinations of the "densities," of oxygen and hydrogen too, as well as of other gases. Regnault was interested also in determining how much heat is necessary to warm up certain materials, such as iron, aluminium, and copper, as well as the gaseous elements, nitrogen and oxygen. Mendeleyev, for his part, worked on his own problems, dealing with the characteristics of liquids instead of solids and gases.

This association with outstanding French scientific thinkers was inspiring to him. On the other hand, his acute mind and ingenious chemical technique aroused the interest of the French scholars.

He worked long hours on his own research, watched other men, thought deeply, observed carefully, visited everything. Not for a moment did he forget the goal of his sojourn abroad—to bring scientific innovation to Russia.

But all too quickly, it was time to move on. The next stop was Heidelberg.

There, perhaps the world's foremost scientific center of the time, Mendeleyev associated with the great Kirchhoff—expert in radiation, the spectroscope, and electricity. There, also, he felt the influence of Bunsen—supreme technician, inventor of the famous gas burner bearing his name, and of a number of other devices for accurate scientific measurements in problems of light.

Outstanding in Mendeleyev's new acquisitions was the spectroscope technique. From the careful meticulous Kirchhoff he learned the use and profound importance of the instrument with which sunlight is broken into colors spread out along a numbered scale. The spectroscope, containing a glass prism, could also break up the light from a burning substance like flaming potassium that glowed with a purple light. Long ago, from Old Andrei the Chemist at the Glass Factory, he had learned something of the colors of substances when they burned, but here, with the sensitive color-analyzing spectroscope, he could see that the purple of burning potassium was actually composed of a number of different colors. In the spectroscope, the prism, breaking the entering purple shaft of light into its constituents, showed, separately, red and blue beams. . . . The spaces between colored beams falling on the screen were black, indicating that the purple of potassium though it actually was not a single unbreakable purple still did not contain all possible colors stretching between red and violet. When burning calcium was placed before the spectroscope, Mendeleyev saw a series of colors spread out in a row along the numbered scale. Similar sets of color lines appeared when air was caused to light up by an electric spark, and also when oxygen was sparked, or hydrogen, nitrogen, and other gases. But each substance, no matter how its color-glow seemed to the eye, revealed in the analyzing spectroscope an absolutely distinct set of lines of color. Thus, every substance could be identified from every other by its set of fiery footprints. And, in fact, an utterly new substance could be discovered by the appearance of a new set of color lines appearing in the spectroscope turned toward some glowing material.

In Heidelberg, besides learning from others, Mendeleyev set up his own laboratory, spending some of his own money—from the Russian government's allowance for his foreign livelihood—on apparatus for experiments, though he built much of it himself. He continued his studies of liquids, making delicate measurements on the effects produced by high and low temperatures, and by increase or decrease of pressure upon the liquid surface. He studied, too, the subtle transition of liquid into vapor, and the reverse process.

Thinking of the smallest particles of which matter is composed—the atoms and the molecules—he always sought a dependence between the chemical constitution of matter and the behavior of its molecules or atoms—their attractions to each other and their mutual effects in general. He studied closely water, alcohol, ether, benzol, and other substances. His experiments in the transitions between liquids and vapors paved the way for the world-famous researches on critical temperatures of Andrews of the University of Edinburgh. In 1860 his researches were beginning to appear in the German, and French, as well as the Russian scientific journals.

And now an event took place which had a profound effect on the twenty-six-year-old Mendeleyev. In September he attended the great Chemical Congress in Karlsruhe and was thrilled by the performance of the Italian chemist Cannizzaro. The principal question of discussion dealt with the weights of atoms of different elements. It was known that an atom of copper is approximately 64 times as heavy as an atom of hydrogen, and an atom of silver is nearly 108 times that weight—comparison usually being made to hydrogen because its atoms are the lightest. But the relative weights—numbers like the 64 and the 108—were not definitely established for all known elements. The principle which could clear away the confusion had been enunciated by Avogadro, and also in a way by Gerhardt and Regnault. Avogadro's principle stated in effect that a certain-sized jar containing a gas has within it the same number of molecules regardless of the nature of the gas. Thus, irrespective of whether the jar holds nitrogen gas or hydrogen or oxygen, there will be the same number of molecules floating inside. Naturally, Avogadro stated that when each gas is considered in turn, its temperature must be the same as in the other cases, and also it must be pumped into the jar to the same pressure. Otherwise one could compress a great amount of gas into the jar in one case and less in another case, and this would destroy all basis of comparison.

The scientific controversy raged about the question of whether or not to accept Avogadro's principle and whether its consequences were to be valid in all branches of chemistry. The evidence was overwhelmingly in the affirmative, but there seemed to be some factors supporting a contradictory idea. A few scientists, speaking from the floor of the assembly at Karlsruhe, tried to promote a compromise so that the contending theories would be somehow reconciled and both factions of scientists placated. In effect, the compromise being sought—especially by Dumas—was this: new atomic weights were to be used in organic chemistry and old atomic weights in inorganic chemistry. Thus the same element would have two atomic weights.

Mendeleyev, sitting tense in the audience, could feel that scientific history was in the making. His own germinating ideas regarding a possible unifying connection between all of the known elements depended on the outcome of the discussion.

Then it was that the intrepid Cannizzaro took the floor. With scientific comprehension and fervent insistence, he forced the detailed reexamination of the evidence pro and contra the contending theories, and defiantly refused to placate all theorists concerned.

Under Cannizzaro's insistence and leadership it was eventually established that Avogadro's idea with its universal consequences was right, and the other idea was utterly wrong.

Mendeleyev was exhilarated. Excitedly he chatted with a young scientist, Leboir.

"How thrilling!" he said, in French. "Science knows no compromise between the true and the untrue."

Leboir, too, was excited.

"*Mais oui!*" he said. "*Vous avez raison.*"

"Science does not care for the feelings of a mistaken scientist," Mendeleyev said. "The truth comes first. And by the way, concerning that other matter—whether atoms and molecules are real or are merely convenient mental constructs. I say they're real."

In a letter to his former professor, Alexander Voskresensky, Mendeleyev described the Karlsruhe Chemical Congress and the battle of ideas that he had witnessed. This letter was printed in the *St. Petersburg News* and aroused widespread interest. The Minister of Public Education who had permitted Mendeleyev to go abroad was now looking forward to his return. Russia needed a shot in her scientific arm.

Russia also needed a shot in her arm of humanity.

In 1859, after much suffering in Siberia, Dostoyevsky was permitted to return to western Russia. In Siberia he had written *Dead House*, the outpouring of a tortured soul confined within the dead house that was his degrading prison camp in the Siberian snows. Upon his return from exile he founded the journal *Time* and after its suppression, *The Epoch*. His hand, when unperturbed by epileptic seizure, wrote quickly, unceasingly; for Dostoyevsky, who had once reckoned on four minutes of time remaining before death, seldom forgot the value of the fleeing moment.

Alexander Hertzen, who had been influenced by Belinsky, was safely abroad producing his weekly journal *The Bell*, and continued to sound the call to social and political reform. But the serf system continued, though many felt that it could not last much longer.

It had taken perhaps one spark to set Moscow burning in 1812.

Were the ineffable human chemicals now building up into the spark that flamed to freedom? Or would the Tsar relieve the imminent tension, release the gathering combustion?

Returning to Heidelberg, Mendeleyev renewed his studies, met Dumas, Odling, and Lothar Meyer, all of whom were working on ideas similar to his, all of whom were destined to become men of scientific achievement in France, England, and Germany.

Suddenly, on February 19, 1861, a Tsarist manifesto proclaimed that the serfs were henceforth free. True, there was practically no land given to the emancipated peasants—but a man was a man. He could call himself "free."

Then, a few months after, came the call to Mendeleyev. From Russia came the summons to put himself into the Russian problems of science.

Now there was really something to work for. He tingled with anticipation. Breathless, he packed his suitcase, and hurried home.

Chapter Nineteen

The Road to 1869. The Climb

IN THE years immediately following Mendeleyev's return from study abroad many things happened to him. Perhaps more happened to him than to his motherland.

First of all, there was the death of Bassargin. The serfs were freed and it was as though Bassargin's spirit saw no further reason for existence. Quietly, he died.

In the fall of 1861, while Mendeleyev was teaching a course on the compounds of carbon, he entered a book contest and in two months wrote a five-hundred page treatise, *Organic Chemistry*. This book won the famous Domidov Prize and the twenty-seven-year-old Mendeleyev suddenly became well known in St. Petersburg and Moscow. His book was widely used; he himself used it in his course on the element carbon. At about this time a great student uprising took place over the question of civil liberties, and Mendeleyev witnessed the spectacle of more than four hundred students being dragged away by police, to be thrown into jail at the Petropavel Fortress. The university closed down. Armed guards patrolled the buildings. Mendeleyev was in the midst of critical research and he continued to work.

He finished his soil analysis for various regions of Russia. This work was intended to help in the scientific planting and growing of crops for the vast, diverse land where periodic famine was unjustified. He analyzed the black earth of the Simbirsk regions, the claylike soil from the Smolensk area, the sandy soil from the Moscow environs, and the peaty soil around St. Petersburg. He sent his report and conclusions to the Imperial Free Economical Society.

He translated technical articles from German into Russian, and expanded these articles by adding his own analysis. He translated the technical encyclopedia of the German R. Wagner, but elaborated by adapting it to the basic problems of Russian national economy—the basic problems of survival. The study was divided into the following sections:

1. Flour, Bread, and Starch
2. Manufacture of Sugar

3. Manufacture of Spirits and Studies of Alcohol
4. Preparation of Glass
5. Manufacture of Oil

In all, the published work totaled more than twelve hundred pages.

He worked almost without rest, and yet his short hours of sleep brought him profound regeneration of strength. Russia needed pure science and Russia needed technology. Mendeleyev was striving for both.

He wrote an essay on the theory of organic combinations, dealing with the limits to be expected in the reactions of the omnipresent element carbon, the element so vital to plant and animal life, the element so dominant in the sugars, the alcohols, the fuels, the crystals of the earth.

He wrote his doctoral thesis, a 120-page dissertation on alcohols, a work of both scientific and technical value, and received his degree. There followed the 70-page study on the density of gases and vapors, then a work on land problems—efficient usage for growing food, for which he submitted a program. Thereafter came a study of the action necessary for the immediate development of a chemical industry in Russia. After that, a report on a new hydrocarbon, a compound of carbon and hydrogen extracted from coal tar, a work done jointly with Fritzsche.

As the years between 1861 and 1869 unfolded, Mendeleyev's intensive scientific labors found only a few interruptions. Once, he had the startling experience with the *izvoschik*—the carriage driver; once, after the completion of one article and before starting to write another, Mendeleyev married; and once, after a luncheon in a Petersburg restaurant, occurred the episode of the horse. . . .

2

Every year since he had reached the city Mendeleyev looked forward to the new issue of the city directory. As soon as the book came to his hands he searched for a certain name. In the fall of 1863 he found it: Stepan Andreyevitch Yusulov. Mendeleyev was thrilled. Jumping up from his laboratory stool, he grabbed his jacket and hat, and leaving the green mixture in the flask to cool without his encouragement, dashed out into the drizzling St. Petersburg afternoon.

It was a long buggy ride to the address given in the directory. The *izvoschik* sitting on his perch seemed to be drowsing and Mendeleyev waited impatiently for the casually trotting horse to complete the journey.

At a small dilapidated house with broken windows and chipped paint, he got out of the buggy and paid his fare.

Mendeleyev

Mendeleyev knocked at the door but there was no answer. He knocked again, then tried the door. It was locked.

For an hour he walked up and down in front of the house. Then a carriage came round the corner, drawn by a gray horse whose hoofs clacked loudly on the cobbled street. On the driver's perch sat a shaggy-haired *izvoschik*, his long brown moustache tinged with gray. He seemed to be about sixty years old, though he had a look of vigor.

Mendeleyev watched the carriage come to a halt before the brown house, then he advanced.

"Stepan Andreyevitch Yusulov?" he said.

The man nodded.

"And who may you be, sir?" he replied from his perch.

"My mother's family name was Korniliev," said Mendeleyev.

The man slowly opened his mouth and stared.

"The Glass Factory," he said barely audibly.

"*Da*," nodded Mendeleyev.

The man crossed himself.

"*Bozhe moi*," he said. "Aremziansk, Aremziansk." He rocked from side to side.

"Why didn't you write home to the village?"

Yusulov stopped rocking and lifted his hands into the air.

"*Akh*, but what for?" he said, lifting his shoulders. "When I heard in 1819 that my mother had died, I began to forget the village."

Mendeleyev drew closer to the carriage. He put his hand on Yusulov's shoe.

"Listen to me, Stepan," he said gently. "Listen carefully."

Yusulov gazed at him. "I'm listening," he said.

"I left Aremziansk in 1849," said Mendeleyev. "Your mother was alive."

Over Yusulov's face came a look of bewilderment. His mouth opened and in his eyes was a look of confusion and hurt. Slowly he put his hands to his chest.

"I'm getting to be an old man," he said pleadingly. "Don't play tricks, brother. That is not humanity."

"Let God strike me dead," said Mendeleyev softly. "Your mother was alive in 1849. I promised I would seek you. She said she could not die until she saw you again. Three years ago she still lived. I had a letter from the Village Elder."

Large tears were coursing down Yusulov's cheeks and running into his moustache.

"*Bozhe moi*," he whispered. "My soul will be damned. *Akh, akh. Akh, akh.*"

"You didn't know."

"She lives," said Yusulov. "She still lives."

Mendeleyev nodded his head.

"I think so," he said. "She said she would live."

Yusulov blew his nose. Then he straightened up on the perch.

"Which way is Siberia?" he asked.

Mendeleyev pointed to the east.

Yusulov pondered.

"Is it still there?" he asked. "They say the earth turns."

Mendelcyev waved his hand in front of his face.

"That's all right," he said. "It's still out that way. I promise you."

"*Khorosho*," said Yusulov. "I believe you."

He fingered the reins for a moment.

"You say out that way?" he pointed.

Mendeleyev nodded.

"All right," said Yusulov addressing the horse and turning him about. "Move along."

Mendeleyev stepped out into the roadway.

"Don't you want to take your things from the house?" he said. "And do you have a family?"

Yusulov shook his big shaggy head.

"There's nothing in there," he said. "Some bread. Onions. Old rags. There's no time to waste."

He turned his gaze to the east and without looking at the horse spoke to him.

"Move, little dove," he pleaded. "Fly. Fly for me. Then I will let you go free. I promise. *Davai*, brother! Give! Give now!"

The horse moved off and the clacking of his hoofs resounded through the street.

Mendeleyev watched the carriage roll out of sight, in the drizzly St. Petersburg afternoon.

Then he returned to his laboratory. The green liquid had cooled.

He added a clear liquid to it and watched the mixture closely. The experiment had turned out well.

"*Akh*," he sighed and wrote the result in a notebook.

A small smile stole about his eyes.

3

In 1863 Mendeleyev married, in 1864 he received a letter from Aremziansk, in 1865 he bought a summer home on top of Boblovo Hill, not far distant from Moscow, and in 1866 there occurred the episode of the horse.

It happened after a luncheon-meeting with university colleagues at an old St. Petersburg restaurant.

Mendeleyev was crossing the street after having bidden good-by to his associates. A heavily loaded wagon, pulled by an old brown horse, was lumbering past him. His glance happened to fall on the horse's head, and somewhat unconsciously he noted the rising and falling of the horse's ears. He crossed the street, stopped, and called to the driver, a young man in a *kaftan*—a long white shirt trimmed with red.

"That horse is thirsty," he said, and started to walk away.

But suddenly he stopped, walked out into the street, and taking the horse by the muzzle led him to the curb. The good-natured young driver in the *kaftan* got down to talk. Mendeleyev was patting the horse's head and talking to him softly. The driver walked up, scratching his head reflectively.

"*Chto takoye?*" [What's going on?] he said. "Do you like horses, little father?"

Mendeleyev nudged his head against that of the horse.

"He was mine," he said. "His name is Soldat. He's from Siberia. Seventeen years ago."

The young driver put his hands on his hips. "I bought him," he said, "for sixty roubles. I bought him at Nizhny where the Volga runs into the Oka. We pulled Eastern goods together there."

"The horse is thirsty," said Mendeleyev. "*Akh*, Soldat, Soldat, what have you been through?"

"We used to haul the tea that came up the Volga," said the young driver. "He is old but strong."

Mendeleyev took out his purse and withdrew some banknotes.

"Here is ninety roubles," he said. "Will you take it?"

The young driver took the money and Mendeleyev began to unharness Soldat.

"You had him too tight," he said. "You'll have to buy another horse. This one has pulled his last load." He finished unharnessing Soldat.

At the university he tied the horse to a wooden post at the curb and went inside the building. In the hallway he met one of the new students, Goldenberg.

"Find me Lozhinsky," Mendeleyev said. "Look in my laboratory."

He went back to Soldat.

Presently the dark-haired, slender Lozhinsky appeared.

"Take the horse to Boblovo," said Mendeleyev. "Do not ride him. Arrange transportation in the new rail-cars. Then lead him from the station the rest of the way to my summer house. Tell my wife this is the horse that brought me from Siberia. He is not to do any work. He is just to wander in the fields. I am coming up in two weeks, as soon as the last classes are over. You can come back as soon as you deliver the horse."

"*Khorosho*," said Lozhinsky.

"Take care of the horse."

Lozhinsky nodded.

"I like animals."

Mendeleyev went to the laboratory and finished the experiment of the electrical current through the copper-sulphate solution.

4

In his classrooms Mendeleyev was giving reviews to help the students for the final examinations. His classes were crowded. Even law and philosophy students came to listen to his lectures. As he stood before them, dressed in his gray jacket and brown trousers, his eyes twinkling and his hands gesturing, the students sat listening carefully, following the arguments. Even in the class of two hundred, everyone seemed able to follow his discussion as it progressed from the first statements to the conclusions. When he did reach these conclusions many of the students, feeling that they understood, and rejoicing in the revelation that they were not stupid, would smile broadly and steal glances at each other.

He lectured in an offhand manner, knowing his subject so thoroughly that it was not necessary for him to stick to a beaten path for fear of getting lost. He explored whatever side roads appeared on his scientific lecture path, and improvised with oral excursions to the left and right amplified by a multitude of verbal footnotes. Always, gradually, the side excursions led back again to the main path, and the principal exploration advanced.

"As we have seen in this introductory course, the principal objective of chemistry is the study of the homogeneous substances of which all objects are composed, of the transformations of these substances into each other, and the phenomena which accompany such transformations. . . .

"By studying the universe using an inductive method—that is, by attempting from the much which is observable to arrive at a little which may be confirmed and is undeniable—science today refuses to recognize dogma as truth. On the contrary, through the use of reason, and by a careful and laborious method of investigation, modern men of science strive for and in fact attain to true deductions.

"One of the wholly refreshing aspects of chemistry that the beginner first meets is this—by mixing two substances, a third one is produced which differs completely from the first two. Thus, when I heat this mixture of iron and sulphur, a single new substance is produced—iron sulphide. And in this new substance the original constituent substances cannot be discerned even under the highest magnification. . . .

"In the same way, mercury oxide does not contain two simple bodies, a metal and a gas. In fact, neither mercury as a metal nor oxygen as a gas is present in mercury oxide, which only contains the substance of these elements, just as steam merely contains the substance of ice but not the ice itself. Or, as bread contains the substance of the corn, but not the corn itself. . . ."

In his classes he performed exciting experiments. Both he and his student-assistants worked long hours in preparing the demonstrations, so that all would go well, precisely, and just as it should.

He loved the colorful demonstrations as much as the students, and like them, he seemed to be exhilarated by the colored flames, the bubbling liquids, the explosive reactions.

"Here we see that burning potassium seems to be of a purple color. And now here we have sodium burning yellow, and copper burns green, and in the same way you can see the colors of the other burning substances. Here each has its name on the large card in front of it. You must come and look closer after class. By looking at the flames through this spectroscope—which, I am sorry to say, is not of the best make available—we can see that the purple flame of potassium is composed of a number of separate colors. You will see these colors spread out along a scale inside of the spectroscope. Original work of this type, especially theory, is being done by Kirchhoff in Germany, and that's where I learned it a few years ago. One can study sunlight and starlight in this way, and observe the colors in the spectroscope and thus recognize the substances burning up there. . . ."

In another class he talked of colors in test tubes—not burning colors, just colors of liquids.

"Here is a solution of copper sulphate. As you see, it is blue in color. On the other hand, this over here is a solution of copper chloride and it is green. If we mix these two solutions like this—we still see a distinct green tint. Therefore, by this color it is possible to recognize the presence of copper chloride in copper sulphate. We get at once—look!—a green color. This proves that copper chloride is formed. It does not happen to precipitate out, but is obviously there.

"Chlorine itself is a gas of a yellowish-green color, and has a very suffocating and characteristic odor. When we lower the temperature to —50 degrees, the chlorine condenses into a liquid. It then weighs 1.4 grams for every cubic centimeter. Furthermore, the liquid chlorine can then be made solid, by cooling it some more, down to —100 degrees. On the other hand, as we raise the temperature after that it begins to boil—at —34 degrees. By the way, you can take the chlorine gas and make it into a liquid without lowering its temperature down to —50 degrees. This can be done at 0 degrees by simply pumping chlorine gas up so tight—six times the normal atmospheric pressure—that the molecules are forced to very close distances from each other and join into a pattern more closely packed than in the gas state. That is, the molecules are close enough to form the liquid pattern. . . ."

The next day, early in the morning, Mendeleyev wrote a report on the naphtha springs of Russia. He told of the feasibility of obtaining oil in a new way from the seeping deposits near the Black Sea. Then he went to lecture again.

"Yesterday we were speaking of chlorine," he began. "I would like to continue with a few remarks and show a few more experiments. Chlorine explodes with hydrogen if a mixture of equal volumes is exposed to the direct action of the sun's rays. This effect of the light is fascinating to me. Sunlight showing its immediate effect on chemical processes. Akh, I like that. How direct and clean. Very nice. Don't you think so? By the way, the light from burning magnesium, and actinic light in general, acts in proportion to its intensity, in the same way as sunlight. They all can make chlorine react violently with hydrogen. However, at —12 degrees light no longer brings about reaction, or at all events does not cause an explosion. It is possible to show that when the ordinary explosive effect occurs at the higher temperature, it is chiefly the violet end of the sun's colors that is responsible.

"If the light is not strong, but diffuse, the reaction is slow and not explosive. Which is a good way to start experiments."

In the next class he discussed the atmosphere—the air surrounding the earth and its extremely varied composition. First he spoke of the various gases that compose air—oxygen, nitrogen, carbon dioxide—then he discussed the question of dust in the air. ". . . A portion of the atmospheric dust is of cosmic origin—that is, it comes to us from outer space. This cosmic dust contains metallic iron, as do the meteorites. The atmosphere is of course full of minute living things, the germs and the spores, for example."

He spoke of the evolution of temperature on the earth, the cooling from a time in the past, and the solidification of the earth's interior, the formation of coal, and the birth of the diamond. Then he returned once more to the atmosphere about us, the air we breathe, and the nature of the ventilation needed in theaters, other public buildings, homes, and mines.

He finished the review lectures and the students took the examinations. Then he left for his summer home at Boblovo. There more scientific work awaited him—experiments and writing; there also was Matvei's horse,

Soldat; and the quiet little woman he had married three years before, in 1863, Feozva Leshcheva, now Madame Mendeleyev.

This was summer of 1866. He was thirty-two years old. His wife seemed older.

5

Feozva was older. She was thirty-eight but, somehow, the difference in age between her and Mendeleyev seemed even greater.

The tiny graceful woman who seemed so pensive was Feozva Nikitichna Leshcheva, from central Siberia. The marriage had been brought about a few years before by Mendeleyev's sister Olga, who had become very concerned about the fact that her scientist brother was apparently leading a life of self-sacrifice.

"You are not obligated to give yourself completely to Russia," she had told him in the spring of 1862. "You are not leading a well-rounded life, Dmitri. You should marry."

Mendeleyev shrugged his shoulders.

"Such things one does not plan quite so closely," he replied. "I mean, if marriage somehow occurs, let it occur. But one does not merely set out to marry. . . ."

Olga shook her head.

"Marriage is planned," she said.

"First," said Mendeleyev, "there must be love."

Again Olga shook her head.

"No, Dmitri. Not necessarily. Far from it. One has to be more realistic. Now in your case, for example, I say, you should simply marry."

To him the conversation was unpleasant but he felt affection for Olga, as for all members of his family, and did not wish to hurt her in any way. Obviously, she was thinking of him. So instead of leaving the room, he stood before his older sister and said patiently, "Olga, I know you are trying to be helpful. But please let nature and events take care of things. If I were to set out and simply marry in cold blood, I wouldn't even have the slightest idea where to turn, whom to wed—"

Olga sprang from her chair and grasped his arm.

"I have the answer," she said. "There is that friend of mine, whom you have met—the enchanting girl from Siberia. You even wrote to her occasionally from Odessa, didn't you? I will arrange some meetings."

Mendeleyev suddenly thought of Katerina the Matchmaker of Aremziansk. But never had he seen Katerina attempt a union between a man and a woman unless there already existed at least the first spark of love. Katerina was a discerning artist whom Timofei could rightly admire.

"Do not arrange any meetings," said Mendeleyev. "I know your friend Feozva in only the most casual way. Please do not arrange any meetings."

But the meetings were arranged—many of them, and Mendeleyev was frequently left alone with the graceful and shy Feozva. He was kind, and Feozva gentle and friendly. She aroused nothing whatever within him.

There were more meetings, again arranged by Olga, and finally one day he made Feozva an offer of marriage.

"*Akh,* you two will be happy!" Olga exclaimed to them.

Mendeleyev stood silent, listening to his sister's exuberance. Feozva was sweet and shy. She stood smiling gently.

Olga made more arrangements, for meetings and short outings.

Then, one day, Olga went to Moscow on some business. Mendeleyev wrote her a letter.

". . . The more I know my intended, the more I feel something wrong. . . . I do not feel about her as a man should about a woman he is to marry. . . ."

Olga replied immediately.

"Know, Dmitri, I was married twice—once to an older man, Medvedev, and the second time, through passionate love, to Bassargin. I will tell you frankly, and you are the first and only one to whom I tell this—I was happier in my first marriage with Medvedev. . . . If this marriage takes place I shall die content. . . . Also, remember what the great Goethe said, 'There is no greater sin than to betray a girl.' You know that everyone knows you are engaged to her. In what situation will she find herself when it becomes known that you now refuse?"

He married.

Chapter Twenty

The Road to 1869. At the Summit

IN 1865 MENDELEYEV had bought for eight thousand roubles a half-interest of three hundred and sixty acres in the Boblovo estate of Count Dyadon. His partner in the purchase was Professor Ilyin of the Technological Institute.

The estate was located on Boblovo Hill, seven hours by rail from Moscow and twelve miles from the station. The house itself was a one-story structure built in the center of a large park. Great towering trees almost entirely hid it from view. The tall pines, spreading birch, and century-old oaks cast a protecting mantle over the wooden building and its large glass porch.

Here at Boblovo the air smelled invigoratingly of the birch trees and the rich mellow earth. Near the house, the rose garden added its scent.

All around stretched the fields and forests and experimental plots of land where Mendeleyev worked during the summer, as he sought to evolve sturdier life-giving crops. There were horses on the estate, too, and cows, and a number of mouzhik-workmen, and a threshing and grinding machine.

In the garden immediately outside the house stood a gauge which caught rainwater and indicated how much had fallen, and near it Mendeleyev had mounted a barometer and thermometer to tell him the condition of the air. A hygrometer indicated the humidity. These were all aids in his experiments with crops.

Mendeleyev, wearing a loose jacket and a straw hat, worked in the wheat fields. His flowing blond hair and fair beard seemed like part of the countryside and his large forehead glistened in the summer sun as he treaded carefully among the plots.

Frequently his riding horse browsed near by, waiting to take him to the more distant fields or into the forest, and nearly always Soldat waited around to see what Mendeleyev would do next, and would follow leisurely behind when Mendeleyev rode the young horse.

In 1866 the yield from the experimental plots was great, and the mouzhik-neighbors who came to look at the ripened rye stood marveling. Mendeleyev's yield was three times that of the mouzhiks' on their own land.

"How is it now, Mitri Ivanitch," a burly redheaded mouzhik asked Mendeleyev, "how is it you have such harvest?"

Mendeleyev straightened up from his work. He stood smiling, his clear blue eyes sparkling at the conceded success.

"How is it?" repeated the redheaded mouzhik. "Is it luck or is it talent?"

"Talent," said Mendeleyev smiling. "Of course, little brother, it's talent. But you can have this talent, too. Let me tell you."

"*Akh*, I have never seen such bread," said a slight mouzhik named Fontov, admiring the wheat.

"Sit down," said Mendeleyev. "I'll tell you about it."

The mouzhiks sat down. There were eight of them. Mendeleyev dropped to his haunches and faced his friends.

"The first thing is this," he began. "The soil can either be good or not good for a plant. If it's not good, it can be fixed."

Fontov, the slender mouzhik, was nodding his head.

"Or a man can pray for rain or sunshine," he said, crossing himself. "Now that's a holy truth, little brothers."

The redheaded mouzhik took Fontov by the ear and pulled it.

"*Ish ti!*" he chided. "Another professor. Let the *barin* talk. Let the sire have his word."

A wizened mouzhik with a tangled brown beard lifted his hand and pointed at Mendeleyev.

"That's a regular one for you," he said. "There's a regular sire for you. A simple *barin, yei Bogu*—honest to God. Let him spin the yarn."

The mouzhiks all turned on Fontov.

"*Ekh*," they said. "*Akh ti.*" "Now look at you."

Fontov stood up to plead. He stretched out his hands.

"What is the matter with you, little brothers?" he said. "What sin have I sinned? 'Rain,' I said, 'is good for the crops' and 'sun' I said, 'is good.' Is this God's fact, Mitri Ivanitch, or shall I hang myself?"

Mendeleyev laughed, and nodded.

"There's no denying the rain and the sun," he agreed. "But there's more to the story."

"And I'll be the first to listen," said Fontov, and turning to his fellow mouzhiks shook his head at them. "*Ekh* you," he chided. "*Ish ti*. What a gang."

Mendeleyev resumed his explanation.

"The soil has to have certain things in it. You can't see them very easily in the earth. But if these things are lacking, then I put some in. Look." Here he took a little corked bottle out of his pocket. The bottle contained a powder. The mouzhiks crowded around.

"Imagine that to yourself!" said one of the group. "That wouldn't be solid sunshine?" suggested Fontov.

The mouzhiks waited for Mendeleyev to answer. Fontov could be right—he'd been to Moscow once or twice. If he were right, it would be best to say nothing. But if . . .

"No," said Mendeleyev. "This is something called 'potassium chloride.' "

The redheaded mouzhik grabbed Fontov by the ear.

"*Ish ti!*" he exclaimed. "Everything pours out of his mouth. God's truth and the devil's lie—all mixed."

"He's got a head like a *baba*," said another. "A cabbage, that's what it is."

"Stupid as a cork," said the redheaded mouzhik, letting go of Fontov's ear.

Fontov sat quietly, resigned to everything.

"Out of respect for the *barin*," he murmured, "I will not cripple you all with an ax. Listen, you *svolatchee*. Let him talk."

Mendeleyev gave the little bottle of potassium chloride to Fontov, to pass to each mouzhik. They looked at it intently and shook their heads in awe.

"What a creation," marveled the wizened mouzhik.

"I didn't make it," said Mendeleyev.

"Yes, but still . . . ," another mouzhik said.

The redheaded mouzhik took Mendeleyev by the sleeve.

"But to smell it—is it permissible?" he asked.

Mendeleyev nodded and took out the cork.

The mouzhiks carefully smelled the bottle.

"*Ai, ai, ai,*" said one.

"*Bozhe moi!*" marveled another.

Fontov sniffed at the bottle vigorously and smacked his lips.

"Like sunshine," said Fontov. "Smells just like sunshine."

Mendeleyev took out his handkerchief and mopped his brow.

"Well," he said. "The potassium is the important thing. If a plant doesn't get this potassium from the soil it won't develop. And the soil has to be studied so that we can find out how much potassium it has. If not enough, we add some more."

The redheaded mouzhik took off his cap.

"Put some in here," he said. "Will you, Mitri Ivanitch? I'll put it in my rye when I get home."

"Can you put this potassium in the flour?" asked one mouzhik. "It's too late for my plants."

"What questions!" said a voice. "The plant has to eat it. Not you."

"Yes, but I eat the plant," replied the first mouzhik. "Ask the *barin*."

The Road to 1869. At the Summit

"*Barin ni barin*," said the redheaded mouzhik. "But a learned one he is, like nobody else. What do you say, Mitri Ivanitch?"

"It should go into the soil," said Mendeleyev. "I'll show you how to mix it. Now let me tell you some more. There are other substances that the roots need for the plant. They are called 'minerals.' Sodium, magnesium, iron, carbon, nitrogen, phosphorus—all in certain combinations, mostly with something called 'oxygen.'"

"Imagine that to yourself," said the wizened mouzhik. "And iron, too, brothers. Did you say 'iron,' Mitri Ivanitch?"

"When I was in Moscow," said Fontov. "Twenty-seven years ago next February third, I saw a black tree twice as tall as any out here." Fontov spread his hands to encompass the fields, the garden, and the surrounding forests. "An honest man told me the tree was that big because it ate nothing but iron from the ground."

The mouzhiks waited, watching Mendeleyev's face.

"Well," said Mendeleyev tentatively. "It's interesting, that's true. But probably the tree nourished itself on other things besides iron."

Now the mouzhiks fell on Fontov.

"*Ish ti!* What a tongue!"

"A professor of sour food."

They pounded him on the head.

"To Moscow he's been!" exclaimed the redhead. "I know a man who's been to Moscow three times, not once. And the last time was ten years ago. Not fifty years ago."

"I said twenty-seven years ago," said Fontov, "not fifty years ago."

"I hope you perish with your twenty-seven years," said the wizened mouzhik.

Mendeleyev looked up. In the distance, across the yellow field, two women were coming from the direction of the house. They carried something in their arms. The mouzhiks followed Mendeleyev's glance.

When the women drew closer, Mendeleyev and the mouzhiks stood up.

The first woman was slender and tiny. She walked gracefully, carrying a fair-haired boy in her arms. The boy held on tightly to a brown paper bag. Mendeleyev stepped forward and took the child into his arms.

"*Akh*, Volodenka," he said. "*Nu*, how are you, my darling?"

The boy murmured happily and put his arms around his father's neck.

The mouzhiks had all taken off their caps and mumbled a greeting to Mendeleyev's wife. She smiled back at them with a pensive shyness. She seemed tired and not disposed to be effusive. Mendeleyev kissed her on the forehead.

The second woman, a maid, had brought a hot samovar and a small teapot. Over her shoulder was slung a straw basket with glasses and cubes of tea.

"There are six letters," said Feozva. "They're in the bag. With *boulkee*. I just made the rolls, so they're hot."

The women departed, leaving the year-old Volodya to crawl over his father. Mendeleyev's face was radiant, and his blue eyes shone as he played with his bubbling son.

"*Akh ti prokhvostik*," [you little scamp, you] he jested. "Where are you crawling now, eh?"

Volodya almost upset the samovar.

Mendeleyev scooped him up.

"Pour the tea," he said, nodding to Fontov.

"Watch now, brothers," said the redheaded mouzhik, "this is the way they do it in Moscow."

From a small pot Fontov poured some dark brown tea into a glass. Then, filling the glass with hot water from the samovar, he gave it to the redheaded mouzhik.

"Here, you stump-head," he said. "Some happy day I'll cripple you with my ax. Here's sugar now, for your poisonous body."

Fontov served tea and sugar to the others, and then passed out the hot *boulkee*. The warm aroma of the freshly baked rolls made everyone's mouth water.

"Here you really have *boulkee*," said the wizened mouzhik, biting into a crackling roll. The rest, too, were eating the rolls with gusto. They smacked their lips, and chewed loudly, and crunched on the sugar, and blew on the hot steaming tea.

Mendeleyev set down his tea in order to open the letters, and almost at once Volodya kicked the glass over, some of the tea spilling on his ankle. Volodya screamed.

"*Chto takoye!*" exclaimed Mendeleyev, grabbing up his son. "What is this! Volodenka. You what! *Ai* you poor little one. *Ai, ai, ai.*"

Fontov, with his shirt, hurriedly wiped Volodya's ankle. Volodya continued to scream. Mendeleyev gave him a lump of sugar, and Volodya, having taken a great breath for a new scream, suddenly changed his mind. He made a few abortive spasms with his chest, and put his fist with the sugar into his mouth.

Mendeleyev read his letters.

His face gradually broke into a wide smile.

2

The first letter was from a professor of chemistry in Germany, and contained information that Mendeleyev needed on the element sulphur. The professor was an expert on the question of the weight of sulphur and had spent a number of years determining precisely how heavy it was. He also had determined a number of other things about it, such as the temperature at which it melts, and at which it vaporizes. All this Mendeleyev would determine himself, but it was of great value to have a specialist's statement to corroborate. The second and third letters were from France, and they brought similar information regarding other elements. Two other letters were from England, also telling of the weights of certain chemicals. The sixth letter was from the new Village Elder in Aremziansk stating that the long-missing Yusulov had arrived safely and his mother, who was still alive, prayed for Mendeleyev's welfare and wished him long life.

Mendeleyev looked up smiling. The mouzhiks, watching him, also were smiling.

"Good news, *ekh, barin?*" ventured Fontov.

Mendeleyev waved the letters in front of his face.

"*Akh*, but good," he said.

He stood up with the slobbering Volodya in his arms.

"I must go," he said. "There are things to write. You boys bring in the samovar when you're through. And you can start working the fields next Tuesday if you're through with your own fields by then. I'll pay you the same as last year."

He walked rapidly toward the house.

Inside, he set Volodya down on the floor and went to his own room. There at a heavy brown table, among his books and papers, he immediately began to work—calculating, and arranging chemical names in certain orders. The new information that had come in the mail fitted his plan—the plan that had been evolving for years, the plan concerning a certain unifying relation among the elements. But there was a long way to go yet. Much more information was needed. Mendeleyev worked late into the night writing more letters to the great chemical laboratories of the world.

In the morning Fontov, the lean mouzhik, came early and waited for Mendeleyev to come out into the fields. When he appeared, Fontov approached him shyly.

"It's about yesterday," he said.

"What?" said Mendeleyev. "What is this sadness on your face?"

"It's about the boys. They laugh at me. Am I very stupid?"

Mendeleyev took Fontov by the arm.

"What nonsense," he said. "Forget that sort of thinking, *batushka. Ekh,* little father, what an idea!"

Fontov scratched his brown head.

"They laugh, Mitri Ivanitch. Makes me feel stupid."

"*Akh,* but that is nothing," said Mendeleyev. "The lads are happy. Drop this, Fontov, don't carry on, old fellow. *Nyet, nyet.*"

"*Khorosho,*" said Fontov.

He started to walk away, but suddenly stopped beneath one of the great oaks.

"It's in me right here," said Fontov pointing to his chest. "Right in here. I still think that everything is made out of sunshine. Crystal sunshine."

Mendeleyev stood silent for a moment.

"Well," he said slowly. "In a way it is. Nothing would grow if there weren't any sunshine."

"I knew it," said Fontov. "I knew it. Crystallized sunshine."

He turned and walked away toward his own small field in the distance.

Mendeleyev watched him go. Then he turned and walked out to his own fields.

The summer recess ended, followed by another intensive year at the university. Daily, hour after hour—when he was not teaching—Mendeleyev performed experiments in his small laboratory. And at night he calculated, wrote articles, answered his mail, and wrote innumerable letters to universities all over the world. In these letters he continued unrelentingly to seek stray bits of information on all the elements known to mankind.

The answers came.

The pieces of the puzzle were fitting.

3

On June 12, 1867, while Mendeleyev was with his wife and son at Boblovo, his widowed sister Ekaterina arrived from Siberia with four children and one grandchild. This was the sister to whom Maria's last letter had been entrusted for final keeping. Ekaterina had lived for many years in Omsk and then Tomsk, where in 1859 her husband, Kapustin, had died. She was now fifty-one years old, eighteen years older than Mendeleyev. She was exhausted from caring for her large family and from the difficult trip. It was at Mendeleyev's urging that the widowed Ekaterina had come with her brood to live at Boblovo. He knew that for many years before her death his mother had poured out her soul in long detailed letters to her daughter Ekaterina whom she frequently called her "wise and reasonable little Katie." All this Mendeleyev knew, and he felt a deep compassion and a strong love for this older sister.

And now Ekaterina had arrived. Mendeleyev dashed out of the glass porch to greet the two tarantasses laden with her family. There were Ekaterina, her three daughters, a small son, and a little granddaughter—through a former marriage of her husband, Kapustin. Two other boys, who lived in St. Petersburg, had already come to Boblovo to await the arrival of the rest of their family.

Mendeleyev embraced his weary sister and admired the brood. Then, in the house, everyone was fed, and the children sent to bed. Late into the night Mendeleyev sat in the kitchen with his wife and Ekaterina, who, though tired, could not go to sleep because of a nervous desire to talk with her brother. She looked at him admiringly. She loved his deep confident voice and the serious but gentle eyes. She watched him as his tall stooped form moved briskly about the house, as he brought books, pictures, and scientific articles that he had written, to show her. She felt that as he was showing her his accomplishments he was really showing them to Maria, his mother. She wept as she looked at his books and pamphlets, and the great stacks of freshly written pages on the table in his room. He talked of the things that he had done, how he had studied, written, planned, hoped, and of how much there was to do for Russia, how short the time was. But it could be done—he would do it. Yes. He told her of a certain great plan about the elements, but the time was not yet at hand.

"You will do it," said Ekaterina embracing him. "You are our Mitenka. She would be proud."

The next night, after supper, Mendeleyev and Ekaterina resumed their conversation of the past. Mendeleyev's wife sat pensive over her sewing, as the brother and sister reminisced.

"And you remember our grandfather, mama's father, don't you?" said Mendeleyev.

Ekaterina nodded.

"Very clearly," she said. "A good old man. Used to give me sugar lumps. And how well he died, Mitenka, how really beautifully. I will always remember."

Feozva looked inquiringly at Ekaterina.

"Do tell," she said. "Please tell about it."

"Yes, Katenka," said Mendeleyev. "Tell about it."

Ekaterina sighed.

"*Khorosho*," she said, turning to Feozva. "This was the little old man Korniliev, our mother's father."

Feozva nodded.

"I know," she said, "Korniliev."

"Well," resumed Ekaterina. "He knew one day that death was near. Somehow he knew. So he dressed in everything new—that was the first thing. Then he sent for the priest. After that he blessed each one of us children. And then he did a very strange thing. *Akh*, my soul, I have thought about it—so often. He asked each person in the room, grownups and children, one at a time, as he spoke to them he asked each to give him a glass of tea. Now he couldn't drink all the tea, but he tried—and he drank quite a bit. But in every case he asked for a glass of tea, and drank some. Then he said *'Praschaitee'* [farewell]. And he waited calmly for death. The gesture of the tea I shall never forget as long as I live. Recently, a few years ago, I suddenly understood it."

Mendeleyev's eyes were fixed on his sister. His wife, too, looked intently at Ekaterina.

"I suddenly understood," said Ekaterina barely audibly, "that his last gesture was a great kindness to us—he asked us to give him tea, which of course he did not need, but he asked each one of us, so that we would feel later that we had done a good deed for a dying man. He wanted us to have this good feeling."

Feozva embraced Ekaterina.

"I love you," she said softly.

Mendeleyev, too, embraced his sister.

"You are good," he said.

Ekaterina looked quietly somewhere into space.

"There are memories—flowers"—she quoted a writer she loved—"and there are memories—wounds."

Mendeleyev embraced his sister again.

"Good night, Katenka," he said. "You are good for us. You are good for me. You're just like mama. I'm going to work now. Good night."

That night, he again sat up late in his room, with his papers about him. The formulas, slowly, slid into place—into a great plan.

4

Nadezhda, Ekaterina's twelve-year-old daughter, intrigued Mendeleyev. She followed him about the fields and asked endless questions. She intrigued him too because her name and even her appearance reminded him of another Nadezhda—Timofei's bride. Mendeleyev had heard that somewhere in the south of Russia Timofei's Nadezhda had died. And he was glad that another similar Nadezhda lived. Nadezhdas must always live. For "Nadezhda" in Russian means "Hope."

The Road to 1869. At the Summit 161

How clever she was, how quaint, how inquisitive and bouncing this little Nadezhda. She made Mendeleyev laugh—and he always looked up when he heard her young voice, so assured, so effervescent.

"What is the name of this flower?" she asked him one day.

Mendeleyev broke off the blue flower with the tiny leaves.

"Dream flower," he said. "Here, if you can't sleep at night, put this under your pillow. Then you'll sleep—and *akh* what delightful dreams you will have."

She looked up at him questioningly. How could one tell when this big man was joking? She took the flower and waved it at Bishka, the amusing hound who liked to smile.

"Here, Bishka," she said, as she waved the flower over his head. "Sleep, sleep, sleep. Go to sleep, Bishka."

Bishka twisted his upper lip into a smile.

Then Bismarck the mastiff came up and growled at Bishka. Mendeleyev scratched Bismarck's head and the growl changed to a pleasant rumbling. Nadezhda put the dream flower on Bismarck's head and ran out into the field to talk to the aged Soldat.

That afternoon Mendeleyev rescued Nadezhda from her older sister Anna who was making her translate the difficult French passages.

"*Akh* now, Annyuta," he implored, "let her be. Languages! *Bozhe moi!* She's got time."

Nadezhda sprang up and ran off to the fields again. Mendeleyev stood laughing as the flying girl vanished.

As he went out to mount his gray horse Nadezhda suddenly reappeared. Mendeleyev helped her to climb up on the horse to sit behind him on the Cossack saddle, and they rode off to inspect the fields and give the horse a run through the forest.

This year, 1867, Mendeleyev had hired Fontov and the redheaded mouzhik as supervisors of his estate. Though he himself had given up working on the agricultural experiments, he gave careful instructions to the two men. Through the summer and until the harvest was in, the neighbor-mouzhiks took time out from their own fields to work for Mendeleyev. Now the harvest was ready and Mendeleyev, with the twelve-year-old Nadezhda bouncing behind him, was riding to watch the mouzhiks at their work in the golden fields under the radiant sun. They were cutting the rye and arranging the sheaves into stacks. Mendeleyev and Nadezhda dismounted and began to help them.

"It's grinding up sunshine," said Fontov, as Mendeleyev began to feed sheaves into a grinding machine operated by a circling horse.

In the evening Mendeleyev, his wife, and Ekaterina again sat in the lamp-lit living room. Little Volodya, a bit feverish and restless, was in his mother's arms. Softly she was singing him a lullaby.

When Volodya was put to bed, Ekaterina spoke of Dostoyevsky and the book *Crime and Punishment* which he had written the previous year.

Mendeleyev frowned a little.

"Too much psychology in it," he said.

"But that's life," said Ekaterina. "He understands life, and minds and hearts of people."

"That's true," said Mendeleyev. "But there's too much inward turning to one's ego. Most of it is futile. A sort of interminable cooking. No. One should turn the heart out to the world, not in to one's self. One needs a large view. That way there is a vast world seen stretching before one, the objective is of consequence—there are people to help, there is work to do. But not when you pirouette around your 'I.' "

Ekaterina pondered.

"I guess women are different," she said.

Feozva nodded, "To a woman a home touches the heart. But the world seems like something cold."

Mendeleyev stood up.

"The home touches my heart," he said emphatically. "And there is work to do for all the homes in the world. Not just one's own. Everything can fit into a plan. I don't despise my home."

Feozva blushed.

"I didn't mean anything wrong," she said.

Ekaterina took Mendeleyev's arm.

"Don't upset yourself, Mitenka," she pleaded. "No one meant anything wrong."

Mendeleyev frowned.

"No, I'm not upset. Well, I have to go to my work. Those letters from France are just what I need."

He kissed his wife on the forehead and left the room, his long stooped form casting a longer shadow in the narrow corridor.

5

This was 1867, and another sister had arrived from Siberia with her family. It was Maria, aged forty. She was married to Popov, former director of Tomsk High School, and at first they had gone to Moscow. There the inexperienced schoolteacher had promptly lost his ten thousand roubles in an obscure big-city business transaction, and now with their seven children they accepted Mendeleyev's offer of help. He gave them a part of his land and some horses and cattle and provided materials and workmen to build a house.

The summer was an especially happy one for Mendeleyev because of the exuberant joy of the children running through the fields, climbing the trees, and strolling in the garden.

The garden itself seemed more radiant because of the healthy, running children, whose rosy cheeks and shining hair made them look like flowers animated by the subtly blowing wind. Mendeleyev frequently joined them in the garden, strolling through the alley of soft purple lilac trees and among the roses and peonies overshadowed by the towering oaks, the maples, firs, and the fragrant lime trees.

Mendeleyev loved all the children almost as much as he loved Volodya, and yet often at mealtime, when the childish babble got out of control, he would rap the table with his long forefinger and exclaim,

"When I eat, I am deaf and dumb!"

This always silenced the children. For a while.

After supper, Mendeleyev usually chatted a while with his wife and Ekaterina, discussing Turgenev's latest work, or Russia's sale of Alaska to the Americans, or the possibility of building a two-story house here at Boblovo, the bottom story of stone and the top story of wood, to replace the present single-story wooden one.

At the end of the summer vacation in 1867, Mendeleyev, Feozva, and Volodya prepared to return to St. Petersburg, to their university apartment. They were taking Nadezhda with them; Mendeleyev was going to send her to high school. Nadezhda at twelve was already interested in art, and Mendeleyev was eager to see what progress she would make.

He went out into the fields for a final good-by to the mouzhik-neighbors who had worked for him all summer.

"Maybe the year will go faster this time," said one of his overseers.

"Come back soon," said the wizened mouzhik. "We'll be waiting for you."

"I'll be back," he said. "A year flies by."

"That's exactly what it does," said an old bearded mouzhik. "Now you take me. Forty-two years ago I married and beat my woman at the end of the first month, and it seems like only yesterday. I was reminding her this morning, and she says, '*Ekh*, you creature, it does seem like yesterday.' "

A young mouzhik stepped forward.

"They say there is a man in another country who can make the time flow backward. Now that is truly a miracle."

Mendeleyev shook his head.

"That's nonsense, little brothers," he said. "We just live and grow, and the body changes and gets worn and the earth moves around the sun. That way things go on, and soon our body is worn out and we die. And nothing flows this way or that, and there's no use talking about flowing time. Things just happen."

"It might be that way," conceded the redheaded mouzhik, "that's true. But now there's about the sun. That puzzles me. Tell me, Uncle, what keeps the sun from falling down?"

Mendeleyev dropped to his haunches and picking up a twig began to sketch in the ground, drawing an ellipse and the moving earth and the sun at the focus. The mouzhiks also squatted, watching intently.

Zassorin, the driver of the tarantass in front of the house, got off and ambled over to listen. Feozva, Volodya, and Nadezhda—all packed and dressed—waited in the tarantass.

After the mouzhiks, Mendeleyev went to say good-by to his beloved Soldat.

"Don't die while I'm gone," he told the aging horse. "You're an animal with a heart, brother. Nothing ever took the Urals like you did, companion. Wait for me. Don't die while I'm gone."

Then he searched for Fontov. He found him at the far edge of the last field. As Mendeleyev approached Fontov was preoccupied with a black box standing on the ground.

"What is it?" Mendeleyev called. "Caught something?"

Fontov, startled, looked up suddenly.

"*Akh*, it's you," he said. "Well, I don't mind. Yes, I caught something. Some sunshine. Come and see."

Mendeleyev drew near and peered through a hole in the black box. Inside, on the bottom, was a piece of broken glass.

"I've been letting the sun shine through the hole," explained Fontov, "and it falls on the glass, and the glass gets heavier."

Mendeleyev straightened up.

"How does it get heavier?" he asked. "How do you know?"

Fontov scratched his brown head.

"Well," he said. "That's not an easy thing to know. But the glass feels heavier. I've had it out here for a week and it feels a little heavier. I'm making crystal sunshine. Right inside that glass. I use the glass to sort of give the sunshine the right idea. You know, to get it started."

Mendeleyev pointed to the box.

"Why do you need that?" he asked. "Why not the glass just out in the open—on a piece of paper to keep it clean."

Fontov shook his head.

"It would be too plain," he explained. "No system. In your University you don't work in the street, do you?"

"No," conceded Mendeleyev.

Fontov was pleased over the victory.

"What a thing it would be," he said, "if I could make crystal sunshine in great amount. Think of it! Much clearer than glass, and cheap. All you want. Of course, on the cloudy days, my factory would have to close. But I could put the men to work making more of these boxes and cleaning the grounds— you know, so they wouldn't loaf. How many men do you think I ought to start with?"

Mendeleyev took Fontov by the arm.

"Fontov," he said. "Listen to me. You're a good workman in the fields, and dependable, and smart with the wheat. That's why you are one of my overseers. Now with this sunshine business you're not very good—"

"How is that—not very good," interrupted Fontov. "This is a real disappointment."

"Well," said Mendeleyev, "I was going to explain. You must do one thing. You must get a very accurate balance to weigh the glass before the sunshine falls on it, and then take it back and weigh it again after the sunshine has fallen on it. I don't think it will be heavier."

Fontov pointed to his chest.

"I have a feeling in here," he said, "that it will be heavier."

Mendeleyev shrugged his shoulders.

"There's only one thing to do," he said. "You've got to perform an accurate experiment. Go tell Ekaterina Ivanovna to show you how to operate the balance scales in my room. She knows how. I am leaving now for St. Petersburg. Good-by, Fontov. Put the men to work in March. Good-by."

Fontov watched Mendeleyev stride away.

"Good-by, Mitri Ivanitch," he called.

Fontov stood quietly for a long time, then presently in the distance he saw the horses go by, pulling the tarantass down the tree-lined avenue.

He sat down and looked long at his box, occasionally glancing at the sun. After a while he looked only at his box, and presently tears began to roll down his cheeks.

6

The year 1868 was a significant one in Mendeleyev's life: a daughter, Olga, was born, but somehow after this Mendeleyev and Feozva drifted apart; Soldat died at Boblovo in the spring while Mendeleyev was away at the university; Mendeleyev became a principal charter member of the Russian Chemical Society; Nadezhda's older sister was married in a near-by town, and Mendeleyev, laden with presents, went to the wedding; Mendeleyev became professor of inorganic chemistry when his former teacher Voskresensky left the university; and Fontov announced his results with crystal sunshine. These results came by letter written for Fontov by a literate acquaintance. Fontov admitted his failure to manufacture pure crystalline sunshine, but said he had another idea, and promised to tell Mendeleyev all about it during the coming summer.

To Mendeleyev, however, the most important thing was the publication of his first volume of *Principles of Chemistry*. This book was the most thorough, the most detailed, and the best-planned of anything that he had done so far.

"The rapid development of the study of the external universe, dating from the days of Galileo (1642) and Newton (1727), led to the separation of Chemistry as a special branch of natural philosophy. . . .

"The minds of the ancients attempted to grasp at once the very fundamental character of the universe, while all the successes of recent knowledge are based on a method of investigation in which it is not necessary to determine 'the beginning of all beginnings. . . .' In the investigation of anything there always remains something which is accepted without investigation. . . . The axioms of geometry are an example in point. . . . Likewise, in biology it is necessary to admit the ability of organisms to multiply themselves, as a phenomenon whose meaning is as yet unknown. . . . Nevertheless, by studying and describing that which is open to direct observation by the organs of the senses, we may hope to arrive first at hypotheses, and then at theories, of that which is now to be taken as the basis of our inquiries. . . .

"By means of the inductive method—attempting from much that is observable to arrive at a little that may be verified—the new science refuses to accept dogma as truth, but through reason attains to true deductions. . . . Thus, the inductive method has been successful for example in making possible acquaintance with much of the invisible world, the molecular motion of all bodies, the composition of the heavenly luminaries together with the paths of their motion, the necessity for the existence of substances as yet unknown to experiment. . . . The knowledge obtainable in all these directions is of course employed in increasing the welfare of humanity. . . .

"In order to be able to express chemical changes by equations, it has been agreed to represent each element by the first or some two letters of its Latin name. Thus we have, for example, oxygen represented by O; nitrogen by N; mercury (hydrargyrum) by Hg; iron (ferrum) by Fe; and so on for all the elements. . . . A substance which is a compound substance is represented by placing side by side the symbols representing the elements of which it is made up. As an example, a mercury oxide may be represented by HgO, which shows that it is composed of mercury and oxygen. . . .

"When a property can be measured it is no longer arbitrary, and makes the comparison objective. . . .

The Road to 1869. At the Summit

"The number of elements with whose compounds we commonly deal in everyday life is not greater than twenty-five at the present time. . . .

"The crystalline form is, without doubt, the expression of the relation in which the atoms occur in the molecules, and in which the molecules occur in the mass, of a substance. . . .

"The separation of ice from solutions explains both the fact, well known to sailors, that ice formed from salt water gives fresh water, and also the fact that by freezing, just as by evaporation, a solution is obtained which is richer in salts than before. In cold countries this is taken advantage of for extracting from sea water a liquor, which is then evaporated to leave the salt. . . .

"It is true, however, that to be free of salt, the ice must be formed in a continuous mass. Whereas, if it occurs as frozen fragments, it will enclose a portion of the salt water. . . ."

At the university Mendeleyev taught classes in the morning. In the afternoon he performed experiments in his two-room laboratory, and at night he worked on his plan to reveal a unity among all the elements and even among their compounds.

Somewhere in between these activities he worked on the second part of his *Principles of Chemistry* and it was going rapidly.

Twenty years had passed since the night of 1848. The fire burning on that night in the Glass Factory seemed to have kindled another fire burning to a climax within Mendeleyev. A book, and a universal plan for the elements.

Between the book and the plan, and providing the catalytic mechanism for a chemical interaction, were the lectures.

"This forms the peculiar charm of chemistry, and especially of physicochemical research. If the astronomer grasps the infinitely great in its highest reality, the chemist embraces the infinitely small, and science strives to attain the infinite and everlasting, unfettered by the finite and temporal. . . .

"In the fashioning of the scientific edifice, the artisan, architect, and creator are very often one and the same individual. . . .

"The natural philosopher of modern times no longer regards man as the pivot of the universe. . . .

"We can get along without a Plato, but a double number of Newtons is required to bring life into harmony with laws of nature. . . .

"It is the function of science to discover the existence of a general reign of order in nature and to find the causes governing this order. And this refers in equal measure to the relations of man—social and political—and to the entire universe as a whole. . . ."

The students sat quietly in the lecture room and watched their tall stooped professor intently as he raised his hands in emphasis or smiled with his blue eyes or in a fleeting gesture ran his hand under his blond beard. As usual, he wore his gray jacket and brown trousers. He moved about casually as he lectured, and spoke in a rapid but informal manner, as though confiding something to a deeply loved friend. His voice was low and resonant and clearly heard by the two hundred students, even when, in a moment of special emphasis, the words suddenly came in an intimate whisper.

7

There was another matter, too, that was using up his time.

In January of this year 1868 a great gathering of Russian men of science, meeting in St. Petersburg, had decided to organize formally into scientific societies. There had been, up to then, few—if any—science groups as such, and the professors and research men finally felt the need for closer communion with their colleagues and possibly scientific exchanges with the world outside Russia.

One of the men who labored for days to bring the Russian naturalists together was Dmitri Mendeleyev.

The scientists who assembled at the Petersburg meetings readily decided to form themselves into specific sections on biology, physics, chemistry, and so on. Mendeleyev and his young friend Nikolai Menshutkin undertook to bring into existence the Russian Chemical Society.

The work of organization continued throughout the year, with a number of meetings taking place in Mendeleyev's apartment. There was the problem of attracting more and more chemists to the plan; of deciding on the nature of the meetings and the constitution of the society, and, above all, the problem of obtaining permission to form a society at all—in the Russia of eternal government suspicion.

Finally, on November 6, 1868, the first formal meeting of the Russian Chemical Society was held, presided over by the ranking charter member, Dmitri Ivanovitch Mendeleyev. Tall, bearded, intense, he gazed down upon the other thirty-four charter members. He stepped forward on the platform.

"On the 26th of October, 1868," said Mendeleyev, "the formation of the Russian Chemical Society was confirmed by the Director of National Enlightenment, State-Secretary I. D. Delyanov."

A faint smile played about his eyes. The chemists in the audience too were proud of their new association.

"Now," said Mendeleyev, "I invite the members to settle problems arising out of the formation of this Society."

The Chemical Society was under way. It would in the future feel the obligation to justify its existence.

8

At night, much of Mendeleyev's time was spent with the white cards on which he noted down information regarding each of the chemical elements. Each had its case history—weight, luster, malleability, melting point, behavior in combination with other elements—all recorded on the cards. Daily, the notations increased, and daily Mendeleyev noted certain relationships among them.

Other men before Mendeleyev had observed certain relationships among the elements. One was the Englishman J. A. R. Newlands who reported his observations at a meeting of the Chemical Society at Burlington House, in 1866. Newlands had observed that if the elements were listed according to the weights of their tiniest particles—the atoms—then the eighth one resembled the first one and the ninth resembled the second, and so on. However, this was only approximately so, and Newlands was at a loss to explain the discrepancies. As a matter of fact, practically all of the chemists who listened to his exposition of "The Law of Octaves," expected from nature only "discrepancies," and considered the few resemblances at intervals of eight as simply coincidences not worthy of a serious scientist's attention.

Newlands had actually compared his table of the elements to the keyboard of a piano. He pointed to the eighty-eight notes divided into periods of eight, or octaves, and declared that the members of the same group of elements stand to each other in the same relation as the extremities of one or more octaves in music.

The very name—"The Law of Octaves"—was considered by the audience as a thing to ridicule, apart from its analogy to the octaves on a piano keyboard. And the further attempt by Newlands to hint at the existence of a parallel harmony between the notes on a piano and the elements was considered childish and silly. Professor Foster, one of the listening scientists before whom Newlands presented his report, asked, "Have you thought of arranging the elements according to their initial letters? Maybe some better connections would come to light that way."

This remark of the sarcastic professor, later bandied about in the scientific world, almost crushed the spirit within Newlands, and undermined his confidence. But, in fact, this loss of confidence could only happen because of something of which Newlands himself had been guilty: he had not put his theory of repetitious resemblances—periodicity—to a thorough test. Newlands had taken many things for granted. He had accepted the data for the elements as quoted in the scientific magazines, he himself checking little. He also seemed to assume that the elements then known were the only ones ever to be known and he tied them into a closed scheme. He also, noting the discrepancies in the law of repetition of qualities, did nothing about them, but merely hoped that the coincidences would outweigh the deviations.

Newlands was like a man touched with the light of modern science but who in a moment of crisis slips back into voodoo. On "The Law of Octaves" could at best resound the metaphysical harmony of the spheres, and at worst, a melancholy dirge—a dirge for the efforts of a man who had tried hard, but not hard enough.

The work that Dmitri Mendeleyev was doing was different.

He was taking nothing for granted. He performed thousands of experiments with his own hands. He made thousands of calculations, wrote innumerable letters, and studied countless reports. Everything in the world that was known about the chemical elements Mendeleyev knew. For months, for years, he searched for missing data, then checked it himself. In many hundreds of laboratories throughout the world, thousands of chemists had labored for years on copper, silver, gold, sodium, lithium, potassium. Mendeleyev knew the results of their work. In French, Spanish, Italian, German, and English he perused their reports and followed their continuing labors. His great blond head absorbed the information and sifted it.

The elements that were a very part of him had long and varied origins. But now they were being brought together on his white cards, grouped in a special way that perhaps recalled their common origin. Here in a cramped St. Petersburg laboratory was a reunion, after ages of scattered slumber in the earth, in the water, in the air, since the dawn of creation.

Long ago, gold had been known, and copper, silver, zinc, tin, lead, sulphur, iron, carbon, and mercury. After that the alchemists in their mystical play had nevertheless discovered a half-dozen more genuine elements.

Almost at the moment when Columbus was discovering a new world, Valentine, a German physician, was discovering antimony—a brittle silver-white metal; and bismuth, a white metal with a reddish tinge. In 1649, Schroeder discovered arsenic, a gray brittle metal of many uses, and twenty years later Brandt described phosphorus, which eventually was known to exist in four colors—yellow, red, violet, and black.

In 1735, in Colombia, the Spaniard de Ulloa established the identity of a new shiny metal—platinum; though the honor for the original discovery may have belonged to Scaliger, a scholar of the sixteenth century. Between the years 1735 and 1800 came the discovery of a considerable number of elements: cobalt, nickel, magnesium, fluorine, chlorine, manganese, molybdenum, and barium. Also, in the fruitful eighteenth century there occurred the discovery by Cavendish of the lightest element of all, the gas hydrogen— "inflammable air"; then came oxygen, chromium, tellurium, tungsten, titanium, nitrogen, beryllium, zirconium, and strontium. In 1789, Klaproth found a metal which was white, malleable, ductile. A day would come when Dmitri Mendeleyev would show that this element was the heaviest of them all. The name given to it was "uranium," because—in weight—it was beyond all the other elements, just as Uranus was considered to be beyond all the other planets in distance from the sun.

Now in 1869, on the white cards before Mendeleyev lay the complete histories and intimate detailed descriptions of more than sixty of these elements. Often, in the middle of the night, he would suddenly waken, walk to his desk piled with the white cards, and after making a notation on one of them go back to bed. Occasionally, too, waking thus at night, Mendeleyev—in his night clothes—would hasten to his study-laboratory to perform an experiment. Presently, sleepy but smiling, he would return to bed. More and more clearly a certain plan was coming into focus.

He had already written an article for the *Journal of the Russian Chemical Society*, telling of a certain plan that he had found to exist in nature and into which all the known elements fitted. On March 6, of this year, there would be a meeting of the Society, and he was to present his findings in person. In the St. Petersburg and Moscow scientific circles interest was growing in Mendeleyev's expected revelations. In addition to writing the *Journal* article Mendeleyev had distributed some preliminary pamphlets among his scientific colleagues. No one knew, however, the full scope that the impending personal presentation might take.

On March 5, the day before the meeting, Mendeleyev was not feeling well. He had a cold and his head felt heavy and feverish. Alone in his study-laboratory, he walked up and down before the wall opposite his desk. On this wall he had pinned his white cards, each dealing with one element. The cards were arranged in a number of columns. Here and there a column was broken off, allowing a patch of brown wall to show through. Below the patch the white cards resumed their sequence. Several such blank spaces were visible.

He stopped before the large arched window.

Snow was falling. The large flat flakes casually descended to the ground, which was already piled high with a puffed blanket of shining white. As far as the eye could see the white snow enveloped the university garden, the pathways, the hunched buildings. In the distance only a single object appeared which the snow had not been able to cover—the shining golden cross surmounting the white cupola of a Petersburg church.

He coughed. Then once more. Then again, and his entire body was shaken by the spasm.

The door suddenly opened, and his wife, the tiny melancholy Feozva appeared.

"It is cold there," she said. "It is cold by the window. Come away."

Mendeleyev paid no attention but for a moment he stopped coughing. Outside, a slim dark figure was coming through the snow.

"It's Nadezhda!" he exclaimed. "How nice! Little Nadezhda."

He rushed to the door and waited.

Presently hearing the footsteps outside, he opened the door.

He helped Nadezhda take off her coat.

"You are not well, Dmitri Ivanovitch," Nadezhda was saying, her pale face frowning in compassion. "I can see you are not well."

Feozva exchanged pleasantries with Nadezhda and then withdrew to her room. Inside could now be heard the voices of Volodya playing with his sister Olga.

"It is beautiful," said Mendeleyev. "How beautiful is the snow."

He walked back to the great arched window and immediately began to cough again.

"*Akh*, Dmitri Ivanovitch!" exclaimed Nadezhda flying to him. "It is cold by that window!"

Nadezhda led him to the little round stove in the center of the room, then walked to the door of Feozva's room and knocked.

When Feozva opened it, Nadezhda asked permission to make tea.

"Make all you want," said Feozva. "Make as much as you want. And take jam."

Soon Nadezhda served her uncle hot tea and a dish of strawberry jam. His cough seemed to have diminished.

"You're fourteen now," he said. "Am I right?"

Nadezhda nodded.

"Yes, Dmitri Ivanovitch," she said. "Time is flying."

He studied her pale face.

"You should eat more," he said. "You are now at the age when every cell in your body cries out for food. Do you eat well?"

Nadezhda nodded her head vigorously.

"*Akh*, but I do eat well, Dmitri Ivanovitch. I simply adore eating."

Mendeleyev nodded toward the bulging jar of strawberry jam.

"Take some," he said. "Take much."

"With your leave," said Nadezhda, and began to spoon jam onto a saucer. She poured herself some tea, and refilled his glass.

"I promised to explain to you my periodic system of the elements," he said and walked over to the wall.

Nadezhda followed him and stood open-mouthed before the rows and columns of white cards.

"How strange," she murmured, "how important. How awfully awfully important."

He pointed at the cards with his long forefinger.

"Every element in the world is made up of its tiny particles which we call 'atoms.' There are now known about sixty different kinds of elements, so there are about sixty different kinds of atoms. Each kind of atom weighs a certain amount. Hydrogen has the lightest atoms and uranium has the heaviest."

Nadezhda drew closer and read the names on the white cards.

"These are the elements," Mendeleyev explained. "They are arranged according to the weights of their atoms. You could have just simply one long vertical column from lightest to heaviest. When you do that then the following is known to be true. The first one that I have here, lithium, resembles the eighth one, sodium. And the second one, beryllium, resembles the ninth one, magnesium. Thus it goes, essentially, with certain refinements. So you see, after a lapse of seven we get an element of similar characteristics again. This lapse or interval I call a period. This is a periodic system. After a certain lapse or period in counting, we get again an element similar to one way above. In this way we get entire groups which resemble each other. . . ."

Nadezhda pointed to the cards.

"But how do they resemble each other?" she asked. "Do they look alike?"

"In many ways," he said. "Chemically, for example. Take the first group. Every element there, lithium, sodium, potassium, and so on, behaves like this: two atoms of lithium will combine with one atom of oxygen. And two atoms of sodium also will combine with one atom of oxygen. And the same is true for potassium, and so on. On the other hand, in another group which I get by that periodic selection, one atom of each element wants to combine with one atom of oxygen, to form an oxygen compound, of course. This is true for the group with beryllium, calcium, strontium, and so on. Then, another group contains elements for which each atom wants to combine with three atoms of oxygen—if given a chance. . . ."

"How clever!" said Nadezhda. "How simply clever of them."

Mendeleyev coughed again.

"Well," he said. "Some day I will explain some more."

Nadezhda hurriedly put on her coat.

"Good-by, Dmitri Ivanovitch," she said. "*Akh*, but I am sorry you are unwell. May I have permission to send your doctor to you?"

"No. Let it be."

But Nadezhda sent his doctor who put him immediately to bed.

At one o'clock that night Mendeleyev arose quietly and, burning with fever, began to wander dazedly about his apartment. The yellow light of the moon sifted through the tall curved windows. There, at the window, he stopped and gazed at the sky. The yellow moonlight enveloped him. It fell upon his wild disarrayed hair, the ill face, the tall stooped frame in dark blue night clothes, gaunt bare feet.

His beard rose and fell rapidly as he struggled for breath.

Then, turning, he seemed to contemplate the study-laboratory before him. Tall glass bottles with many gullets stood on the upper shelf of the broad experiment table. The bottles, filled with colored liquids, were surrounded by rows of test tubes resting in wooden holders. A large glass dome sat upon a metallic plate leading to a pump. Under the glass dome was a tiny crucible. On the experiment table there were clamps, supports, funnels, and stacks of filter paper; on the upper tier of the table, on a level with a man's eyes, small bottles of acids—sulphuric, nitric, and hydrochloric—sodium and ammonium hydroxide, other chemicals. Surrounding the central laboratory space stood the cabinets filled with glass tubes of every sort—curved, straight, short, long, narrow, wide, tapering. Other cabinets and shelves were laden with books, and one cabinet stood bulging with sorted letters. The work-desk was piled high with books, manuscripts, written pages. . . .

Mendeleyev walked out into the corridor, almost impassable because of the piles of scientific books and journals. In the dark he tripped over a stack of journals and fell. Before he could scramble to his feet, Feozva, tiny and frightened, appeared at her door. Terrified she flew to him.

"To bed," she begged. "To bed, Mitenka, to bed."

She placed a vinegar compress on his forehead, then, for a moment darting outside the apartment, she roused the Gontarov family and begged them to summon Lentov, the doctor.

In his bed Mendeleyev stirred uneasily. His four-year-old son, Volodya, had come to him and sat sleepily on his bed. Feozva took the boy back to his room and once again returned to Mendeleyev.

For an instant a gleam of comprehension came in his eyes.

"This is March 6. In the morning I must present my paper—my plan," he whispered hoarsely.

The doctor came. But the crisis had already passed, and the fever was dropping.

This was March 6, 1869, the day he was to read the paper before the Russian Chemical Society, on "The Dependence between the Properties and the Atomic Weights of the Elements."

Chapter Twenty-one

The Blank Spaces

BEFORE THE audience—the members of the Russian Chemical Society—stood Professor Menshutkin, Mendeleyev's colleague and friend.

"Professor Mendeleyev is ill," he said. "This I deeply grieve. However, I have the honor of making an announcement in his behalf."

Menshutkin turned his eyes to the notes before him and began to read.

"The properties of the fundamental substances, as well as the forms and properties of the compounds of these elements, are dependent in a periodic way, on the magnitude of the atomic weights of the elements."

The weights of the atoms of a substance—Menshutkin went on to elaborate—determine the chemical attributes of a substance. Furthermore, there is a way of arranging the substances on a chart so that certain heavier ones are seen to resemble certain lighter ones in their chemical behavior, this repetition of properties being called a "periodicity."

"Professor Mendeleyev wants everyone to know that he has drawn on the labors of a great many workers all over the world. I will now display a huge chart to show the way in which the elements are grouped by our illustrious, unfortunately ailing, colleague. There are many remarks to make. These were just being prepared by him last night when the fever overtook him. I regret that I am not able to make the necessary remarks. We shall have to await his recovery. I do know that we shall have many puzzles in our minds until we hear from him. All right, here's the chart."

The audience leaned forward to gaze as Menshutkin unrolled the chart on the wall.

After half an hour the audience filed out.

Berlikov, the young analytical chemist from Kazan University, took Menshutkin's arm.

"Those blank spaces," he said. "They bother me. What is the meaning?"

Menshutkin shrugged his shoulders.

"As I said," he replied, "Mendeleyev listed the substances in this order, but had to leave blanks so that the relationships which he has found would not be spoiled."

Berlikov was puzzled.

"But can nature have blank spaces?" he asked.

Menshutkin smiled.

"Apparently she has everything," he said. "She might as well have blank spaces. My mind is one of them."

Berlikov frowned.

"*Akh*, but this is puzzling," he complained; "this is puzzling to leave blank spaces just to make the answers come out right. I feel badly."

"Go have some tea," advised Menshutkin. "And wait for Mendeleyev to recover."

Berlikov continued to wonder about the blank spaces. The Moscow scientist Kotinsky began to talk about certain research that Mendeleyev's chart seemed to call for. Menshutkin listened to both of these men as the three wandered slowly to the Chemical Society luncheon.

2

When the summer vacation arrived, Mendeleyev set out for Boblovo with his little niece Nadezhda. Feozva was already there with Volodya and the year-old Olga. Mendeleyev's sister Ekaterina would spend the summer at his university apartment. She would have a good rest, for Mendeleyev had asked that she leave her children at Boblovo. He looked forward to a joyous time, his fields and garden alive with the boisterous youngsters.

He and Nadezhda took seats in the train of the Nikolayev Railroad, and settled down for the seven-hour run to Klin. From there, by carriage, they would ride to Boblovo. How much thrill there was on this trip, Nadezhda knew already. She could hardly wait.

They were traveling third class. Mendeleyev always traveled that way, with the simple mouzhiks, their *babas*, and other plain people. The wooden seats were narrow, and Mendeleyev occupied a seat alone. Nadezhda sat across the aisle from him, holding a brown satchel on her lap. As soon as the train got under way she opened it and took out the food, glasses, utensils, and the greenish teakettle. At the first stop Mendeleyev hurried out to the station with the teakettle and soon returned with steaming water. A few minutes later they were drinking tea, and eating the *pirozhkee* stuffed with meat.

All the other passengers too were carrying boiling water—the two nuns, the sailor, the old woman at the end of the car, the deacon, the merchant in the blue pants and brown jacket, the three soldiers, and the high-school boy with his dark-eyed girl.

In half an hour a mouzhik came over to borrow a lump of sugar from Mendeleyev. Presently another one came to ask for lemon and gave a huge plum in exchange. Then the sailor came to smile at fourteen-year-old Nadezhda and started to tell about the Caspian Sea. Soon, from the conductor, word got around that Mendeleyev was a professor, and now the deacon came over to ask if any more schools would be built soon in the Petersburg area.

"Our young ones need better care," he said.

Mendeleyev nodded and poured the deacon a glass of tea.

Now suddenly another station was reached. It was a large station and the train would stay twenty minutes. Mendeleyev, the deacon, and the sailor left the train to eat at the station buffet, and Mendeleyev ordered hot dishes to be taken to Nadezhda.

Back again on the train they listened to the mouzhiks at the front of the car sing a round of songs about going to the fair and what they saw there. Then two mouzhiks came to talk to Mendeleyev about their crops. From the other end of the car came several more, and all stood in the center or climbed about, blocking the car entirely. It had been unanimously decided, apparently, that one does not travel with a professor every day, and now was the time to improve one's head.

"They say tea may be harder to get," said a bearded mouzhik. "Is this a fact, little father, or is it foolishness?"

Mendeleyev shook his head.

"There's no reason to believe that," he said. "Our trade with China goes well. Boats are coming up the Volga regularly."

"Where is this China?" asked a fat *baba* in a green cotton shawl.

"Over that way," said Mendeleyev, pointing southeast. "A great distance. They have yellow skin, those people, and narrow eyes."

The *baba* shook her head.

"*Bednyazhkee,*" [the poor little ones] she said, "how do they live in that condition?"

Mendeleyev smiled.

"It's all right," he said. "It doesn't hurt."

One of the soldiers asked Mendeleyev about Tolstoy.

"Where is he now? He was at Sevastopol when I was there. During the Crimean War."

Mendeleyev nodded.

"He's a writer—have you read *War and Peace?* It was published in the magazine of Katkov."

The soldier didn't know about that.

"But he's a good-hearted man, this Tolstoy," he said. "He gave me a small apple tart one time. It was a little sweet, to be sure, but then, I'm no fine one to pick things over. But the meat ones I like real well. With a glass of tea. There you really have something."

Mendeleyev

"You're a regular artist in foods," said the *baba* of the green shawl.

The soldier was slightly confused.

"Artist or no artist," he said. "But I eat with the best of them. When I can get it."

An hour later, a larger crowd had gathered about Mendeleyev and Nadezhda. The questions were nearly all about nature now. It came about this way: a young husky mouzhik with a ruddy complexion had said that everything in the world was made of little round spheres.

"I myself am not literate," he said, "but an old man of my acquaintance once read this in a book."

An older mouzhik with a drooping brown moustache would not believe this. His large green eyes sparkled with objection.

"If everything is made of round things," he asserted, "then nothing could feel smooth. Now feel this kopek. Go ahead."

The young mouzhik appealed to Mendeleyev.

"It was in a book," the young mouzhik said. "How could it be wrong? I saw the book with my own eyes."

"It could be wrong anyway," said Mendeleyev.

The mouzhik of the green eyes was jubilant, the young one chagrined.

"But in this case it's probably not wrong," added Mendeleyev.

The younger mouzhik now was jubilant and the other was chagrined.

"Yes, we think that everything is made up of tiny particles. But they may not be round. And actually there is no direct way of proving yet that these tiny particles exist. But it seems like a right idea."

"Then why isn't everything the same?" asked the sailor, who had now returned from helping the old woman at the back of the car drink tea and eat *pirozhkee*.

"The particles for one substance are one kind," said Mendeleyev. "And for another substance they are another kind. For iron, the particles are the iron kind, and for lead, they are the lead kind. We call them 'atoms.'"

"Atoms," said the young healthy mouzhik. "Sounds like that's what the man read in the book. I think so."

The train jerked to a halt.

Mendeleyev descended to buy Nadezhda a crisp red apple.

For a while after the train resumed its journey everyone in the car sang, and Mendeleyev louder than anyone else. Some of the songs were gentle, emotional ones, like "Volga, Volga, Native Mother," but most were boisterous rollicking songs. The deacon himself began the never-ending song of the priest and his dog. This song, known all over Russia, was sung with reckless abandon and lifting of spirits.

A priest, possessed a dog,
And this dog thrilled him.
But he ate up a hunk of meat once,
So he killed him.
He killed him, buried him,
And carved on the gravestone:
"A priest possessed a dog,
And this dog thrilled him.
But he ate up a hunk of meat once,
So he killed him.
He killed him, buried him,
And carved on the gravestone:
'A priest possessed a dog,
And this dog . . .' "

Round and round went the song with everyone coming into it at some time or another. After five rounds, the emboldened nuns joined in, listening to themselves in astonishment. Nadezhda had come in on the third round, and the old woman at the end of the car on the fourth.

Just before the train came in to Klin, Mendeleyev finished an explanation of the formation of the earth and the origin of the sun and its planets.

The mouzhiks shook their heads in wonderment.

"And now if another war comes," said a new mouzhik, a sad one who had gotten on one station back, "can we go up there to one of those planets as you call it? To get away?"

Mendeleyev, looking the sad mouzhik in the eye, shook his head slowly.

"No," he said. "No. We can escape from everything except our own evil."

The sad mouzhik shook his head.

"I've lost four sons in war," he said. "There is only Vasska left. I want him to live. What must I do? What can we do? Isn't the earth soaked enough with our blood? What can we do?"

"Pray," said the woman of the green shawl.

"Work hard and live honestly," said the young healthy mouzhik. "Am I not right, little father?"

Mendeleyev sat silent.

They waited quietly for him to speak.

"I don't know the answer, little doves," he said. "All I know is that among the scientists of the world there is a deep understanding. All are seeking the same truths. All are together in their wish to know only the truth about nature, about the world. And they have a language which they all can understand. In mathematics there is a language. In physics, in biology, in chemistry. So small a thing as a tiny chemical formula is a meeting of the minds. . . ."

The sad mouzhik pressed forward.

"Then let us all be scientists," he said. "I want my boy to live."

Silence fell again.

"Perhaps we are too old," said a mouzhik with a graying beard.

"No," said Mendeleyev, "no one is too old. Yes—be scientists, all of you. Everyone. Men and women and children."

The mouzhik with the graying beard was dubious.

"It is not easy," he said. "How is this done, little father?"

Mendeleyev stood up. A new idea suddenly occurred to him.

"It is easy," he said. "It is very easy. . . ."

"*Akh*, but we do not even know what a scientist is," said the gray-headed mouzhik.

Mendeleyev took the old man's arm.

"Listen to me, *dedushka*," he said. "Listen to me, little grandfather. A scientist is a man who does something where no question of making money is involved. Understand? And two scientists who deal with each other are dealing about something, about anything which does not concern money."

The old man thought for a while.

"I can be that kind," he said. "That is not difficult. And it is even a thing of interest."

"I can be that kind, too," said the sad mouzhik. "But now about the rest of the world. Who will tell them this good thing, *ekh?*"

Mendeleyev slowly put his arm about the old man's shoulders.

"I will try to tell them," he said. "Pray for me, little father."

The train arrived at Klin.

3

Mendeleyev and Nadezhda were met at the station by Zassorin, the driver from the Boblovo estate. Zassorin had left the carriage and the three horses just outside the station, and now he took the suitcases and satchels that Mendeleyev and Nadezhda had brought.

"Now here is a day of magic for you, Mitri Ivanitch," said Zassorin, filling his lungs with the cool early evening air. His red shirt swelled as he breathed, and his blue eyes smiled.

He departed to arrange the baggage and check over the harnessing of the troika, a three-horse team.

This was the high point for Nadezhda in her trip with her uncle. It was something that Mendeleyev took for granted, having ridden the troika so often, but this was only the third time for Nadezhda and she thrilled at the prospect.

Zassorin made the final adjustments, and checked all the straps, and looked at all the wheels. Then he climbed up on his seat.

"*Gotovo*," [she's ready] he said.

For a moment Mendeleyev and Nadezhda stood admiring the young gray horses.

"Let's go," said Mendeleyev, and helped Nadezhda to climb in.

"*Khorosho*, Zassorin," said Mendeleyev. "All right. *Davai*. Give, brother, give."

"*Khorosho!*" called Zassorin. "Yes, Mitri Ivanitch."

He turned to the horses. The ride would be a conversation with them. To no one else would Zassorin speak until the trip was over. This was between Zassorin and the three grays. They knew it, and they waited for the conversation to begin. The horses loved and feared Zassorin, but their best efforts were forthcoming solely if Zassorin talked to them as only he knew how—talked with his heart, talked with his hands and his feet, talked with gentle reproach and magnanimous praise. The horses knew their man and they waited.

"*Nu chto*," said Zassorin in a casual way, "what do you think, little doves, shall we go for a promenade?"

The carriage began to roll.

Out in the clear, beyond the station, the horses began a light prancing.

"To dance, we will dance," said Zassorin, "but now, little brothers, let's move along a little."

The lead horse picked up speed and the side horses at once followed.

Nadezhda leaned forward to listen to Zassorin. Mendeleyev, smiling, relaxed in the carriage.

"This is like a cripple," chided Zassorin, "now let's have some legs."

Barely perceptibly the speed picked up.

Now Zassorin began to reason.

"What is it with you, my companions? The *barin* has come home. The master is here. Can you move?"

This was not enough.

"And a young lady has arrived," pleaded Zassorin. "*Chto takoye?*" [What is the matter?]

This, too, had no effect.

Zassorin stood up.

"Come on," he began in a threatening undertone. "Come on, I say. Come on, little doves, come on, you criminals. . . ."

The lead horse again picked up speed and the side horses responded.

Zassorin remained standing. He handled his long whip and cracked it explosively way out front over the head of the lead horse. Nadezhda jumped at the sudden crack of the whip.

"*Davai!*" shouted Zassorin in a mountainous voice. "Now, give!"

The horses flew.

Zassorin kept up the whipcracking and now he stamped his feet. Then suddenly he stopped the urging and with whip upraised in his right hand studied the speed. The horses were flying at the maximum. This speed they could maintain for twelve miles, but a greater speed would break them. The fine balance had been reached.

In the open, the horses raced through the countryside, their hoofs hardly touching the ground.

Mendeleyev took off his hat and stood up in the carriage. The wind blew through his hair and beard.

"*Akh*," he said as it tore at his teeth. "*Akh*, how relaxing."

Zassorin stood straight at his place, the whip hand still poised high in the air.

Now he was satisfied, and gently he paid the animals. Gently he spoke, and smoothly, cautious not to break the stride and the maximum constant speed.

"*Goloubcheekee,*" [little doves] he soothed. "How smooth you are, how strong, how clever. Fly, my darlings, fly over God's earth."

On the troika raced.

Then suddenly, it was Boblovo Mountain—the estate, with the new two-story house. The horses came to an abrupt halt.

"*Akh, akh,*" sighed Nadezhda breathlessly.

Zassorin got down to help with the baggage.

Mendeleyev embraced him.

"You're a great one," Mendeleyev said.

"But why, Mitri Ivanitch?" he said. "It's the horses."

Zassorin stepped over to the horses and talked to them.

"You took a little while to get started, companions," he said. "But you did all right. I'm proud of you."

4

During the next two years—1869 and 1870—Mendeleyev's life, as well as the life of Russia, was full to overflowing.

The summers at Boblovo were spent in furious writing, and occasional walks about the estate in the bright happy sunlight. The rest of the time was spent in St. Petersburg, in experiments, lectures, and in more furious writing.

The Blank Spaces

On August 22, 1869, Mendeleyev went to Moscow to attend the Second Congress of Naturalists. The next day, in the division on chemistry, he presented a report dealing with far-flung agricultural experiments that he had been supervising for more than two years. He told of results of experiments in four parts of Russia, and made recommendations for the special treatment of the various soils in order to increase the harvest. He stressed the need for artificial enrichment of the soil with nitrogenous substances. In certain cases the use of ammonia salts and of lime was more advantageous. During the current year of 1869, without further enrichment, the increase in the yield of rye in certain farm districts was clearly noticeable. As expected, where two years ago nitrogenous enrichment had been used, no increase in harvest occurred this year, the nitrogen effect lasting only one season. Enrichment due to potash availed little, and the same was true for phosphorus in the Moscow and Simbirsk districts. But in Smolensk a significant increase in the harvest occurred, an increase of 15 per cent.

Chemical analysis of the soil was carried on in the St. Petersburg laboratories by five research men under Mendeleyev. These investigators—Vreden, Oliv, Pitov, Schmidt, and Jacobi—studied the amounts of phosphorus in the soils from various districts.

Mendeleyev concluded the report with an indication of the localities where nitrogenous deposits would best serve the soil and those where lime and ash would be most beneficial.

Much bread could grow in Russia. One needed only to think. One needed only to negotiate with the soil.

Before the meeting of the Chemical Society on December 4, 1869, Mendeleyev read a paper on his elements, their atomic weights, and how the various elements combined with oxygen. This was a part of the large problem which overshadowed all others—the problem of completing the plan of unity among the elements. In this problem loomed the blank spaces which had puzzled the youthful Berlikov at the March 6 meeting.

For the January 8, 1870, meeting, Mendeleyev had the research paper on a law in the study of heat and on the constitution of carbon crystals.

On March 5, he reported for the student P. Bauer on the digestion of substances by rabbits.

For himself, on the same day, he reported on his work with ammonia.

At the May 7 meeting, Mendeleyev, eager to extend scientific horizons, proposed the institution of an exchange of Russian chemical literature with a society struggling into existence in Prague. This suggestion was unanimously adopted.

At the October 8 meeting he proposed that the Chemical Society encourage master's- and doctor's-degree chemical students to submit their theses to the

Society for printing at the latter's expense. Copies would then be distributed among the Society members, and the balance given to the candidates. This suggestion too was adopted. After that, he presented a report on certain acids.

On December 3, 1870, the roll of Chemical Society members stood at sixty-seven. Gradually the list was growing. More and more young men were hearing of the Chemical Society, more and more freshmen were enrolling in chemistry.

Mendeleyev, at the December 3 meeting, presented a short report, indicating certain changes in his system of the elements. He indicated a new position for the element indium and placed the elements cerium, thorium, and uranium in his scheme.

There was also a paper by him on those elements for which one atom, when combining with oxygen, takes two oxygen atoms.

In 1870 he managed to steal away for a trip to western Europe. He was fascinated by the Isle of Camarga, at the mouth of the River Rhone, where he contemplated the extraction of "summer-salts"—salts of the element potassium.

The writing went on. *Principles of Chemistry*, the second part, 951 pages, *On the Question of Manufacture of Cheese in Artells, Dependence between the Properties and the Atomic Weights of the Elements*; a paper titled "Solutions"; a report on the atomic volumes of simple bodies; a report on earth analysis; a paper on heat associated with chemical combinations; a critique of Thomsen's thermochemical investigations; remarks on the investigations of Andrews on the compressibility of carbon dioxide, more papers on soil analysis. . . .

5

In March, 1869, in the report which Menshutkin briefly discussed for Mendeleyev while he was ill, Mendeleyev had set forth the following ideas:

1. The elements, if arranged according to the weights of their atoms, exhibit an evident periodicity of properties. For example, the ninth element, sodium resembles the second, lithium . . .

2. Elements which have similar chemical properties have atoms of nearly the same weight (platinum, 196.7; iridium, 197; osmium, 198.6), or which increase regularly (e.g., potassium, 39; rubidium, 85, or 46 higher than potassium; caesium, 133, or 48 higher than rubidium).

3. The arrangement of the elements, or of groups of elements, in the order of their atomic weights corresponds with their so-called *valencies*; that is, the ability to combine with other elements. Thus, for each member

of one group, like potassium, rubidium, and caesium, two atoms will combine with one atom of oxygen; for another group, only one atom may be necessary to combine with three atoms of oxygen, and so on.

4. The elements which are most widely distributed in nature have *small* atomic weights, and all the elements of small atomic weight are characterized by sharply defined properties. They are therefore typical elements.

5. The *magnitude* of the atomic weight determines the character of an element.

6. The discovery of many yet unknown elements may be expected. For instance, elements analogous to aluminium and silicon, the weights of whose atoms would be between 65 and 75.

7. The atomic weight of an element may sometimes be corrected by the aid of a knowledge of those of the adjacent elements. Thus, the weight of an atom of tellurium must be greater than 123 and less than 128; otherwise tellurium would find itself in a group of strange elements.

8. Certain characteristic properties of the elements can be foretold from the weights of their atoms.

It was now November, 1870, and Mendeleyev was putting his plan into final form. Certain changes had to be made if the scheme was to be consistent. Boldly he changed the atomic weights of a number of elements, since, as they stood, they did not fit in with his plan. Gold, with a quoted weight of 196.2 should have been placed *before* such elements as platinum, iridium, and osmium, of atomic weights 196.7, 196.7, 198.6. But Mendeleyev, feeling that their weights were wrong, put gold after these elements. He proved to be right, and eventually the order was osmium, 190.2; iridium, 193.1; platinum, 195.2; and gold, 197.2. He made many other changes too, among them uranium, from 120 to 240. This change he had already announced some time before.

"The laws of nature admit of no exception," he wrote, "and in this they clearly differ from such rules and maxims as are found in grammar, and in other inventions, methods, and relations of man's creation.

"It is necessary to do one thing or the other—either to consider the periodic law as completely true, and as forming a new instrument in chemical research, or to refute it."

November 20, 1870, had come. Mendeleyev was working incessantly on his plan. As fast as he could tear himself from his lectures, he rushed, as though in a trance, to the private study of his university apartment.

There was no time for anything else now. There was hardly time for food. He no longer came to the table to eat. With nervous energy, the tall shaggy Mendeleyev, head and hands in quick movement, concentrated upon his problem. Stooped and gaunt from late work during the nights, he strode about his study, pen in hand, now stopping to gaze upon the array of white cards pinned upon the wall across from his desk, now dropping down onto the yellow sofa to jot down an elusive idea.

Occasionally the study door creaked open, and tiny Volodya came tiptoeing into the room, carrying a tray in his slender hands. Only the five-year-old Volodya could thus dare to intrude upon his father. Slowly he would come forward, quietly place the tray on the desk on top of Mendeleyev's papers, then, still on tiptoe he would leave. Often, as he closed the door behind him, he would peek through to catch a glimpse of his father's pleased face, then the door would creak shut. And at once Volodya could be heard shouting in triumph to his mother and bounding down the hallway. Mendeleyev would eat. His mind eternities away from food, but he would eat because his beloved Volodya had brought it, and because it was necessary to clear his desk. Down went the bowl of borsch, down went the piece of fish, the warm milk, and the strong tea. All went down, down somewhere for reunion below—out of his way. Now he could write again.

On November 29, 1870, the long article, "The Natural System of the Elements and Its Use in Determining Properties of Undiscovered Elements," was almost finished.

"In a previous arrangement that I had, certain elements did not have a place in the system. I refer to uranium and indium. That was one defect of my grouping. In addition, my previous system seemed to place such diverse groups near each other as the alkaline metals and the halogens—chlorine, iodine. . . .

"Now it becomes possible to eliminate both these defects.

"First it will be recalled that in *Principles of Chemistry* I recently proposed to change the atomic weight of uranium from 120 to 240. . . ."

He had tried to determine the atomic weight of uranium by direct experiment, but it was impossible to get an appropriate sample of the element. Nevertheless, Mendeleyev's table could find no place for uranium unless the weight of its atoms be considered about 240 and not 120. He adopted the weight that he needed.

"To determine the atomic weight of this element, it will be necessary to determine the heat capacity or crystalline structure of its compounds, or the density of its vapor. . . . As soon as a proper sample becomes available, I expect to perform the necessary experiments. . . .

"I have found it necessary also to change the atomic weight of thorium from 116 to 232. Cerium must also be changed, from 92 to 138, and this value agrees with that actually obtained in the laboratory by heat capacity measurements.

"It is likewise necessary to change the value of the atomic weight of indium, from 75.6 to 112. The experimental values for cerium and indium conform with the values I consider they must have, through the requirements of the periodic table, which I now submit. . . . It now becomes possible to predict the properties of undiscovered elements. . . .

"A look at the table of the elements reveals a number of empty places.

"I am now going to make such predictions of the existence of certain elements as yet unknown in order to make a test of my system. . . .

"In the row of more or less ordinary elements there seem lacking analogues of boron or aluminium, as a glance at the table shows. In the third group there is an element lacking right after aluminium. From studying the table, and from considering the nature of the elements which surround this blank space I conclude that the weights of the atoms of this undiscovered element is about 45. This can be seen by interpolating between the values of calcium, 40, and of titanium, 48. As is obvious, two atoms of this unknown, X, will combine with three atoms of oxygen to form the oxide X_2O_3 . . . The unknown will combine with sodium, lithium, and so on, and will not be dissolved by water. With acids this unknown will form permanent salts. . . . In any case, ammonia will not dissolve it. . . . I propose to call this undiscovered element 'ekaboron.' The prefix 'eka' means 'one' in Sanskrit, and here it is used to indicate 'resemblance to.' Thus, ekaboron or Eb 45.

"Eb will be metallic in appearance. And the weight of 1 cubic centimeter of Eb will be 3 grams. It will not be volatile, and therefore it is not likely to be found by the spectroscopic method where it is necessary to have the substance glowing as a vapor to emit its characteristic colors. Ekaboron will not break up water into hydrogen and oxygen at ordinary temperatures, but at somewhat higher temperatures it will do so.

"Of course Eb will dissolve in acids.

"One atom of Eb will combine with three atoms of chlorine to produce $EbCl_3$, (possibly two atoms of Eb will prefer six of chlorine, Eb_2Cl_6). This chloride must be volatile. . . . The weight of 1 cubic centimeter of this chloride will be 2 grams. Ekaboron will offer two atoms against three, of course, in forming a combination with oxygen, Eb_2O_3. This must be nonvolatile, and not soluble in water . . .

"I shall now predict the nature of another undiscovered element, also in group 3; in fact an element right below ekaboron. To this one I shall give the temporary name of 'eka-aluminium.' The weight of its atoms will be 68. Its salts will be more stable than those of aluminium. . . . The weight of 1 cubic centimeter in the metallic state will be about 6. Eka-aluminium will be more volatile than aluminium, and a spectroscopic discovery is possible."

Mendeleyev then made a brief prediction as to a few more elements.

"But now I wish to take up a most interesting one. This one I will call 'ekasilicon.' It is at present a blank space in the fourth group. We may write this element as 'Es,' and the weight of its atoms should be 72. The oxide of course is EsO_2. The weight of 1 cubic centimeter of free ekasilicon will be about 5.5 grams. It will be a fusible metal, capable of vaporizing in strong heat. . . . The weight of 1 cubic centimeter of EsO_2 will be about 4.7 grams. The chloride $EsCl_4$, must be soluble in water. The weight of 1 cubic centimeter of it will be about 1.9 grams. Ekasilicon will also form an ethide $EsEt_4$ and this will boil at 160°. The weight of 1 cubic centimeter of the ethide will be about 0.96 grams. Ekasilicon will form the compound EsH_4 with hydrogen.

"I will now indicate where this element ekasilicon might be discovered. . . ."

Suddenly there were loud voices outside of his door and he found it impossible to finish his thought. The phrase "arrested student" stuck sharply in his mind. Mendeleyev, with his pen in his hand, walked to the door of his study and opened it. He was just in time to see the figure of a woman disappear beyond the corridor.

In a moment Feozva appeared. She seemed tired and alarmed.

"I'm sorry," she said, her eyes cast down. "We disturbed you."

Mendeleyev pointed down the corridor with his pen.

"Who was it?"

"Madame Golikov. She came to tell of the Akhmatov boy. Wasn't he a student of yours last year?"

Mendeleyev nodded.

"Akhmatov, yes," he said. "What is this about an arrest?"

"There was a student meeting last night at the Akhmatov home. The students were printing handbills, apparently. Madame Golikov says it was about freedom of speech. The police raided about two o'clock. Many students were beaten."

Mendeleyev stood in his doorway and gazed silently upon his wife.

Through the open doorway she could see the wall with the white cards pinned on it, and the writing desk piled with papers.

"I'm sorry," she said. "We didn't mean to disturb you."

"Tell me the rest," he said.

Feozva shrugged.

"Only this," she said. "The student Akhmatov was taken by the police. He has not returned home yet."

The pen in Mendeleyev's hand broke with a snap.

"*Khorosho*," he said, and stepped back through the doorway, into his own room. "Why don't they just study! *Akh Bozhe moi.*"

Mendeleyev's Chart of the Elements
Year 1871

Each number refers to the weight of one atom of the element compared to the weight of the lightest atom, that of hydrogen

GROUP I Two atoms of any element (R) here combine with one atom of oxygen (O) R_2O	GROUP II One atom of any element (R) here combines with one atom of oxygen (O) RO or R_2O_2	GROUP III Two atoms of any element (R) combine with three atoms of oxygen (O) R_2O_3	GROUP IV One atom of any element (R) here combines with two atoms of oxygen RO_2	GROUP V Two atoms of any element (R) here combine with five atoms of oxygen (O) R_2O_5	GROUP VI One atom of any element (R) here combines with three atoms of oxygen (O) RO_3	GROUP VII Two atoms of any element (R) here combine with seven atoms of oxygen (O) R_2O_7	GROUP VIII One atom of any element (R) here combines with four atoms of oxygen RO_4
Hydrogen = 1							
Lithium = 7	Beryllium = 9.4	Boron = 11	Carbon = 12	Nitrogen = 14	Oxygen = 16	Fluorine = 19	
Sodium = 23	Magnesium = 24	Aluminium = 27.3	Silicon = 28	Phosphorus = 31	Sulphur = 32	Chlorine = 35.5	
Potassium = 39	Calcium = 40	—— = 44	Titanium = 48	Vanadium = 51	Chromium = 52	Manganese = 55	Iron = 56, Cobalt = 59 Nickel = 59, Copper = 63
Copper = 63	Zinc = 65	—— = 68	—— = 72	Arsenic = 75	Selenium = 78	Bromine = 80	
Rubidium = 85	Strontium = 87	?y = 88	Zirconium = 90	—— = 94	Molybdenum = 96	—— = 100	Ruthenium = 194, Rhodium 104 Lead = 106, Silver = 108
Silver = 108	Cadmium = 112	Indium = 113	Tin = 118	Antimony = 122	Tellurium = 125	Iodine = 127	
Cesium = 133	Barium = 137	?Di = 138	?Ce = 140	……	……	……	……
……	……	……	……	……	……	……	
……	……	?Er = 178	?La = 180	Tantalum = 182	Tungsten = 184	……	Osmium = 195, Iridium = 198 Platinum = 97, Gold = 197
Gold = 197	Mercury = 200	Thallium = 204	Lead = 207	Bismuth = 208	……	……	
……	……	……	Thorium = 231	……	Uranium = 240	……	……

"Mitya," asked his wife gently, "was he a good student, Akhmatov?"

"A fair student," he said and closed the door behind him.

Slowly he walked back to his writing desk and picked up another pen. He dipped it into the inkwell and leaned over the incompleted pages on ekasilicon. But thought would not come. He bit his underlip and stared at the pages. They were meaningless. He flung down the pen and picked up another but it would not move over the paper. He ran his hand through his hair, tugged at his beard, and stared at the wall of white cards.

In an empty place among them a face appeared, a young face. The eyes were black, the hair was black too, and curly. The nose was ordinary, and the lips were small and thin. It looked at Mendeleyev quietly from its blank space surrounded by the columns of white. It now seemed to be behind white bars. It was the face of the student Akhmatov.

He put down the pen. "For whom am I doing all this?" he said aloud, his glance taking in the roomful of books, magazines, and the white cards on the wall.

Before his mind appeared the vision of Bassargin and for a fleeting moment the image of Matvei the Night Watchman, and his wrinkled Marfa. A crowd appeared and an old mouzhik was saying, "We have nothing, but if you succeed, we shall all be rich."

Now a telega was moving through a village crowd.

"Give it to them, little boy!" someone was calling.

On the slope of a strong mountain, a tireless brown horse was pulling a telega.

In a small dark room, on a bed, a woman with narrow eyes held an ikon in her hand.

"I bless you, Mitenka," she said.

In a dismal cold hospital a worn exhausted girl lay on a bed coughing.

At a small flower shop, a woman, weeping softly, was holding out a bouquet.

"Take it," she said. "So long as I live you can have these free. From an orphan one does not take money."

A crowd of mouzhiks was gathered round.

"What keeps the sun up there, Uncle?"

"How do you get such crops, little father? Is it luck or is it talent?"

"Some day I will make crystal sunshine, Mitri Ivanitch. I feel it in my heart."

The train. An old mouzhik has Mendeleyev's arm.

"I've lost four sons in the war," he is saying. "Only Vasska is left. I want him to live. What shall I do?"

Then an old man with white locks appeared. And before him a brave man with a great chest.

"Once there lived and existed," says the old man to a little boy on his knee —"once there lived and existed a little boy with blue hair and strong brown shoes. . . ."

Then all the faces together were before him.

"Strength," says one. "Love," says another. "Science," says a voice. "Freedom," says another.

"We have nothing," repeats the mouzhik, "but if you succeed, we will all be rich."

"For whom am I doing all this?" again Mendeleyev spoke aloud.

The young dark face remained on the wall, in the space behind the bars.

Mendeleyev stood up. He walked out of his study and reached for his rubber boots, his overcoat, his hat. Outside, in the eleven o'clock St. Petersburg night, snow was falling.

6

A white wind was blowing through the streets. It came down at a cutting angle and hurt Mendeleyev's face as it swept across it. The streets were laden with snow. In the whipping lash of the wind the darkened city slept. One by one, lights in the windows continued to vanish.

Through the falling snow Mendeleyev strode rapidly along the sidewalk. No carriage was in sight.

For a long time he walked till he reached the home of the assistant registrar of students. He hadn't time to go in.

"Forgive me," he said, "but I'll wait out here. I must hurry. Please look up for me the home address of Sergei Akhmatov."

In a minute the corpulent Shostenitch returned to the porch. "It's number eleven Vinogradny Drive," he said. "He was not in school last term, and I have his address from the last registration. He'll be in the directory next time."

Mendeleyev nodded.

"*Bolshoye spaseebo*," he said. "A great thanks to you. Peaceful night."

"Peaceful night," replied the puzzled Shostenitch, watching the retreating figure striding through the snow.

At the home of the student Akhmatov Mendeleyev learned from the weeping woman that her son had been taken to the main police center.

"They won't let me see him," she wept.

"What was he printing exactly on those handbills?"

The weeping woman looked about the room apprehensively.

Then, stealthily, from under the hallway carpet she withdrew a folded circular and handed it to Mendeleyev.

"Students!" he read. "When Will We Be Free? All Meeting Permits Have Been Denied Us Everywhere. We Demand the Right of Self-Expression About Our Mother Country and How to Improve Our Lives. Do Not Give Up!"

He returned the circular to Madame Akhmatov.

"I'll do everything I can," he said, and turned to go.

The weeping woman made the sign of the cross over the doorway where Mendeleyev had stood.

In a few minutes, a carriage drawn by a black horse came through the snow.

"*Izvoschik!*" called Mendeleyev. "Driver! Eh!"

The *izvoschik* did not hear.

Mendeleyev ran through the snow and caught up with the carriage. The drowsy driver wakened and stopped the horse.

"Which way?" he asked.

Mendeleyev climbed in.

"To the main police center," he said.

The *izvoschik* was shocked. He turned and looked closely at Mendeleyev.

"This is no time to play tricks," he said. "Where will it be, a cafe, *ekh?*"

"Drive to the main police center."

The *izvoschik* shrugged his shoulders. He brushed the snow from his nose.

"I'll take you within one block of it," he said. "I don't want to have anything to do with them. I'm a peaceful man."

"Drive," said Mendeleyev.

The clock inside the main room was striking twelve as Mendeleyev, taking off his hat, opened the door.

Three uniformed gendarmes were dozing at their desks. None noticed his entry.

"I have come for the student Akhmatov"—Mendeleyev's voice had a quiet strength.

The three gendarmes suddenly sat up as though they had been struck. With mouths open they stared at the figure in the doorway.

In his great fur coat, Mendeleyev stood tall, broad-shouldered, erect. His great head with the mass of long blond hair reflected the yellow light of the lamp near the doorway. The broad forehead glistened and the blue eyes were narrowed. The high cheekbones too seemed forceful, adamant. He breathed deeply. The lively quick temperament was concealed, and in its place was a look of determined command. The usual stoop of the shoulders was missing now. He stood towering.

"I have come for the student Akhmatov," he repeated evenly.

The gendarme at the right desk stared at him in awe.

"It is Christ," he whispered.

The gendarme at the left desk glanced nervously at the clock. It stood at twelve. He could not detach his eyes from it.

"Twelve," he whispered. "Twelve."

At the center desk, a strong red-faced gendarme gazed intently at Mendeleyev.

"The student?" he asked.

Mendeleyev did not answer. He fixed all his attention on the man who had spoken.

"The student Akhmatov?" repeated the gendarme. "Well, yes. But who are you? Who speaks?"

Mendeleyev kept his eyes on the man. Now he took a step forward. The gendarme at the right crossed himself. The gendarme at the left gazed with fascination at the clock.

"Twelve," he mumbled again. *"Bozhe moi twelve."*

The red-faced gendarme put his hand to his ear, and scratched it.

"Akh," he said, *"ekh,* that is. May I be so bold. Who speaks?"

"A citizen of Russia," said Mendeleyev.

The red-faced gendarme spoke to the man on the right.

"Get the student," he said.

The gendarme disappeared through a doorway and in a minute returned with a thin, dark-faced youth. His black curly hair hung over his forehead. A dark line of dried blood stretched from his mouth down his chin.

"The Christ has come for you, little brother," whispered the gendarme leading young Akhmatov.

Akhmatov smiled at his former professor.

"Come," said Mendeleyev, and putting his arm about him, led him through the doorway.

The gendarme standing near by, crossed himself. The gendarme at the left desk tore his eyes away from the clock.

"Was it a dream?" he said.

The red-faced gendarme clawed at his ear.

"Perhaps it was the Tsar," he said jerkily. "Or a priest."

He shrugged his shoulders. "How is one to know?"

The gendarme at the right crossed himself again.

"It was the Christ," he said. "This was the Christ."

Out in the snow Mendeleyev picked up the student Akhmatov and carried him to the waiting *izvoschik*.

"*Ekh, bednyazhka*," said the driver. "The poor little one. What is it, my little one?"

Mendeleyev settled Akhmatov in the carriage, then got in next to him.

"What did they beat you with?" he asked.

"Wooden sticks," said Akhmatov. "Long round ones."

"All over?"

"Yes. And once on the face. They beat my arms they said so that I could never print circulars again. But I will print them."

Mendeleyev gave the *izvoschik* the address of Doctor Lentov.

Akhmatov had no broken bones. Lentov put him on the bed, applied compresses to his bruised body, then bandaged him. He gave him an injection and wrote down his address.

"I'll visit him tomorrow," he said to Mendeleyev. Then turning to the student, "You stay in bed," he said, "when you reach home."

"Yes," said Akhmatov. "*Khorosho*."

Mendeleyev carried him back to the carriage and drove him home.

His mother wept incessantly and wrung her hands.

"*Nitchevo*," consoled Akhmatov. "No broken bones."

Mendeleyev put him to bed.

"I must go now," he said. "Come to see me when you are well."

At home Feozva was sitting up waiting.

"Did you get him out?" she asked.

Mendeleyev nodded.

"Yes," he said. "But for how long I do not know."

"Go to bed," she said. "It is three o'clock."

He shook his head.

"I must finish something," he said, and entered his study.

Mendeleyev bent over his desk. He picked up the pen, and it wrote well. His hand moved quickly across the page.

"To discover ekasilicon one might well look among the compounds of titanium and zirconium. . . ."

Presently the article was finished. He looked up at the wall of white cards and spaces before him. He looked at the spaces intently. They remained blank. He walked to the wall with several white cards in his hand. On one he wrote "ekaboron" and pinned it up. On another he wrote "dviboron" and pinned this up, too. On a third he wrote "eka-aluminium" and on the fourth "ekasilicon."

He was tired. He stretched out on the couch and slept.

Chapter Twenty-two

The Planet Neptune

OTHER MEN had thought about a unity among the elements. Others had made schemes and plans tending to show relations among the fundamental substances of the universe.

In France, there had been De Chancourtois; in Germany, Lothar Meyer, in England, Newlands. None had dared challenge the then-accepted figures for the atomic weights of the elements, or change these figures to obtain a more logical scheme of unity. None had dreamed of prophesying the existence of undiscovered elements, or of giving their attributes in minute mathematical detail.

But Mendeleyev had done it.

His report containing the prophecies appeared in the *Journal of the Russian Chemical Society*, in the issue of January 7, 1871.

When the details of the predictions became known, chemists and physicists looked at each other and silently wondered. What was there in the character of a man who, having a successful career in science, suddenly risks his reputation in so bold and perhaps unnecessary a way?

Nothing like these predictions of undiscovered elements had ever been known in science. Nothing, except. . . .

Through the heavens, around the sun, swung the planet Uranus. The path of its motion caused astronomers deep concern. It did not move as they expected it to. It continually deviated from the orbit computed for it. All known influences had been taken into account, all the perturbations caused by the known planets had been considered, but these did not account for the strange heavenly life of the puzzling Uranus. Then, after many and long calculations, two scientists, the Englishman Adams and the youthful Frenchman Leverrier, independently predicted that an undiscovered planet was pulling gravitationally on Uranus. They concluded that the unknown planet should be found in the constellation of Aquarius. A telescopic search of this region of the heavens was begun by the German astronomer Galle, who followed the predictions of Leverrier. In England, Challis of Cambridge was making the search on the basis of the predictions of Adams. To Challis fell the first observation of the hitherto unknown planet, but he failed to recognize it until after Galle had announced the discovery on September 23, 1846. The new planet was named "Neptune." Its discovery was regarded as one of the overwhelming successes of Isaac Newton's theory of gravitation which was used in making the calculations of prophecy.

In Russia they wondered about Mendeleyev. Abroad, the few who bothered to think of the work of a Russian shrugged their shoulders.

2

On March 4, 1871, at the meeting of the Russian Chemical Society, Mendeleyev was presiding. This was because Zinin, the president, was not able to attend, and it was Mendeleyev's turn on the membership list to be the substitute.

On this occasion, a unique announcement was made by Menshutkin, the Society's director.

"Gentlemen," he said, "we have received an invitation from the English Chemical Society to enter into scientific exchange with them."

The members of the Russian Society were jubilant at the announcement. The advanced English were beginning to notice the groping Russian chemists who had organized only three years before. The learned English Society was the first foreign group to express a wish to become acquainted with the status of chemical knowledge of Russia and the original research of Russian chemists. Somebody in England was beginning to struggle through the *Zhurnal Russkovo Khimicheskovo Obshchestva*. Someone was beginning to notice the recurring names Zinin, Menshutkin, Beilstein, and—Mendeleyev. Eternally, Mendeleyev. Who were these primitive Russians? Who was this audacious prophet of the undiscovered terrestrial planets?

The Russian Chemical Society voted to send the bound volumes I and II of their work to their English colleagues.

Mendeleyev proposed that these volumes be also sent to the German, A. Strecker, who might include some abstracts in his *Yearbook of Chemistry*.

At the monthly meeting, on September 16, 1871, announcement was made that a communication had come from America. The Russian chemists beamed at each other. The Smithsonian Institution in a place called "Washington, D.C.," had sent some of its publications and was inviting scientific exchanges.

They eagerly voted to accept the invitation. After the meeting the professors crowded around the table to gaze at the American letter and look at the journals sent by the Smithsonian Institution. "U.S. Department of Agriculture," read one of the multilingual professors. "Reports for 1868 and 1869."

"What is this Washington, D.C.?" asked the young Barodin.

" 'Washington' is the city," said Frontovitch. " 'D.C.' I don't know. Maybe those were Washington's initials. What was his name?"

"Grigor," said someone. "This D.C. I don't know."

There was also a publication from England, *The Journal of the Chemical Society of London*, Series 2, Volume IX.

But the interest was in the American gesture now. England had the greater scientific prestige, but America was America. There was no other way to say it.

At the university in St. Petersburg, professors and students discussed Mendeleyev's predictions regarding the undiscovered elements. At the University of Moscow, too, the prophecy was debated at the meetings of scientific groups, and also at the university in Kazan. Even the students in the high schools had heard of the predictions and questioned their chemistry teachers. The teachers shrugged their shoulders.

"*Kto znayet?*" they said. "Who knows? If you're lucky even your roosters will lay eggs."

Mendeleyev's January, 1871, article prophesying the existence of undiscovered elements became more and more widely known abroad. In France, in Germany, in England, in a few places in America, shoulders were shrugged, but the article was read.

Mendeleyev worked. In his study at his university apartment, he sat up late into the night. No one disturbed him, and the hours were fertile, pregnant with ideas. At three or four in the morning he would lie down to sleep on the wooden sofa with the thin mattress. In the morning at nine he would waken and go to lecture at his ten o'clock class. Month after month and year after year the unbroken regime of work went on.

With all his scientific work he still found time to help students in their personal problems. As a moderator he sought to make life possible for the "radical hotheads."

"There exists everywhere a medium in things, determined by equilibrium," he wrote. "The Russian proverb says, 'Too much salt or too little salt is alike an evil.' It is the same in political and social relations."

He found time for his children, too. Dropping to the floor on all fours he would play a growling bear to the delight of shrieking, scampering Olga and Volodya. Cagily, Volodya would attack the great grisly bear, and then tiny puffy Olga would come forward to battle.

For his niece Nadezhda Mendeleyev found time, also. In 1872 she finished high school and then one day came to chat with her uncle.

"I want to study art now thoroughly, Dmitri Ivanovitch," she said. "What do you think of that?"

Mendeleyev was pleased. The fair-haired Nadezhda had always looked flowering, refreshing. Now, at seventeen, she was radiant.

"Why, yes," he said, "why certainly. A woman is born for art. And music."

"I want to know everything," said Nadezhda. "I want to be a cultured person. To know everything."

Mendeleyev put down his pen.

"Well, now, look at you, little mother," he said. "One person can't know everything. You must unravel yourself, Nadenka. You can be cultured with your art. There is enough in that. Even a carpenter is cultured—if he is a good carpenter."

Nadezhda smiled. She liked to listen to her uncle's deep, resonant voice. She treasured the serious manner with which he considered her problems. He gestured with his hands, and let his mobile features play, and reasoned about everything.

In the spring of 1872, and every spring after that, Mendeleyev sent his family to the Boblovo estate. Ekaterina and Nadezhda would spend the summer at his university apartment and Nadezhda would go to art school.

Occasionally a student would come to Mendeleyev's home at night, for advice. Somehow the students preferred to come at night, for then a discussion seemed to lie on a more human plane. Always Mendeleyev advised more devotion to work, less side-slipping, more purpose and concentration. Always he counseled that a man ignore futile rumors about himself.

Mendeleyev always deplored hearing evil spoken of anyone and he would threaten to terminate the conversation on such occasions.

"It is not good for your character, to speak evil of him," he would say.

This was his attitude toward his colleagues as well as the students. However, with a sensitive, bewildered person he would soften the blow with some gesture or remark.

"Put a good word in occasionally even for the devil," he would say. "You never know whom you may please."

Occasionally Feozva became restive with their quiet life. "We never go anywhere together. To the theater for example."

Mendeleyev held a cup of tea and a slice of bread.

"I must work," he said.

"But the theater—for relaxation. . . ."

He shook his head.

"No," he said. "Why should one seek diversion from without? The theater —too much of it—fills life with trifles and foolishness."

"But we practically never go," said Feozva, sitting down on the chair at the table. "Once in a while, surely. . . ."

"Once in a while we do go," he said. "To the university dinner and functions. Every February 8, for example. But—you know I must work."

"We are married," said Feozva softly. "And yet it seems we aren't. Are you married to science or are you married to me?"

"To both," said Mendeleyev. "Unless that is bigamy. In that case—to science."

He set the cup of cooled tea down on the table, and placed the bread on a saucer. Then he turned and walked into his writing room.

3

Mendeleyev's scientific work went on. In August, 1871, at the third annual meeting of Russian Naturalists held at Kiev, he presented five research reports. At the Chemical Society meeting in October, he presented another paper. In November Mendeleyev, always devoted to the Chemistry Society of which he had been the principal founder, announced that the Physics Society, through its president, Petrushevsky, was seeking closer association with the chemists. There was the suggestion of publishing a joint journal. Other news was of interest. The French Society—the Paris Academy of Sciences—was reported as another of the foreign groups seeking exchange with the Russians. The Paris Academy requested the Russian journals. A certain audacious Russian prophecy had been reported somewhere. The Russian chemists were jubilant—the Paris Academy was an outstanding scientific group—so they sent their journals and in return asked for the *Comptes Rendus*. The Russian scientists, reluctant to thrust themselves forward, waited for invitations of exchange. They waited for recognition. When it came, they smiled.

"How is it, Professor Mendeleyev?" said the research man Berlikov after the meeting. "Have you regretted your predictions? Perhaps your plan of unity is good—but not quite that good."

Mendeleyev shrugged his shoulders. "We shall see," he said. "I had no choice but to express my thought."

4

In the years 1871 to 1875 an avalanche of research and written work flowed from Professor Dmitri Ivanovitch Mendeleyev.

There were papers on "The Periodic Law of the Chemical Elements," "On Crystallization and Water Trapped during the Process"; "The Atomic

Weight of Yttrium"; "The Temperature of the Upper Layers of the Earth's Atmosphere."

In addition, another type of investigation attracted his attention. In the year 1875 a strong wave of interest in spiritualism was sweeping over Russia. Tables were being tilted in numerous salons and apparitions of many kinds were welcomed from "the other world."

Among the professors of the university who were strong believers in spiritualist phenomena were N. P. Wagner and A. M. Butelerov. Together with their friend A. N. Aksakov they published articles in several journals setting forth their beliefs. Mendeleyev offered to the Physics and Chemical Societies to investigate the alleged phenomena under controlled laboratory conditions.

The investigations were undertaken. The "mediums" Blavadskaya and Bredif agreed to perform and Aksakov brought the famous Petti boys from London.

The séances first took place in Mendeleyev's rooms with a presiding commission composed of the scientists Krayevitch, Petrushevsky, Borgman, and others. Also invited were the intellectual sponsors, Butelerov, Wagner, and Aksakov.

During the séance the Petti brothers brought a musical box which they wanted to have play while they performed.

"It's for the mood," said the older one.

The lights were put out, the music began to play, and some peculiar sounds soon emanated from somewhere.

Mendeleyev lit a lamp and began to examine the Petti brothers. The younger one's face was moist with droplets.

"Spiritual droplets," someone whispered.

Mendeleyev brought up a tray of chemicals and test tubes, and rapidly tested the drops on the face of the younger Petti. The audience waited in silence.

In a few minutes Mendeleyev raised his head.

"Saliva," he said, and wrote an entry into a notebook.

At later séances Mendeleyev provided all materials requested by the mediums—tables, slates, and jars. He insisted on being near by, on lighting the lamp when he wanted to, and on making physical and chemical tests on the spot. He made entries in the notebook and had them witnessed by the audience.

In all, nineteen séances took place through the entire year, and then Mendeleyev wrote a book of 382 pages called *Information for Critical Judgment of Spiritualism:* "Spiritualist phenomena, so-called, operate best at night, or in the dark, when deception can't be so readily noticed. . . .

"The only thing there is, is the trance—if not faked—and even this is of interest only for study from the point of view of medical men. . . ."

In the introduction he had written, "Whatever sum of money may be forthcoming from the sale of this work is hereby designated for the construction of a balloon and in general for the study of meteorological phenomena of the upper layers of the atmosphere."

Later, at a lecture on his findings, he said, "The most all-penetrating spirit, before which will open the possibility of tilting not tables, but planets, is the spirit of free human inquiry. Believe only in that."

5

Then late one night in November, 1875, while Mendeleyev was writing his pages there came a loud knock on the door of his apartment. He was about to rise when he heard Feozva leave her room and go to the door. Someone was running down the hallway to Mendeleyev's study. He waited. The door flew open, the man had not even knocked. It was Professor Menshutkin, Mendeleyev's friend and colleague. He was breathless, grinning, wild-eyed, and waving a journal.

"Mitya!" he exclaimed. "Mitya! Mitya! They have found it! They have found your terrestrial Neptune! They have found eka-aluminium. *Akh Bozhe moi!* It's perfect. Perfect prediction."

Mendeleyev stood up.

"*Akh*," he said. "*Akh*, God. I've been waiting a long time. Four years. . . ."

Menshutkin embraced him.

"You great fellow, you," he said. "Look. In this report. They don't say it. But I'm almost positive. I think they're going to call it 'gallium.' Here—read."

Mendeleyev read the article giving the proceedings of the Paris Academy of Sciences. It was before this scientific organization that the discovery of the new element had been announced.

"They are not sure of the density," mused Mendeleyev. "I must write to them. Yes, it is really my 'eka-aluminium.' "

"Of course," said Menshutkin. "*Akh*, but this is news. *Akh*, what a confirmation! You must report at our next meeting."

The discovery had been made by the French chemist Lecoq de Boisbaudran.

De Boisbaudran had done much work in spectrum analysis. One day, while flaming a zinc blende from the Pyrenees, he observed a brilliant violet line in the spectroscope. This color fell at the place marked 417. The length of these violet waves of light was thus 417 millionths of a millimeter. De Boisbaudran knew that this was a new line. The French scientist, believing that he had found a new element, began the investigation of the substance hidden within the zinc blende. He separated out something and recognized its difference from zinc, and from cadmium and indium, as well as the other companions of zinc. This, too, he did by the spectroscope, matching and comparing the various glowing lines. Then De Boisbaudran began to perform chemical tests on the new substance. He determined as many properties as he could. It was difficult work, for he had been able to extract only a very small amount of the new element as yet. He tried to determine the atomic weight, the weight of 1 cubic centimeter of the material, the boiling point, reactions with other substances. . . . De Boisbaudran and two of his colleagues remembered something. They got out a Russian journal of 1871, and turned the pages. With a Russian-French dictionary the three Frenchmen went to work on the article by D. Mendeleyev. Late at night they sat staring at two columns on a sheet of paper. In one column they had listed the already determined properties of De Boisbaudran's new element. In a parallel column they had just finished listing the properties of the predicted eka-aluminium. The Frenchmen stared. The match was very close.

"*Mon Dieu!*" said one. "*Mon Dieu!* But he is some fellow, this Russian!"

His colleague reached into a glass cabinet and produced a bottle of champagne. He poured three bubbling glasses.

"To this Russian," he said. "To this Mendeleyev."

Lecoq de Boisbaudran named the new element "gallium" in honor of the ancient name of his country. But it was Mendeleyev's "eka-aluminium."

After the excited talk with Menshutkin, Mendeleyev sat down and wrote out more properties to be expected from the element eka-aluminium, or gallium. These, too, were confirmed. And Lecoq de Boisbaudran admitted a mistake in the value of the density. Now there was no question that it was in fact the predicted eka-aluminium.

The Frenchmen poured more champagne.

"To this Mendeleyev," they said. "A man!"

Now almost the entire world of science read Mendeleyev's old article. He had predicted other elements. The shoulders now did not shrug.

At Princeton University, a gray-haired man sat staring at a scientific report.

"Mendeleyev," he said. "I wonder how he pronounces that. Mendeleyev. So it has been found. Well, well, well."

He turned in his chair and spoke to a young woman at a desk.

"Miss Jackson," he said. "You better fill out an order card for that Russian magazine mentioned in this footnote. Get it on a regular order. Get all the issues from now on. And the back issues."

He rose to enter the laboratory, then stopped for a moment.

"And, Miss Jackson," he said. "You better buy me a dictionary. A Russian-English dictionary. Yes. And a Russian grammar. A good one."

The young woman stared.

"Russian?" she said. "You mean Russian?"

The gray-haired man gave a look of hopelessness.

"Yes," he said. "I'm afraid so. One has to keep up in one's field."

Chapter Twenty-three

Baku, Nizhny Novgorod, America

It was 1876 and Russia was suffering a crisis in oil. In a land of vast subterranean seas of oil, a shortage of the fuel was rapidly developing. In the region of the Black Sea and the Caspian, marsh gas was seeping in abundance from the earth. The people in the immediate vicinity carried the crude product away for lighting and warming their homes. The excess was poured during holidays onto the Caspian and set afire to burn with mountainous blue flame.

But no significant oil-well developments existed, no refineries worth the name, no scientific techniques of extraction and purification. Much of the vast Caucasian oil regions had come into the possession of a few landowners who knew nothing of scientific extraction of oil and its related products and who, furthermore, refused to develop these natural resources. They were awaiting guarantees of high-price purchase by the government and the people of Russia.

The members of the Russian Chemical Society were worried. Dmitri Mendeleyev stayed up later during the nights. Among the written pages overflowing his desk now appeared pages with chemical formulas concerning oil products. On the pages also appeared drawings of installations, refineries, schemes depicting extraction processes.

"Russia's eventual modernized culture must be based on dominion over nature's gifts," he wrote. "The proper usage of the wealthy naphtha seas will eventually alleviate in a measure the poverty of the people. Power over nature will bring leisure for a creative life."

The government learned that Mendeleyev knew what to do about the oil situation, so he was sent to the Caucasus to make a tour of inspection, a study, and a report.

"After the Caspian, Black Sea, and the Caucasus analysis, the government wants you to go to Amerika," he was told, "to report upon the best methods of working the oil wells."

He packed a suitcase and set out to explore the oil regions of southern Russia. Then would come America. Mendeleyev was now forty-two years old.

Time was passing. It was necessary to do many things—quickly. He hurried southward to Baku.

Mendeleyev took samples of the oil, made measurements, studied the soil, sounded the depths, sighted the courses, drew charts and wrote entries in black notebooks.

"When a pipe line has been laid from Baku to the Black Sea, then the entire mass of the Baku naphtha will furnish safe illuminating oils of immense application. . . . At present pyronaphtha is hardly manufactured at all, and we, as well as the whole world, are consuming the unsafe kerosene."

2

On the return trip to St. Petersburg he sailed up the Volga on a tiny steamboat with a huge clanging bell. He leaned forward at the wooden rail as the tiny steamboat suf-suffed past Saratov where Maria and Ivan had once lived, past the hillside and the rock with the name of Stenka Razin, the Russian Robin Hood, past Kazan of the middle Volga.

At Nizhny Novgorod he disembarked to see the Fair.

Kirghiz, Turkmen, Georgians, Great Russians, Ukrainians, fair-haired, dark, narrow, and tall—all the two hundred tribes of Russia were there. And the peoples of the Orient, the Chinese, Hindus, and the varieties of Mongols. Trading, selling, cajoling, brow-beating, thieving, loving, displaying their wares, informing, threatening, persuading—in groups, in masses, and in twos. Rugs, carpets, trees, silks, purses, parrots, shawls, robes, human hair, wild animals—all was there for exchange, for sale, for show.

But the greatest attraction of all lay to the left. In the milling human stream Mendeleyev was carried leftward with the crowd. There, on a high platform, a great old man with white locks held them entranced. The sturdy old man was fashioning articles out of glass. With a mighty breath he blew through a glowing tube of glass and in a twinkling fashioned a huge swan. The crowd gasped. Now he blew once more, into another tube, and suddenly made a flower, with petals.

Mendeleyev stared unbelieving. His heart stood still. Only one man in Russia could blow glass like that. He forced his way through the crowd, it resisted, but he pressed forward and came through.

Now the old man rested. As though looking into space he came down the stairs of the platform and stepped behind a curtain. Another act went on in his place on the stage—a younger man was blowing figures of glass.

Mendeleyev stepped behind the curtain. The old man sat before him, resting; he did not see him.

Mendeleyev looked at the aged figure in front of him.

"Timofei," he said. "Timofei."

The blind man was startled. His body stiffened. The great chest held the breath. Slowly he stretched out his hands. His unseeing eyes were fixed on space.

"Who is it?" he said. "Who?"

"Mendeleyev. Mitya Mendeleyev."

"Mitya," said Timofei. "Mitya, take my hands."

Mendeleyev came forward and took the old hands. Tears were flowing down his cheeks.

"Your eyes," said Mendeleyev. "Timofei, your eyes."

Timofei held Mendeleyev's hands tightly and drew him closer. Slowly his hands touched Mendeleyev's shoulders, then his beard, the cheekbones and nose, and then the great wide forehead.

A quiet smile came over Timofei's face.

"Mitya," he said. "You have grown. You are a strong man."

Mendeleyev looked closely at Timofei's eyes.

Timofei felt the glance.

"I have seen much sorrow over the face of Russia," he said. "The Lord thought I had seen enough."

There was a silence. Then Timofei spoke.

"I have heard your name mentioned," he said. "Once or twice, through the years. Your work must be good, Mitya. You have kept your faith with us."

"I am making the effort," Mendeleyev said.

Timofei told of the death of the strannik, then of the death of his beloved wife, Nadezhda.

Mendeleyev asked about Timofei's son.

"I had heard that a boy was born," he said.

"Yes," said Timofei. "He is on the platform now, blowing objects of glass. Some day he will blow better than I do. He is an artist. And his heart is great with love."

"Timofei," said Mendeleyev, "come and live at my country home. Your time for resting has come."

But Timofei shook his head.

"The time of resting shall come unannounced," he said. "In a few days, when the Fair ends, Stepan and I will go back over Russia."

Mendeleyev was silent.

"Russia needs you, Mitenka," said Timofei.

Soon Stepan came down from the platform and stood before Mendeleyev. He had a great chest. He was strong and his eyes were clear like his father's had once been.

Baku, Nizhny Novgorod, America

"Good-by, Mitenka," said Timofei. "It is my turn with the blowing glass. Good-by, God guard over you."

Stepan led his father to the platform.

The next day Mendeleyev packed his suitcases and started for America, to visit the Philadelphia World's Fair in which the Americans were celebrating the one hundredth anniversary of the declaration of their independence. Specifically, he would study the oil techniques in Pennsylvania. It was June, 1876.

In France he boarded the vessel *Labrador*.

3

The ship plunged downward between mounds of green water, and suddenly rose again with a shudder. Then down again and in a moment once more tore itself violently out of the depths of the sea. A small thin man stood on deck. He did not feel well. Every day, immediately after breakfast, he appeared on deck. Silently, grimly, he struggled against the sea. Mendeleyev was sorry for him.

"*Bednyazhka*," [the poor little one] he said.

The pale little man glanced at Mendeleyev. He knew that the big hairy Russian was sympathizing.

"Don't you feel anything?" said the man.

Mendeleyev did not understand what the Englishman said. But he understood the Englishman—at the moment. He went downstairs and came back with lemons. He sliced one and offered the man a piece. The Englishman took the lemon and ate it.

"In Roshia," said Mendeleyev, "limon ees good."

Mendeleyev stood in the tearing wind. He breathed deeply, as his narrowed eyes shielded themselves against the streaming cold air.

"*Akh*, how relaxing," he said in Russian. "How relaxing."

One day the Englishman was suddenly well. He strode smilingly on the tossing deck searching for the big man of the lemons. He found him, way up front, peering westward.

"Good morning."

Mendeleyev nodded. He smiled and patted his companion on the back.

"Ees much good—limon," he said.

The Englishman laughed.

"By the way," he said. "You are the great Mendeleyev, who predicted the element gallium."

Mendeleyev brightened.

"Gallium," he said. "You science?"

"I'm an engineer," said the Englishman. "J. G. R. Russell. But I know about chemistry. Captain Sanglie told me you were Mendeleyev. Well, well, well."

Mendeleyev nodded. "Ees nice Capitan," he said.

"They're talking about you in England," said Russell. "All the technical societies are sending for the journals of your chemical society."

Mendeleyev noted many things about the ship. He learned that its normal speed was 13 knots, the screw—of diameter 5.68 centimeters—was making 58 revolutions per minute, the coal was being consumed at the rate of 2500 kilograms per hour. He wrote this information down in his black notebook.

Then one day, as he stood at the front of the pitching ship, a dark, diffused mass appeared far ahead. He came forward to the rail, his eyes on the distant mass.

"Amerika," he said.

4

This was the land of America. Many things were being done well here.

In northwestern Pennsylvania the presence of oil underground had long been known, even as Russia had known of its existence in the region of the Caspian Sea and Baku. In Pennsylvania, similarly, the amount of oil that came to the surface had not been great, and so in 1858 E. L. Drake, of the Seneca Oil Company, sought an underground reservoir of the precious illuminant. Drake struck oil at a depth of sixty-nine feet, on August 27, 1859. At that time Mendeleyev had been studying in western Europe, and the news of the spectacular American achievement reached him there. The enterprising Americans were actually bringing up ten barrels of oil a day. News of Drake's strike started a "flowing gold" rush and within three years the production of oil had become one of the leading American industries. Over much of the land wooden towers suddenly sprang up from the ground, and the oil rose up the pipes in an endless stream. Mendeleyev planned to go first to Titusville in Pennsylvania, then to travel over the entire state, and study the role of the Alleghenies in the origination of Drake's well. The Sherman Well at Oil Creek would be worth seeing too, and also every technical process used by the Americans.

But America was much more than its oil wells. There was said to be an elevated railway in New York! In 1869 the country had been spanned by railroad. This could be done in Russia, too. In the very city of New York there was reputed to be a gigantic railroad station with several stories, and a dome reminiscent of Russia's churches. This Grand Central Depot would be a phenomenon to see, with its many parallel trains puffing and chugging in the colossal tunnellike interior. Mendeleyev had been told not to miss the giant department store of Lord and Taylor, which was five stories high. Almost anything could be bought in this store. The question was how to find "Broadway and 20th Street" in the large, widespread New York. It was said that one costume of silk clothes for a lady cost three hundred dollars, in this new store. Dollars, not roubles. That would be equivalent to the net profit made by twelve mouzhiks working one year each.

City Hall Park was also a place to see. Cars were pulled along railroad tracks by pairs of horses; carriages, carts, people promenading, huge widely separated buildings between which lived the park itself—all this one must see. And exclusive Fifth Avenue where men in top hats, dark coats, and checkered trousers gallantly escorted bustled ladies with parasols. Also—somewhere in this city—was Stewart's store, the largest retail enterprise of all.

For Volodya and little Olga at home Mendeleyev would have to see the American Museum of Natural History and the Metropolitan Museum of Art.

But one could not see everything. There was no time to seek out the great Vassar College, an institution of higher learning for women! That would really be something to see. And yet Mendeleyev himself had already established chemistry courses for women. It was the first time in Russia's history that women had been accorded such recognition of equality with men.

Way out, in the American West, new sunlit land beckoned enterprising Americans. In Russia, no new sunlit lands beckoned anywhere. Siberia was the only possible region of full-scale expansion, but to win Siberia against its deadly cold would be a task of more than Herculean dimensions.

In Pennsylvania, he would visit the foundries and steel mills of Pittsburgh. Russia was far outclassed in this domain. But she had iron. And she had people. Would the government actually do something, would the iron be taken out of the Urals, would the coal be taken out of the Donetz Basin? It must be done and on a huge scale, comparable to the hugeness of the land and the needs of the people. If he studied the Bessemer process of making steel, would it be adopted in Russia?

The financial panic of the previous year had caused wide contrasts between rich and poor suddenly to loom on the national scene: on the one hand, soup kitchens came into being, while on the other, elegant parties were given in New York and shining carriages rolled through Central Park. In Russia no startling contrast between poverty and affluence suddenly came to life—it was always there.

In food problems, too, the American people had found ingenious solutions. The Russians, by and large, ate from hand to mouth, but in America they were able to store food for long periods by canning milk, packing meat, and bottling liquids. The Americans were even working on machines to heat small chickens out of eggs. In Russia, the sentimental mouzhiks permitted the hens to get the chickens out of the eggs in their own way.

But Mendeleyev's main objective was the study of the technique of oil production. There was plenty of oil in both countries, but the Americans knew the answers to most of the questions of surveying, drilling, refining, storing, and shipping.

As he gazed now at the approaching American shore he tingled with excitement.

5

Together with the Englishman Russell, Mendeleyev saw many of the things in New York that he had thought about on the ship.

As he strode along with the diminutive Russell people gazed in astonishment. First of all, Russell practically had to trot to keep up with the long-legged Mendeleyev. Mendeleyev could not slow his pace—somehow the attempt upset his mental equilibrium. Then, of course, there was his appearance—the massive hairy head and the great beard. His peculiar loose jacket and rough gray trousers were also unusual on Fifth Avenue. Moreover, in the summer sun Mendeleyev did not wear his hat, but carried it. The slight breeze through his hair raised it up and down as he hurried along. In addition to all this, he cracked *semochkee* loudly as he strode along.

That evening Mendeleyev was introduced to another side of the American picture. In front of a certain building he saw a veiled woman drop a baby into a wicker crib and hurry away. In a moment the door opened and a nun appeared. She picked up the baby and took it inside. Mendeleyev was amazed.

"Amerika," he said. "Much machine teknika. This small children, lady leave to vash? Like machine teknika?"

Russell shook his head.

"No, not to wash," he said. "This is a Foundling Hospital."

Mendeleyev did not understand.

"Small child no papa," said Russell.

Mendeleyev stood pensive.

"In Russia?" said Russell.

Mendeleyev shrugged his shoulders.

"In Roshia," he said, "no papa, nu, no papa. Bot ees always mama."

They walked along the darkening street.

6

Later in the evening, at the Continental Hotel, Russell introduced Mendeleyev to Gerard, the manager.

"This is Professor Mendeleyev," he said.

The men shook hands.

Gerard was elated.

"I heard about your work from a friend of mine, a college professor," he said. "That was remarkable about those peas. How did you ever think of it? And from the green ones, sometimes come the yellow ones, don't they? I think three are green and then one would be yellow. And in the second generation would there be more yellow ones?" Gerard smiled at Mendeleyev's blank face. "I've forgotten," he said.

The man talked so rapidly that Mendeleyev had not understood a single word. But he was a good man, one could see that. Mendeleyev smiled.

"Ees much nice," he said, pointing to the spacious and clean hotel interior.

Gerard took him by the arm and led him into the dining room.

"I have eat," said Mendeleyev, protesting.

"I would like you to meet someone," Gerard said, bowing slightly.

Russell was following behind Mendeleyev.

At a long sparkling table a great many women and men were chatting, laughing, and eating. A solid paunchy man at the head rose to greet Gerard and his companions.

"Senator," said Gerard proudly, "this is the great Mendeloo, the great French monk who discovered the heredity of peas. A professor friend of mine predicts his work will be world-famous. I have the honor. Monk Mendeloo, meet the Honorable Senator J. R. McAuliffe of the great state of New York."

Mendeleyev, comprehending nothing, shook hands with the genial Senator.

Russell squirmed uncomfortably, and slowly ran his hand over his cheek.

Senator McAuliffe beamed.

"I am delighted," he said.

He turned to his dinner companions. The senator tinkled his spoon against his glass.

"Ladies and gentlemen!" he said. "Rarely does it come in a man's life to make such an announcement. We have here a man about whom I admit I know nothing. However, Mr. Gerard informs me that his friend, a noted college professor, predicts that the work of this man whom we are privileged to meet tonight will some day be world-famous. Friends, we have here the man who discovered heredity and environment!"

The Senator's guests applauded and looked at each other in awe.

A tall dark woman at the end of the table said,

"My God! James Darwin himself!"

Up and down the table the murmur ran.

"Darwin," someone said. "Elsa says it's James Darwin the English heredity and environment scientist. How exciting to meet him."

Senator McAuliffe again tinkled his glass with the silver spoon. The diners quieted down.

He spoke in careful measured tones, "I give you the one and only Professor Mendelyou, the great monk of the European continent, our neighbor across the wide benevolent ocean. I give you the monk of monks, Mendelyou of the green peas and the yellow ones and every color under God's sun. Professor, we are at your feet. Speak, good monk!"

The audience applauded violently.

"It's not Darwin," the whisper went up and down. "They say he missed the boat," someone explained. "Wait till I tell Fred," said a voice. "If there is anything to know about peas, this is the man, so help me," a voice whispered. "They say that these very peas here on the plate are his," said an elderly woman.

Mendeleyev was in complete confusion. Imploringly he turned to Russell. The little Englishman was standing as though frozen. His lower lip was in his mouth and his upper teeth were tightly closed over it.

"Vot ees?" said Mendeleyev to him.

Russell glanced at the hushed audience.

"Speak," he whispered to Mendeleyev. "Say something. Anything. You know, 'ees nice Amerika.' Say anything. Volga, borsch, vodka. Say 'limon'!"

Mendeleyev did not understand; but the people seemed kind and generous so he spoke.

"Ees nice Amerika," he said. "Roshia science, Amerika science—much frend. Roshia porson lov all Amerika porson. Ees free science in all vorld. Ees hope vorld free every porson like free science. Ees vorld peece. My heart ees lov you."

The people around the table applauded.

Russell patted Mendeleyev on the back.

Gerard, the hotel manager, came forward to press his hand. The Senator said something to him, and Mendeleyev bowed.

"I'm going to get the reporters," said Gerard hurrying out of the dining room. "Mendeloo and the peas, this happens once in a lifetime."

Russell grabbed Mendeleyev's arm.

"Come on," he said. "We've got to run for it."

Mendeleyev did not understand, but in their room upstairs, Russell packed furiously. He packed Mendeleyev's things as well as his own.

"Oh, God," he kept murmuring. "Oh, God."

Mendeleyev was stupefied.

"Vy ees go?" he said. "I speak not good? Ees come gendarme?"

But Russell continued packing.

"You speak good," he said hurriedly. "Ees good speak. But we go quick. Ees come much reporter. Much bother professor. Ees please pack your things, for Christ's sake. Don't just stand there!"

Mendeleyev packed.

Russell brushed aside the assistant manager, "The professor has been suddenly called away; he has to make a small discovery," he said.

7

Russell established headquarters for himself and Mendeleyev at the Jefferson Hotel. And now he was careful not to introduce Mendeleyev to too many people. When he did make introductions he always said something like this:

"You know about chemistry, Mr. Jones. Well, here we have a chemist, the famous Russian chemist, Professor Mendeleyev. Some people confuse him with someone called Mendel who works with peas. But no, he is a Russian chemist. Professor Mendeleyev, may I present Mr. Jones."

Sometimes this served to establish the idea that Mendeleyev was a chemist, but usually people preferred to believe that he was someone called Mendel who worked with peas.

Among the engineers and chemists of Russell's acquaintance however, the situation was different. Most of them had heard about the Russian Mendeleyev, and there were many invitations to dinners and meetings. He accepted only one or two, for he was busy studying New York. And New York was busy studying him. Each gaped at the other.

He wandered through the department stores and bought toys for his children. Invariably crowds collected about him. He always bought the best things, though he complained with his *"tse tse tse"* at the high prices.

The first night in the Jefferson Hotel Russell retired early, and Mendeleyev sat down to write. First he prepared charts and columns dealing with oil questions—the things that he would have to find out in Pennsylvania. After that, he wrote a paper on the difference in composition of air at different altitudes; then a study of the temperature of the atmosphere high above the ground.

At four o'clock he drew his bed a little further from the window and went to sleep.

When Russell awoke at eight, he stared unbelieving at the great mound of written pages piled on the little writing desk. He picked up a few and examined them. Vainly he searched for at leat one word that he could comprehend in this mountainous mass of Russian script. Finally, he thought that he recognized the word "limon," but he wasn't really sure about it. Mendeleyev was snoring regularly and deeply, like a rumbling volcano, or a steam engine laboring under a heavy load. Russell dressed and went to breakfast, then out into the city on his engineering business.

When he returned at ten, Mendeleyev was still sleeping in exactly the same position.

There was a timid knock on the door, and Russell opened it. It was the maid.

"Cheerio," said Russell.

"I came to clean before," said the maid, "but this, er, man, was sleeping. It frightened me a little. Sounded like he might explode."

"Come on in and clean," Russell said.

"What if I wake him?"

Russell nodded. "That's what I want to see," he said. "Go on and clean. And do a jolly good job of it."

The maid began to make Russell's bed, then she dusted and swept. She tiptoed around. Russell sat on his bed watching. The maid grew bolder and pulled the bureau around. She swept under Mendeleyev's bed. Finally, just as she was leaving, the broom accidentally struck the water pitcher on the bureau and it fell to the floor with a crash. Both Russell and the maid stared at Mendeleyev. Nothing whatever happened. The same snores came in and out and the whiskers rose and fell.

The maid looked at Russell in profound wonder. He shrugged his shoulders.

"Must be sleepy," he said.

Mendeleyev woke up suddenly at eleven o'clock.

"*Akh*," he said. "Ees nice sleep in Noo York."

"I'm glad, old chap," said Russell. "I tried to keep everything quiet for you."

"Tea," said Mendeleyev. "Ees now tree hot cops tea. With booter-brod."

Russell barely perceptibly twisted his face. His right hand was drumming on the little table at the head of the bed.

"How about caviar?" he asked.

Mendeleyev lifted his eyebrows with pleasure.

"*Akh!*" he commented. "Ees like hom!"

Russell stood up. "That's our specialty," he said. "Make everybody feel like ees hom."

He went to the door.

"I'll see what I can do," he said. "The maid likes you. Three hot cops of tea with booter and bread, and caviar."

"Ees nice," said Mendeleyev. "After those I eat brake fast."

8

Mendeleyev was delighted at the fact that Russell planned to return to Europe on the same ship with him. That is, after Mendeleyev returned from Pennsylvania.

"I'll be at the same hotel," Russell said. "Maybe the same room."

"I much happy you go same sheep," said Mendeleyev.

"*Au revoir*," said Russell.

"*Au revoir*," said Mendeleyev as the conductor bellowed something at the people near the train on the ferry.

Mendeleyev had tried to buy a third-class ticket for the train.

"Ees always feel gooder," he said. "Much frend people."

Russell had bought him the most uncomfortable seat he could get.

"This will be all right," he had said. "A jolly stinkhole, old chap."

On the train Mendeleyev gazed through the window at the water flowing past.

In half an hour he stood up to examine his fellow passengers. In turn, they examined him.

Ten minutes later he stopped the passing conductor.

"One minoot," said Mendeleyev, lifting his finger.

The conductor waited. Mendeleyev opened a suitcase and took out a teakettle. The conductor stared.

"Ees vader," said Mendeleyev. "Much boil. You please? Vill give you teep."

The conductor stood as though stunned. He looked confused.

An old man in a neat blue suit stood up.

"Get it for him," he said. "What's it to you?"

The conductor shrugged his shoulders. He took the teakettle and, somewhat embarrassed, walked through the car.

Mendeleyev stood up and bowed to the old man.

Fifteen minutes later the conductor returned with the teakettle, steam issuing from the nozzle. Every head in the car turned as the teakettle went past. Then people stood up to see better.

Mendeleyev took the teakettle.

"Anything else?" said the conductor. "You know, like a stove, and flour to make bread . . ."

"Ees not now," said Mendeleyev. From his suitcase, he took three glasses and a lemon, and cubes of white sugar. The people were standing up staring, their eyes and mouths wide open. Mendeleyev looked up at the old man in the blue suit and nodded to him.

"Ees ready," said Mendeleyev. "Please."

The old man smiled and came over. Mendeleyev took out a cube of black tea, and peeled off a layer. He made strong tea in a little green pot and poured the old man a glass giving him two cubes of sugar.

"Limon?" asked Mendeleyev.

"Never use it," said the old man.

Mendeleyev poured another glass and looked up inquiringly at the conductor. The conductor shook his head.

"He can't take it," explained the old man. "He works here."

Mendeleyev shrugged his shoulders.

"In Roshia ees dreenk," he said. "Vork and dreenk."

Now Mendeleyev looked at the other faces. A redheaded boy with freckles stepped tentatively forward. Mendeleyev encouraged him, and poured him a glass of tea and gave him two cubes of sugar. Then a young woman, giggling a little, stepped forward, too. Then a fat lady with a Napoleonic hat, and two sturdy men, who appeared to be brothers.

"You vait for glasses," he said.

Then he passed out small flat rolls that Russell had bought for him, and pieces of yellow cheese. The people stood in the aisle and drank, and ate. The red-haired boy had a difficult time with his glass. It was too hot for his hands. Mendeleyev broke off two pieces from a roll, and placing one on each side of the redheaded boy's glass he made them stick. The boy held the glass through these insulating pieces.

The old man in the blue suit sat next to Mendeleyev and talked to him about New York, and asked about Russia. The people strained to hear, and smiled at each other when Mendeleyev spoke. His soft resonant voice carried through the car. He always spoke as though saying simultaneously, "And what do you think? How does it seem to you?"

"Ve do not have many teknika," said Mendeleyev. "Ve can have, ees not right?"

The old man nodded his head. "Why not?" he said. "Now you take our own case. I remember twenty years ago there wasn't an iron wheel spinning around here, worth mentioning. You wouldn't see smoke out of a steel-mill chimney for hundreds of miles. It's a question of resources and desire I would say."

Gradually more and more questions were being asked about Russia. Most of them Mendeleyev understood, and answered as well as he could. About the people, how they worked, what they ate, what was this Siberia, how is the Tsar?

Suddenly the train stopped at a station.

"Ve go buffet," said Mendeleyev. "Make eat."

Everyone followed him off the train to the station restaurant.

9

In Pennsylvania Mendeleyev saw everything that he wanted to see. He talked, in a fashion, with many engineers, visited the fields and the plants, made surveys, collected samples, and asked for data. In Philadelphia he was impressed especially by the magical factory "Alladin" where wondrous petroleum by-products were produced—special lubricants, oils, paraffin-like substances. Mendeleyev was very much interested in a certain hard yellow substance which did not melt until a temperature of over 300 degrees was attained. "Petrocin," the Americans seemed to call it. "Much nice petrocin." Each evening, after a trip, he made calculations and wrote reports. Later, in Russia he would make another survey of the Caucasian oil lands. But already something could be written.

"Naphtha, or petroleum, in Pennsylvania has been found only on the western side of the Alleghenies, but the Caucasus is full of naphtha from the north, south, and on both sides, at the Black and Caspian seas. This must be explained in the following manner. In the first place, the old beds had many natural opportunities of getting opened, of letting out their naphtha supply, of being washed away and becoming lost for the use of the people. But the younger naphtha deposits of the Caucasus had less chances of this. In the second place, near the Alleghenies and near the naphtha wells of Pennsylvania there are no mud volcanoes—like the active Kyr-Maku—which are very often found in Baku, and generally near the Caucasus. These mud volcanoes are in a sense the natural satellites of naphtha. That is, they are apparently the breathing holes of the earth interior, which evolve mud, water, and steam, and let out the burning gas. In Pennsylvania this process terminated long ago, while in the Caucasus it still continues. One finds naphtha both in Pennsylvania and in the Caucasus in similar conditions with regard to space distribution, but the conditions of geologic periods in the two countries are very different. . . . With regard to the Caucasus, as long ago as in biblical times, and indeed long before the Russians came there, the inhabitants of the place used the naphtha which rose to the surface, for illuminating oil. . . . There is every expectation for the abundant flow to continue for a great period of time yet. As the proverb has it, 'From good no one will expect anything else but good to spring.' . . .

"In certain districts, particularly in those where petroleum is found, as for example near Baku, where a temple of the Indian fire-worshippers was built, and in Pennsylvania, and other places, marsh gas issues from the earth in abundance, and is usable, like coal gas, for purposes of lighting and warming. . . .

"In Pennsylvania, beyond the Allegheny Mountains, many of the shafts sunk for petroleum only emitted gas, but many useful applications for it were found and there is a project of conducting it in metallic pipes to works hundreds of miles distant, especially for metallurgical purposes. This can be done at Baku. . . ."

Back in New York, Mendeleyev found Russell still at the Jefferson Hotel. They made a few more excursions and then prepared to leave for Europe.

In their stateroom Mendeleyev noticed for the first time that Russell had brought along a large brown paper bag.

"Vot ees?" he asked.

Russell opened it. It was full of lemons.

"Ees limon," he said.

Mendeleyev roared.

During the crossing Russell used up the entire supply.

The men conversed almost fluently whenever Russell was strong enough to speak, but Mendeleyev was using more and more of his own English, and Russell—whose resistance was low—adopted Mendeleyev's English.

Mendeleyev infected others, too, and just before they landed at England, when the captain gave a dinner in honor of "that intrepid Russian scientist of the elements, the compounds, and other things," the first mate said "Ees nice speak." And the captain himself, speaking to the first mate later, said, "Ees von much nice guy."

Before Russell disembarked he and Mendeleyev exchanged addresses and spoke of a possible reunion some day.

Mendeleyev went on to Russia. Everything had gone well. The Pennsylvania oil techniques had been observed, the land had been studied, and the reports written. Now he was ready for Russia's slumbering oil resources. He would go again to the Caucasus, and make recommendations as to what ought to be done.

The vast sea still stretched ahead.

Chapter Twenty-four

Anna Ivanovna Popova

IVAN EVSTAFYEVITCH POPOV was born in the year 1827.
When Ivan was still a little boy he fell ill with inflammation of the lungs. A little white-haired man, Dr. Volzov, worked day and night to save Ivan's life.

Ivan never forgot.

"Some day I want to be a doctor," he said when he recovered, "to save some other little boy's life."

Ivan grew up in the city of Voronezh, and after finishing secondary school, began to plan a medical career. He awaited an opportunity to go to Moscow for study, but events unfolded in such a way that Ivan had to work incessantly to help support his family, and the opportunity never came. Instead he followed in his father's footsteps and became a military man—a Cossack in the region of the Don.

With the frustration of his ambition, something within him seemed to change forever. For the remainder of his life Ivan, who had previously been a very joyful lad, was never known to laugh again with the complete abandon of his soul. One idea thereafter sustained him. It was a promise he had made to himself that if he ever married and had children, nothing should be permitted to frustrate their ambitions.

After nine years in the Caucasus, in 1855, he married. This was the year in which Mendeleyev was seeking health in the near-by vineyards of the Crimea.

The woman whom Ivan married was Anna Logginovna Efremova, daughter of a Russian engineer. She was three years younger than her husband.

Their first child, a girl, was born in 1858 and was christened Maria.

On February 27, 1860, another girl was born and this girl was named Anna.

When Ivan was able to retire from the military service he settled his family at Ourupenskoy Station in the Don Valley. There he waited for his girls to grow up, so that he could turn his attention to their proper education. In

1868, he decided that the time had come. Maria was ten and Anna eight. He took them to Moscow, and in the fall of the year placed them in a girls' boarding school directed by Countess Elena Sergeyevna Gorchakova, a relative of Count Leo Tolstoy.

Ivan and his wife continued to live at the Station in the Don, because life was cheaper there and also very pleasant.

The two Popov girls stayed at their school for five years and then entered the higher Bauer Institute for the period 1874 to 1875.

Anna, who had begun to be interested in drawing, also attended Sunday classes at the Stroganov Art School. Although she received here only ten lessons she became convinced that she wanted to make art her career. She wrote to her father and Ivan remembered his vow.

"You will study art," he wrote her. "Now come home for the summer. Both of you. Then we will make a plan."

In the fall of 1875, Ivan, scraping together his remaining resources, which he had been saving for just such an event, took Anna to the capital, to St. Petersburg. There facilities for art and music study for women were good. At first, Anna took an examination in "forte piano," and entered a musical conservatory, where she met Alexandra Vladimirovna Sinegoubova. The two girls roomed together in the home of the retired general A. K. Erdberg.

After Christmas Anna left the music conservatory and sought the best lessons in drawing that she could find. She studied at the Vasilievsky Ostrov and also studied drawing and sculpture at the Academy of Art.

And it was here that she met the twenty-year-old Nadezhda Yakovlevna Kapustina, Mendeleyev's niece.

2

Anna Ivanovna Popova was seventeen years old, a tall, stately girl unusually graceful in her movements. Her thick golden braids were tied with black ribbon, and her large eyes, light blue in color, seemed serious, giving her round girlish face an unexpectedly mature aspect. Her cheeks were rosy and the thick, stern eyebrows complemented the expression of her eyes. Her voice somehow was shy.

At the Academy of Art she soon surpassed the other young women. She painted with a verve and force which was regarded at the Academy as masculine. Somehow one expected the feminine Anna to produce paintings of delicate flowers. Instead she produced strong vigorous human figures and terrifying mountain chasms, blazing with excitement and rugged color. People came to look. Anna smiled, and painted on, rapidly, dashingly.

For the summer of 1876 Anna went home to the Don Valley, and there she received a written proposal of marriage from the local doctor, Vladimir Platonovitch Rubashkin. Anna's sister Maria had already married and gone to live at Novocherkassk. Thus Maria was off her parents' hands. Because Anna felt sorry for her father, who was spending his money on her, she considered the marriage proposal carefully. But it was not in her heart to accept; she told her father that she wanted to continue with her studies, unless . . .

Ivan took his daughter's hand.

"So long as you live," he said, "never give up what you want. If you do, you will die inside. Go study your art. The money will be found."

So Anna wrote to her devoted and kindly suitor,

". . . I cannot consider marriage until I finish my course at the Art Academy. . . . Believe me, Vladimir Platonovitch, I regard your proposal as an honor. . . ."

When she returned to St. Petersburg in the fall of 1876 she went to live at Nadezhda's home. The Kapustins now lived on Glinka Street.

She was happy there, and her art work progressed. Though the Kapustins had thought of taking nothing from her, Anna insisted on paying twenty-five roubles per month for room and board.

In this home, the name of Dmitri Ivanovitch—Mendeleyev—was practically never mentioned. Ekaterina considered it bad form to speak too much of her brother. He was now very famous, and to Anna his name suggested something abstract and eternal somewhere in Russia's culture. She had never met him and did not even think of him as a person, but as some great name. Occasionally Ekaterina would go to visit him, but he himself never came; there was never time.

The Kapustins sometimes had costume and dancing parties. Always the most thrilling event of the evening was Anna's matchless performance of a Russian dance, in the costume of a nobleman's daughter. The costume did not matter. Once when the artist Feodor Aleksandrovitch Feodorov was present, he sat entranced.

"I have never seen a better expression of the Russian dance," he said after having seen Anna perform.

When the young Kapustins and their friends played Faust extemporaneously, Anna was Marguerite.

Then, one evening, on February 8, 1877, Nadezhda took Anna for the first time to the University of St. Petersburg, to witness the annual academic gathering, open to the public.

Anna and Nadezhda sat upstairs in the gallery and waited for the speeches to begin. But before that they would watch the professors arrive. Now they were coming. First came the rector, Andrei Nikolayevitch Beketov, with his mop of gray hair; then came Menshutkin, Buteler, Inostrantzev, Sovetov, Wagner—the physiologist-writer Kot-Mourlika (who nearly always carried a pet white rat in his pocket), then came Dokoutchaev, Ovsyannikov; then—

Suddenly—a whisper went fleetingly up and down the rows; in a twinkling the entire auditorium was buzzing in confidential snatches.

"There's Mendeleyev." "There he is—Mendeleyev."

"Here he is—here, now look . . ."

Into the room strode Mendeleyev, his great blond head reflecting the yellow lamplight, his full beard stirring in the breeze of his fast walk.

The people in the auditorium smiled with pride, and strained to get a good look at this man Mendeleyev—whose fame was increasing every day.

"Gallium," said a young man to his lady companion. "He predicted it."

"Plan of unity," someone else whispered; "the Periodic Table."

"More scientific papers than anybody in Russia," a thin man with dark spectacles said to a woman next to him.

"His book is a treasure house, there's nothing like that *Principles of Chemistry* in the world."

"He saved the student Akhmatov," another explained. "Just walked into the station and folded his arms. They say twenty gendarmes fell trembling to their knees. *Ai, ai, ai,* imagine that to yourself."

"He's the one," said a whispering voice. "He's the one who founded our Chemical Society. We are getting recognition from all over the world."

"They say he's to give chemistry courses to women! Or maybe he already is. Imagine that to yourself—for the first time in Russia's history."

"He's been to Amerika," said a loud voice, and people turned round and slowly shook their heads.

Anna, sitting next to Nadezhda, leaned forward and stared at Mendeleyev as he continued to stride, his body leaning forward slightly.

"Nadenka," said Anna, "is it possible that this is your own uncle?"

Nadezhda nodded.

"Nadenka," said Anna, "look how the people regard this man! Look, Nadenka!"

"I know," said Nadezhda.

Anna's large round eyes continued to follow the tall figure.

"He's thinking," said Anna. "He's not even conscious of the people."

"He's always conscious of the people. . . ."

"Well you know what I mean."

"Yes, I know," said Nadezhda.

Anna leaned back in her seat, and looked at Nadezhda.

"I had no idea he was like that," she said. "And to think that he is your uncle! How strange, Nadenka, how strange and difficult to think that this man has nieces, and nephews, like other people."

"He buys me brushes and paints," said Nadezhda. "He says that music and art are the natural expressions of a woman's heart."

Anna was looking meditatively far down below, toward the front. There Nadezhda's uncle was speaking to some professors. He was speaking intensely, gesturing with his hands. The professors were nodding.

"His appearance is inspiring," she said softly.

Nadezhda nodded.

"I have always felt that," she said. "And *akh*, Nutochka, you should see him at the country home—at Boblovo. It's as though he belonged to the land."

"How old is he?" asked Anna. "I mean one so promising, and yet not so very old. . . ."

"Forty-three," said Nadezhda. "Or forty-two. No, I think he's forty-three. We can ask my mother."

"No, no, no," said Anna. "I didn't mean—I meant—I didn't—*akh*. So much promise for Russia."

A man next to Anna leaned toward her.

"That's Russia's pride and glory," he said. "That tall one standing there. Look how he tells them. Just look how he tells them."

Anna nodded.

"Such a person can say anything," she said. "He can even scold—and it would be forgiven."

Anna and Nadezhda looked again toward the front, where Nadezhda's uncle was standing.

"What do you think?" she asked. "Am I not justified in being proud of him?"

"You know," said Anna. "You know what I was thinking. He is so different from the others."

A man on the platform began to speak.

3

The friendship of Nadezhda and Anna grew. Together they went to the opera to listen to Nilsson and Patti, and they also went to various St. Petersburg balls.

Through their art school Anna and Nadezhda met the promising artists Shishkin, Polenov, and Maximov, the pianist, a student of Liszt.

Anna herself played exceptionally well on the piano and even gave occasional lessons. This had been arranged through Professor Adrian Viktorovitch Prakhov, who lectured at the academy on the history of art and who was also editor of the journal *The Bee*. Nadezhda assisted Prakhov on this journal, and so she attended his socials. Soon Anna, too, was attending the socials and once after Prakhov heard her play he sent her the eight-year-old Mamonov boy for lessons. He came with his mother and Anna received three roubles for each lesson, but she could not sleep nights because the child made so little progress.

But the boy was very happy as he banged away at the piano, frequently hitting the right notes. And Madame Mamonov was happy too and sat continuously beaming as her baby struck the keys so forcefully with his tiny fists. She talked to Anna about St. Petersburg and Paris and London, and about clothes and furs and her hopes for her little musical boy. All the time Anna was trying to lead the boy in his lesson. But he, too, enjoyed the conversation, occasionally turning his attention back to the piano which he pummeled happily. No matter what he did—even if he shut his eyes—he could still strike the keys and bring forth sounds. Madame Mamonov smiled.

"More expression," she would say. "Now make it from your heart."

But there were other, perhaps more exciting, events. Once Anna and Nadezhda stood trembling in a line of fellow art students—men and women—as Tsar Alexander II made an inspection of the Academy of Art. The Tsar was amazed to find women here—they were, in a sense, illegally enrolled, but he made no objection and the women were permitted to remain at the Academy. Now women were permitted legally to study both chemistry and art.

It was the spring of 1877 and Mendeleyev, as usual, had sent his family to the Boblovo estate. Twelve-year-old Volodya remained in St. Petersburg to go on with his schooling until summer. Ekaterina took over the apartment as she had done in previous years. This time, however, because Ekaterina was building a new house, Mendeleyev told his sister to bring her entire household with her. This meant Ekaterina's children, including Nadezhda, and it also meant Anna.

Mendeleyev's university apartment was divided into two parts. The first consisted of his bedroom, study laboratory, hallway, and an entrance; the second had other rooms and another entrance. Thus it was possible for occupants of the two parts not to see each other for long periods of time—unless they made use of the connecting hallway. When Ekaterina first came with her household Mendeleyev saw Anna once or twice, but thereafter a long time passed before he saw anyone except Ekaterina, who cooked special meals for him at special times, since Mendeleyev studied and worked late hours.

Once when Mendeleyev was eating in the kitchen he heard piano music from the other side of the house. It was Beethoven's Concerto Number 5 in E-Flat Major, a composition that Mendeleyev loved.

He stood up with his huge cup of strong tea in his hand.

"Who is playing?" asked Mendeleyev.

Ekaterina buttered some bread for him and spread red caviar on it.

"The art student Anna," said Ekaterina. "That blond girl."

Mendeleyev listened.

"Art student," he said, "and musical, too."

Ekaterina nodded.

"Yes. She is also a beautiful dancer."

Mendeleyev drank the tea, picked up the bread with the caviar, and ate rapidly.

Ekaterina later told Anna that Mendeleyev had seemed to enjoy her playing. At this the girl became so self-conscious that for a long time she would not go near the piano.

"Why doesn't she play any more?" Mendeleyev once asked at his ten o'clock breakfast.

Ekaterina explained what had happened.

"*Akh*, Katenka!" Mendeleyev roared. "Why did you tell her I was listening!" He banged his cup on the table and flew out of the kitchen.

Anna was just coming in, and hearing Mendeleyev's roaring voice, nearly collapsed with fright. She caught a glimpse of him as he stalked out. He did not see her.

But the same day Ekaterina begged Anna to resume her piano playing.

"Please. It will soothe him," she explained. "Don't be bashful. Please, go and play."

Nadezhda too coaxed Anna to play.

"The students are having examinations this week," she said. "Maybe it will be easier for them if Dmitri Ivanovitch is happy."

So Anna played and Mendeleyev in his study held his pen above the page and listened.

Soon Anna really began to understand to what extent the house revolved around Mendeleyev. Ekaterina waited on him hand and foot, and Nadezhda, too, scampered around the kitchen helping to prepare things that he might like to eat. There were, for example, pancakes of precooked rice which had been soaked in red wine. This was Mendeleyev's own idea, and Nadezhda knew how to make them to please him. Anna's place seemed to be at the piano, where more and more she obliged and Mendeleyev listened from a distance.

But everything moved according to Mendeleyev's disposition.

"Dmitri Ivanovitch is resting now," Ekaterina would say. "Everybody tiptoe."

"Dmitri Ivanovitch is now getting up. Hurry his breakfast, Nadenka, hurry, my dear."

"Dmitri Ivanovitch has just come back from classes—Anna, run to play. Hurry, darling."

Gradually Anna became terrified in this household, fearing that something might go very wrong and then Dmitri Ivanovitch might explode and the whole house might fly to pieces. She was mortally frightened that she might make a mistake on the piano and then surely the wall behind her would come crashing down. Frequently, as she played, she gazed at this wall, knowing that on the other side a large hairy man with penetrating eyes was standing, listening.

At the Sunday dinners the whole household would gather and Mendeleyev presided. He was invariably in good humor then, but still Anna was afraid to look at him. At the first such Sunday dinner she scarcely breathed as she ate little morsels of a cutlet. Not once did she look up from her plate. Mendeleyev was in a talkative mood: he spoke of an amusing incident with a student, commented on the remarkably exhilarating weather, told of his research and the present writing. Ekaterina and Nadezhda carried the conversation with him, and little Volodya talked of his Maritime School. Volodya wanted to be a sailor.

After dinner Ekaterina coaxed Anna to play chess with Mendeleyev. Anna could not escape and tried to play, but she seemed to be paralyzed. Once or twice she looked up with a frightened expression as though to say,

"But, Dmitri Ivanovitch, how can I play against you? I am just a little girl. Let me run, *akh*, let me run from here!"

But Mendeleyev kept the game going, corrected Anna's moves, and stopped before he had won. Then, abruptly he got up and went to his study.

There, at the table, he took a sheet of paper, and wrote a letter. The letter was to Anna Ivanovna Popova. He sealed it and put it in a small cedar box on his desk. He took a key out of his pocket and locked the box.

4

From behind the wall, from the other end of the house, came the rolling notes of Beethoven's Fifth Concerto—the *Emperor*.

Mendeleyev straightened up and listened.

Onward rolled the music, up, gathering strength, rolling, weaving—Mendeleyev stood straight, his great head weaving back and forth. How that young girl played! What heart and strength! How sure and imperious. Only an understanding heart could love Beethoven that much. Now the entire house resounded! Here was life flowing, all of life, at once in an unchecked flood—Mendeleyev stood peering through the wall.

Once Nadezhda had told him that Anna painted pictures the same way. Every restraint was broken—she poured out her heart; one could sense it as she mixed the colors and put the brush to the canvas.

Mendeleyev wondered. Strange how such a shy, such a painfully bashful girl, could give herself so forcefully in art, and here now in this music. Ekaterina had said that Anna danced the same way. Why had he not seen her pictures? Why had he not seen her in that Russian dance that everyone talked about?

Through the wall poured the music and Mendeleyev stood at his writing desk, his eyes fixed on the wall.

He walked out of his room and softly through the hallway. At the open door of Nadezhda's and Anna's room, he stood and watched. The girl at the piano kept on playing. She was dressed in blue. The golden braids were wound about her head.

But suddenly the music ended. The girl sighed and wiped her eyes. On tiptoe Mendeleyev retreated to his room. There, at his desk he sat with his pen in his hand and looked at the opposite wall. He took a sheet of paper and wrote another letter to Anna Ivanovna Popova. Again he sealed it and locked it in the cedar box. Then he picked up his pen, and began the revision of the manuscript for the third edition of *Principles of Chemistry*. In the late evening he switched for a while to the article "Our Future Petroleum Industry."

Somehow occasions arose now where Mendeleyev met Anna in the kitchen, in the hallway, in the large guest room.

Frequently he carried his chess box with him.

"Will you play a game?" he would ask.

Anna played. She was learning to play well. After one game Mendeleyev would hurriedly gather up his chessmen and disappear into his study.

Occasionally he would now come to Nadezhda's and Anna's room and talk to them—about politics, about science, about his visit to America. Everything that he said entranced the girls, the twenty-two-year-old Nadezhda and the nineteen-year-old Anna.

Mendeleyev now often asked her to play, and after the first few times in his presence she recovered her natural assurance.

"You remind me of Marguerite," Mendeleyev once said to her.

Nadezhda was there.

"And you resemble Faust, Dmitri Ivanovitch," she said, and then suddenly was confused.

Mendeleyev abruptly left the room.

It was the spring of 1877, and Mendeleyev arranged a trip for everybody on a ship, to Kronstadt. He was gay and jubilant, and laughed aloud at the antics of his Volodya who pretended to be the captain.

Anna's blue eyes sparkled, and the flush of her face deepened under the strong bright sun. Nadezhda made sketches of the passing boats, and graying Ekaterina sat back happily to contemplate the restful sea.

After that trip Mendeleyev came more and more to the girls' room to play chess, to listen to Anna's music. He talked more, too.

One day, in the kitchen, Ekaterina said in a casual way, "Anna has received a beautiful bracelet from her suitor."

Mendeleyev looked up suddenly, then bent down over the brown cutlet and the sliced tomatoes on his plate.

"From her suitor?" he said.

"Yes," said Ekaterina. "A certain Dr. Rubashkin, at the Station on the Don where her parents live."

Mendeleyev finished his food.

"He will be a lucky man," said Ekaterina. "Anna is going home in a few days—as soon as her art examinations are over. I suppose they will then marry."

Mendeleyev nodded.

"Naturally," he said, "that's splendid. Just simply splendid."

He left to deliver a lecture.

That evening he brought his box of chessmen to Nadezhda's and Anna's room. Anna was there alone.

"Anna Ivanovna," said Mendeleyev, "could you play a game?"

"Yes, Dmitri Ivanovitch," she said. "If you like."

The game began.

Mendeleyev moved a pawn.

Anna was trying to play carefully. She pondered for a while. Then she moved a pawn too.

Mendeleyev countered rapidly with another pawn move.

Anna put her fingers on a knight. But here she began to think deeply. For a long time she figured, gazing intently at the board. Still she would not move the knight. She looked up for a moment at the man sitting opposite her, and on her face there slowly appeared an expression of bewilderment. The big man opposite her sat with one hand over his eyes. Between the fingers of that hand Anna could see large tears rolling slowly down his cheeks into the great blond beard.

She sat petrified. Her breathing seemed to stop. Mendeleyev's eyes lifted and from behind his hand he could see Anna watching him. He took his hand away from his face.

"I am alone," he said. "I am alone in the whole world."

Anna sat speechless, her large blue eyes seeming larger now.

"All my life I have been alone," said Mendeleyev, "but I have never been so ill with loneliness as now."

Anna could not utter a word.

Mendeleyev stood up.

"Forgive me," he said. "I did not mean to embarrass you."

He gathered up his chessmen and left the room.

The next day Anna started for her home, to the Station on the River Don.

5

Mendeleyev did not expect Anna to return. Daily he wrote a letter and locked it in the small cedar chest.

At the Station on the Don, Dr. Rubashkin came to see Anna and they reached an understanding.

"It would be improper for me to accept the honor of being your wife," she said. "It is not within my heart."

Dr. Rubashkin understood. He asked her if she loved someone else. Anna shook her head.

In the fall she returned to St. Petersburg.

The Kapustins were still at Mendeleyev's university apartment, and Anna moved in again with them.

By now Ekaterina could see that a very complex situation might develop. Mendeleyev could not conceal his feeling for Anna, and soon his wife would return from Boblovo. The worried but masterful Ekaterina went out and rented a four-room apartment, made arrangements for a servant to cook for Mendeleyev, and moved out, taking Nadezhda and Anna with her.

But this did not end anything at all. Mendeleyev visited the Kapustins and Anna at their new home. He developed an intense interest in art, and began buying the best pictures. He also began to have socials on Friday nights, and invited the foremost artists and musicians of the capital—and Nadezhda, and Anna.

In his study, daily, he wrote a letter.

". . . I want to serve as a step for your rise in the world of art, for your rise upward into the world of human freedom. Into the universe of freedom of the human soul. . . ." He locked the letter in the box on his desk.

To his socials came the artistic and the musical visionaries: the artist

Koundzhi, the art historian and writer Prakhov, the sculptors Lemokh and Posen; Kramsky and Makovsky, Kouznetsov and Klodt; also the Professors Volkov and Wagner; the physiologist who as "Kot-Mourlika" wrote fairy tales. There came, too, the Rector Beketov, the great physicist Krayevitch, and the chemist Menshutkin.

Frequently the gatherings spontaneously became hilarious instead of serious and then Kouznetsov imitated the zhouzhanye of a fly on the wing, and Klodt performed a Caucasian dance.

Gradually Anna began to feel herself part of the advanced Petersburg cultural life, and she understood that Mendeleyev was planning it that way, for her. Once he came to the Academy of Art to speak with the Director Chistyakov.

"Pavel Petrovitch," he said. "I am deeply interested in having a copy of a painting made—'The Last Day of Pompeii.'"

Chistyakov nodded.

"I can put one of my clever young men to work on it for you," he said.

Mendeleyev was embarrassed.

"The situation is like this," he said. "There is a certain style that appeals to me especially. How shall I put it?"

"Yes?" encouraged Chistyakov.

"It's approximately this way," went on Mendeleyev. "The style should be that of a certain lady—Anna Ivanovna, for example."

"*Khorosho*," Chistyakov said. "I will commission her."

"And, Pavel Petrovitch," hurried Mendeleyev, "perhaps it would be best not to say who it is for. That is, it is not for me, in any case. It is for a friend. And perhaps two hundred roubles," suggested Mendeleyev. "Would that be enough?"

"For two hundred roubles," said Chistyakov, "we can give you not only Pompeii's last day, but its last five years."

Anna went to work on the picture.

When it was nearly done Mendeleyev came to see it.

"It's for a friend of mine," he said to her. "It's splendid! I will tell him."

Mendeleyev had suggested to Chistyakov that the artist—Anna Ivanovna, for example—could take the picture over to him when it was completed. This, Chistyakov did not like. He was the Director, and he himself transmitted pictures.

Anna gave the picture to Chistyakov, who gave her Mendeleyev's money, and took the picture to him.

Mendeleyev looked at "The Last Day of Pompeii," and all he could see was Anna's blue eyes, her golden braids, her serious young face, and sympathetic glance.

He wrapped the picture again in the brown paper and hid it on top of his bookcase.

But nothing was being resolved. Mendeleyev's wife had arrived and she scarcely spoke to him. He watched her, and wondered, and suffered. His work was beginning to slip.

One day he sat down at his desk to find a solution. He attacked the dilemma as a problem in science.

"One," said Mendeleyev. "Forget her. This I refuse. Two. Marry her, if she will have me. This requires permission of her father, then agreement for a divorce by my wife. There is nothing else to do."

He wrote a letter to Anna's father, asking permission to ask Anna to be his wife, if everything else worked out well.

In reply, Ivan Evstafyevitch Popov, Anna's father, arrived in person.

"Dmitri Ivanovitch," he said, "you are a famous man, and I am nobody."

"You are her father," interrupted Mendeleyev gently.

"I am nobody," repeated Ivan. "My mind is not great. I can only act according to my simple ideas. I want you to leave my daughter alone."

Mendeleyev staggered. Piteously he gazed at the stern little man.

"You are married," said Ivan. "You have a family. By one look at your wife I can see she will not give you a divorce. My daughter means my life to me. I don't want her to be hurt. She wants to study art. Leave her alone. Do not frustrate her with meaningless diversion and suffering. I know what frustration means. Once I wanted to be a doctor. You are old enough to be her father. She is so pitifully young. You are in your middle forties. I say leave her alone."

Ivan drew himself up.

"Do you promise?" he asked.

Mendeleyev stood crushed, staring blankly at the little man.

"I promise," he said.

Ivan moved his daughter out of the Kapustin house back to the room in the apartment of her friend, Alexandra Vladimirovna Sinegoubova.

In his study Mendeleyev held his hands to his head. His head rocked to and fro.

6

Mendeleyev was unwell. The food did not interest him. Even the beloved tea had no taste. In his lectures the joyful energetic sound was gone from his voice. The students looked at each other. The professors, too, were disturbed.

He broke his promise. He began to meet Anna in the halls of the Academy of Art and at the gateway. The students pointed. . . .

Anna went home for vacation, but when she returned, Mendeleyev sought her out again.

"Encourage Dmitri Ivanovitch to seek a divorce," Nadezhda pleaded. "Otherwise, he will die."

Anna wept. She didn't know what to do.

"Don't you love him?" Nadezhda once demanded fiercely. "Do you want to kill him?"

Anna sobbed. "I love him," she said. "I love him deeply. But I cannot—how can I cause trouble—scandal."

"There's more scandal this way," retorted Nadezhda. "I beg you, encourage him to obtain a divorce."

Anna stood with head bowed.

"My father sacrificed much money," she said softly. "A great deal of money on my art education. I must make a career for myself. I must not betray my father."

Nadezhda dropped down impatiently on a chair.

"You have told me more than once," she said quietly, "that your father wants you always to do what you want in life. Remember?"

Anna was looking into space. "But I can't hurt him," she said. "He thinks that this is all wrong. He wants me to end this business. I don't know what to do. I don't know."

At his home, Mendeleyev stood gazing into his wife's eyes.

"You better forget her," Feozva said. "I will never give you a divorce. I helped to make you what you are. Why should she come to steal like a common thief?"

In his study the pen rested for a moment but presently he wrote a letter. Tears were streaming down his cheeks. He placed the letter with the others in the cedar box.

Now Mendeleyev was really ill. He was losing weight rapidly. One day his old friend Sergei Petrovitch Botkin came to see him.

"Mitenka, you better go abroad. Go to Biarritz for the winter."

"My work," said Mendeleyev.

Botkin shrugged his shoulders.

"You're not doing any work," he said.

Mendeleyev took his cedar chest. He sat down and wrote a will, and another letter to Anna Ivanovna Popova. Then he took the locked chest to his friend Beketov, the rector of the university.

"Please keep this for me," he said. "If I die, give the letters to Anna Ivanovna. Then take care of the will."

Beketov embraced Mendeleyev.

"Go abroad," he said, "but do not die. Come back strong. We need you.

Everything here will lose force if you do not recover. Keep faith with us."

Mendeleyev went to Biarritz. Suddenly, in midwinter, he returned for three days to see Anna. Then he went back.

Anna tried to forget him. She tried to divert herself—to give herself completely to her art work. But it was impossible. The image of Mendeleyev stood before her.

It was the summer of 1879 and Anna went home to her parents.

Mendeleyev returned from abroad, his health improved.

Then, as had happened four years before, another event occurred that rapidly became well known all over the world.

7

Once more Menshutkin stood knocking at Mendeleyev's apartment door and again Feozva let him in. He came bursting into the study.

"Mitya, Mitya," he said. "They have found another one of your predicted elements."

Mendeleyev stood quiet, pensive.

"Which one?" he asked.

"Ekaboron. It was found by Nilson. They say he is going to call it 'scandium' for Scandinavia."

Menshutkin enumerated all the properties of the newly found element. They were exactly the same as those of Mendeleyev's ekaboron.

The news reached all Russia and soon all the world. In France, England, Germany, Italy, and in America, too, chemists shook their heads in awe. Not only a plan of unity, but that Russian had boldly foretold the detailed quantitative characteristics of supposedly hypothetical elements that were now being discovered. This was the second one.

Frenchmen recalled their beloved Danton, *"L'audace, et encore l'audace, et toujours l'audace!"* The Frenchmen loved a brave courageous man, an intrepid and imaginative thinker who spoke forthrightly, openly. Above all, audaciously. A man who risked his reputation and career to make predictions if his reason told him he could. A man who did not mince words or make qualified safe statements.

In America, too, the scientists were saying, "The greatest living chemist."

The University of St. Petersburg had become one of the world's great centers of scientific learning. Letters came from all over the world. Congratulations, inquiries, requests for the Russian chemical journals.

In classes students rose and applauded when he walked in. In the streets people turned and pointed.

In his study Mendeleyev sat before the cedar box.

8

A year passed. In the fall of 1880 Anna realized that something would have to be done. She was seeing Mendeleyev by prearrangement at the art galleries, at her school, at other public places, and she knew that his health was breaking. She wrote to her father for advice. Ivan somehow scraped together some money.

"Go abroad," he wrote her. "Maybe the poor man will forget you. And you must do the same. Study hard, perhaps at Rome."

So Anna went to Rome and Mendeleyev buried himself in his work.

In his junior class he related the history of all the elements—where and how each was discovered.

Tungsten had been found by Scheele in 1781 . . . ; lithium was obtained from petalite, in 1817, by Arfvedson . . . ; vanadium had been unearthed by Del Rio at the beginning of the nineteenth century. . . . Mendeleyev told of eka-aluminium, or gallium, and finally he told about ekaboron, or scandium.

"We must expect more discoveries," Mendeleyev concluded. "Many more. Within the borders of the Periodic Table there are still empty places. These I discussed in detail in 1871. Outside the present borders of the Periodic Table other elements may appear. This, one cannot foretell."

In another class where he was discussing the element iron, Mendeleyev spoke of meteors.

"The question arises as to why the iron in meteorites is in a free state, while on the earth it is in a state of combination. Does not this tend to show that the state of our globe is very different from that of the rest? In my opinion, inside our earth there is a mass similar in composition to meteorites. . . . When the whole mass of the earth was in a state of vapor, the substances of denser vapor accumulated about the center and those with lighter vapors at the surface. . . . It thus becomes clear why such light elements as hydrogen, carbon, nitrogen, oxygen, sodium, magnesium, aluminium, silicon, sulphur, phosphorus, potassium, calcium, and their compounds predominate at the surface, and thus largely constitute the earth's crust. There exists also now much iron in the sun, as spectrum analysis shows, and therefore iron must have entered into the composition of the earth and other planets, but would have accumulated at its center because the vapor of iron is very dense and it condenses easily. . . .

"All these things an educated man should know. The time has arrived when a knowledge of physics and chemistry forms as important a part of education as a knowledge of classics did two centuries ago. . . ."

In the outside world things were happening which somewhat distracted Mendeleyev from his almost incessant thoughts of Anna.

Tolstoy had written *A Confession,* and this study advocating Christian living without theology and mysticism was causing a sensation and provoking violent discussion. On June 8, 1880, Dostoyevsky made a stirring speech at the unveiling of a monument to Pushkin. The speech affected all Russians profoundly. It called for humanity, sympathy, and unity among the people. Mendeleyev felt the speech deeply and returned to his work with an emboldened spirit. This uplift in spirit was not affected by the fact that the St. Petersburg Academy of Knowledge blackballed Mendeleyev because he was too liberal in his views.

On January 28, 1881, a great national catastrophe occurred. Dostoyevsky, who had spent his life analyzing the human spirit and dreaming of the moral evolution of man, suddenly died. Death was caused by rupture of an artery in the lung, but there were many who said that his great heart had burst from the pressure of human woe. The funeral, on January 30, was larger than that ever accorded any Tsar. The people came simply out of their homes —the whole city came out to walk bareheaded behind the casket. . . .

Anna was still in Rome.

Through the heavy snow Mendeleyev walked in the dark St. Petersburg streets. It was February, 1881. At this moment he felt a loneliness that he had never experienced since the death of Maria and the fragile Elizabeth. He walked to Volkovo Cemetery and stood before the snow-laden grave of Maria. And yet, somehow, he felt that he could not call on the spirit of his mother. He was forty-seven years old and this was a struggle that he must make himself. The twenty-one-year-old girl possessed his life completely. But a woman stood in the way, Feozva, who had ceased being his wife in 1868, after the birth of their second child, Olga. Thirteen years ago Mendeleyev had ceased having a wife, and yet he was married and the woman would not consent to a divorce. This was no problem for the spirit of a dead mother; it was a problem for him. But where, and how, did one come to grips with such a problem? What was there to do?

He went home to work. In his study he sat down at his desk and bent over his papers. Suddenly, through the wall came the rolling notes of the *Emperor* Concerto.

Mendeleyev's heart froze. He rose, and walked slowly toward the wall. The music continued, higher, onward. . . .

His hands trembled. The pen spattered small drops of ink onto his trousers. Still the notes continued. He walked through his room, through the hallway, to the other side of the house. In front of the door he stopped, but when he opened the door, the piano stood alone, and the music had ceased.

Mendeleyev stared at the lone piano. He took his head in his hands and rocked it to and fro.

Slowly he went back to his room. Once more he sat down at his desk, and again he dipped the pen into the inkwell. He began to write. Then suddenly there were voices. One voice—what was it saying? He arose and followed it —there to the parlor. *Akh,* yes, there in the corner stood someone in front of the easel. How she applied the color! With such strength and depth of expression!

Mendeleyev approached. Where, where are you? Where have you gone? There was no easel. There was no one.

He tore at his hair.

He walked back to his room, to his bedroom. He put on his overcoat and left the house.

The house of the rector, Beketov, was near by. Mendeleyev knocked. Beketov had retired, but from his room he heard Mendeleyev speak with the servant and he came out in his bathrobe.

"I am ill," said Mendeleyev.

For a long time they talked. There seemed, however, to be no solution. Beketov gave Mendeleyev some sleeping pills and he went back home.

The next evening he decided to work in his laboratory instead of writing at his desk. He was working on some Baku petroleum. He started to make an analysis. Suddenly, on the surface of the large flask on the chemistry table, Anna's face appeared. Mendeleyev stared, his hands trembled, he felt ill. He put on his hat and coat and galoshes, and started out of the apartment. Feozva appeared in the doorway of her bedroom.

"Where do you run to these nights?" she asked.

Mendeleyev walked out without answering. Aimlessly he plowed through the St. Petersburg snow.

He began to lose weight. The spirit seemed to be entirely gone.

The Rector Beketov was worried. Again he advised him to go away for a long rest. Perhaps to Algiers. Mendeleyev agreed. Secretly he was hoping to drown in the sea on the way over. Again he gave Beketov his cedar box with the letters to Anna and his will. His eyes had lost luster, his frame was gaunt, he seemed listless.

Beketov was seriously alarmed. Now he was afraid to let Mendeleyev leave. Hurriedly he called together the Professors Inostrantzev, Krayevitch, and Dokutchaev.

They made a plan. That afternoon, while Mendeleyev was away at a doctor's office, the four professors came to call on Mendeleyev's wife, Feozva.

"Come in," she said. "This is an honor,"

They entered, and Beketov began speaking without removing his overcoat or sitting down. Everyone remained standing.

"Your husband, that is, Professor Mendeleyev is in a serious condition," said Beketov. "Are you aware of this, Madame?"

Feozva looked at him.

"It could be," she said. "He seems unwell."

"It is possible that he will soon die," said Krayevitch the physicist, who had been Mendeleyev's colleague years ago at the Pedagogical Institute.

"What do you want me to do?"

Dokutchaev and Inostrantzev pointed out the need for a divorce.

"It is not fair to me or our two children," she said. "The man has become famous, and we have helped in a way. He has fair earning power now, too. One must be realistic. Why should some young girl come along and entice him away? Is this humanity?"

Beketov was gentle.

"There is perhaps a truth of a sort in your remarks," he said. "But let us only deal with the truly important fact. Mitya is very seriously ill. He has been examined by several doctors already. He has a very serious disease—he does not wish to live. You must save his life."

Feozva raised her thin eyebrows.

"I am not a tyrant," she said. "If this is truly serious, all right. All I want is to be taken care of—my children, mostly."

"That can be done with the alimony," said Krayevitch.

Feozva considered.

"Well," she said. "I will accept on one financial condition. His entire University salary is to go to me and the children."

The professors were stunned.

"He makes money through his writing," said Feozva. "And besides, his intended one can work. She's young."

"He makes money only from his book *Principles of Chemistry*," said Krayevitch.

But Mendeleyev's wife would accept nothing less.

Beketov consulted with the professors. They agreed to accept the condition.

Mendeleyev was almost delirious with joy at this sudden development and commissioned the lawyer Golovin to start divorce proceedings immediately

In a frenzy of haste, he grabbed the suitcase that had been destined for Algiers and started out for Rome.

In January, 1882, Dmitri Ivanovitch Mendeleyev was married to Anna Ivanovna Popova, daughter of the former Don Cossack Ivan Evstafyevitch Popov.

Chapter Twenty-five

Mendeleyev and Anna

IN THE university apartment of Professor Dmitri Ivanovitch Mendeleyev nearly everything was different now. Feozva and her children lived in a distant section of St. Petersburg.

At night, in the apartment, Mendeleyev often burst out singing, usually "La Donna e Mobile." Anna's easel stood in the front room and, in the evening, she would stand in front of the canvas and paint furiously in her "masculine manner."

The socials, too, were resumed, and every Wednesday evening the leading St. Petersburg artists and musicians gathered there. Foremost among these were Nikolai Alexandrovitch Yaroshenko and Arkhip Ivanovitch Koundzhi. Yaroshenko, a thin man of medium height, had wavy black hair, interspersed with gray which stood on top of his head like a Cossack hat. On the whole, Yaroshenko's features were irregular, but no one noticed this. Everyone knew only that this artist-idealist was very *sympatichny*. He promised Anna that he would paint the portrait of her first child "in the immediate future."

Yaroshenko's wife, Maria Pavlovna, was a tall solid woman, an amiable brunette who considered her husband the best painter in the world. Occasionally Anna would visit them at their studio home in the Chinese section of St. Petersburg and Yaroshenko would give her impromptu lessons and show her his own techniques in mixing paints.

On one occasion Anna returned home in a hilarious mood after visiting the Yaroshenkos, and Mendeleyev, taking her in his arms, asked her the cause of her merriment.

"At Yaroshenkos'," laughed Anna so bubblingly that Mendeleyev bent down to kiss her, "at Yaroshenkos', just outside their apartment there was a peculiar odor. I came in and asked them what it was. *Akh*, Mitya, that Nikolai is so amusing—you know what he said?"

"Tell," said Mendeleyev.

"He said that the Chinese were frying a crocodile." And here Anna laughed and laughed and laughed. "It was actually only some sort of bean butter, I later found out," and again Anna laughed.

Mendeleyev, too, began to laugh, and gathered her up in his arms. He loved to see his young wife laugh. But he also loved her when she was serious, standing in front of her easel, giving all of herself to it, and when she played the piano, so feelingly. He also loved Anna when she was neither laughing nor serious, but somewhere in between.

Koundzhi, the other artist whom Anna so admired, was also a simple and friendly man, like Yaroshenko. Anna would always tremble as she awaited Koundzhi's opinion of her efforts.

In his university work Mendeleyev became more spirited, and students who needed counsel came to him more and more frequently. Something about his eyes had grown softer, and instinctively the students noticed it.

Then, suddenly, came the announcement from England that Professor D. Mendeleyev had been awarded the Davy Medal for the year 1882. All of St. Petersburg and Moscow talked for days of this honor, this recognition from the Royal Society of Great Britain. Mendeleyev knew well the work of Humphrey Davy, the chemist who in 1807 and 1808 had discovered certain elements besides isolating a number that had been discovered by others. But the significance of the Davy Medal went deeper than this. In the coal mines of England a great many disastrous explosions had occurred up to 1813. A society, formed with the object of investigating these mine explosions, engaged the chemist Humphrey Davy to study the problem. Davy invented a miner's lamp which was safe and could not ignite any accumulated gases. The miners' society was grateful, and Davy received silver plate worth 1500 pounds. Davy willed the silver plate to his wife, brother, and other relatives in succession, but he also presented the alternative proposal—that the plate be given to the scientific Royal Society to be used for making medals, one per year to be awarded for the most important discovery in chemistry made in Europe, England, or America.

Together with Mendeleyev, the German, Lothar Meyer, received the Davy award. Meyer, too, had worked on the periodic system, though he had never assigned atomic weights to elements whose values were not known with certainty, nor had he ventured to predict the existence of definite elements. He was, however, a very thorough worker in chemistry and well known on the Continent.

At home, Mendeleyev gave the medal to Anna to keep in her chest of letters.

Occasionally, when someone would come to inform Mendeleyev of some infringement of student rights, he would jump in fury from his chair at his study table.

"Why!" he would roar. "What again!"

Once, when a group was gathered at a Wednesday evening social an excited pale-faced student arrived to tell that the police were about to break up a meeting of students at the home of the president of the Student Council.

Mendeleyev roared in fury, while Anna went scampering. He put on his overcoat and fur hat. Everyone sat silent, watching. Presently Anna returned.

"Must you go?" she pleaded.

"I'll go. But I wish those students would keep themselves busy just studying. Yes, I'll go."

"It's the police," said Yaroshenko. "Dmitri Ivanovitch, I urge prudence."

Mendeleyev stopped a moment at the door.

"Last night," he said, "my little Anna read me a line from a book. You remind me of that line. 'Prudence,' it said. 'A man may carry his prudence so far as to forget his courage.' "

Mendeleyev left with the student.

Anna frequently read translated American books of adventure to her husband, and Cooper was one of his favorites.

Occasionally, while he worked in his study, Anna would sit in her own room reading the letters which she took one by one out of the chest that he had given her.

His hours of sleep still depended on how his writing was going. Now, however, after finishing an article in the middle of the night, he did not lie down to sleep on the yellow couch in his study, but went to their bedroom.

Within a year a little fair-haired girl was born to Mendeleyev and Anna. They named her Liubov—Love.

2

On the first day of spring in 1883 Anna accompanied Mendeleyev to the Boblovo country home for his annual haircut. This was to be Anna's first attendance at the shearing ceremony.

"It's foolish," said Mendeleyev on the train. "I merely go there to be trimmed by Nikita and they go and make a fuss. But Nikita is clever with the shears."

"He would have to be," said Anna looking up at her husband's overgrown head and face.

They rode in third class and Mendeleyev, as usual, was soon surrounded by peasants, who asked questions about the crops, the universe, and the new Tsar. Tsar Alexander II had been assassinated in 1881, and now, two years later, the peasants were still talking about the coronation of the new Tsar, and what his attitude toward the peasants might be.

"We need more land," a young mouzhik was telling Mendeleyev. "Can you tell the Tsar about us?"

Mendeleyev nodded.

"At my first opportunity," he said. "I give you my word. If I ever see him."

The mouzhiks and several *babas* then began to talk about Anna.

"Where did you get her?" asked a wiry wrinkled *baba* with a green kerchief. She stood in front of Anna and pointed at her.

Anna sat silent.

"I found her," said Mendeleyev, "in St. Petersburg."

"She's a likely one," said an old mouzhik with white whiskers. "Give her a chance, *barin*. Let her prove her worth, Sire."

Mendeleyev nodded.

"All right," he said. "I'll keep her for a while, and see how things go."

The mouzhiks laughed. In a moment one of them gave Mendeleyev a cucumber, and the entire company suddenly began to eat. Then there was the inescapable tea.

Just before the station at Klin, where Zassorin would be waiting with the troika, a tall red-faced mouzhik in a red shirt made his way through the crowd surrounding Mendeleyev and Anna.

"This is your day, isn't it, Mitri Ivanitch?" he said. "This is the day of the cutting of the hair, isn't it?"

Mendeleyev nodded.

"*Akh*, now," he muttered. "What's this fuss?"

"What time will it start?" asked the red-faced mouzhik. "When the sun is high, or after?"

"Well, maybe at three o'clock," Mendeleyev replied.

"I'll be there."

Anna sat staring at the crowd about her. The train lurched to a stop.

"Come on," said Mendeleyev. "It's Klin."

3

At Boblovo the mouzhiks had already begun to assemble. They came from the adjoining farmlands, and from the more distant farmlands, too. They came on foot and on telegas and a few even came in ancient tarantasses apparently cast off by someone. The *babas* came too, in green and red and blue shawls and long dresses of many colors. The mouzhiks wore trousers stuffed into their boots and colored shirts that hung outside their pants. Many wore belts or had ropes tied about their waists. Many children had come too, and were now gazing at the flower gardens, and peering at the house. Every family had brought a picnic lunch.

It was now eleven o'clock, and the sun was warm, and the earth smelled with the fragrance of spring. Mendeleyev and Anna made their way into the house.

Outside, more telegas were arriving, with men, women, children, and lunch baskets. The peasants walked about the estate, chatted, talked, waited.

At three o'clock the barber Nikita arrived and was greeted with loud acclaim. Nikita, a thin mouzhik with very dark eyes, had curly hair and an enormous Adam's apple. He was confident, serious, and impeccable in his appearance. His white blouse was spotless, the green pants were sparkling, and the patent leather boots shone with the reflected sunlight. There was an odor of powder about him, and the crowd of mouzhiks sniffed with pleasure.

Nikita came to the back door and knocked. The crowd suddenly quieted. Mendeleyev smiled.

"Mitri Ivanitch," Nikita said, "I just happened to be passing by. And I said to myself why not call on the *prostoy barin*, why not go to the plain sire and see if his hair needs a trimming."

"Thank you," said Mendeleyev. "I appreciate it."

He walked out onto the high open porch and sat down on a chair. There was no railing on this porch, and Mendeleyev, as though on a platform, was in full view of the mouzhiks.

Now the crowd relaxed, and everyone sat down on the grass. The women began to unwrap the lunches. Hard-boiled eggs were passed around everywhere, then papers of salt, black bread, tomatoes, and cucumbers, and small bits of fried meat.

Nikita began his haircutting of the year.

Nikita, the expert self-made barber, had gotten his invaluable training shearing lambs on the estate of Count Prakhnovsky. For ten years Nikita had deftly performed on the lambs, and never had been known to draw blood. Peasants used to say that Nikita was the best shearer for miles around. Then, one day, Nikita suddenly announced that he would never shear another lamb.

"How is this—never shear another lamb?" asked his unbelieving wife. "And how will the children be fed?"

Nikita shrugged his shoulders.

"Lamb-shearer," he said. "That's all I am. That's all I will be till the day I die. I refuse. I am going to shear people now."

Gradually Nikita built up a clientele among the landowners. There was never any work among the peasants—they always cut their own hair—when they cut it.

THE NEW SUMMER HOME AT BOBLOVO: Feozva at left, with Volodya seated above her between two columns, and Olga at right, leaning against the pillar.

Mendeleyev with son Volodya and daughter Olga. At Boblovo in 1878.

"Man does not live for himself alone. . . . Only man or being on a lower level lives for himself alone, like a microcosm or infusoria."

One day, five years ago, Nikita came to Boblovo when Mendeleyev was there. He brought a letter of recommendation from the Antonov brothers, municipal employees at Klin.

Mendeleyev habitually had his hair cut in St. Petersburg, but he liked Nikita's friendly and confident manner.

"Let's cut right now," he said.

There and then was born a relationship that lasted for years. Mendeleyev saw Nikita once a year. Never more than that.

Now, as Anna watched through the open window of the door, Nikita opened a box, took out a white sheet which he wrapped about Mendeleyev, then long scissors and a comb, and in a moment began the trimming of the mass of hair.

The peasants sat below, carefully watching, and eating their hard-boiled eggs.

Nikita worked dexterously, but on the whole slowly. Frequently, with the shears snipping the air he stepped back to view his work.

A mouzhik stood up from the seated crowd below.

"Nikita!" he called. "Take a little off the left. Near the ear!"

Nikita glared.

"Sit down and eat your egg," he said sternly. "Are you a barber? If you're a rooster, crow. Sit down."

The mouzhik sat down.

A little later the aging Fontov stood up and told how in Moscow, forty-three years ago last February 3, he had seen a barber cutting the hair of Count Dolgorouky.

"He used golden scissors," said Fontov.

Nikita glanced at his iron scissors, and then stole a glance at Mendeleyev.

"Nitchevo," said Mendeleyev. "That's all right. Cut. I'm not a count."

Nikita brightened and resumed his work.

The haircutting had now reached a stage where everyone felt comfortable. The sun was warm, the lunches satisfying, and Nikita was working well, even humming a tune.

Now a mouzhik stood up. His little blond boy stood up at once also.

"Mitri Ivanitch," said the mouzhik, "they say you've been to the great Amerika. Is there truth in this, *barin?*"

Mendeleyev started to nod, but Nikita held his head.

"I've been there," said Mendeleyev. "The Amerikans know many technical things. I went to learn about their petroleum work. We too have much petroleum—we must get it out."

"Is it far, this Amerika?" asked the mouzhik.

"Far, yes."

A woman stood up. She took off her kerchief.

"My boy has a soreness in his belly," she said. "The poor little thing, *bednyazhka*, is ailing. I had hot leaves on his body, but nothing comes of it."

"A doctor!" barked Mendeleyev, "you need a doctor, not leaves. Take him to Dr. Vorontsov in Klin, and say that I sent you. You won't have to pay anything. I'll arrange it. Go at once. Take him now."

The woman put on her kerchief and picked up her pale little boy. A mouzhik followed them through the crowd.

"Mitri Ivanitch," said a heavy woman without rising, "my daughter will not marry the merchant Davilov. He is kind and generous, but she will not listen to me, her own mother. If my old mouzhik were alive, she would listen."

Mendeleyev blew some hair off his nose.

"She has a right to decide for herself," he said. "You won't be the one to sleep with him—it will be she."

The woman shook her head.

"But he is good and kind."

"Well, why don't you marry him?" asked Mendeleyev.

The heavy woman blushed.

"It is a possibility," she admitted. "He loves to eat. And the *pirog* that I make is the best meat pie in the province."

A murmur ran through the crowd as the mouzhiks and their *babas* discussed the virtues of the *pirogs* made by various *babas* of their acquaintance.

Now a boy stood up. He was blond and thin, not more than fifteen years of age.

"I have finished the schooling around here," he said. "I want to learn about how to get petroleum out of the ground. I want to help. What shall I do?"

Mendeleyev straightened up in his chair.

"Come to me at the University in St. Petersburg next week, on Monday, at five o'clock in the afternoon. Bring all your papers."

"I'll be there," said the boy.

Many more questions and answers followed. After an hour Nikita had finished. Mendeleyev stood up. The peasants stood up too.

"Turn around, Mitri Ivanitch," they called. "Let's see the other side. My, my, how pleasant it looks."

Mendeleyev shook hands with Nikita and paid him. Then he turned to the peasants.

"Good-by," he said. "I will see you next spring. Good-by."

"Good-by," they called. "Good-by, Mitri Ivanitch."

Mendeleyev went into the house.

Outside, the peasants cleaned up the grounds, and climbed back onto their telegas, and drove away.

4

On December 13, 1883, Mendeleyev's and Anna's second child was born, a boy. He was named Ivan in honor of Mendeleyev's father and of Anna's father as well.

A few months later, more happiness and honor came to the Mendeleyev home: Mendeleyev was invited to England to receive the honorary degree of Doctor of Laws from the University of Edinburgh. The especially exciting feature of this honor was that Edinburgh, the home university of the famed chemist Andrews, now made a certain admission: the great researches of its favorite son on liquids and vapors and the critical temperatures at which the one changed into the other, were based on the work done long ago by D. Mendeleyev of Russia.

In England, besides receiving his degree, Mendeleyev attended a dinner given for the chemist William Henry Perkin. It was Perkin who at the age of seventeen had produced from coal the first artificial dyestuff—aniline purple, or mauve. Perkin for long thereafter had engaged in the commercial manufacture of dyes, but in 1874, grown rich, he disposed of his factory and devoted himself to pure research. In 1879, when Lecoq de Boisbaudran received a medal from the Royal Society for discovering one of Mendeleyev's predicted elements—gallium—Perkin, too, received a medal for his researches.

Mendeleyev arrived early at the dinner. There was only one other scientist there. This was the impeccable, goateed William Ramsay, English chemist famed for his researches on the properties of gases and liquids and currently studying the decomposition of ammonia gas under the action of heat. Ramsay was also famed for his aristocratic bearing and his reputation as a linguist.

Mendeleyev did not know him. Bowing, he approached.

"How do you do?" said Ramsay. "We will presently have quite a gathering, I should presume."

Mendeleyev smiled.

"I do not spik English," he said.

Ramsay raised his eyebrows.

"Vielleicht sprechen Sie Deutsch?"

"Ja," replied Mendeleyev. *"Ein wenig. Ich bin Mendeleyev."*

For some reason Ramsay laughed. *"Ich heisse Ramsay,"* he said.

The men then shook hands and chatted in German about chemistry.

Many other scientists were now arriving and Mendeleyev and Ramsay drifted apart.

In a corner of the great dining hall Ramsay stopped to chat with the young French chemist Lebrun.

"You really must enjoy something," Ramsay was saying. He glanced about the hall.

"I don't see him," he said. "But it is amusing. A short while ago a peculiar hairy foreigner came up to me bowing. He said, 'I am Mendeleyev.' Just like, 'I am Jones, the only Jones.' Very entertaining, you know. For my part, I did not say, 'I am Ramsay.' I said perhaps more modestly, 'My name is Ramsay.' Well, we chatted in German, but his German is not perfect, I would say."

The thirty-two-year-old Lebrun, sandy-haired, short, and amiable stood nodding.

"I've met him," he said. "True, he is somewhat different."

Throughout the dinner Mendeleyev and Lebrun talked of Byron.

"I read him practically every night," said Lebrun, speaking in German.

Mendeleyev nodded.

"I read him often," he said. "The poems on Greece. And 'Darkness.' It is full of images, and seems dreadfully prophetic."

Lebrun nodded.

"I haven't read that one for a long time," he said. "I'll read it when I get back to Paris."

"And if you ever learn Russian," laughed Mendeleyev, "you must read the poem 'Silentium,' by Tutchev. *Ach*, it is wonderful. My most favorite of all."

"I'll read it in translation," said Lebrun. "Better than nothing, I suppose."

Mendeleyev wanted to know the appropriate time for smoking. "It is such a very proper dinner," he said, looking about him, "I do not wish to offend."

"I'll tell you when," laughed Lebrun. "I have learned all the rules."

Lebrun told of his work in chemistry, especially his mathematical treatment of chemical problems, and of the way in which he considered that atoms grouped themselves into molecules.

Mendeleyev told of his latest ideas in his plan of unity—the Periodic Table.

"By the way," said Lebrun, "they say that our LeChaplain could not come because his wife would not let him leave France alone. How do they feel in Russia about such matters?"

"In Russia," said Mendeleyev, "we have a saying. 'A crab is no fish among fish, a bat is no bird among birds, and a henpecked man is no man among men.'"

Lebrun laughed.

"That's good," he said. "Good grief, here come the speeches!"

After the dinner Mendeleyev went to a reception with Lebrun, and then back to his hotel. He was lonesome. He tried to look up Russell, but the Englishman was once more in America.

In the morning he strode about London, buying presents. Then he hurried to the wharf, boarded the ship, and impatiently waited for the Channel crossing.

He felt strong and vigorous, anxious to get home, and somehow inspired to greater scientific efforts than ever. He was now fifty years old.

5

In 1886 Mendeleyev was president of the Russian Physical and Chemical societies. The Chemical Society, in the formation of which in 1868 he had played the dominant role, now numbered about 180 members—professors and research men in chemistry. The initial membership had been thirty-five.

The applications of chemistry also were growing. Once again the government called on Mendeleyev for his services in behalf of the petroleum industry. There was fear that the Russian fields were on the verge of exhaustion. Mendeleyev investigated.

"Unfounded rumor," he wrote. "Completely unjustified. Russia abounds with subterranean seas of oil."

Then he told once again what must be done to increase the output, and how to refine the crude naphtha. Now the government was listening. The prestige of the name Mendeleyev was soaring. His suggestions led to results.

In this same year, 1886, he drew up a slightly revised form of his periodic chart—including the recently discovered elements. This chart was printed in quantity, and presently began to appear on the walls of Russian high schools and colleges.

In this year too the twins Maria and Vassili were born, named in honor of the mother sacred in Mendeleyev's heart, and her brother—Mendeleyev's uncle.

As he sat now with Anna, Liuba, and Vanya gazing upon the newly arrived twins, Mendeleyev, though happy, thought also of his first son—Volodya—and his daughter Olga, who were not now with him.

"What are you thinking?" asked Anna.

"I'm just thinking in general," said Mendeleyev. "Of all the things in life, I love nothing more than to have my children about me."

Also in this year another significant event occurred.

In Freiburg, Saxony, the German chemist Clemens Winkler found a new element. Winkler had set out to follow the clue given by the Russian Mendeleyev in his predictions of 1871. The Russian had actually suggested where to seek for an element which he named "ekasilicon." The German scientist was seeking a grayish element whose atoms would be about seventy-two times as heavy as those of hydrogen.

According to Mendeleyev's prediction, the weight of the new element was expected to be about 5.5 times that of water—that is, 1 cubic centimeter of it should weigh 5.5 grams. There were of course a great many other properties predicted. The element, for example, would be slightly susceptible to acids.

Winkler examined the silver ore argyrodite and extracted a grayish substance. Its atomic weight was 72.3 and 1 cubic centimeter of it weighed 5.5 grams. When Winkler made the substance combine with oxygen he found that the resultant oxide weighed exactly what Mendeleyev had predicted. Then Winkler made an ethide and found that it would boil at Mendeleyev's predicted temperature. Winkler made other tests, and finally he flamed the new substance and looked through the spectroscope. The set of bright colored lines was new. No known substance could emit this particular set of colors. This was a new element. Winkler wrote, "There is no doubt that this is Mendeleyev's 'ekasilicon.' The correspondence is remarkable. Even amazing." He named the new element "germanium."

When the news reached Russia, people in the universities and students in the high schools felt a thrill of pride. The news also reached England, France, Holland, Italy, and America. And in these lands, too, both scientists and laymen stopped a moment to marvel as they had before. In England, the scientific commotion was great. Three elements that the outlandish hairy foreigner had predicted in detail, had been found—eka-aluminium in 1875 by Lecoq de Boisbaudran, and named "gallium"; ekaboron in 1879 by L. F. Nilson, and named "scandium"; and now in 1886 ekasilicon by Clemens Winkler, and named "germanium."

In 1846 the existence of the planet Neptune had been predicted accurately. But this Mendeleyev had in great detail predicted the three terrestrial "planets" which had now been found.

There was more marveling when the final tables of comparison between Mendeleyev's ekasilicon and the newly named germanium became known:

	EKASILICON (Es)	GERMANIUM (Ge)
1. Weight of atoms (compared to hydrogen)	72	72.3
2. Weight of 1 cubic centimeter (compared to water)	5.5	5.469
3. Heat required to warm the 1 cubic centimeter by 1° C (compared to water)	0.073	0.076
4. One atom will combine with 2 atoms of chlorine to form	$EsCl_4$	$GeCl_4$

Mendeleyev and Anna

		EKASILICON (Es)	GERMANIUM (Ge)
5.	Weight of 1 cubic centimeter of the oxygen compound (compared to water)	4.7	4.703
6.	One atom will combine with 4 atoms of chlorine to form	$EsCl_4$	$GeCl_4$
7.	The compound with chlorine will melt at about	90° C	86° C
8.	The weight of 1 cubic centimeter of the chlorine compound (compared to water) will be	1.9	1.887
9.	The ethide compound will exist	$Es(C_2H_5)_4$	$Ge(C_2H_5)_4$
10.	The above compound will melt at	160°	160°
11.	The weight of 1 cubic centimeter of the above compound (relative to water) will be	0.96	1.0

Several other comparisons also matched, and in Russia the name "Mendeleyev" rang with a golden magic. The Tsar sent for him.

6

The personal courier from the Tsar came in gilded finery and knee breeches.

Anna, who opened the apartment door, nearly fainted from apprehension and excitement. Mendeleyev led her to a chair.

"Come in," he said to the imperial courier. "Come in, my good man, and close the door."

"Professor Dmitri Ivanovitch Mendeleyev," said the courier in measured formal tones.

"That's me," said Mendeleyev. "Go ahead. And sit down."

The courier remained standing. Once more he began.

"Professor Dmitri Ivanovitch Mendeleyev—tidings from the Tsar!"

"*Akh!*" exclaimed Anna.

"Behave," Mendeleyev said, "and listen to the man."

The courier began to read.

"We, by the Grace of God, Emperor and Autocrat of All Russias, Moscow, Novgorod, Kazan, Siberia, Astrakhan, Smolensk, Podolia, . . ."

"Who's that?" asked Mendeleyev.

The courier stopped and glared into space.

"The Tsar Alexander the Third of the Dynasty of Romanov," he said.

"*Khorosho,*" said Mendeleyev. "Now to the point."

The courier continued to gaze into space.

"His Highest and Most Exalted Majesty requests the presence of the Professor Dmitri Ivanovitch Mendeleyev at the court."

Mendeleyev stood up and patted the courier on the back.

"Very well done," he said. "Tell him I'll be there." For a moment the courier brought his eyes from out of space and wrinkled his brow.

Mendeleyev was amazed.

"*Bozhe moi!*" he exclaimed to Anna. "My God! The man's alive! Look!"

Anna sat speechless.

"Mitenka," she begged. "Be careful. Please."

The courier was frowning at the floor.

"But my good man," said Mendeleyev. "This is so out of character. Have you lost that point in space at which you were looking?"

The courier looked up at Mendeleyev.

"I'm sorry," he said. "It's my job."

Mendeleyev shrugged his shoulders.

"There are better ways to make a living," he said. "However, what's on your mind now? Anna, dear, bring some tea, please?"

"*Akh*, but yes!" exclaimed Anna and hurried out of the room.

"Well?" said Mendeleyev.

The courier cleared his throat.

"Professor Mendeleyev. I don't know how to tell you something additional."

"Just tell it in the simple direct way. That will be good enough."

"All right then," said the pale man, dropping down onto a chair. "The court people and the Tsar expect you to appear for presentation but only after you cut your hair considerably and also shave your beard. That is, the beard should be cut to reasonable size. You understand—"

"*Akh*, but of course," said Mendeleyev. "I understand. I am to clean up, as it were. *Pravda?* Isn't that the truth?"

The courier was now more embarrassed than before. Anna came in with the samovar.

"Well, isn't that true?" repeated Mendeleyev. "I am to clean up and put on a formal frock coat, and so on."

The courier nodded.

"That would be simplest," he said softly. "And safest."

"Tell the Tsar," Mendeleyev said, "that I will not cut a single hair on my head nor shave or trim my beard. Also I will wear my ordinary everyday clothes. These corduroy trousers and this jacket. If this is not agreeable, I will not appear at court."

Anna stood frozen in the middle of the room.

The courier sat open-mouthed, his right hand holding the glass of tea before him.

"Is that clear?" asked Mendeleyev.

Slowly the courier nodded.

"But you do get your hair cut once in a while, don't you?" he said. "So why not now?"

"I have my hair cut in the spring," said Mendeleyev. "You can tell the Tsar that I can come then if he wants, but the clothes will still be just my ordinary ones."

The courier rose and placed his full glass of tea on the table.

"I will deliver your message," he said. "I don't know what else to do."

"You're not supposed to do anything else. Good-by, my good man. God be with you."

Anna still stood motionless in the middle of the room.

"Mitenka," she pleaded. "Mitenka, what have you done?"

Mendeleyev picked up the glass of tea that the courier had failed to drink, and drank some of it.

"Well, I've got work to do," he said, and went to his study.

7

Two weeks later the courier from the Tsar returned. Anna was frightened. In a moment Mendeleyev emerged from his room.

The courier now was smiling.

"That looks better on you," said Mendeleyev.

"The Tsar wishes me to inform you that you may appear in your own attire and the hair as it is. His Majesty suggests the third Monday at five in the afternoon."

"*Khorosho*," said Mendeleyev. "I'll be there. Convey my regards, please."

8

At the palace Mendeleyev was escorted to a large hall with gleaming mirrors and chandeliers. There were many men in frock coats and ladies in elegant attire, chatting in dignified tones, bowing endlessly to each other and to the mingling courtiers, couriers, and men in military uniforms. From somewhere in the background came strains of music. Mendeleyev, in his gray jacket and corduroy trousers, stopped and listened.

Suddenly a courtier appeared at his side.

"Professor," he said. "His Majesty will receive you now."

Mendeleyev followed the tall man.

In the center of a great shining room stood Tsar Alexander III, a handsome powerful man with a black beard. He nodded to Mendeleyev. Mendeleyev nodded back and approached.

"Dmitri Ivanovitch Mendeleyev," said the Tsar. "We are pleased to have you here."

"I am pleased to be here," said Mendeleyev. "It's a fine place you have."

The Tsar frowned. The courtier at the door gazed fixedly at the opposite wall.

"You have brought great honor to Russia," said the Tsar. "Your name is on the lips of the entire scientific world. It is an honor to reward you, with one of our stars of the saints. A golden star on the sash of the blue, white, and red colors of Russia. This will be done before the assembled witnesses in the Great Hall from which you have just come."

Mendeleyev shrugged his shoulders.

"If you like," he said. "But the stars are very expensive and it's a shame to waste value that way."

The Tsar gently rapped on his right epaulet.

"Well, perhaps. But your country wants to honor you. Tell me," said the Tsar. "Why didn't those men name the discovered elements for Russia or for you? You predicted them!"

"That's a sort of unwritten law in science," Mendeleyev explained. "The discoverer has the thrilling reward of naming the thing discovered. I think it's very nice that way."

"I understand," said the Tsar. "Now what is your work for the future? What is your Chemical Society doing, or planning?"

"Next year," said Mendeleyev, "there will be a total solar eclipse visible over a wide belt of Russia and across the entire length of our country. We are getting ready for it now. We have been, in fact, preparing for two years with the astronomers, physicists, and other scientists."

"Wonderful," said the Tsar. "I will see you again after the presentation of awards and the supper. I should like to talk with you more in private."

At nine o'clock Mendeleyev was once more conducted to the Tsar. Mendeleyev now wore a colored sash diagonally across his chest, with a large golden star pinned on it.

The Tsar bowed.

"I merely wished to bid you good night and good fortune," he said.

"Good night," said Mendeleyev. "Except just a moment, if you do not mind. I promised some friends of mine that I would speak about them to you, if I ever should meet you."

"Yes?" said the Tsar, tapping his left epaulet. "What is it?"

"There are several matters," said Mendeleyev. "First, the peasants need more land. Land of their own. A man should have not only a bit of ground to be buried in, but also a spot of land to live on. The serfs were freed, that's true. But they never received enough land for growing their own bread."

The courtier at the door was biting his under lip.

"Go on," said the Tsar.

"We need more schools. More teachers. The country will go forward only if the youth go forward. And the youth cannot go forward without education. The teachers need better pay. Also there should be more money for the building of laboratories and for purchasing equipment. I have been to Amerika. There they spend effort on technical devices, factories, installations. That's part of the reason they have a higher standard of living."

"What else?"

"We need more educational opportunities for women. More art schools, music schools, and scientific laboratories."

The Tsar tapped his right epaulet.

"Well," he said, "this is all very interesting. Will you please send me a report on these matters. Write something on this."

"I write something on this every day," said Mendeleyev. "I'll send you some of my reprints."

"Good night," said the Tsar.

"Good night," said Mendeleyev.

The courtier at the door stared as Mendeleyev strode past him. Outside the door, without breaking his pace, Mendeleyev took off the sash and the star and stuffed them into the pocket of his trousers.

Inside, the Tsar walked to the window. Beyond, lay the brightly lit palace grounds, and there a tall bearded man was striding along past gaping gentlemen in frock coats and elegant ladies in evening gowns. The man marched boldly forward into the dark night.

9

Between the discovery in 1875 of Mendeleyev's eka-aluminium—that became known as "gallium"—and the discovery in 1886 of his ekasilicon—that became known as "germanium"—he produced a great many published scientific writings. True, there were times between 1877 and 1881 during which he suffered so greatly when the matter with Anna threatened to end badly that his work did not go well. But after his marriage to Anna, his drive returned in even stronger measure, and once more the problems of science and the crying technological problems of the Russian land gripped him completely.

The works that Mendeleyev produced between 1875 and 1886 ranged from problems of the earth, "The Status of the Petroleum," to problems of the air above, "The Temperature of the Upper Layers of the Atmosphere."

Russia finally was listening to this man. They were extracting the petroleum from the ground—as he indicated—and manufacturing fuels—according to his method—in large quantities for the great cold land. They were beginning to listen, too, to his plea for better laboratory facilities for students, even as over the world men were listening to his scientific pronouncements.

Chapter Twenty-six

To God on a Bubble

ON AUGUST 7, 1887, a great shadow fell upon the land of Russia.
A mantle of hushed darkness, a mantle of black, swept over the vast Eurasian continent.

The moon—for an instant in its eternal life—stood before the earth in such a position that it blocked off the light from the sun.

All over the land birds screeched in terrified flight as they flapped wildly through the suddenly darkened air. Mouzhiks in their fields dropped to their knees and gazed in supplication at the gloomy heavens and the black disk over the face of the sun. The women in the izbas knelt before the ikons.

The complete blocking of the sun occurred for observers in a central east-west belt girdling the country. The belt was 140 miles wide. Here the total shadow raced across the continent, spanning its full width from the Baltic Sea to the Sea of Japan. This was the region of the totality. Above and below this zone of complete obscurity stretched progressively the regions of lesser eclipse.

For three years Russian scientists had planned and labored to be ready for the total solar eclipse. Though the chief labors fell to the lot of the astronomers, nevertheless, physicists, chemists, and mathematicians stood in constant readiness with assistance to help extract every iota of information possible during the event. At the time of the eclipse, when the bright disk of the sun was obscured, the luminous flames dashing wildly into space from the sun's periphery would be visible. A study of this solar crown—the corona —would yield information regarding the gases that flamed on the sun, the heat and activity of the great star itself. From all this would come an increase of man's knowledge of the universe in which he lived.

The Russian scientists had built a temporary observatory in the path of the totality, and established hundreds of observers in distant stations over the entire land. They had appealed to all volunteers—intellectuals, merchants, wayfarers—to be on the alert, to observe, sketch, and send in information concerning the event.

To Russia had come scientists from England, France, Germany, Italy, and the United States. Concentrating in the region of Moscow, they set up their instruments together with the Russians and prepared to record the eclipse.

At Moscow, the totality would be under way at 6:46 A.M., and would end 150 seconds later. At Tobolsk, the full phase would commence at 9 A.M., for 192 seconds. In Siberian Tomsk the full darkening would begin at 10:30 A.M., and last about 213 seconds.

Seven days before the eclipse it became certain that a balloon would become available for the rise into the heavens to study the corona and the changes in the atmosphere. The balloon would carry an army operator and one scientist.

Thus seven days before the eclipse a meeting took place at the home of M. N. Ghersevanov, the president of the Russian Technological Society. It was brief and to the point: a scientist was to be selected to make the ascent in the balloon.

"Gentlemen," began Ghersevanov, "first of all we must set down the characteristics desired for the man whom we invite. As you know, this will be a hydrogen-filled balloon and the possibility of explosion, such as has occurred in the past, cannot be denied. The man we need must therefore be supreme in courage, otherwise he will not work well in the air. Second, he must have acute perceptions, and mental and physical agility of a high order —for as you know the totality will continue little more than two minutes. Finally, he must be a man whose love for science will animate his mind and his hands during any critical situation that may develop—so that the entire flight from start to finish may be successful in every way."

The old retired scientist Polkonov stood up. Slowly he smoothed his white beard.

"Let us not waste time," he said. "You know very well who that man is. I suggest that you go and invite him at once."

Ghersevanov sent the telegram to Boblovo.

2

On Sunday, August 2, Mendeleyev sat down in his room and wrote his will. He was fifty-three years old, strong, vigorous, and still rapid in his walk. His narrow long hands with straight fingers and strong nails were renowned for the dexterity that lived in them.

After writing his will he went to look for Anna. He had not yet told her of his decision to make the flight. He found her in the front room and took her in his arms as he told her of his plan. For a long while he tried to console her.

To God on a Bubble

"It is safe," he kept repeating, "absolutely safe. The army is sending its principal aeronaut to take me up. Lieutenant Kovanko."

He began to assemble the necessary apparatus—thermometers, barometers, a special clock. The barometers were of the type that he had himself invented. After that he sat down to augment the calculations in the meteorological papers that he had written through the years, papers on the layers of the atmosphere.

The next day Volodya and Olga arrived. Volodya, still somewhat narrow-eyed but handsome, was twenty-two and serving in the Maritime Corps. Olga was nineteen, quiet, with large eyes. The brother and sister were worried about their father's impending flight. Volodya at once became Mendeleyev's aide, and went to Klin—where the ascent would take place—to study the terrain, then to St. Petersburg where he conferred for a long time with the physicist Krayevitch, Mendeleyev's long-time friend. The two men began to plan all sorts of precautions.

They wondered about the strength of the ropes that support the gondola suspended under the balloon. Volodya was especially concerned over the descent. A rope would have to be pulled which would open a valve and let out the hydrogen gas, causing the balloon to partially collapse and sink toward the ground.

"Everything will be all right," Kovanko assured Volodya and Krayevitch. "All is my business."

That evening Mendeleyev came to his laboratory and tested his thermometers and barometers. Then he repacked the basket that he had set aside for these instruments, placing the thermometers in a special box. After that he returned to Boblovo.

Late into the night, in a dark room, he practiced certain maneuvers. Squatting beside the basket with the instruments he suddenly reached out his hands without looking at the basket. Rapidly he lifted the cover on the basket, drew out the principal thermometer, and held it up before his face. Then he replaced the thermometer. He repeated this operation many times. Likewise, he practiced with the barometers that would indicate the pressure of the air and the height of the balloon above the ground. One barometer would be affixed to the side of the gondola, and the other, an aneroid, Mendeleyev would carry in his pocket.

The next morning Krayevitch the physicist came with Volodya, then a number of foreign scientists who wanted to pay respect to Russia's man of science.

The night before the ascent, Mendeleyev played for a long time with his children. Anna stood by, crying silently.

Then, while Krayevitch and Volodya waited outside, Mendeleyev embraced Anna.

"You're always in my heart," he said. "Always."

She wept on his shoulder.

Mendeleyev had to leave now. The rest of the night would be spent at Klin, at the home of the mayor, Voronov. At four o'clock he would have to arise. The ascent would begin about six.

"Be careful," pleaded Anna. "Be careful. You are our whole life."

He kissed her again.

"Everything is well prepared. And remember, my darling, you are not to watch the ascent. You would worry. Do you promise?"

Anna nodded her head.

"I promise," she whispered.

Mendeleyev left.

Early next morning, Anna left to watch the ascent.

3

It was 5 A.M. The great open square at Klin was filled with thousands of people—citizens of the town, vacationists, peasants, spectators from Moscow and St. Petersburg who had arrived on special trains. In the center an area had been roped off, and there, wallowing like a mountainous yellow whale, was the great balloon, now being filled with hydrogen.

The morning was cold and damp and gloomy. Overhead the sun was disappearing behind clouds.

Anna, sitting in her carriage and concealing her face with a veil, searched the space near the balloon. A few men were standing there, but not the one she was seeking.

"Yefim Khrisanovitch," said Anna, "please drive to the mayor's house. But don't let anyone see us. I just want to know where Dmitri Ivanovitch is."

Lavrov, the gaunt, long-whiskered gardener who was driving the carriage, nodded his head and spoke to the horses.

At the house of the Mayor Voronov, he quietly climbed onto the porch and peeked through the window. Suddenly, as though shot from a cannon, he bounded over the railing onto the ground and jumping to his perch set the two horses into a wild run. Away went the carriage. Anna was terrified.

"*Chto takoye?*" she whispered. "What is it?"

Far away, at the edge of the crowd on the square, Lavrov stopped the horses.

"He was just putting on his hat," he said. "He must be coming now."

A great roar went up from the crowd.

"Oorah!" thundered the voices. "Oorah!"

Anna turned.

From the mayor's house came a tall man in a round hat and a long dark coat. Anna's heart beat violently.

"Oorah, Mitenka," she said softly, "oorah."

Next to Mendeleyev was Volodya in his blue midshipman's uniform, then the Mayor Voronov, and the physicist Krayevitch.

The crowd pushed and swerved and roared its welcome as the group made its way toward the balloon, where Lieutenant Kovanko was supervising its inflation with hydrogen.

Anna came across Nadezhda, but she did not converse with her. She could not take her eyes off Mendeleyev. She watched him as he stood gay and calm, chatting with Lieutenant Kovanko. She watched his hands as he pointed to the balloon, to the tanks with the hydrogen, to some mechanism near the tanks. Now he took off his hat. *Akh,* how nice he looked, how strong, and confident. Fifty-three years old, but such a youthful man in spirit, in heart, —be careful, Mitenka, it is high up there, be careful.

"Look!" said Nadezhda, "look at the mouzhiks!"

Anna stared. A group of ten or fifteen peasants suddenly had made their way into the reserved space where Mendeleyev stood with his friends, while the balloon was swelling to greater and greater size.

The gendarmes were trying to herd them away, but apparently Mendeleyev was intervening.

He approached the mouzhiks.

"It's a good day, brothers," he said. "A little cold maybe. What is the question here?"

An old man came forward.

"I'm a tired old man, Mitri Ivanitch," he said. "I don't want anything for myself. But they say you are going up to see God. Will you ask help for my woman? She is dying at home. Tell Him to be ready for her. Will you do that?"

Mendeleyev scratched his head.

"I'm going up to study about the sun, little father. That's all I am going for."

"But if you see God, will you tell?"

"I'll tell."

The old man turned and walked away.

"I'm going to tell her," he called over his shoulder.

Now a short woman in a green shawl came forward.

"My son is about ten years old," she said. "There is trouble in his chest. He coughs day and night. Will you seek help from God? The name is Ferasantavna—tell Him I live in the house of the green roof at the edge of Klin."

"Listen, little mother," said Mendeleyev. "Go to the house of Doctor Vorontsov and tell him I sent you. Tell him about your boy. The doctor is my friend; he will help your son. He lives down that street, right at the end. Go later. He's probably in the crowd here now."

The woman nodded.

"But will you also speak to God?" she asked.

"I will," said Mendeleyev. "If He calls me to Him, I will speak."

The woman wanted to kiss Mendeleyev's hand, but he drew it away.

"Go to your son, little mother," he said.

Now a sturdy mouzhik came forward.

"I am not literate," he said, "but a man who knows letters wrote this petition for me. Will you present it to God?"

Mendeleyev stretched out his hand and took the paper.

"If I see God, I will present it," he said.

"That is the reason for your healthy beard," said the mouzhik. "You knew that some day you would come before God."

Now six or seven others presented petitions to Mendeleyev. Then they calmly withdrew and Mendeleyev returned to the hydrogen tanks. The balloon was filled and was held by ropes tied to stakes. The sky was growing darker—the moon was slipping gradually across more and more of the disk of the sun. People somehow felt constrained to whisper. The heavens were growing gloomy and increasing numbers of dark clouds were beginning to appear. A few clouds during the time of totality would destroy the work and hope of years.

It was six-thirty and the full phase would begin in twelve minutes. Lieutenant Kovanko climbed into the gondola. Mendeleyev shook hands with the pale Volodya and followed into the basket.

"Cut the ropes!" called Kovanko.

The crowd stood with hushed breath.

Four mouzhiks chopped the great ropes, but the balloon did not rise.

Occasionally it seemed to make a feeble effort to go up, but at once again sought the ground.

"It's the dew," said Mendeleyev. "The balloon has soaked up great quantities overnight."

Kovanko was frowning.

"I don't know why I didn't have it covered," he said.

They began to throw out the sandbags. All were now out except two. Still the balloon would not rise. At least two sandbags had to be left, so that later, by pouring out sand, the rate of ascent could be controlled.

Mendeleyev turned to Kovanko.

"You better get out," he said. "It will lift me alone."

Kovanko shook his head.

"That's impossible," he said. "You know nothing about the controls."

The sky was growing darker. It was now six-thirty-five. The full phase would start at six-forty-two.

"Lieutenant," said Mendeleyev, "I am asking you to get out. I am flying alone."

Kovanko frowned.

"The War Ministry ordered me to take you up," he said. "I have my orders."

Mendeleyev took a step toward Kovanko.

"I am not going to lose a total solar eclipse just because of orders by the War Ministry. Get out!"

Mendeleyev suddenly put his hands on Kovanko's shoulders.

"All right," said Kovanko, "all right," and he sprang out of the basket.

Immediately the balloon came to life. It began to rise, straining toward the heavens. Mendeleyev threw out a stool, and a heavy board on which he had wanted to rest his basket of instruments. The balloon continued to rise. It was six-thirty-eight.

Suddenly the tension was broken in the observing crowd.

"Oorah!" thundered the voices. "Oorah!"

Mendeleyev stood at the side of the basket, smiling, and waving his hat.

In the crowd now, a few people sank to their knees and began to pray.

At the edge of the crowd Anna stood petrified, staring at the rising gondola.

"Alone," she whispered. "He's going alone. He doesn't know anything about the controls. Nadenka, he's going alone!"

Nadezhda, too, stood as though hypnotized.

"Don't fear," she said with pale lips. "Don't fear, Anna."

Higher went the balloon, higher and higher.

Anna's eyes followed the diminishing mass in the heavens. Now it was only a spot, now smaller, a dot. In the crowd, someone screamed.

Anna watched. A dot, a dot. Gone.

She fell to the ground, unconscious.

4

In the balloon Mendeleyev felt that the rate of rise was not great. It would be desirable to pass through a considerable vertical height while recording temperature and pressure, especially during the total part of the eclipse. He took out the pocket aneroid barometer and observed that the pressure of the surrounding air was dropping slowly.

The balloon was climbing into the thinner atmosphere at too slow a rate. It was necessary to throw out some of the sand. Rapidly he grabbed one of the sacks and cut it open. He lifted the open end over the edge of the basket. The sand would not pour—it had soaked up the dew and was now stuck into a lump. He clawed at the sand and threw it out by handfuls. The balloon rose more rapidly. It was now thirty seconds before the beginning of the full phase. Working at fever pitch Mendeleyev brushed his hands off on his trousers and squatted next to his basket with the instruments. With his eyes fixed on the moon and the almost-vanished sun, he lifted the basket cover and withdrew a thermometer. Around the moon was now visible a bright ring of clear silver. This was the corona. The full phase was on. The corona was all one color, but the intensity was smaller farther out from the moon. There was no red, violet, or yellow light in the corona. The intensity of the light was approximately equal to that of ordinary moonlight. The width of the corona was not the same in all directions. It was widest at the bottom. Mendeleyev observed no rays of the kind often supposed to emanate from the sun. Now there was some red visible in a projecting section of the solar crown. This was the gas hydrogen excited into a red glow. There were no stars visible in the sky. The seconds were ticking away on Mendeleyev's watch. The full phase had been on now for about fifteen seconds. Mendeleyev's eyes did not deviate from the eclipse. The darkness all around was not greater than that at twilight, because of the reflection from the clouds. For an instant, Mendeleyev observed the running shadow of the eclipse passing him from the right. The flight of the shadow seemed discontinuous —jumpy. Then, suddenly, to Mendeleyev's horror, a small cloud began to pass over the face of the moon and over the solar crown. For still a few seconds the corona could penetrate through the thin cloud, but in a moment an edge of a massive cloud entirely shut off the view.

There was now little to do but to take more readings of pressures and temperatures, though these would be less valuable than those observed before the clouds intervened. Mendeleyev jotted down the temperature readings he had made just before the full phase began. The balloon was still rising. He read the temperatures at the various passing altitudes. —1.2 degrees centigrade, read the thermometer; now 0 degrees; now 3 degrees; now 5 degrees; now the temperature dropped again, 2 degrees, 1 degree. The balloon had reached the maximum height of 11,375 feet. He had time now to reflect on the strange rise and fall of temperature that he had observed, and concluded that the effect was due to variation of cloud distribution in the sky.

The maximum temperature had been observed under clouds, the minimum under a cloudless sky. But the more valuable observations had been the clear views of the corona, the nature of the flaming protuberances. Every bit of such information contributed to the ultimate knowledge of the reactions taking place on the sun, and this in turn would one day help reveal the great secret of the source of the sun's tremendous and seemingly undiminishing energy.

Now there was time to think about descending to the ground.

Mendeleyev sat down to think about the controls. A breeze was blowing, carrying the balloon to the side.

Sitting in the gondola, he suddenly thought of the petitions that the peasants had given him. He took them out of his pocket and began to read. One asked God to find a missing son who had gone to the Northland somewhere five years ago; another asked God for money—twenty roubles—to buy good food and medicine for an ailing girl. Mendeleyev searched the paper for an address. He found it. Another petition asked God to send "Mitri Ivanitch" back home safely.

Mendeleyev stood up. After all, the balloon was a scientific apparatus, and he was accustomed to working with apparatus of science. And furthermore, there was nothing to do but pull this rope which hung from the balloon and was tied to the side of the gondola. The rope led to a valve on the balloon that, if opened, would permit the hydrogen to escape, and the balloon to collapse and sink to the ground. But it was necessary to open the valve slowly.

He took the rope and pulled. The barometer showed that the balloon was dropping too rapidly. He released the rope to close the valve. All seemed well, but strong wind was now blowing, taking the balloon with it. Once more he pulled at the rope. The valve must have opened—the barometer showed that the altitude was decreasing. . . .

He had been up more than two hours. The balloon was sailing along and gradually dropping. Mendeleyev pulled the rope again, and again the balloon dropped. But this time it must have dropped too rapidly, for, suddenly, below, a great forest seemed to rush up furiously toward him. He released the rope quickly but the forest of trees was almost upon him. Quickly he grabbed the half sack of sand and threw it overboard. The balloon shot up.

5

Throughout Russia, during the eclipse, 150 observers had been stationed in the zone of totality, 106 others were scattered throughout the regions of partial eclipse. In distant Irkutsk the observer Shevitch noted carefully that during the total phase the corona did not change in color—the rays remained fiery red. There had been no silver shine, and no stars were visible in the sky. The artist Smirnov made a rapid sketch of what he saw. Near the Irtysh River rings of light were observed surrounding the dark disk of the moon, and in Tobolsk the talented and agile Korotkevitch made several drawings. In Vladimir province drawings were made by Deeman; photographs by Khamantov, and photometric studies carried out by Rogovsky. The spectroscope was used by Borgman, and telescopes by many Russian and foreign scientists.

On the outskirts of the city of Tomsk, near a wood, an old blind man with white hair lay on the ground. It was Timofei, the former chief glass blower at the Glass Factory in the village of Aremziansk. Next to him knelt his great-chested son, the blue-eyed thirty-seven-year-old Stepan.

On his sightless eyes Timofei felt the darkness of the eclipse.

"Night," he whispered, "night has come."

Stepan held his father's left hand.

Timofei lifted his right hand above Stepan's head.

"I bless you, Stepan," he whispered. "Be brave; stay strong."

Stepan drew closer to his father.

"I leave you nothing," continued Timofei. "Nothing except my cane. It belonged to the strannik of whom I have told you. Take it. Go over the land. Help the people."

The sun was emerging from behind the obscuring moon. The light was coming upon the earth.

In the afternoon Stepan built a cross over the mound. On it he carved "Timofei of Aremziansk."

Then he prayed, and picked up the cane.

6

At Klin, Anna finally regained consciousness. Nadezhda and Dr. Vorontsov had worked over her frantically, and Yefim, the gardener, who had driven her to Klin, took her home to Boblovo. The children were waiting there. Kneeling in the front room, Anna gathered them to her.

"Where is *papachka?*" asked the blue-eyed Liuba. "Where is our *papachka?*"

"He'll be back," she consoled them. "Pray, Liubachka. Pray. He'll be back."

The maid Katerina prepared an early luncheon.

"Nitchevo," she kept calling to her young mistress. "Nitchevo, Anna Ivanovna. God will bring him back."

Nadezhda and the physicist Krayevitch remained at Klin, at the home of the mayor. The nervous Krayevitch paced incessantly up and down in the front room. Nadezhda sat in frozen terror.

"He knew nothing about the controls," Krayevitch muttered occasionally. "He left all that to Kovanko. *Bozhe moi, Bozhe moi.*"

Outside, it was growing lighter, the eclipse was ending. The reemergent light of day resembled a dawn, and in the near-by yards roosters were crowing.

At four-fifty-five Volodya came in.

"No news," he said grimly, his narrow eyes seeming narrower, his blue uniform splattered with mud. There were bits of straw on his trousers. "Is there anything new here?"

Krayevitch tugged silently at his ear.

Then, suddenly, a wild-looking man burst into the house.

"A telegram!" he exclaimed breathlessly. "A telegram!"

Krayevitch, Volodya, and Nadezhda leaped at the messenger and reached for the paper in his hand. From another room the mayor came rushing. Krayevitch read the telegram. It was sent from a station along the Nikolayev Railroad.

"Balloon was sighted," read Krayevitch in a trembling voice. "Mendeleyev not."

In the house of the mayor they began to discuss a plan for searching the countryside for miles in every direction. Outside, people were arriving from every house in Klin. They gathered silently and waited. Voronov, Krayevitch, and Volodya stepped out onto the porch. Nadezhda watched through a window.

"Citizens," said the mayor. "We are worried."

The men and the women shook their heads.

"We are worried," repeated Voronov. "It is necessary to search."

"*Tse, tse, tse,*" said the crowd. "*Bozhe moi.*"

Voronov waved for silence.

"Please begin the search," he said. "This section—to the north, this, to the south. This group, east, and this group, west. And spread out. Go."

The crowd divided. The people hurried. In carriages, telegas, on foot.

At Boblovo, the mouzhiks heard of the search. From every house came every mouzhik, calling to Anna as they hurried past.

"*Nitcheve!*" they called. "That's all right! Don't worry, lady. We're going for our Mitri Ivanitch!"

"*Davai!*" they roared at their horses. "*Nu chto!* [What's up!] Are you playing the fool, brother! *Davai!* Give now!"

Anna, in panic, stood at the darkened window. It was seven o'clock.

7

When Mendeleyev threw out the half sack of sand, the balloon rose violently into the air above the forest. The gondola barely escaped a crash with the tall trees.

As the balloon, sailing on the wind, passed over the forest, Mendeleyev saw a clearing ahead. Again he pulled on the rope leading to the hydrogen. The gas was again escaping, and the balloon descending. Below, people were running. Mendeleyev glanced at the coiled rope lying in the bottom of the gondola, one end being tied to it. Rapidly he bent down and threw out the rope. Then he turned back to the rope leading to the hydrogen valve. Now was the time. With all his strength, using both hands, he pulled on the rope leading to the hydrogen escape-valve. The gas blew out of the balloon and it descended rapidly.

The rope from the gondola was dangling, sweeping along the clearing, almost touching the ground. A boy came rushing across the field, and from the other side a hearty mouzhik. The mouzhik grabbed the rope and the balloon came down, then suddenly bounded up again. The mouzhik hung on to the rope, and floated through space. Mendeleyev, straining with all his force, held the hydrogen valve open all the way. The balloon came down and the mouzhik bounced, but he held on. Now the boy was near and Mendeleyev threw him the end of the rope leading to the hydrogen valve.

"Grab it!" he hollered. "Grab it, and pull, little brother! Pull steady!"

The boy grinned and dove for the rope. He caught it and hung on, scrambling somehow to his feet. Now the mouzhik with the rope from the gondola dashed for a tree and in a frenzy of haste circled twice round it. The rope held.

The grinning boy continued to pull on the hydrogen valve. The gas was hissing in escape. The mouzhik with his rope wound it once again around the tree. The balloon bounced up and down, and finally came to rest. Mendeleyev mopped his brow.

Mouzhiks, children, and barking dogs rushed into the clearing from all sides.

"Step out, *barin*," said a lean brown peasant. "Step out. All will be good. These are friendly people. Have no fear. Step out."

The mouzhik who had wound the rope from the gondola around the tree now made a knot and came forward.

"My name is Egor," he said. "Come on, *barin*. You did good. These are your friends."

Another man came forward. He was tall and dark. His face was alert.

"My name is Makar," he said. "I understand your studies."

Crowds continued to arrive, and now the entire clearing was overflowing with peasants.

Mendeleyev stepped out of the gondola. He took off his round hat and crossed himself.

"God be with you all," he said. "What place is this?"

The village Starosta came forward, old, whitebearded, and serene.

"Kalyazinsky District," he said. "Province of Tver. Between the villages of Olghino and Malinovetz. Where did you go up?"

"At Klin."

"At Klin," repeated the Starosta. "Well, this is about one hundred and fifty miles away."

Mendeleyev looked at his watch. It was 9:20 A.M. Now he took a reading on the barometer. It read 750 millimeters of mercury pressure. The temperature was 16.2 degrees centigrade.

He glanced at the yellow balloon. Slowly it continued to deflate. The gas was still rushing out of the valve being held open by the rope in the hands of the boy.

"The Northern Volga branch is not far away," someone said. "Suppose you had fallen into the Volga?"

The peasants were beginning to approach the balloon. Mendeleyev spoke to the Starosta.

"Tell them there is a dangerous gas in the balloon. They must not smoke near by. It is better to keep away. There could be a bad explosion."

The Starosta appealed to the people and they withdrew a few paces.

Makar took Mendeleyev by the arm.

"There is an educated man in the village of Spas Ougol. It is four versts from here. You could rest at his place and decide how to return home. His name is V. D. Saltikov."

Mendeleyev nodded.

"I know him. I'll go there. But first it is absolutely necessary to make certain that no fire is brought near the balloon—no smoking."

"I will see to that," said the Starosta. "You go in peace."

Mendeleyev started out on foot with two guides, but almost at once a wagon came toward him. There were three men on it.

"There he is!" exclaimed a freckled mouzhik. "There is the man who sailed on the comet."

The other two mouzhiks shook their heads back and forth.

"To think," said one, "to think I would live to see a comet." He stood up and gazed at the deflating balloon.

"Come on, comet-man," said the freckled mouzhik. "Come on, we'll take you anywhere. But not so fast as the comet."

At the home of the friendly Saltikov, Mendeleyev wrote a message—a telegram—on a white card. Saltikov gave it to the freckled mouzhik to send from the nearest station. Then Mendeleyev went back to the balloon. It had completely deflated. Makar and Egor and the boy were folding it. Others were helping. Mendeleyev made arrangements with Saltikov to give money to various peasants for their help.

He took his basket with the instruments and the notebook with the data and mounted a telega for the first lap of the journey home. The balloon would follow later. He stood up in the telega and waved to the peasants.

"Good-by," he said. "You are God's people. I thank you for the welcome."

"Good-by," said the voices.

"You had some bubble there," someone called out. "Good-by, cometman," called out the freckled mouzhik.

"*Nu, davai,*" said the driver calmly, to the gray horse.

The telega rolled.

8

Mendeleyev's telegram arrived at Klin at 7 P.M. It was brought to the mayor's house, where Nadezhda was still waiting. When the messenger arrived with the white paper—the second of the day—Nadezhda grabbed it.

"Came down safely at 9 A.M. in Kalyazinsky District," she read. "Glory to God!"

She flew out of the house. The mayor stood in the middle of the room. Then, suddenly, he began to dance.

"Oorah!" he yelled. "Oorah! oorah!" and he pranced about the room.

Nadezhda arrived at Boblovo in a flying troika and burst into the house.

"Safe!" she screamed. "Anna! Anna! Safe!"

Anna came rushing out of a back room. In a frenzy she read the telegram.

"He's alive!" she exclaimed with tears rolling down her cheeks. "My Mitya! *Akh! akh!*"

"Now just be calm," soothed Nadezhda.

Anna took Nadezhda's hand.

"I love you," she said with a smile. "I love you. I met him through you."

In a moment Volodya arrived.

"Yes, I heard," he said. "Certainly I heard. I am going to Moscow to meet him. I'll bring him tomorrow."

The next evening, when Mendeleyev and Volodya arrived at Klin, a great crowd was swarming about the station.

Mendeleyev and Volodya climbed into a troika and were about to start, but the crowds prevented the horses from moving. The people themselves

wanted to draw Mendeleyev through the streets. He arose in the carriage.
"I forbid it!" he called out. "I forbid it! Such a thing is immoral!"

The troika passed through the crowd. In a moment it was flying through Klin, the driver rising in his seat to talk to the strong horses. The bells of the troika tinkled and the wind raced through Mendeleyev's beard.

At Boblovo, suddenly, everyone in the house jumped up. Outside the bells of a troika rang clearly. Anna rushed out, followed by Nadezhda, her brothers, and Katerina the maid.

On the porch, in an ecstasy of joy, Anna fainted once more. Nadezhda's brothers hurriedly carried her into the house, to her room. Nadezhda ran after them and began to work furiously over Anna.

"*Akh, Nutochka*," moaned Nadezhda. "Anna darling, what a time for you to pick."

Volodya ran up the stairs of the house.

"I have brought the airman," he laughed. "I have brought the airman."

Now Mendeleyev came bounding up to the house, and onto the porch.

"Where is Anna Ivanovna?" he demanded.

The maid Katerina tried to divert him.

"She'll be right out," soothed Katerina.

"*Akh*, but no!" roared Mendeleyev. "Something's wrong!"

Wildly he dashed into Anna's room. Anna had just opened her eyes.

"Mitenka," she pleaded, "Mitenka, how could you go up so high and leave me?"

That evening, in the village of Spas Ougol, a little peasant boy in a hut could not fall asleep. His tired, worn mother bent over him.

"Sleep, my young one," she implored. "Sleep."

"A story," pleaded the boy. "Tell a story."

The woman bent over her boy and kissed his cheek.

"Once there lived and existed," she said, "a great learned man with a beard almost as long as God's. And one day the people came to this man and said, 'Go to the Lord our God, and tell him of our misery.' 'I will go,' said the man. So he caught a great bubble, and sat down on top of it, and flew up and up and up, higher still, until he pierced the very heaven above us. And there he saw God and told him of our misery and God pardoned our sins and lightened our burdens. Then the great bearded man came down from the heavens on his bubble, and the people were happy, and the land was gay. And for this, the authorities and the Tsar made this man a very great scientist."

The little boy slept.

Chapter Twenty-seven

The Faraday Lecture and Vassya

Two days after the eclipse, having written a description of it, Mendeleyev left for England with Menshutkin, to attend a meeting of the British Scientific Association. But upon his return, he gave himself to his family at his every leisure moment.

Anna played the piano—the *Emperor* Concerto and other Beethoven music—after the children were asleep, and Mendeleyev stood next to her as she played. Occasionally, too, relaxing before entering his study, he sat next to her on the couch while she read to him of Cooper's American Indians or the exploits of the daring people created by Jules Verne.

For his entire family Mendeleyev liked to bring surprise gifts. Once, when Liuba received a large blue-eyed doll with blond hair, she came running excitedly to her mother.

"Papa brought you a great big doll, too!" she exclaimed. "A very great big one."

Anna found a full-sized mannequin from Paris standing in the front room.

"*Akh*, Mitenka!" she exclaimed flinging her arms about Mendeleyev's neck. "How nice! how nice it is!"

Anna had wanted such a model for some time, not only for making clothes, but also for serving as a posed figure for her painting. And here was the best mannequin available in the world.

Whenever Mendeleyev had to deliver a public lecture, he expressly forbade Anna to go. He feared that she would become nervous and might even faint. Anna always promised that she would not go, but she never could resist. However, she would sit in a distant spot in the gallery and sometimes wear a veil, or hold her hand in front of her face. She trembled slightly as he began with a slow probing delivery, but as he warmed to the subject, she felt at ease. Toward the end of the lecture he would be speaking without restraint—on the need for more public schools, or more teachers, or the necessity of exploiting the Ural mineral wealth—then he was at his best. The audience sat hushed, and Anna completely happy. After the lecture she would rush home, and it was not until the next morning that she would dare tell him that she had been to the lecture.

"How did you like it?" he would say, and was never angry, for it was water over the dam and all had gone well. The next time the same thing happened again. Anna was amazed at how trusting he was in this game of deception.

Mendeleyev's light brown hair was beginning to be tinged with gray, but his full mouth and strong blue eyes bespoke a deep and almost flaming vigor. To Anna it seemed that he was perpetually on fire inwardly. Even in his leisure moments she was aware that the great head was calculating, planning, evolving formulas and schemes, or seeking ways of ameliorating the plight of neglected peasants or persecuted students.

Mendeleyev's sympathy for all oppressed, weak, and helpless was now as well known as his scientific plan of unity among the elements and the discoveries which he had predicted. In his university associations he guided numerous students and associates, and himself bowed to no authority to see that justice was done wherever he turned. The roar that emanated from him was so great whenever he heard of a persecution or a police raid that those who heard him trembled and spoke of "the lion in his lair." But together with this trembling at the roar, men around Mendeleyev felt a deep inexplicable pity at this spectacle of a great man bellowing against the wrongs of the world.

Occasionally, to protect a student meeting where the eternal questions of freedom of speech were to be discussed, Mendeleyev would consent to be present. Sitting on the stage, he bent over a notebook and made calculations on his chemistry research, while the student orators addressed their audience. In the background stood the frowning police who knew it was impossible to do anything violent while Russia's great man of science sat busy with his calculations on the stage.

Mendeleyev's glance almost never turned within himself. As always, he paid no attention to his clothes, and practically never looked in the mirror. There was a great world outside of him, and as he once told Nadezhda there was no humanity in pirouetting around one's "I" while the world needed help.

Help to the world was coming. In Baku a fountain of oil more than a hundred meters high was spurting skyward. In his laboratory Mendeleyev had determined how to tap this oil, how to purify it, how to use its various components for numerous purposes. In his purely scientific work he was continuing his unceasing labors, and this work, too, was performed for the betterment of the present Russia or because of a memory of the past. In October, 1887, he wrote the preface to his work on solutions.

"This research is dedicated to the memory of a mother by her youngest offspring. Conducting a factory, she could educate him only by her own work. She instructed by example, corrected with love, and in order to give him to the cause of science she left Siberia with him, spending thus her last resources and strength. When dying, she said, 'Be careful of illusions. Work. Search for divine and scientific truth. . . .' She understood how often arguments deceive, how much there is still to be learned, and how, with the help of science, without violence, with love but firmness, all superstition, untruth, and error are removed bringing in their place the safety of discovered truth, freedom for further development, general welfare, and inward happiness. Dmitri Mendeleyev regards as sacred a mother's dying words."

2

In the spring of 1888 a new assignment came from the government. Now that he had made Baku the most productive oil region in the world and had developed a new method for the commercial distillation of the southern oil, thus saving Russia great sums of money, Mendeleyev was asked to look into the problem of coal.

He made a tour of the coal areas on the banks of the Donetz River, and in the adjacent vicinity. His report on the world importance of the Donetz coal made it clear that if his suggestions for working the coal areas were followed, not only would another great source of fuel become available, but Russia could enter into advantageous world trade—if only men put themselves to the task.

In St. Petersburg, scientific courses for women were increasing steadily since the days when Mendeleyev founded the first chemistry course for them. But now, suddenly, in the winter a domestic heartache developed—two-year old Vassya caught cold and became seriously ill with pleurisy. An infection set in and Vassya was expected to die.

The family was now at the university apartment, and a number of doctors were summoned. Dr. Beistrov recommended an immediate operation, and named the man best qualified, Dr. Moultanovsky. Anna, in a panic, grabbed up her coat and dashing out immediately into the St. Petersburg winter ran all the way to Moultanovsky's house.

Dr. Moultanovsky was just leaving. He had on his *shuba*—his full-length fur coat—and his fur hat. In his hands he carried a box containing surgical instruments.

"I'm on my way to an operation," he said. "What is your trouble?"

Hurriedly Anna explained.

"Well maybe after this operation. I do not know, however, how long it will take."

Anna looked up at Moultanovsky with pleading eyes. Snow was falling on her bare head.

"Dr. Beistrov says there is no time to waste," she said softly. "No time to waste."

Moultanovsky shook his head.

"I am sorry," he said.

Anna stepped out of the doctor's way. Silently she stood in the snow and wept.

Moultanovsky took her by the arm.

"All right," he said. "Let's go to your little son."

On the way, Moultanovsky stopped a neighborhood boy and sent a message to Dr. Kondratyev to come at once as an assistant.

The operation was successful.

Vassya recovered slowly. Anna and Mendeleyev worried.

3

Another great honor now came from England.

The Royal Society, one of the greatest scientific bodies in the world's history, sent an invitation to Mendeleyev to read an address at a historic meeting in London. Professor William John Anderson, president of the Mechanics Section of the Royal Society, brought the invitation in person to St. Petersburg. Anderson, who had once studied in Russia and knew the Russian language well, loved to call himself "Vassili Ivanovitch Anderson." Mendeleyev was delighted with him. Anderson presented the formal letter of invitation—it included Anna. She was unable to restrain her joy.

"I'm going to London," she sang excitedly, "I'm going to London. *Akh, Bozhe moi,* to London!"

Anderson and Mendeleyev beamed.

Then, a short while after this invitation, there arrived another one from London. This was from the British Chemical Society, which asked Mendeleyev to deliver the annual Faraday Lecture.

No Russian scientist had ever received comparable honors.

Anderson volunteered to translate Mendeleyev's Russian speeches into English so that they could be read to the English audience after some sort of ceremony. The first speech was to be given on Friday, May 31, of the following year, 1889, and the second on Tuesday, June 4.

In answer to the invitations Mendeleyev wrote that in the name of Russia he was thrilled at the honors.

The British invitations had come not only because Mendeleyev had founded the plan of unity, had successfully and in detail predicted the existence of three unknown elements, as well as having published many scientific papers through the years, but they came also because he had inferred the formula for beryllium in its combination with oxygen, BeO—one atom with one—and had inferred that the weight of beryllium atoms was nine times that of the hydrogen atoms. In 1884 this inference had been confirmed. He had also inferred the weight of the atoms of cerium as about 138, and this was confirmed in 1875 by von Buhrig and in 1885 by Brauner of Prague. Mendeleyev had also insisted that the weight of the atoms of tellurium compared to those of hydrogen was less than 128 and greater than 122; and this too was being confirmed. In addition, the statement made by Mendeleyev many years previously that the atoms of uranium must be about 240 in weight, not 120—and his insistence upon placing uranium at the 240 position in his plan of unity—was also now confirmed. The first confirmation came in the years 1882 to 1886 by Zimmerman and Rammelsberg, and in this very year of 1888 Nilson and Petterson proved and announced that "Mendeleyev was right about uranium."

May, 1889, came. Mendeleyev and his family were at Boblovo. The fair-haired Liuba and Vanya, and the twins Vassya and Maria—Mousya—were gay. Vassya seemed well.

Mendeleyev and Anna left their children in Nadezhda's care, and started for London.

4

On March 2, at the meeting of the Russian Chemical Society, the new president, Beketov, had made a special statement. He related how twenty years before, on March 6, 1869, a plan of unity concerning nature was announced by Dmitri Ivanovitch Mendeleyev. "Not to many scientists comes the opportunity to live through such a brilliant confirmation of the intellectual labors submitted to them," said Beketov, "and to witness how the conception of a system created by them aided in the progress of science."

There was long applause.

At the following meeting on March 30, the Doctors Trapp and Pell had brought tribute from the Medical Council of Interior Affairs: "Deeply esteemed Dmitri Ivanovitch: Today marks the end of the twentieth year. . . . Your chemical law concerns biology too, where we deal with the elements of nature. . . . The Medical Council wishes you many more years of productive labor which already has surrounded you with an aureole of glory . . . constituting the pride of our Fatherland."

That was in Russia. It would be good now to meet new English friends—foreign colleagues in science.

If the Channel were an indication of the reception awaiting, then Anna

Mendeleyev, Anna, and the artist Koundzhi. Sketch made by Anna from a photograph.

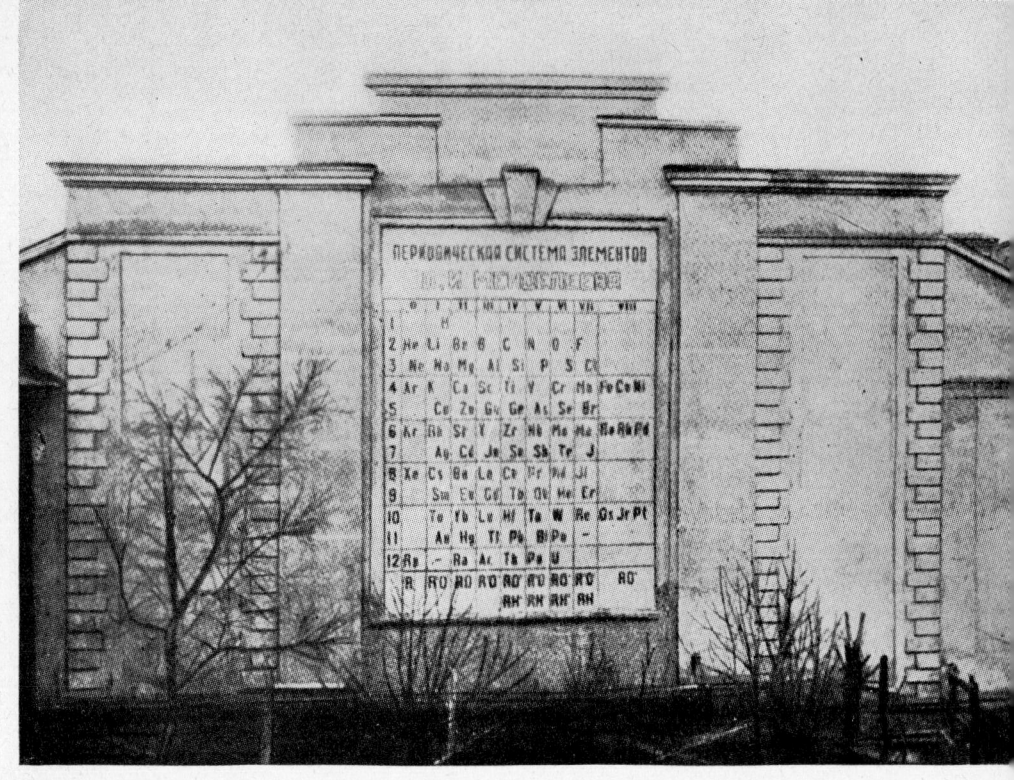

Monument erected in 1934 to Mendeleyev on the one hundredth anniversary of his birth by the Institute of Meteorology of U.S.S.R. Located near the Main Chamber of Weights and Measures, Leningrad. The tablet reads, *"The Periodic System of the Elements of D. I. Mendeleyev."*

The Faraday Lecture and Vassya

could look with terror to the immediate future. She was deathly ill on the tossing green sea. Mendeleyev procured a lemon. It seemed to help. But the only thing that could actually rally her was the eventual arrival at the English shore.

"How good," she whispered. "How good that land exists. *Akh*, the good English soil."

At the Charing Cross Hotel, just as she fully recovered from memories of the Channel, Anna developed a sore throat and high fever. Anderson, who had met Mendeleyev and Anna at the ship, went out and brought a doctor. After examining Anna the doctor sent up huge green pills. Mendeleyev's first lecture was three days away, and Anna was to lead the line of honor on the arm of the president of the Royal Society. She struggled against her illness but secretly laid aside the monstrous green pills which terrified her by their size and reminded her of the sea. On the third day, by accident, the doctor discovered Anna's hoarded pills on a shelf in the bathroom. He was amazed.

"How original!" he exclaimed after he had recovered himself. "How original you Russians are. You are cured merely by sight!" He took the thermometer out of Anna's mouth. "Madame, your temperature is normal," said the doctor.

Mendeleyev, Anna, and the doctor laughed, and when he had gone, Anna jumped out of bed and began to get ready for the evening's reception and lecture.

Anderson, who had thought of everything, had warned that the ladies would be in décolleté and the men in tuxedos. It had taken some time to convince Mendeleyev that purely for the sake of international good will he should wear a tuxedo. This argument was originated by Anna, and it impressed him.

"*Khorosho*," he said. "For the sake of peace between England and Russia I will wear this monstrous aristocratic phenomenon. But for no lesser reason."

No one, however, on any grounds at all, could pry Mendeleyev's boots off him.

"The boots stay," he said. "That's for the sake of peace between me and me. Not another word, please."

At the Royal Institution Anna and Mendeleyev met many men of scientific fame. Sir Frederick Abel, president of the Royal Society, was there with Dr. Russell, president of the Chemical Society; Dr. Mond, president of the Chemical-Technical Society; Sir Frederick Bramwell, president of the British Association; and Professors Frankland, Crookes, Thorpe, Gladstone, Armstrong, Newlands, and many others.

Anna received the central chair opposite the platform on which Mendeleyev and Professor Dewar were standing. Other guests were filing in and taking their seats. Now Dewar began to read the English translation of Mendeleyev's speech, "An Attempt to Apply to Chemistry One of the Principles of Newton's Natural Philosophy." There were many in the audience who were surprised and intrigued at Mendeleyev's attempt to apply to chemistry a famous law of physics—Newton's third law: to every action there is an equal and opposite reaction. There were those in the audience who felt that Mendeleyev was treating all chemistry as a special branch of physics, and they were pleased. These were the physicists. Others in the audience whispered the names of certain of Mendeleyev's investigations which tended to show that he actually treated physics as a minor branch of chemistry. These people, too, were pleased. They were the chemists.

Professor Dewar was reading for Mendeleyev.

"Nature, inert to the eyes of the ancients, has been revealed to us as full of life and activity. The conviction that motion pervaded all things, which was first arrived at with respect to the stellar universe, has now extended to the unseen world of atoms. No sooner had the human understanding denied to the earth a fixed position and propelled it along its path in space, than it was sought to fix unmovably the sun and the stars. But astronomy has shown that the sun moves with unswerving regularity through the star-set universe at the rate of about fifty kilometers per second. Among the so-called fixed stars are now discerned manifold changes and various kinds of movement. Light, heat, electricity—like sound—have been proved to be aspects of motion; to the realization of this fact modern science is indebted for powers which have been used with such brilliant success, and which have been expounded so clearly at this lecture table by Faraday and by his successors. As, in the imagination of Dante, the invisible air became peopled with spiritual beings, so before the eyes of devout investigators, and especially before those of Clerk Maxwell, the invisible mass of gases became peopled with particles: their quick movements, their collisions, and impacts became so manifest that it seemed almost possible to count the impacts and determine many of the peculiarities or laws of their collisions. . . .

"But the invisible world of chemical changes is closely analogous to the visible world of the heavenly bodies, since our atoms form distinct portions of an invisible world, as planets, satellites, and comets form distinct portions of the astronomer's universe; our atoms may therefore be likened to the solar systems, or to the systems of double or of single stars: for example, ammonia, NH_3, may be represented in the simplest manner by supposing the sun, nitrogen, surrounded by its planets of hydrogen; and common salt, $NaCl$, may be looked on as a double star formed of sodium and chlorine.

The Faraday Lecture and Vassya

". . . Some chemists forget that there is the possibility of motion in the interior of molecules, and therefore represent them as being in a state of deathlike inactivity.

". . . Numerous considerations force us to renounce the idea of static equilibrium in molecules, and the recent yet strongly supported appeals to dynamic principles constitute, in my opinion, the foundation of the modern teaching relating to atomic studies. . . .

"The immediate object of this lecture is to show that, starting with Newton's third law of motion, it is possible to preserve to chemistry all the advantages arising from structural teaching, without the necessity of building up molecules in solid and motionless figures, or to ascribe to atoms definite limited valencies, directions of cohesion, or affinities. . . .

"Newton's third law, which is applicable to every system, states . . . 'the actions of bodies one upon another are always equal and in opposite directions.' This simple fact constitutes the point of departure for explaining dynamic equilibrium. . . .

"Let there be a molecule containing atoms ABC; it is clear that according to Newton's law, the action of A on BC must be equal to the action of BC on A, and if the first action is directed on BC, then the second must be directed on A, and consequently then, where A can exist in dynamic equilibrium, BC may take its place and act in a similar manner. . . . Let us call this consequence of an evident axiom 'the principle of substitution,' and let us apply it to those typical forms of hydrogen compounds which we have already discussed. . . .

"Thus, by applying the principle of substitution, we can, in the simplest manner, derive not only every kind of hydrocarbon compound, such as the alcohols, the aldehyde-alcohols, aldehydes, alcohol-acids, and the acids, but also combinations analogous to hydrated crystals which usually are disregarded. . . .

"The discovery of the laws which govern this harmony in chemical evolution will only be possible, it seems to me, under the banner of Newtonian dynamics, which has so long waved over the realms of mechanics, astronomy, and physics. In calling chemists to take their stand under its peaceful and universal shadow I imagine that I am aiding in establishing that scientific union which the managers of the Royal Institution wish to effect, who have shown their wish to do so by the flattering invitation which has given me—a Russian—the opportunity of laying before the countrymen of Newton an attempt to apply to chemistry one of his immortal principles."

Dewar finished reading. He turned to Mendeleyev and bowed. The applause of the audience was thunderous. Mendeleyev shook hands with the man who had read his speech and now he turned and bowed several times to the rising and applauding audience. Anna tried to stop the tears in her eyes, but they spilled over and ran down her cheeks. From the platform, for an instant, Mendeleyev gazed down upon her and smiled.

He was invited to say something, and for the first time in history the hall of the Royal Institution resounded with the speech of Russia.

5

The formal reception began in the adjoining Assembly. Professor Dewar, who had read Mendeleyev's lecture, came and offered his arm to Anna.

"There is a surprise," he said. "Will you accompany me?"

In the Assembly Hall, Dewar and Anna stopped. Before them on the wall hung a great painting of the Russian chemist—Dmitri Ivanovitch Mendeleyev, 1934– .

"*Akh*," said Anna, turning to Dewar, "*kakiye vi sympatichniye luedi—Anglichani.* What heart-warming people you are, you English."

Mendeleyev found Anna.

"Well?" he said. "What do you think?"

She put her hand in his.

"You were wonderful," she said. "They'll never forget it."

"I'll never forget them," said Mendeleyev. "Such a humane atmosphere—everywhere I turn here."

The next day Anna and Mendeleyev were entertained by Anderson at his country home. Anderson had a genuine surprise—a full-course Russian dinner that he had prepared himself. As a student in St. Petersburg he had learned many things. There was borsch now to eat—the kind with beets and floating sour cream. There was also genuine *pirog*—the delicious meat pie that years ago the strannik had prized above all foods. The conversation was in Russian, with Anderson translating for his wife and daughter.

The following day, Sunday, Mendeleyev went to Professor Mond's laboratory to look at his newly invented battery. With Mendeleyev went Ramsay—who had once called him "an outlandish creature." Also in the party were Professors Frankland, Brauner of Prague, and Nazzini of Italy.

At dinner Anna sat between Mond and Nazzini. Anna spoke Italian passably well, having learned it nine years before when she studied in Italy while Mendeleyev despaired in St. Petersburg.

On the following day, Monday, Mendeleyev visited Ramsay's laboratory at University College, and the private research rooms of the great physicist Crookes. Meanwhile, Mond's wife took Anna to inspect London—the Museum, Westminster Abbey, the shopping districts, and the slums.

That evening a telegram came from Boblovo.

6

Anna stood petrified as Mendeleyev read the message to her. The English and Continental scientists rose silently from their chairs in the parlor of the home where a party had been in progress.

"Vassya desperately ill," read Mendeleyev. "Abscess on left lung. Wire permission for emergency operation. I beg you. Nadezhda."

Mendeleyev held Anna to keep her from falling to the floor. But she recovered in a moment. He clutched his head in his hands and rocked it to and fro. He gave Anderson the answer—permission granted for the operation.

Mendeleyev and Anna rushed from the party. The Faraday Lecture, foremost scientific honor, was scheduled for the next day. But at home little Vassya was ill.

In a fury of haste Anna and Mendeleyev started for the waterfront. Someone, if it mattered, might later forward to them their clothes from the hotel.

Anderson rushed along with them, hiring a carriage, buying tickets.

The crossing of the Channel began. Anna was not ill this time. That is, not from the tossing water. Mendeleyev, standing in anguish at the front of the ship, gazed eastward through the blowing dark night.

Meanwhile their telegram had reached Boblovo.

Dr. Ivan Ivanovitch Orlov, with two doctors assisting, disinfected Mendeleyev's study upstairs and cleared the desk. Nadezhda and Katerina the maid brought in little Vassya.

Presently Orlov was ready. He crossed himself and reached for the scalpel.

Nadezhda, her lips reciting a prayer, stood by to help. She, who had brought Mendeleyev and Anna together, now assumed parental responsibility over their child. If need be, she was ready with her blood, with her life. Nadezhda stood by.

7

The next day at the Faraday Lecture, President Russell of the Chemical Society explained to the audience why Professor Mendeleyev was not able to be present. Above Russell, on the wall, hung the Periodic Chart of the Elements. Professor Armstrong prepared to read the English version of Mendeleyev's Faraday Lecture. Before he began he said,

"I would like you to imagine that this man who is flying to the bedside of his little sick boy instead of glorying in the Faraday honor—I want you to imagine that he is standing here beside me, under his chart of the elements." Armstrong turned his gaze sideways. The audience, hushed, followed his glance and fixed its attention on the space beside him.

Armstrong, before the Fellows of the Chemical Society assembled in the theater of the Royal Institution, began to read the address entitled "The Periodic Law of the Chemical Elements."

"The high honor bestowed by the Chemical Society in inviting me to pay a tribute to the world-famed name of Faraday by delivering this lecture has induced me to take for its subject the Periodic Law of the Elements. . . .

"It was in March 1869 that I ventured to lay before the then youthful Russian Chemical Society the ideas upon the same subject which I had expressed in my just written *Principles of Chemistry*. . . .

". . . Strecker, De Chancourtois, and Newlands, stood foremost on the path toward the discovery of the periodic law, and . . . they merely wanted the boldness necessary to place the whole question at such a height that its reflection on the facts could be clearly seen. . . .

"Kant said that there are in the world 'two things which never cease to call for the admiration and reverence of man: the moral law within ourselves, and the stellar sky above us.' But when we turn our attention toward the nature of the elements and the periodic law, we must add a third subject, namely, 'the nature of the elementary individuals which we discover everywhere around us.' Without them the stellar sky itself is inconceivable; and in the atoms we see at once their peculiar individualities, the infinite multiplicity of the individuals, and the submission of their seeming freedom to the general harmony of nature.

". . . In the republic of scientific theories freedom of opinions is guaranteed. . . .

"We now know three cases of elements whose existence and properties were foreseen by the use of the periodic law. I need but mention the brilliant discovery of *gallium*, which proved to correspond to eka-aluminium of the periodic law, by Lecoq de Boisbaudran; of *scandium*, corresponding to ekaboron, by Nilson; and of *germanium*, which proved to correspond in all respects to ekasilicon, by Winkler. When, in 1871, I described to the Russian Chemical Society the properties, clearly defined by the periodic law, which such elements ought to possess, I never hoped that I should live to mention their discovery to the Chemical Society of Great Britian as a confirmation of the exactness and the generality of the periodic law. Now that I have had the happiness of doing so, I unhesitatingly say that, although greatly enlarging our vision, even now the periodic law needs further improvements in order that it may become a trustworthy instrument in further discoveries. . . .

"Although it is but a recent scientific generalization, it has already stood the test of laboratory verification, and appears as an instrument of thought which has not yet been compelled to undergo modification; but it needs not only new applications but also improvements, further development, and plenty of fresh energy. All this will surely come, seeing that such an assembly of men of science as the Chemical Society of Great Britian has expressed the wish to have the history of the periodic law described in a lecture dedicated to the glorious name of Faraday."

Armstrong finished reading. Glancing at the empty space beside him, he bowed, then joined in the prolonged applause of the rising audience.

The Chemical Society voted to send greetings and sympathy to St. Petersburg, and Anderson was given the Faraday Medal to take in person to Mendeleyev. Anderson was given also a purse worked in the Russian national colors—blue, white, and red. The purse contained many golden coins. This, too, was to be transmitted to Mendeleyev. Anderson turned to the audience.

"Last evening, while Professor Mendeleyev was hurrying to the waterfront, I happened to mention to him that a splendid award of money would be transmitted to him. He took me by the arm and told me to convey a message. Gentlemen, I see him standing here under his chart of the elements. I see the vision that Professor Armstrong evoked. There stands the greathearted Mendeleyev. He is being given this purse and he pours the golden coins into his left hand. The hand is open—it does not hold money as a man holds it who wants it. He looks at it. Now he tumbles the coins onto the table. He speaks. It is in Russian, but he says, 'I cannot contemplate accepting payment for a work of love, in the hallways made sacred by the memory of Michael Faraday!'"

Silently the audience continued to gaze at the empty space on the platform.

Presently, a motion was accepted that besides the Faraday Medal the two societies before whom the addresses had been given join in sending certain mementos to Professor and Madame Mendeleyev. It was decided to send two vases marked with the initials of Anna Ivanovna Mendeleyeva, and a goblet of aluminium and gold, wrought with the initials of Dmitri Ivanovitch Mendeleyev.

8

In the train tearing through the night over Germany, Mendeleyev made his way through car after car to the engine. After much discussion with a workman he entered the locomotive.

"*Mein Sohn ist krank*," [My son is sick] he said. "In Russia—far away."

"*Wir fahren ja schon schnell*," [We are traveling already fast.] replied the engineer.

In the train rumbling through Poland, Mendeleyev stood at the elbow of the engineer.

In Russia, all the way to Klin, Mendeleyev and now Anna, too, stood next to the engineer.

Night had passed, the day had passed, and a second night was aging. Klin.

There was a troika, but Mendeleyev had the bells tied up—this was no time for merriment, nor the occasion to waken a child who may be alive and resting.

The troika flew through the night. The driver talked to the team.

"Faster!" called Mendeleyev. "Faster!"

The horses flew through black space.

"Faster!" called Mendeleyev.

And now he made his way to the driver's perch. Anna merely stared ahead through the night.

"My boy is sick," said Mendeleyev.

The bearded driver shook his head.

"*Bednyazhka*," [the poor little one.] he said.

Mendeleyev put out his hand.

"Give me the reins."

Carefully the driver transferred the reins.

Mendeleyev stood bareheaded in the wildly blowing black night. Somehow, for a fleeting instant, a vision out of the past coursed through his mind. A great crowd of people driving frantically toward a glowing sky.

Mendeleyev took a breath of rushing cold air.

"*Davai!*" he roared unto the night.

The horses seemed to leave the ground completely.

At Boblovo, the maid Katerina bounded out of the house. She ran down the incline to the approaching troika.

"Vassya lives!" called Katerina. "Vassya lives!"

Mendeleyev flew to the house with Anna close behind him.

Grim and worn, Nadezhda stood at the open door of Vassya's room.

On tiptoe Mendeleyev entered the room and turned to the little bed. He made the sign of the cross over the little boy.

"Vassya," he whispered. "Vassya, your *papachka* is here. Your little papa has come home."

In all her life Nadezhda had never heard such a tone in a man's voice. Tears ran down her face.

Vassya stirred. He opened his eyes.

"*Papachka*," he said.

Chapter Twenty-eight

The Petition

VASSYA RECOVERED. Anna and Nadezhda nursed him to complete good health.

Mendeleyev was so grateful to Nadezhda for her devotion to his little boy that he could not thank her enough. He gave her a gilt-edged volume of his *Principles of Chemistry,* inscribed to her.

Again everything seemed serene in Mendeleyev's home and when the family returned to the university apartment he began to devote an occasional hour to his hobbies. He arranged photographs and engravings in albums, and made boxes of various sorts to store pamphlets, and also for traveling purposes. For Nadezhda he made a traveling chess set. The board had holes so that the cardboard chessmen could be set firmly and would not slide or topple when the train jolted.

He also bound books and articles, and nearly always brought nonrelated subjects together in one final volume. There were volumes containing articles on art, geology, history, chemistry, plant life, and music.

"Life is divergent but is one," he would say. "These things belong together—they are the components of a single universe."

Mendeleyev still avoided all festivity whenever he could. But he loved the public baths. There he could relax from his laboratory work and from his writing. Undressing, he would bathe and be beaten by twigs with long leaves in the hands of an attendant. Entering the steam room he would occupy the bottom row of bleachers, and then would gradually make his way to the top. On the way up he would encounter other steamed and nearly parboiled creatures. Some of them he might recognize as old acquaintances, habitués of this domain of hot fog. Others were newcomers. But always everyone was mellow and cordial. Stripped of their vestments, the men also seemed to be stripped of affectation and chatted in a casual unaffected manner, and never about the weather. Occasionally, on the way down from maximum steam Mendeleyev might encounter an especially interesting person going up, and then it was worth while to go back up with him one row to finish a conversation.

After the return to the lowermost bleachers he would emerge into progressively cooler rooms. Then there would be massage and drying, and after that a group would sit around in their bathrobes and have supper. Everything was always agreeable here. The steam had apparently dissolved away every trace of any possible meanness in character. The men would finish supper with endless glasses of tea, and then most of them would sleep in private rooms through the night. In the morning they emerged to come to grips with the world. In a week most of them would rush to the baths again.

Back at his work, beaming, Mendeleyev would resume his writing. Frequently now he either stood and wrote behind a tall desk standing next to his old one, or sat on the corner of the divan. The lectures continued. The laboratory work with assistants also went on. Mendeleyev in this year of 1889 was fifty-five years old and the years were sitting well.

The Russian Physico-Chemical Society continued to grow. The work of the men was good and yearly growing better. Mendeleyev attended every monthly meeting that he possibly could. Many people came merely to see him there, to listen smilingly as he tore after a complex problem in chemistry. Mendeleyev, who was largely responsible for the founding of the Chemical Society twenty years before, supported it now with all his strength and enlivened the meetings with his intense participation in them. Even students appeared unobtrusively at the meetings to watch the man whose love of knowledge imparted a unity to the proceedings.

The problems of Russian oil and coal were now being solved. For his friend Professor Mond, in England, Mendeleyev wrote a letter of six thousand words text and two thousand words in footnotes on "The Present Position and Prospects of the Caucasian Petroleum Industry." Mond was the editor of the *Journal of the Society of Chemical Industry* and was glad to print Mendeleyev's letter. Mendeleyev discussed geography, explorations in the Caucasus, tests, statistics of yield, and urged construction of a pipe line to the Black Sea. He also urged the manufacture of benzene, heavy oil, vaseline, and tar in addition to the currently produced kerosene and illuminating oil. He pointed out that the construction of a Caucasian pipe line was opposed by "Baku people because of their supposed interests, which oppose themselves to the general interests of Russia, and more or less to that of the world at large. . . . The Russian petroleum will suffice for the whole world. . . . And nothing should stop the English and Russian people who have commenced operation with Caucasian petroleum. . . ."

At home he continued to write on many subjects, including "The Need of a Chemical Laboratory at St. Petersburg University."

But the University of St. Petersburg was suffering more dire needs. An ominous shadow was falling over the principal center of Russian learning.

2

In the spring of 1890 a series of student uprisings began at the university. The uprisings and student strikes were occasioned by police suppression of any semblance of free thought. Wherever the students met for discussion the police appeared to break up the meeting and jail the leaders.

In the midst of this unrest, notice came from England that Mendeleyev had been elected Foreign Member of the Royal Society. But he could not think about this honor. The plight of the students tormented him. Anna worried too. To seek peace she turned frequently to the box of letters that Mendeleyev had long ago given her. He had wanted to be a step for her, to lift her to art and freedom. In the letters he had not even entertained hope of marriage, nor had he ever mentioned it. Now Mendeleyev wanted to be a step to freedom for the students.

The unrest increased. The students marched about the university grounds and refused to attend classes unless their rights were respected and the government guaranteed free assembly. Professors came out onto the university steps and pleaded with the students to return. The students insisted on freedom of speech. Police charged in with clubs and dragged away as many as they could. The students fought back.

Then came a day when the entire mass of students milled about the university grounds, carrying placards and shouting "*Svobodou!*—Give us freedom!" "Economic Support for Students!" "No Obligatory Uniforms!" "Decrease the Matriculation Fee!"

The rector of the university stepped out to plead.

The students raised their hands to him.

"Mendeleyev!" they called. "Give us Mendeleyev."

Far away in his university office, Mendeleyev heard the call.

He rose from his desk and walked through the long corridors. The students knew he would come. They waited.

Mendeleyev opened the great front doors and stood on the top step of the stairway.

Every voice was now silent. The great mass of students stood watching their friend, Mendeleyev.

Mendeleyev spoke. "Well," he said pensively, "are we going to make noise or are we going to study?"

"We can't study," answered a dark-eyed student. "We need help. And we need protection from the police."

"What precisely do you want?" asked Mendeleyev.

The dark-eyed student spread out his arms. "We don't want birds' milk, Dmitri Ivanovitch. No, our wants are clear. They are on these placards."

"Tell us how you feel!" called a voice from the crowd. "Tell us what you believe, Dmitri Ivanovitch."

Mendeleyev came forward.

"I have achieved an inner freedom," he said. "It has somehow come about. There is nothing in this world that I fear to say. No one nor anything can silence me. This is a good feeling. This is the feeling of a man. I want you to have this feeling, too—it is my moral responsibility to help you achieve this inner freedom. But I am an evolutionist of a peaceable type. I want you now to proceed in a logical and systematic manner. Elect several representatives and have them draw up a petition stating clearly your requests. Bring this petition to me, and I will take it to the Minister of Public Enlightenment, Mr. Delyanov. In a few days, or perhaps tomorrow, I shall bring you the answer. But pending this, I want you to return to your classes."

The students returned.

In a few hours, Mendeleyev received the petition.

3

He took the petition to the home of Minister I. D. Delyanov. He was not there, and so Mendeleyev left it for him.

The next day Mendeleyev received a package. It contained the rejected petition together with a note.

"Neither the Minister of Public Enlightenment, nor you, nor any other person in the employ of the government has a right to receive such a petition. Accordingly it is now rejected and returned to you."

The students heard that their petition had been rejected.

"I do not know how I can aid you further," Mendeleyev told them. "For myself, I now resign my position as Professor in the Universities of Russia."

The students stood aghast.

It was August 17, 1890. Mendeleyev sat down and wrote out his resignation. His door was open, and the hallways filled with silent watching students.

Professors arrived, and the Rector. They begged Mendeleyev to reconsider his decision.

"It is impossible," he said. "I cannot breathe in this atmosphere. I will finish out the year, and this is all."

He finished writing and began to pack his books. For almost thirty-five years his heart had lived in this university. Now it could live there no longer. Mendeleyev was leaving. He summoned two caretakers to carry away his books and manuscripts.

He took up the remaining handful and walked through the corridors. The students watched.

4

Soon there remained only one more lecture to present in order to complete one of the chemistry courses. Word of the last lecture spread through St. Petersburg. The Minister of Public Enlightenment, Delyanov, was alarmed. Nervously he chatted with his aide, Neftyansky.

"Do you suppose he may incite the students to an uprising?"

Neftyansky shrugged his shoulders.

"Many hundreds are coming to the lecture tomorrow," he said. "It is a delicate situation."

Delyanov pondered.

"It would be desirable to have the police ready," he said. "To preserve order—if you know what I mean. Is this a time to permit sentiment about the great Mendeleyev? Perhaps police could be alerted to watch for remarks tending to incite."

The next day the chemistry lecture room was completely filled with townspeople and students. The hallways were packed, and before the doors of the university stood great crowds who could not find room inside.

When Mendeleyev appeared, a hush fell over the audience. But in a moment the tension was broken by thundering applause as the students and city people rose to their feet and clapped energetically.

Mendeleyev walked to his lecture desk and stood facing the people. They applauded for a few moments more, then sat down.

"So many have come to study chemistry," said Mendeleyev.

The audience laughed nervously.

Now Mendeleyev straightened his shoulders and began.

"Manganese," he said.

An uncertain laughter came from the center of the audience. Abruptly the laughter ceased.

"Manganese," Mendeleyev resumed. "I must today give the concluding remarks on manganese and the other substances we have been discussing."

In the front row the student Weinberg was taking the lecture down in shorthand.

"Until now," lectured Mendeleyev, "just as with the deposits of manganese, so also with practically all developed Russian riches—beginning with gold, lead, iron, coal, petroleum, and others—all of them, one might say, are found merely because they stare us in the face—they lie before our eyes. Mouzhiks, Circassians, Persians, Cossacks find these riches. That's not the way it should be, and it is not that way in those places where practical methods are developed to any degree at all—that is, methods which depend on more than the mere accident that some of these riches have come to the surface.

"There are tremendous masses of wealth within the depths of the earth, in the nadir, and one has to have a lamp of knowledge to illumine these depths in order to see in the dark. And if you bring this lamp of knowledge into Russia, you will in fact do what Russia expects of you. . . ."

The door at the right creaked. Mendeleyev stopped for an instant. The audience followed his glance. There, just outside, District Captain of Police Mourganov stood listening intently. Mendeleyev could not see who stood behind the slightly open door.

Mourganov whispered to the police about him.

"I think he's inciting them now," he said. "Listen."

Mendeleyev resumed his lecture.

"On what does the well-being of Russia depend?" he said. "On what do the riches and poverty of the people depend and the people's freedom?"

"Get ready," whispered Captain Mourganov. "He's inciting them about freedom."

"Only economic lack is the real lack. All other is fictitious. Many a nation has done damage to itself where people have gone chasing after the imaginary or wishful, letting go of that which it is in fact necessary to develop for the welfare of the people. Introducing industrial goals we will give work to people and will increase their well-being. We will accomplish that which is lacking at the present time in Russia. The country, being agricultural, one might say receives her resources—to say it curtly and clearly—from robbery of the topsoil. Sending our grain abroad, emaciating our soil and not returning to it that mineral value which is taken from it, our country loses. . . ."

The police now burst into the auditorium.

Mendeleyev stopped, petrified.

The gendarmes moved along the aisles.

"That's enough," they said, "go on home. That's enough."

More police were rushing in.

Through the open door Mendeleyev could see great numbers of policemen invading his sacred university corridors. He stood quietly at the lecture desk. Tears rolled down his cheeks.

Slowly, he made his way out of the building.

Chapter Twenty-nine

Twilight

MENDELEYEV MOVED his family out of the university apartment to a house on Cadet Row. There Anna immediately fixed a study for him, a duplicate of his university study.

Enough money was coming in from his book, *Principles of Chemistry*, to live on, but a part of this would have to go to Feozva.

About this time Nadezhda's niece became ill, and now Mendeleyev, remembering how Nadezhda had helped to save Vassya's life, brought money to send the ailing girl to the Crimea. There she recovered, even as Mendeleyev had, many years before.

He tried to start a newspaper—to be called *Uplift*—but it was necessary to petition the government for permission to establish a new publication. His petition arrived at the desk of the same Minister of Public Enlightenment, Delyanov. The Minister ruled that only a trade newspaper might be permitted, and that only if submitted for censorship. Mendeleyev refused this condition.

In the university bigger student strikes were in progress than before.

Mendeleyev settled down to writing. There was much to do regardless of the nature of the governing regime. He wrote far into the night. The mounds of pages appeared as before.

Between 1886 and 1890 Mendeleyev produced twenty-five published works. They dealt with atoms and the Donetz coal, with analysis of meteorites and with the need of scientific facilities for Russian universities. He continued both purely scientific and technological labors.

Men in the Russian government overcame the prejudice of Delyanov. Mendeleyev was asked to analyze the question of the tariff. He wrote a report of 730 pages. The Navy Department urged him to work on explosive powder. Mendeleyev agreed but insisted on its use only for defense, if need be. He also advocated the scrapping of warships and the building of a merchant marine fleet. He pleaded for growing trade with England and America.

Scientific societies abroad which learned of Mendeleyev's resignation from the university sent messages of sympathy to him. He replied, and wrote on—about ferroaluminium, crystalline glycerine, Russian laboratories, need of certain types of factories, change of water with temperature, manganese, a theorem in geometry, the World Exposition in Chicago and the machinery scheduled to appear there, what to build and where. He suggested experiments of importance and gave away scientific ideas. There had long existed in the lives of scientific men of the past a jealous guardianship over their ideas. Men wrote down their discoveries or intended programs of research in code, so that later they could claim priority to discoveries—if the ideas turned out sound. Even between the great Newton of England and Leibnitz of Germany a scientific intrigue of priorities and secret codes existed in the matter of the invention of the new mathematical development—the "calculus." Vestiges of such scientific innuendo persisted, and Mendeleyev ridiculed them; he told of everything of scientific value that occurred to him and shied from the secret hoarding of ideas.

"They belong to the world," he said. "They do not belong to any individual. Least of all to the man whom fate entrusts with an original thought. It was given to him in trust for the welfare of all."

The Minister of Finance, Sergei Witte, understood Mendeleyev.

"He belongs to Russia," said Witte. "We had better hustle to right a great wrong."

In 1893 Witte asked Mendeleyev to become the director of the Russian Bureau of Weights and Measures. Mendeleyev accepted.

2

Mendeleyev's first act as director was to ask that several buildings be erected for the poorly housed employees. The request was granted. Mendeleyev himself, with his family, moved to the third floor apartment of one of the bureau buildings.

The employees, awed by the repute and fame of the new director, called him "Your Excellency."

"In what way do I excel you?" Mendeleyev chided. "That is, speaking as one human being to another. Please stop calling me that."

Some of the employees—those from peasant origin—reverted to the term "*barin.*"

"And I don't want to be 'sired,'" Mendeleyev responded. "I have always disliked that. Let's all just be people. Shall we?"

He revolutionized the functions of the Bureau. New standards of all sorts were introduced—special balances, measuring devices, weights. Everything was intended for the purpose of standardizing the helter-skelter weights and measures of the great land. Mendeleyev introduced devices and standards utilized in Germany and England and America. He invented standards of his own, when the need existed. He sent for advanced foreign equipment—laboratory furnaces, batteries, a great new refrigerating machine. The employees marveled and delighted in their new "circus land of modern techniques."

But though they admired their new director, they also feared him. Mendeleyev insisted on work. On good careful work. It was hard for some of the men to cast off habits of "good enough" philosophy. Occasionally Mendeleyev lost his temper and roared at a persistently muddling worker. The man would tremble in his boots, and Mendeleyev would at once beg forgiveness. He could not stand to see fear in the eyes of men.

He employed a number of women at the Bureau. The news spread through St. Petersburg and even reached Moscow. This had never been done before. Women had never been used at the Bureau for skilled, precise, scientific work. Mendeleyev trained them and encouraged them. Many stayed after hours to master techniques in weighing and measuring. The women turned out to be superior to the men.

Outsiders were amazed when they learned of this.

"You should only be amazed at your limited point of view," Mendeleyev told the incredulous merchant Nikolayev one evening. "The sooner we emerge from feudal thinking, the better off we will all be."

Later that evening Volodya came with his wife, the daughter of the artist Lemokh. They spoke of Olga, Mendeleyev's oldest daughter, and her husband Trirogov, of the maritime service.

Finally, when all had gone, Mendeleyev went to his study. There was work to do. There was also a letter to answer.

3

From England had come further honors. The universities of Cambridge and Oxford wanted to award Mendeleyev honorary degrees of Doctor of Laws. This was 1894 and Mendeleyev was sixty years old.

Again Anna accompanied him on the journey, and again was ill on the Channel crossing. Mendeleyev attentively supplied her with pieces of lemon.

Once more they stopped at the Charing Cross Hotel, and then left for Cambridge to be guests at the home of the rector, Peel.

The ceremonies at the two universities lasted a week. In the auditorium of Cambridge University Mendeleyev wore a red academic robe with blue trimming. The English called him "Faust." Mendeleyev and Anna met Princess Alice of Edinburgh, the mother of the English monarch, and Prince George, the Duke of York, who also received the Doctor of Laws degree.

The presentations were in Latin, and Mendeleyev squirmed in his chair as he recalled his youthful years of suffering with the grammar books.

By English tradition, the spectator students felt free to make loud remarks at any time during the presentation of honors. When Prince George received the award, a student called out "Long live the new father!" When Mendeleyev stood before the rector and listened to the Latin liturgy, a student called out "That's enough of Latin, sir. Talk English." Mendeleyev could not conceal his delight.

There were days of celebrations and festivities, then the presentation of degrees at Oxford, by the rector, Odling.

When it was all over, Mendeleyev somehow felt depressed.

"It is good," he said to Anna when they were alone. "It is all well. But let us go home. There is work."

4

At home, in Russia, he relaxed for only a brief while. Soon after they arrived and had greeted the children, he threw himself down on his yellow couch and Anna began to read to him Hugo's *The Octopus*. It was very relaxing, in his own home listening to Anna's soothing voice.

"The octopus is in fact vulnerable only in the head. Gilliatt was not ignorant of this fact.

"He had never seen an octopus of this size. He found himself seized at the outset by one of the larger species. Any other man would have been terrified. In the case of the octopus as in that of the bull, there is a certain moment at which to seize it; it is the instant when the bull lowers his neck, it is the instant when the octopus thrusts forward its head—a sudden movement. He who misses that juncture is lost. . . ."

Mendeleyev stood up.

"I will work now," he said.

He stood at his desk, his gaze lost beyond the wall before him.

"There is an octopus that for centuries has held Russia in its grip," he thought. "The monster is ignorance. The tentacles of this monster are famine, lethargy, selfishness, conceit, inefficiency, contempt, unreliability, and insipid exuberance. It is hopeless to attack a mere tentacle. Nothing would come of that. The tentacles are vigorous and cruel, and there are too many of them. One must strike at the very monster himself."

Now Mendeleyev saw clearly that all his life, instinctively, he had been striking at the monster himself, at ignorance. The blows must continue. It could be done through education, through science.

He sat down at his desk and picked up his pen.

"Man is not born for himself—but rather like an atom of an organism, for the organism. . . . Some people say, 'If I don't know what life is and what for, then no use living.' This is wrong. . . . Life is given me, so I live. And if I don't know why, then I should be finding out why. . . .

"Christ taught of the inner world of the man, Socrates taught of the relation of man to the State, and the New Religion will teach of the relation of man to society. The chief principle of the New Religion is the following: Man is one unit, particle, or cell. One man is part of an organism and the organism is the society, and that is why a man must consciously live for the society and this is the logical link of individual man with society.

"Of course each man lives for himself as a cell of the brain lives for itself and not for the whole man, but at the same time serves the man. Only man on a lower scale of development lives for himself alone, like a microcosm or infusoria. . . ."

Then Mendeleyev turned to the preparation of a program for the weekly work at the Bureau of Weights and Measures, and later that night he worked on an article arising out of the work of the Bureau: "The Weight of a Liter of Air."

As the months passed into years the work of the Bureau grew and Mendeleyev's pen maintained its pace. The assault on the octopus of ignorance proceeded: "The Change in Density of Water Between 0° and 40°," "Progress in the Production of New Standards of Length and Weight," second edition of the *Principles of Chemistry*—in English, "The Place of Argon in the Periodic System," "Experimental Investigations on the Oscillations of Balances," *Thoughts on the Development of Farm Industry.* . . .

In 1896, Mendeleyev attended the All-Russia Fair at Nizhny Novgorod. He had been invited to be present as a member of a committee whose duty it was to assign locations at the Fair to the various exhibitors, and to determine also the tax the government could expect. There was great competition for choice spots where many wares could be sold to the great throngs. This was not unusual. However, Mendeleyev was surprised to find that a certain large group of the wealthier exhibitors had worked out a plan by which they could have the best locations and also pay the lowest taxes.

"Well, well," he said. "We'll have to fix this. A little more equitable distribution."

"No, it's all right," said the merchant Khabarov, leader of the majority group. "We have it all figured out."

Mendeleyev laughed. "You certainly have," he said. "But I'm afraid it won't work—your tax must be higher."

"No," replied Khabarov. "It's all fixed. Or, I'll tell you what we can do—let's vote on it to see who's right."

Mendeleyev jumped up and banged his fist on the table.

"Vote!" he exclaimed. "Vote! For the first time in my life do I hear that truth is to be decided by majority vote!"

Khabarov and his men retreated from their position. The taxes and locations were apportioned according to Mendeleyev's plan.

After the meeting he wandered silently among the gay crowds of the great Nizhny Fair. There were no glass blowers.

He left for St. Petersburg.

Another call came from the government: "In view of the achievements accomplished by you in opening the oil industry of the Caucasus, and the coal industry of the Donetz Basin, will you undertake the investigation of Russia's resources of iron?"

Mendeleyev left again for the Urals.

At the summit he stood gazing over the vast expanse below the mountain top.

"I am tired," he said to the space about him. "You have made me tired."

The sun had set beyond the distant horizon. The color of twilight caressed the heavens.

Twilight had come.

Chapter Thirty

The Urals, Tobolsk, Aremziansk

MENDELEYEV SPENT a month inspecting the Urals and the lands lying about them. He made voluminous notes to be used later for a report he planned to call "The Iron Industry of the Urals in the Year 1899." He estimated that the story of the Urals and its iron could be told in about six to eight hundred pages, but he made many preliminary notes.

". . . I may add that the Urals, Donetz area, and the Kouznets coal fields of western Siberia offer the greatest advantages for the development of a vast iron industry, because these localities not only contain enormous supplies of excellent iron, but also coal, which is necessary for smelting it. The Ural area with its cheap charcoal is best suited for the production of the higher grades of steel. . . ."

On the western slopes there was coal at Kizel, near Perm. Brown coal was abundant at Yegorshino, and also at Chelyabinsk.

No idea of the real quantitative potentialities of the Ural iron actually existed. Now this was being determined. Here were entire mountains of high-grade magnatite ore, for example, Mount Blagodat, Mount Visokaya, and the Magnetnaya Mountain. The ore here had a 60 per cent iron content. The Magnetnaya Mountain by itself had a potential yield of 450 million tons. Then, stretching to the northwest of this magic mountain of iron were the Zigazin areas with potential yield of 150 million tons. The Bakal district, too, was a treasureland of iron, as well as other minerals.

On the eastern slopes of the Urals too there were overflowing deposits of iron, as well as copper, chrome, gold, platinum. More to the east still were fields of coal, oil, phosphates, potassium salts.

Mendeleyev's gaze turned still more to the east. Suddenly there came over him an overwhelming desire to see the place of his origin—Tobolsk, where he was born—and Aremziansk, where once burned the Glass Factory.

2

In Tobolsk Mendeleyev found several former student companions: Grigoriev, and Varnikov, and Luetin. The friends stood and studied him, and he looked into their eyes and tried to recapture the glance of bygone years. It was not there. The men were sixty-five years old, too. There was little actually to say. The long years had carried away the fragile links of friendship.

Alone, he climbed the mountain overlooking the city. Into a bonfire on this mountain, fifty years before, he had tossed a book on Latin grammar.

He descended into the city once more and made his way to the Church of the Archangel Mikhail, in the parish of which he had once lived. Everything was the same; everything was different. Outside, he walked to the rear window of his old home and gazed upon the ledge where once Bassargin had placed bread for the unfortunate fugitives in the black Siberian night.

Then he visited the cemetery, the grave of his father, Ivan, and of his deeply religious sister, Apollinaria, Maria's "Polya."

Then he made his way to the village of Aremziansk.

On the hill stood the church in whose bell tower one night Matvei the Night Watchman had rung a bell. This was Maria's church, and there lay the schoolhouse, also built by his mother. He went to the site where the Glass Factory had once stood. The roaring scene of the fire raced before his vision. Here was Bassargin, here the strannik, there was Maria, and now the flaming door was opening and out came Timofei bearing a glass-polishing table on his great back. And there, in a sled, sat a weeping boy with a little pig in his arms.

In the village, the izbas seemed different—because the people were different. And yet they were similar. Gray-bearded men, strong young mouzhiks, girls in kerchiefs, the simple *babas*. . . . They asked about Moscow and St. Petersburg and the Tsar.

"The greatest Tsar," said one mouzhik, "must be put to bed with a shovel at last." "Even in hell," said another, "the mouzhik will have to wait on the landlord, feeding the fire under him."

There was no one to remember here in Aremziansk—not among the living. Long ago most of the younger villagers had gone to seek a better livelihood in Tobolsk and other cities. Others had not gone. They slept there in the graveyard beneath the crumbling crosses.

Mendeleyev, with bowed head, walked through the graveyard. The names —how the names gripped his heart!—Oblontov; Maroosya, Marfa, Matvei; Anton the Furnace Man; Pavel the Gatherer; Old Andrei the Chemist; Katerina the Matchmaker. And there stood another grave.

HERE LIES OUR VANYA
WHO COULD NOT LIVE IN THIS WORLD

Mendeleyev stood silent for a moment.
Then he left for St. Petersburg.

3

Immediately upon his return home he began to write the report of the iron potentialities of the Urals. It was eight hundred pages long and told the story of iron for the land of Russia. Oil, coal, iron, and pure science. These things had been done. There was still more to do.

He stood in front of the great cage containing a parrot that Volodya had brought him from India.

"Will you have some tea?" asked Mendeleyev.

"With lemon," said the parrot.

"And jam, perhaps."

"Jam," said the parrot.

"And *boulkee*—some nice hot rolls?"

"With lemon," said the parrot.

In the afternoon Mendeleyev attended the theater with Anna. It was an academic function and university professors and assistants were there. As soon as Mendeleyev entered his loge, the eyes of the audience turned on him, and many looked on him through their binoculars. The young scientist Kapustin came and called Anna out of the loge. He whispered to her. She stared at him, blankly.

Volodya had died. The news was in the papers, but Anna and Mendeleyev had not known it. Mendeleyev was stupefied. With Anna he hurried dazedly outdoors. Volodya was thirty-four years old. He had been ill only a few days and was apparently recovering from influenza when suddenly pneumonia set in. Volodya had become a gentle and devoted husband and an admired officer in the Maritime Corps. He had recently retired, and become interested in engineering projects. When he was a little boy with slightly narrowed eyes Mendeleyev had loved him so much that whenever he liked anything supremely, he would say, "I love that as much as I love Volodya."

Now Volodya was dead. Mendeleyev stood near. His hands stole to his head and the head rocked to and fro. Volodya was buried in Volkovo Cemetery. Maria, Elizabeth, Volodya. Mendeleyev bought a plot of ground near Volodya's.

It was the first of January of the year 1900. Mendeleyev stood at the window of his office in the building of the Bureau of Weights and Measures. In a year a new century would come upon the world. How would it be with this century? Was the struggle against the octopus of ignorance being won? Would this be the century of scientific enlightenment? Was this destined to be the century of peace? Was there to be less misery in the twentieth century, less bloodshed in the world?

Chapter Thirty-one

Shadow

In 1900 the Prussian Academy of Science celebrated its two hundredth anniversary. Mendeleyev was asked to attend as the delegate of the University of St. Petersburg. At the banquet to be held in connection with this meeting it would be proper to appear in formal attire. Mendeleyev did not wish to embarrass the German scientists—and so in leaving Russia he took along his tuxedo, the special suit reserved only for life's most inescapable festivities.

At the banquet he appeared in the dress suit, but he still wore his boots.

He sat at one of the small tables presided over by his friend, the Dutch chemist van't Hoff, and they spoke of Byron, whom van't Hoff also loved. Many familiar faces were scattered about the room: Ramsay and Thorpe of England, Cossa of Italy, Ladenburg of Breslau—and, near the head of the table, Winkler of Germany. This was Clemens Winkler who in February, 1886, had discovered a new element, which he had named "germanium." The element had been found in a peculiar silver ore called "argyrodite," and after making many tests and rechecking himself, Winkler had written in the *Journal für Praktische Chemie*, ". . . there can exist no more doubt that the new element is none other than that predicted by Mendeleyev fifteen years ago and called ekasilicon by him."

Van't Hoff, brushing back his yellow coarse hair, leaned over to Mendeleyev and touched his arm.

"I've been anxious to ask you something," he said. "What exactly made you resign from the University?"

Mendeleyev shrugged his shoulders.

"To put it briefly," he said, "the government considered me too liberal. The students of course did not share this view; they probably thought I did not go far enough."

"It's an eternal problem," said van't Hoff. "To know how to steer a proper course."

"As you know," said Mendeleyev, "I'm an evolutionist of a peaceable type. My kind always suffers from the fact that we are bound to come into the path of some who do not want to be peaceable and some who do not want to be evolutionists."

Van't Hoff and Mendeleyev understood each other. Both worked toward more scientific education throughout the world.

"The scientists understand each other," said van't Hoff, "because they deal with undistortable truth. It is their bond of fraternity."

"And language," added Mendeleyev. "Language is paramount in the peaceful life of nations. Scientists perhaps understand each other because of the common mathematical language. As I used to say to my students, 'A chemical formula is an international language. Therefore it achieves a meeting of minds.' And everyone knows that knowledge of another man's language at least helps achieve knowledge of another man's heart."

There were speeches by many delegates, in several languages, and then the banquet concluded with the posing for official photographs. Somehow Mendeleyev felt a desire to return home as soon as possible. He nodded to a few younger chemists and he and van't Hoff left the banquet room.

Immediately outside the room he stumbled and almost fell. He had not seen the step. As he put on his coat and hat and walked out into the night there seemed to be a mist hanging in the air.

"How foggy it is," he said to van't Hoff.

"No," said van't Hoff. "It seems like a clear night to me."

They shook hands and parted. Mendeleyev went to the railroad station. On the train he met the young Englishman Brighton and chatted with him, but he retired early. He felt strong and well, and fell at once into his usual profound sleep. At one o'clock the train came to a sudden halt. Brighton, who was sleeping in the next compartment, awoke suddenly. The cars up ahead were on fire. For an hour the blaze was fought and when it was finally brought under control, Mendeleyev was still sleeping.

The next morning Brighton told him of the fire. Mendeleyev was amazed.

"Why didn't you wake me?" he asked.

Brighton smiled.

"The fire had not reached our car," he said.

At Prague Mendeleyev got off to visit Professor Brauner who was working on certain rare elements.

"I am bringing out a new edition of my book in a year or two," said Mendeleyev. "Will you write a chapter for me on your work?"

Brauner agreed.

The men strolled along a boulevard in the city, and Brauner pulled Mendeleyev into a photographer's studio.

"Another picture," laughed Mendeleyev. "There are too many celebrations for me on this journey."

In the late afternoon Brauner escorted Mendeleyev to the train. Mendeleyev looked about him just before he mounted the steps.
"Why is everything so foggy?" he asked.
Brauner looked about.
"It seems clear," he said. "I think . . ."
The train started.
"I'll see you next year!" called Brauner. *"Bon voyage!"*

2

He was glad to be home. He greeted Anna and his children, visited the Bureau laboratories downstairs, and then entered his study.
"Too much parading," he said aloud. "I must stop parading around. There is work here."
He took up his pen. But, for a moment, he turned in his chair. On a copper table stood a statuette of Peter the Great. On this table too reposed the medallion of Alexander II who had freed the serfs, and a medallion of Faraday—the award of the English chemists. Anna's portraits and pencil sketches were on the wall. The sketches seemed dim, and even the portraits had lost their usual clarity. He narrowed his eyes and studied the pictures. Diderot, Suvurov, Raphael, Beethoven, Lavoisier, Descartes, Gerhardt, Shakespeare, Dante, Glinka, Galileo, Newton as a young man, Copernicus, Rose, Newton as an older man, Weller, Krayevitch, family groups, professors in a group —Mendeleyev, Butelerov, Menshutkin, Somov, Bogdanov, Wagner, and the rector Andreyevsky. The portraits were of his children, and an old portrait of Ivan, Mendeleyev's father, and one of Maria, drawn by Anna from Mendeleyev's description.
He rose and drew closer to the drawing of his mother. Why was it so dim? Why was everything dim? Mendeleyev did not want to alarm Anna.
He sat down at his desk and picked up his pen.
At supper he ate a little bouillon, and a cutlet. There was also his favorite rice, cooked in red wine. Then he went back to his study to plan the work of the Bureau and write up results of certain experimental studies.
At nine o'clock Anna brought him his regular large cup of strong tea and bread and butter, and before he retired he drank a cup of milk.
The next morning, after breakfast, Mendeleyev started down the stairs to the Bureau laboratories, but he missed the last step and fell. Anna came running, but he had already scrambled to his feet.
"What is it?" called Anna in alarm.
Mendeleyev shook his head.
"Nothing," he said. "I kicked the wall. By accident."

That evening he was jubilant.

"Mikhail is getting married," he said. "What an unexpected family rejoicement for us."

Mikhail was a handy man in the laboratories. Mendeleyev was always glad to know that people were marrying.

"A man must have a family," he would say. "Everyone should marry."

That evening he ate a little fish, a few spoonfuls of *kasha*, and corn cakes fried in butter. He drank a glass of *kvahs* and then went to his study.

A little later in 1901, Mendeleyev's sister Ekaterina died.

She had lived to become a gray little old woman with a look of distant hope and love in her eyes.

Mendeleyev stood over her grave and silently wept.

Walking with Anna out of the cemetery he stumbled on a small projecting root. Anna had avoided it. She stopped and took him by the arm.

"Your eyes, Mitenka," said Anna gently. "Is something wrong? You are stumbling too often."

"It's nothing," he said shaking his head. "There's a little mistiness before my eyes—but I have wept for my beloved Katenka. It's the tears."

Anna waited until the next day. In the morning she came into his study.

"The doctor is here," she said. "I called him to examine you. And your eyes."

Mendeleyev rose from his desk. He lowered his head.

"*Khorosho*," he said. "It had to come."

3

This was Dr. Nikolai Alexandrovitch Orlov—a thin tired-looking man with golden pince-nez which he kept putting on and taking off as he examined Mendeleyev. The examination was thorough. The doctor had brought instruments to test his blood pressure, his heart, his eyes.

Anna was waiting outside behind the closed door when the doctor came out.

"His body is sound," said Orlov. "Very strong. Very hearty. He is sixty-seven and I see no old-age infirmities whatever." He stopped.

"Finish," said Anna, her hands on her bosom. "Finish your remarks."

Orlov frowned. He took off his pince-nez and immediately replaced them.

"Well," he said. "His eyes are failing. It's not really a question of eyeglasses."

Anna leaned against the wall. Orlov led her to a chair.

"I don't know what actually to make of it. It may be development of cataracts. It seems as though his eyes had burned themselves out."

"Perhaps," said Anna, "perhaps from writing for fifty years."

"It is possible," said Orlov.

Anna went into Mendeleyev's study. He was at his desk, writing. She put her arms about his neck.

"Mitenka," she said, "rest. Rest, Mitenka."

Mendeleyev wrote on.

"There will be time for that," he said. "I must write. I told the doctor to send me some glasses. This is nothing. Just a little eyestrain. Please let me write."

Anna left.

"Remarks on Public Instruction in Russia. The fundamental direction of Russian education should be living and real, not based on dead languages, grammatical rules, and dialectical discussions, which, without experimental control bring self-deceit, illusion, presumption, selfishness. . . ."

On November 27, 1902, Mendeleyev wrote a new preface to his *Principles of Chemistry*. It was the seventh Russian edition.

". . . In previous times sciences, like bridges, could only be built up by supporting them on a few broad buttresses and long girders. In addition to the exposition of the principles of chemistry, it has been my wish to show how this science has now been built up like a suspension bridge, supported by the united strength of a number of slender, but firmly fixed, chains—individually of little strength—and has thus been carried over difficulties which before appeared insurmountable.

"To conceive, understand, and grasp the whole system of the scientific edifice, including its unfinished portions, is equivalent to experiencing that enjoyment only conveyed by the highest forms of beauty and truth. Without the material for building the edifice of science the plan alone is but a castle in the air, a mere possibility; while the material without a plan is but useless matter. . . . In the work of science the artisan, architect, and creator are very often one and the same individual. . . .

". . . The natural philosophy of modern times has the additional merit over that of former ages, that it no longer regards man as the pivot of the universe, but consciously submits itself to harmonious, coherent, and logical laws embracing all time and space, and extending alike over the immensity of the heavens and the infinitesimal atom. . . ."

It was 2 A.M. Anna, in her bathrobe, stood in the doorway.

"I can't sleep," she said. "Mitya, I can't sleep. You are burning your eyes."

He looked up at her. Her face was pleading.

"*Khorosho*," he said, laying down the pen. "I will stop. For tonight. But I feel a driving need to write everything out, quickly. While there is time."

4

In the weeks that followed Mendeleyev read and revised many portions of the seventh edition of his *Principles of Chemistry*. Anna continually tried to diminish his hours of work, but he wrote on.

One evening when she entered his study, she found him bent close over his work, his left hand holding a large magnifying glass over the paper while the right hand held the swiftly moving pen. The shadow was growing darker, but the pen continued to write.

"I regard Winkler, Brauner, Thorpe, Nilson, Lecoq de Boisbaudran . . . the true confirmers of the periodic law, whose further development still awaits many new workers. . . .

"But nothing, from mushrooms to a scientific dependence, can be discovered without seeking and trying. So I began to look about and write down the elements with their atomic weights and typical properties, analogous elements, and similar atomic weights on separate cards, and this soon convinced me that the properties of the elements are in periodic dependence upon their atomic weights. . . .

"In proclaiming this result—showing themselves that they were wrong—Nilson and Petterson proved that in science truth is equally precious to all, although it may have first been denied by those who afterwards established it.

"There exists everywhere a medium in things, determined by equilibrium. The Russian proverb says, 'Too much salt or too little salt is alike an evil.' It is the same in political and social relations."

Occasionally, to rest his clouded eyes, Mendeleyev got up from his desk and made his way to a table laden with pieces of wood strips, boards, cardboard, paper, a pot of paste that he had made by his own formula, and some tools. At this worktable, groping, or with eyes closed, he made little boxes for his children and his friends, and frames for pictures. Then, after the lapse of an hour, he would return to his writing desk.

On the day that he wrote of the work of Becquerel, the room seemed unusually dark. Mendeleyev lit the lamps, then sat down again.

In 1896 Henri Antoine Becquerel had discovered that the element uranium can make spots on a photographic negative. The uranium could be at some distance from the negative enclosed in black paper and yet something apparently came out of the uranium, traveled through the air, and affected a well-covered negative, so that when it was developed, a spot or spots were clearly visible. Even if wood were placed between the uranium and the photographic negative or thin pieces of metal, still the negative was affected. The mysterious radiation from the uranium had therefore considerable pene-

Mendeleyev's Periodic System of the Elements in Groups and Series — 1902

Each number refers to the weight of one atom of the element compared to the weight of the oxygen atom taken as 16

SERIES	GROUP 0 — These substances do not combine with anything	GROUP I — Two atoms of any element (R) here combine with one atom of oxygen (O) R₂O	GROUP II — One atom of any element (R) here combines with one atom of oxygen (O) RO or R₂O₂	GROUP III — Two atoms of any element (R) combine with three atoms of oxygen (O) R₂O₃	GROUP IV — One atom of any element (R) here combines with two atoms of oxygen (O) RO₂	GROUP V — Two atoms of any element (R) here combine with five atoms of oxygen (O) R₂O₅	GROUP VI — One atom of any element (R) here combines with three atoms of oxygen (O) RO₃	GROUP VII — Two atoms of any element (R) here combine with seven atoms of oxygen (O) R₂O₇	GROUP VIII — One atom of any element (R) here combines with four atoms of oxygen (O) RO₄
1	……	Hydrogen H 1.008							……
2	Helium He 4.0	Lithium Li 7.03	Beryllium Be 9.1	Boron B 11.0	Carbon C 12.0	Nitrogen N 14.04	Oxygen O 16.00	Fluorine F 19.0	……
3	Neon Ne 19.9	Sodium Na 23.05	Magnesium Mg 24.3	Aluminium Al 27.0	Silicon Si 28.4	Phosphorus P 31.0	Sulphur S 32.06	Chlorine Cl 35.45	……
4	Argon Ar 38	Potassium K 39.1	Calcium Ca 40.1	Scandium Sc 44.1	Titanium Ti 48.1	Vanadium V 51.4	Chromium Cr 52.1	Manganese Mn 55.0	Iron Fe 55.9 Cobalt Co 59 Nickel Ni 59
5	……	Copper Cu 63.6	Zinc Zn 65.4	Gallium Ga 70.0	Germanium Ge 72.3	Arsenic As 75	Selenium Se 79	Bromine Br 79.95	……
6	Krypton Kr 81.8	Rubidium Rb 85.4	Strontium Sr 87.6	Yttrium Y 89.0	Zirconium Zr 90.6	Niobium Nb 91.0	Molybdenum Mo 96.0	……	Ruthenium Ru 101.7 Rhodium Rh 103.0 Palladium Pd 106.5
7	……	Silver Ag 107.9	Cadmium Cd 112.4	Indium In 114.0	Tin Sn 119.0	Antimony Sb 120.0	Tellurium Te 127	Iodine I 127	……
8	Xenon Xe 128	Caesium Cs 132.9	Barium Ba 137.4	Lanthanum La 139	Cerium Ce 140	……	……	……	……
9									
10	……	……	……	Ytterbium Yb 173	……	Tantalum Ta 183	Tungsten W 184	……	Osmium Os 191 Iridium Ir 193 Platinum Pt 194.9
11	……	Gold Au 197.2	Mercury Hg 200.0	Thallium Tl 204.1	Lead Pb 206.9	Bismuth Bi 208	……	……	……
12			Radium Rd 224		Thorium Th 232		Uranium U 239		

Periodic Chart of the Atoms 1948

Note: Arrangement follows atomic numbers, not atomic weights

Number in upper corner is "atomic number," equal to net positive electrical charge on nucleus
Number at bottom is weight of atom compared to that of oxygen taken as 16.0000

Period	Group →	I	II	III	IV	V	VI	VII	VIII			
1		1 H Hydrogen 1.0080							2 He Helium 4.003			1
2		3 Li Lithium 6.940	4 Be Beryllium 9.02	5 B Boron 10.82	6 C Carbon 12.010	7 N Nitrogen 14.008	8 O Oxygen 16.0000	9 F Fluorine 19.00	10 Ne Neon 20.183			2
3		11 Na Sodium 22.997	12 Mg Magnesium 24.32	13 Al Aluminum 26.97	14 Si Silicon 28.06	15 P Phosphorus 30.98	16 S Sulphur 32.06	17 Cl Chlorine 35.457	18 A Argon 39.944			3
4		19 K Potassium 39.096	20 Ca Calcium 40.08	21 Sc Scandium 45.10	22 Ti Titanium 47.90	23 V Vanadium 50.95	24 Cr Chromium 52.01	25 Mn Manganese 54.93	26 Fe Iron 55.85	27 Co Cobalt 58.94	28 Ni Nickel 58.69	4
4		29 Cu Copper 63.57	30 Zn Zinc 65.38	31 Ga Gallium 69.72	32 Ge Germanium 72.60	33 As Arsenic 74.91	34 Se Selenium 78.96	35 Br Bromine 79.916	36 Kr Krypton 83.7			
5		37 Rb Rubidium 85.48	38 Sr Strontium 87.63	39 Y Yttrium 88.92	40 Zr Zirconium 91.22	41 Cb Columbium 92.91	42 Mo Molybdenum 95.95	43 Tc Technetium 99	44 Ru Ruthenium 101.7	45 Rh Rhodium 102.91	46 Pd Palladium 106.7	5
5		47 Ag Silver 107.88	48 Cd Cadmium 112.41	49 In Indium 114.76	50 Sn Tin 118.70	51 Sb Antimony 121.76	52 Te Tellurium 127.61	53 I Iodine 126.92	54 Xe Xenon 131.3			
6		55 Cs Cesium 132.91	56 Ba Barium 137.36	57 La* Lanthanum 138.92	72 Hf Hafnium 178.6	73 Ta Tantalum 180.88	74 W Tungsten 183.92	75 Re Rhenium 186.31	76 Os Osmium 190.2	77 Ir Iridium 193.1	78 Pt Platinum 195.23	6
6		79 Au Gold 197.2	80 Hg Mercury 200.61	81 Tl Thallium 204.39	82 Pb Lead 207.21	83 Bi Bismuth 209.00	84 Po Polonium 210	85 At Astatine 211	86 Rn Radon 222			
7		87 Fa Francium 223	88 Ra Radium 226.05	89 Ac** Actinium 227.05								7

*58-71 Rare Earths	58 Ce Cerium 140.13	59 Pr Praseodymium 140.92	60 Nd Neodymium 144.27	61 Pm 147	62 Sm Samarium 150.43	63 Eu Europium 152.0	64 Gd Gadolinium 156.9	65 Tb Terbium 159.2	66 Dy Dysprosium 162.46	67 Ho Holmium 164.94	6
	68 Er Erbium 167.2	69 Tm Thulium 169.4	70 Yb Ytterbium 173.04	71 Lu Lutecium 174.99							
**90-103 Rare Earths	90 Th Thorium 232.12	91 Pa Protactinium 231	92 U Uranium 238.07	93 Np Neptunium 237	94 Pu Plutonium 239	95 Am Americium 241	96 Cm Curium 242	97	98	99	7
	100	101	102	103							

trating power. The invisible something which came out of uranium could be used to warm up water slightly. But although the warming was not great, still the amount of energy coming out of the uranium could eventually add up to a very great deal, because the radiation continued to come out over very great periods of time and declined in strength very slowly as time passed. Here was a substance acting like a dam with water dribbling out slowly through a hole in the retaining wall. Eventually a great amount of water would come out. This discovery of the fact that energy comes out of the atoms of uranium excited the attention of chemists and physicists the world over. The uranium was said to be "active," and it emitted a "radiation." Hence the uranium was described as "radioactive." Mendeleyev had thought a good deal about this newly known event in nature. He was especially interested because many years before, using his system of the elements, he had decided that the weight of one atom of uranium must be about 240 times that of one atom of hydrogen (which has the lightest atoms). It had been supposed that the ratio was 120 to 1. But Mendeleyev had been later proved right by the experiments of Roscoe, Rammelsberg, Zimmerman, and others. Now he wrote,

"Uranium has the highest atomic weight of all the analogues of chromium, and indeed of all the elements yet known. . . .

"Sodium uranate is used for imparting the characteristic yellow-green tint to glass and porcelain. . . .

"Of the various compounds most frequent is the noncrystalline earthy brown uranium ore known as pitchblende. . . . This ore is found at Joachimsthal in Bohemia, and Cornwall. . . .

". . . It appears to me that there is much significance in these facts concerning uranium, more especially since its connection with two of the most important—in many respects—discoveries in physics and chemistry made in our days, i.e.; the discovery of the argon elements (especially of helium) and of the radioactive substances. Both present much that is unexpected and extreme in some yet deeply hidden way, connected with the extreme nature of the evolution of the element uranium itself. . . .

"The greatest known concentration of mass of ponderable matter in the indivisible mass of the atom of uranium should already, a priori, produce peculiar qualities. . . . Being convinced that the investigation of uranium, starting from its native sources, will lead to many new discoveries, I am bold enough to suggest to those who seek new subjects of research to occupy themselves with the uranium compounds. . . ."

Mendeleyev's new edition of the *Principles of Chemistry* appeared in January, 1903. In this year the scientists Marie and Pierre Curie received the

Davy Medal for their work on other substances which of their own accord emitted energy from their atoms.

Mendeleyev thought of the time when he received the Davy Medal, and he somehow compared the French couple to himself and Anna. The Curies, too, seemed exceptionally devoted to each other. Only Anna was a musician and an artist. But still the comparison was good and gratifying. It was said that Pierre had keen clear eyes, and Mendeleyev, too, had once had keen clear eyes.

He rose from his desk. It was dark in the room. A day was coming on which he wanted to appear great and strong. It was a day on which he would need to do much to make up for his lack of clear sight. Mendeleyev was planning to wear his tuxedo and his medals.

5

It was August 17, 1903. Mendeleyev's daughter Liubov—Love—was marrying the poet Alexander Alexandrovitch Blok.

Liubov and Blok had known each other for many years. Often, as mere children, when Liuba was five years old and Blok was seven, they had stood in the street and chatted with Professor Nikolai Petrovitch Wagner, who carried the pink-eyed white rat under his long overcoat. Wagner, himself small, wearing large dark glasses, used to discuss the white rat with the golden-haired blue-eyed Liuba. With the blond Blok, whose big light eyes stared at the famous physiologist and writer of fairy fables, Wagner would occasionally discuss literature.

Now Liubov was marrying her friend Alexander.

Mendeleyev arrived late. Every head in the reception hall turned to view him. His gray hair was puffy and brushed, his tuxedo fitted well, and his chest was adorned with a broad ribbon and medals.

Liubov, gazing at the dim eyes of her approaching father, could hardly hold back the tears. Mendeleyev, escorted by Anna, walked straight and resplendent.

Liubov came forward.

"Papa," she said, "*akh,* how I love you."

Mendeleyev took his daughter's hand.

"This glitter," he said. "I am wearing this glitter on my chest for you. To make up for my eyes."

For a moment Liubov bowed her head.

"Go on, dear," he said. "Go get married."

Liubov kissed her father on the cheek and turned away.

Friends urged Anna to have Mendeleyev examined abroad by German and French specialists.

"I have already made plans," she said.

The opinion of the foreign doctors was that Mendeleyev had "dark water" in his eyes—the inner fluid was deteriorating, they said.

"Hopeless," they told her. "Resign yourself. There is nothing to do. In three months everything will fade for him, completely."

Mendeleyev guessed at the verdict.

"Take me home," he told Anna. "I have to finish my work."

On the train he took her hand.

"It's all right," he said. "I only regret one thing. The Christmas tree this year at the Bureau—how will it be? Will I see the lights at all?"

At home Anna sat down next to him in his study.

"Mitenka," she said, "there's something I want to tell you."

He turned to his wife. He could barely see her.

"Yes?" he said.

"Mitenka—our Dr. Kostenitch. There is something about him. Recently he told me that it seemed to him you merely had cataracts. You told me once that your father had cataracts and regained his sight through an operation. Let us call Kostenitch now. For another examination."

Mendeleyev bowed his head.

"The German specialists did not offer hope," he said.

"I offer hope," said Anna.

"All right," said Mendeleyev. "Call him."

Despite the foreign specialists' warning that Mendeleyev would be blind at once, Kostenitch performed an operation in Mendeleyev's study.

The doctor was nervous. His two assistants, too, were nervous, thinking of the great scientist on whom they were working.

Anna was waiting outside the closed door.

While the critical cut was being made on the left eye, Mendeleyev raised his hand and grabbed Kostenitch by the elbow. The action was inexplicable. It merely occurred. When he finished, Kostenitch, pale and aghast, dashed out of the room and flung himself on the corner sofa. Anna was petrified.

"It's over," wept Kostenitch. "It's over. But he pushed my hand. Before God I swear, Anna Ivanovna, he pushed my hand."

Anna sank to the floor and hid her eyes in her hands.

Kostenitch went back into the study.

In fifteen minutes Mendeleyev came out. His eyes were bandaged. Anna, weeping, put her arms about him.

"*Nitchevo*," he consoled, "that's nothing. A little darkness, that's all."

The doctors wanted him to go to bed for three or four days. Or perhaps a week.

"Nonsense!" he grumbled. "I'm as strong as you are."

Anna, too, tried to persuade him to go to bed; but he refused.

For two weeks he groped about the apartment. Often, for long periods of time, he stood at his desk holding the pen in his hand, waiting.

The day came, the day for the removal of the bandages. Kostenitch and his two assistants stood with Mendeleyev in his darkened study.

Mendeleyev called to Anna to come in.

"Anna, my heart, I want you to be the first one in this world toward whom I gaze. It will help me, Anna."

She stood before him, too frightened to weep.

"And the children," he said. "Have them wait outside."

"They are waiting," said Anna.

Mendeleyev nodded.

"*Khorosho*," he said. "Take it off."

Kostenitch cut the bandage at the back and removed it.

Before Mendeleyev stood a woman of beauty. She had not seemed so beautiful in years. Her face smiled with radiance upon him. Her eyes held tiny sparkles of tears.

"Anna," he said, "Anna, I can see."

For several moments he held her close and then called for the children, one by one, looked at each, and pressed them to his heart—Liubov, Vanya, Vassya, and Moussya.

He embraced the doctors too.

"You will nevertheless have to wear glasses," said Kostenitch. "Several different kinds. And no reading or writing for some time. I will see you on Friday."

That night, when Anna was asleep, Mendeleyev softly got out of bed.

In his study he lit the lamp in the corner, sat down at his desk, and took up his pen.

"Knowing how contented, free, and joyous is life in the realm of science," he wrote, "one fervently wishes that many would enter its portals."

Chapter Thirty-two

"Once There Lived and Existed . . ."

ON JANUARY 27, 1904, Mendeleyev was seventy years old. He had labored fifty years in the service of Russia and the day of his birthday was also declared the day of the Fiftieth Jubilee.

In the rooms of the Bureau of Weights and Measures the sixteen employees were busy officiating at the reception in honor of their director. Hot chocolate was served in beakers and glass rods were used for stirring. Filter paper was used as napkins, and many types of food were served in chemical vessels. Delegations came from all over Russia and endless speeches resounded through the laboratory rooms. From all over the world messages of good will and congratulations poured in all day.

"Yours is a spirit of ultimate scientific integrity."

"A spirit of universalism."

"Express our deep appreciation of the unending credit you give in your writings to scientists of all the races of the world."

"We firmly shake your hand and shall always recall your remark that a chemical formula is an international language."

"In a conversation, especially on the philosophy of science, you have no peer."

"Appreciate deeply your 'Science strives to attain the infinite and everlasting, unfettered by the finite and temporal.' "

"May God grant you fifty more years of labor in science."

Mendeleyev was remembered by all the societies that had honored him through the years. There were scores of these societies and many had been the honors:

Doctor of Laws, St. Petersburg, Edinburgh, Göttingen, Oxford, Cambridge, Member of the Royal Society of London, Edinburgh, Dublin, Member of the Academy of Sciences of Rome, America, Denmark, Yugoslavia, Czechoslovakia, Cracow, Ireland . . .

The letters and telegrams piled up on Mendeleyev's table in his study. Friends came and suggested that he acknowledge his thanks in the newspapers.

"The machine age has not progressed that far yet," he said. "Not for me." He sat down and began to answer the letters personally.

That night news of a disturbing event reached the celebrants in the Bureau of Weights and Measures. War had broken out between Japan and Russia. Much of the Russian fleet had already been sunk.

Mendeleyev stood at his desk. His hands stole to his head and his head rocked to and fro. Before him lay the first pages of the new manuscript, *Intimate Thoughts,* dealing with people, industry, factories, high schools, the need for more teachers and professors. Before him lay messages of congratulation. About him the world he had been building threatened to tumble.

2

On Sunday, January 9, 1905, the workers of St. Petersburg marched to the Imperial Residence to ask for improvement in their working conditions. The Imperial order of Nicholas II was a reply with gunfire—the same reply that had been made by Nicholas I in December, 1825, when Bassargin had stood in a crowd and had called, *"Constitootsiya!* Give us a Constitution!"

Mendeleyev hurried outdoors and for hours tried to make his way through the milling crowds to the residence of his friend Sergei Witte, the Minister of Finance, who had power to attempt a peaceful negotiation.

When Mendeleyev returned to his home, he took the portrait of Witte off the wall. Outside, gradually, "Bloody Sunday" subsided.

From time to time Mendeleyev still lectured in chemistry in the course he had founded, "The Higher Course for Women." Occasionally, when he returned from this lecture, he glanced at a portrait on the wall of his study, the portrait of Maria. And a sketch of her, too, made by Anna. Anna was drawing again, finally having found leisure as her children married and left home. Before that, she had felt as though she were stealing from the family's time and robbing the children of attention they needed, and her stolen moments of art produced forms of constraint and small horizon. Now the work was good again. Once more she stood before the easel and gave color to it and life in a bold "masculine manner."

In this year of 1905, Mendeleyev began to write a book he called *Knowledge and Art of Russia.* Joyfully, Anna read every word. She was now forty-five, but still slender and youthful looking. Her face was that of a woman of radiant health, a woman happy and mature and free.

In this year, too, appeared the third edition in English of Mendeleyev's *Principles of Chemistry.* Previously, in 1892, a German edition had appeared, and a few years later there had been an edition in French.

Mendeleyev was busy now thinking once more of the new groups of elements recently discovered by Ramsay. These were the so-called rare gases, present in minute quantities in the air. Helium was one, and neon, argon, krypton, and xenon were others. All of these gases had the peculiar common property of aloofness—they refused to combine with other elements. They were considered inert. Mendeleyev, who had once been characterized by Ramsay as "a peculiar hairy foreigner," and "an outlandish creature," could not help permitting himself an occasional jest.

"The elements that Ramsay has discovered are as aloof and snobbish as he is. They will associate with no other element. Especially a foreign one."

But Mendeleyev actually had become very good friends with Ramsay and considered the Englishman's discoveries remarkable scientific performances. Moreover, the rare gases, since they would not combine with any elements, constituted now the "zero group" of Mendeleyev's Table of the Elements. All other groups consisted of elements which offered one, two, or more atoms in combining with atoms of oxygen, for example. The discovery of the zero group constituted a profound expansion of Mendeleyev's Periodic Table, and was completely compatible with it.

On March 26, 1895, Ramsay had written to the Paris Academy of Sciences:

"I did not doubt for a minute the full correctness of the periodic law. I was convinced that in the system of my friend, Mendeleyev, there must be found a little place for the inert gases too."

In October there occurred a great general strike in Russia and also in October, on the 17th, the Russian people were granted a few civil liberties, a constitution, and a representative legislative assembly—the State Douma. There was grave doubt that the manifesto meant in practice what it said in print.

In November Mendeleyev went to London—encouraged by the Russian government to be away so as to diminish the liberal influence during a time of strife. But he only consented to go because the Royal Society was awarding him its highest honor—the Copley Medal.

The president of the Royal Society, Sir William Huggins, in making the award to him, quoted the words of the English chemist Thorpe. In the magazine, *Nature*, in June, 1889, Thorpe had written:

"Mendeleyev's *Principles of Chemistry* is one of the classics of chemistry; its place in the history of science is as well assured as the ever-memorable work of Dalton."

For himself, Huggins said, "Mendeleyev stands high among the great philosophical chemists of the last century."

Mendeleyev returned to Russia. At the end of December an abortive armed insurrection occurred, and blood flowed in the streets.

Old and tired, with his books and medals about him, Mendeleyev stood at the window of his room. From the eyes which had received new sight flowed tears born of the twentieth century's new sights. New, and forever old.

3

In 1906 Mendeleyev was still the director of the Bureau of Weights and Measures. During the daytime he inspected the laboratories, advised the men and women scientists, and planned the course of future work. At night, he sat for long hours at the writing desk in his study. He wore glasses, but with them his vision was good and his pen wrote well.

In June he finished *The Map of Russia*. He had made a study of the location of cities, giving their exact meridian positions and population distribution, designated the wooded areas and the barren ones, and prepared a huge map sprinkled with dots.

In July the representative assembly—the Douma—was dissolved and a deep undertone of discontent rumbled through Russia. In August Mendeleyev suddenly felt the need to think over and arrange certain details for his family. He started to write his biographical notes.

"I am beginning to put my books and papers in order—this is important to me—before death—although I feel well. . . ."

He worked with great concentration on his book *Toward Knowledge of Russia*. This contained the first proposal for a plan of commercial and industrial development, based on an intimate knowledge of Russian resources and scientific and technical potential.

"Our peasants make 50 to 60 roubles per year, while in the United States of America the average workman, through factory and machinery, is able to make the equivalent of 350 roubles per year . . . Our mouzhiks work only during summer . . . and if the weather is bad, the loss is acute. . . .

"Work can be done by wind, water, and animals, but man must work in a different way—for the good of others. . . .

"Nothing political, no force can help—only honesty and good, education and friendly agreements. We Russians as yet labor very little and work according to methods already outgrown. . . .

"We need a merchant fleet instead of a fleet for war, and peaceful agreements with China. . . . Russia is a great fair for foreign countries. . . . The resources of our Urals are more than abundant, and the oil of the Caucasus. . . .

"The philosophy of Jean Jacques Rousseau and now of Tolstoy for a back to nature existence is semichildish. . . . Because in a patriarchal society as well as among higher animals there is a definite limit to growth, but human beings taken as a whole recognize no such limit. . . .

"The figures I give here show that for the United States of America and Russia the total number of professional workers, fishermen, woodsmen, breeders of livestock, shepherds, diggers, servants, and other feeders and supporters of the nation is the same. These persons constitute the true strength of a country. And yet the population of the United States is 76 million whereas that of Russia is 128 million, so that we have $1\frac{2}{3}$ times the number of people but the feeders and supporters are only the same as in the United States. In Russia the feeders and supporters constitute 24 per cent of the population, while for the United States the figure is 38 per cent. This is where we must seek the root of all our suffering and poverty. For this, no laws can do anything. We must have love of work, which comes from freedom. . . ."

People were listed here, their age groups, occupations, distribution of population according to language. Seemingly everything was here to be knit into a system, a group, and this group might be brought into harmony with others, foreign ones, into one plan of unity, a table of the elements of humanity. Perhaps there would be gaps in this table, perhaps one could predict the undiscovered elements and describe them in detail. Were they science, and art, and love? Were they freedom and equality? Where did they lie hidden? Who would find them?

4

In October, 1906, Mendeleyev went to sunny Cannes, to recuperate from an attack of influenza. He stayed a month and returned feeling well. He wrote again some biographical notes.

"In the fall I finished the last edition of *Principles of Chemistry* and began the 4th edition of *Toward Knowledge of Russia,* and went to Cannes due to weakening by influenza. The money arrangements are all made."

Old friends came to see him. They sat about the samovar on the table in the front room. Anna served tea, and the men chatted. Later, out on the street the men talked about Mendeleyev, and marveled that at seventy-two his walk was still fast and the movements of his hands and body were quick—though more nervous than before. They recalled how his deep guttural utterances fascinated people even up to last year. But now there was more mellowness in his voice, and he spoke less. When talking of good, Mendeleyev still had a low, clear voice, held his head up, and opened his eyes wide. And when speaking of bad, he still had the habit of bowing his head, of frowning, and of saying *"okh, okh,"* between words.

In mid-December, Nadezhda, who had married a man named Gubkin, received a letter from Mendeleyev. It was a short letter and spoke of casual things. She wept as she looked at it. It was written in a trembling hand, and it frightened her.

5

On January 11, 1907, Mendeleyev, though he was unwell, attended the Minister of Commerce and Industry, D. A. Filosofov, on his tour of inspection of the Bureau of Weights and Measures. There was a strong draft in one laboratory, and Mendeleyev suddenly felt chilled. For a moment he stood and shook, then continued to guide the Minister through the rest of the rooms.

At home that evening Anna saw that Mendeleyev was ill and begged him to go to bed early, but he sat down at his writing desk and resumed the revision of *Toward Knowledge of Russia*.

For a number of days he carried on his normal activity though he was pale and shaking.

One evening Anna could no longer stand seeing him working at his desk while his body trembled. She placed her hand on his right arm.

"Mitenka, my darling," she begged, "please rest. Go to bed. Or at least lie down on the divan for a while. Please, Mitenka."

Mendeleyev bowed his head.

"*Khorosho*," he said. "But I must finish this."

He glanced at the last words written on the paper before him.

"In conclusion I consider it necessary, although in the most general terms, to say . . ."

Mendeleyev put down the pen.

Anna helped him to the divan standing a few feet away and he lay down.

Later, she helped him to his bedroom next to his study. As he walked past the wall hung with pictures and photographs, his eyes fell on the portrait of his mother, Maria. In her eyes he saw courage and faith.

Mendeleyev lay down on his bed.

His daughter Liubov came the next evening. She was amazed at his pallor, but said nothing to her mother. Anna herself had had a bad dream the night before. At the end of this dream Mendeleyev had stood before her and said, "Farewell. Christ be with you." But Anna did not speak of this dream to her daughter, nor did she wish even to think of it.

When the doctor, Professor Yanovsky, came and examined him, he found that Mendeleyev had pneumonia, the same illness which had attacked him so often many years ago when he was a student at the Pedagogical Institute.

It was Friday, January 19. Mendeleyev was drowsy all day, and occasionally lapsed into unconsciousness.

But each time he regained consciousness he asked Anna to read to him.

Anna read the story of the journey to the North Pole by Jules Verne. Only three weeks before Mendeleyev had expressed the desire to accompany the balloonist Wellman on a flight to the North Pole.

Once Mendeleyev tried to sit up.

"Give me my comb," he said.

Anna brought him the comb.

He combed his white hair and ran his hand down his beard.

"Put the comb back into its proper place," he said. "In the little table. Or otherwise later you won't find it."

Anna replaced the comb.

"Now read," said Mendeleyev.

Later, when she stopped, he immediately opened his eyes.

"Why don't you read?" he asked. "I am listening."

At 1 A.M. on Saturday, January 20, Mendeleyev asked for a cup of warm milk. In his mind's vision he saw himself on the great oven in the hut of the village of Aremziansk. Maria was giving him a cup of warm milk.

"Drink, Mitenka," she said.

He drank a little.

"I won't drink any more," he said, and lay back. Near him stood his beloved Anna, and the maid Katerina.

"I won't drink any more," Mendeleyev repeated gently.

It seemed to Anna that he did not wish to upset her.

"Read," he said.

And Anna read:

"Hatteras thought night and day of his brig, and full of anxious forebodings and questionings as to the state in which he might find her, he hurried impatiently forward, always in advance of others.

"On the twenty-fourth of February, in the early morning, he came to a sudden stop.

"About three hundred paces distant, he saw a bright red glare, from which an immense volume of black smoke rose up toward the sky.

" 'Look at that smoke!' he shouted. His heart beat violently, and again he shouted to his companions.

" 'Look! Down there! All that smoke! My ship is on fire!'

" 'It can't be the 'Forward,' said Bell. 'We are more than three miles away.'

" 'Yes, it is,' replied the Doctor. 'It is the mirage which makes her seem so near us!'

"Bell and the Doctor came up that same instant, and found the Captain overwhelmed with despair. But suddenly he roused himself, and said in a strong, cheery voice—

" 'Friends! The cowards have fled! Fortune favors the brave. Johnson and Bell you have courage; Doctor, you have science. I have faith . . .' "

"Once There Lived and Existed . . ." 317

It was 5 A.M., January 20, 1907. Anna stopped reading and took Mendeleyev in her arms. In a moment, the heart within Dmitri Mendeleyev stopped. He had come into the world on February 7, 1834. Now he was leaving.

Anna laid him down gently. She glanced at the book.

"I have faith," repeated Anna.

The thumb and fingers of Mendeleyev's right hand were curled, as though in them he held a pen.

6

On January 25, Dmitri Ivanovitch Mendeleyev was buried by the state.

In the snow-laden streets of St. Petersburg thousands of people joined the procession. A light snow was falling, and the street lights, shrouded in black, were burning in mourning. The great multitude escorted the metal coffin to the Church of the Technological Institute where they knelt for the services.

Now the procession started for Volkovo Cemetery. There rested many of Russia's great. There rested Maria, Elizabeth, Volodya, and Ekaterina.

At the head of the procession two students carried high in their hands a huge tablet—The Periodic System of the Elements. Behind them came fifty pairs of students, each pair bearing a great wreath.

Then came the coffin borne by university students.

After that came thousands of bareheaded, serious, high-school and college students. Under their arms the students carried their books. Many carried the *Principles of Chemistry*. After them walked the bareheaded fathers who years ago also had studied from the same book.

In the crowd following were mouzhiks from many parts of Russia, and nearly all of those from Boblovo and Klin.

Continually, telegas were arriving with anxious mouzhiks who had come from miles away.

At the cemetery, not far from his loved departed ones, Mendeleyev's coffin was lowered into the grave. The tablet of the Periodic System was set down among the wreaths and flowers as the dirt was shoveled into place. The snow continued to fall.

There in the crowd stood professors, students, city people, mouzhiks. There, somewhere also, stood a woman, who once, as a girl at Boblovo, had been encouraged to study chemistry, and a man who as a boy had also been encouraged to come to St. Petersburg to study. There in the crowd stood also a graying man—the man who was once the student Akhmatov, rescued from the police. All had come.

There in the ground lay Mendeleyev, close to the heart of his mother. Both close to the heart of Mother Russia.

7

That night, snow continued to fall in St. Petersburg and a soft wind blew over the face of Russia. It blew over Moscow and over the Urals and over Siberia. It blew over the Irtysh River and passed over Tobolsk; over the Crimea, too, and over the Caucasus, the Caspian Sea, and the Donetz Basin. Gently, it explored the shafts where the oil came out of the ground, the fields where the coal was worked, the mountains from which the treasures were taken, the fields near Boblovo where better crops grew. And if it could have penetrated the locked schoolrooms, it would have blown over the charts of the elements of the universe that hung on the walls.

Over the village of Aremziansk it blew, over the crumbling crosses in its cemetery, and over the site where once had stood a great enterprise.

And over the Volga blew the wind, at whose frozen bank lay the hardly discernible mound of the grave of the strannik.

Over the vast Russian plain it blew, toward a village, where a tall man with graying long hair and a great chest, carrying a cane, was walking. This was Stepan, the son of Timofei, the former glass blower of Aremziansk.

The children of the village rush toward him.

"Strannik," they plead, "tell us a story."

"Once there lived and existed," begins Stepan, "a little rich boy with blue hair and strong shoes. . . ." But in the heart of Stepan lives a sadness. Who will take up his cane when he is gone? Tears run down his cheeks and he embraces the children. Who will take up his cane?

And lastly that night the wind blew over a village near central Russia where a mother was putting her boy to sleep.

"So this great bearded man flew on a bubble and pierced the very heavens. And for this the Tsar made him a great chemist."

"And where is he now?" asks the little drowsy boy. "Where is he now?"

The woman covers the child.

"They say, little dove, they say he is in heaven presenting a petition to God for our mouzhiks. Sleep, my heart, sleep."

Author's Note

Concerning This Biography— How Much Is Fiction?

IN GENERAL, every significant event is factual—I have read considerable numbers of Russian books and documents and have based the unfolding of the life of the great scientist on this material. For example, the catastrophe of the first chapter actually occurred, although not all the people mentioned may have been present at the time. And of course some of the minor characters are invented, but such types as the wanderer—the strannik—certainly existed in Russia, as elsewhere.

Bassargin, Olga, Elizabeth, Maria, and of course Mitya are depicted as true to life as I could infer from my research. The sufferings of Maria are accurate, as is the fate of Elizabeth. The attempts to place Mitya in a university are also correctly set down. Mendeleyev's incident with the purple grapes is invented, but he did go to the Crimea for the purpose stated. And of course his scientific studies are described faithfully, I trust, although an occasional invented incident may be thrown in for the sake of unifying the events in the life of the man. Such an incident, for example, is the story of the valiant horse, as well as the story of the man who tried to make crystal sunshine. There are others.

The story of the woman Feozva is substantially right, and the events connecting Mendeleyev with the Cossack maiden Anna are accurate. I read her own story. The story of the extraordinary letters which were guarded in a box is accurate, and I regret to say that they mysteriously disappeared—at a time after my story ends.

The various scientific predictions are accurately related. In the incident with the Tsar I let my imagination go a little, although the Tsar did send for him and also there was some unofficial discussion of the matter of the haircut. The flight on the "bubble" is accurate, and taken from Mendeleyev's own words. I must say, however, that the petitions to God are my inventions, although the spirit of the peasant-people was compatible with such an event. Vassya's illness is truthfully set down, as is the story of the petition by the students, the dangerous operation by Kostenitch, and substantially everything that follows to the end, including the great silent procession in the streets of snow.

DANIEL Q. POSIN

Appendix I

Principal Published Works of Dmitri Ivanovitch Mendeleyev

Key: *J* means *Journal of the Russian Chemical Society*, later associated with the Physical Society, article in Russian
B means *Berichte der Deutschen Chemischen Gesellschaft*, article in German
C means *Comptes Rendus*, article in French
Z means *Zeitschrift für Chemie*, article in German
I means Free Imperial Economic Society, article in Russian

All other publications are as indicated but when necessary R means article (or work) is in Russian, G in German, F in French, E in English

1854

"Chemical Analysis of a Sample from Finland," *Proceedings Russian Mineralogical Society*, St. Petersburg, pp. 234-239, R

1855

"Pyroxen from Finland," *ibid.*, 1855-1856, pp. 207-209, R
"Isomorphism in Dependence on Other Relations between Form and Constitution," *City-Journal*, pp. 229-400, 405-467, R

1856

"Dissertation for the Completion of the Pedagogical Institute," 234 pp., R
Specific volumes. Dissertation for master's degree, St. Petersburg, 224 pp., R

1857

"New Events in Science," *Journal of the Ministry of National Enlightenment*, St. Petersburg, R
"Concerning the Book of E. Hoffman, *The Northern Urals*," *ibid.*, R
"Concerning the Translation of the *Chemistry* of A. Strecker," *ibid.*, R
"Regarding Liquid Glass," *ibid.*, R
Technical article in *Manufacturing and Mining News*, St. Petersburg, R

1858

"Newest Metallurgical Investigations," *Leaflet of Industry*, R
"Regarding the Burning of Smoke," *ibid.*, R
"The Drying of Egg White," *Economic News*, St. Petersburg, R
"The Connection between Certain Physical Properties of Substances and Their Chem-

ical Reactions," *Bulletin de la classe physikomathematique* 17, pp. 49–68, G. *Melanges physiques et chimiques*, T. III

1859

"On Sulphurous Acids," *ibid.*, pp. 350–352, G; also, *Liebigs Annalen*, 110, pp. 251–254, G, and *Chemical Journal of Sokolov and Engelhardt* 1, pp. 146–158, R

1860

"On Molecular Cohesion of Certain Organic Liquids," *C*, pp. 50, 52

"On Cohesion of Certain Liquids," *C*, 51, 97; also *Chemical Journal of Sokolov and Engelhardt*, 3, pp. 81–97, R; also Z

"On Cohesion of Certain Liquids and Its Relation to Chemical Reactions," *ibid.*, 4, pp. 65–95, R

"A Note on the Expansion of Homologous Liquids due to Heating," *Liebigs Annalen*, 114, pp. 165–169, G

"The Chemical Congress in Karlsruhe," a letter to A. A. Voskresensky, *St. Petersburg News*, R

1861

"The Expansion of Fluids Due to Heating above their Boiling Points" ("Absolute Boiling Point"), *Liebigs Annalen*, 119, pp. 1–11; also Z

Organic Chemistry, 502 pp., St. Petersburg, R

"Theory Regarding the Limits of Organic Combinations," *Bulletin de l'Académie de Sciences*, 4, pp. 245–250, St. Petersburg, F

1862

"Optical Saccharimetry," *I*, 52 pp.

"Technical Encyclopedia," ("Technology" as by Wagner, translated and enlarged by Mendeleyev), *General Welfare*, 1862–1867, R

Analytical Chemistry, Gerhardt and Chancel, translated and enlarged by Mendeleyev, 1864–1866, *ibid.*, R

1865

"Combination of Alcohols with Water," doctor's dissertation, St. Petersburg, 119 pp., R
Also published in *Pogg. Ann.*, 1869, G; and Z, 1, 1865

1866

"Determination of the Density of Gases and Vapors," 74 pp., R

"Organization of Agronomical Research," *I*, 2

"Program for Agronomical Research," *ibid.*

1867

"First Report on Agronomical Research," *ibid.*, 4

"On Contemporary Unfolding of a Chemical Industry in the Development of Russia," R

"A New Hydrocarbon," Fritzsche and Mendeleyev, First Congress of Russian Naturalists, R

1868

Principles of Chemistry, 1st ed., 1868–1871, 2 vols., 816 and 951 pp., R

1869

"Manufacture of Cheese in Artells," *I*, 2, 3, and 4
"The Dependence between the Properties and the Atomic Weights of the Elements," *J*, vol. 1, pp. 35, 60–77, 229–230 (communicated March 6, 1869); also in *Z*, 5, pp. 405–406; also in *B*, 2, p. 553
"Research on a System of Elements according to Their Atomic Weights and Chemical Functions," *Journal für praktische Chemie*, 1, p. 251, G
"Atomic Volumes of Simple Bodies," work of the Second Congress of Russian Doctors and Naturalists, R
"Earth Analysis," *J*, 1, pp. 227–229
"Heat Capacity and Complexity of the Carbon Molecule," *ibid.*, vol. 1, pp. 216–217; vol. 2, pp. 10, 28–46, R; also *B*, 2, pp. 662–664

1870

"Determination of Specific Heat of Chemical Compounds," *Z*, 6, p. 200
"The Place of Cerium in the System of the Elements," *Bulletin of the St. Petersburg Academy of Sciences*, 16, p. 45, 1870–1871, R
"Concerning the Support of Agronomical Work," *I*, 2
"Examination of Court Matters," *Juridical News*, R
"Remarks on the Researches of Andrews on the Compressibility of Carbon Dioxide," *Pogg. Ann.*, 141, p. 618, G
"Agronomical Work of the Free Imperial Economic Society, Report on the Chemical Investigation of the Soil," R

1871

"Specific Volumes of Hydrocarbon Combinations," *J*, 2, p. 292
"The Natural System of the Elements and Its Use in Determining Properties of Undiscovered Elements," *J*, 3, pp. 7 and 25–56; communicated Dec. 3, 1870; also *B*, 3, pp. 990–991, 1870
"Regarding the System of the Elements," *B*, 4, pp. 343–352
"The Periodic Law of the Chemical Elements," *Liebigs Annalen*, Suppl. 8, G
"The Effect of Time on the Progress of Chemical Reactions," *J*, 3, p. 250
"A Note Regarding the Question of Improving the Gymnasia," *St. Petersburg News*, R
"On Crystallization and Water Trapped during the Process," *J*, 3, p. 249
"Regarding the Super-oxide," *J*, 3, pp. 221, 284–286
"On the Necessity for Increasing Facilities in the Chemical Laboratory of St. Petersburg University," R

1872

"Pulsating Air-Pump" (together with M. Kirpitchev and G. Schmidt), *J*, 4, pp. 34, 139–204; also *Liebigs Annalen*, p. 165, 1872–1873, G; also *B*, 5, p. 328, 1872

Principles of Chemistry, 2d ed., vol. I, 827 pp., 1872; vol. II, 932 pp., 1873, R

"The Atomic Weight of Yttrium," *J*, 4, p. 7

"Concerning the Compressibility of Gases," *J*, 4, pp. 102–103, 309–352; also *Artillery Journal* No. 8, R; also *B*, 5, p. 332

"Answer to the Remarks of N. Lavrov Concerning the Article: 'Heat Capacity and Complexity of the Carbon Molecule,'" *J*, 4, p. 104

1873

"The Verification of Meters and Kilograms," *J*, 5, p. 14

"The Torsion Balance and the Determination of the Average Density of the Earth by Bell," *J*, 5, pp. 15–16, 48

"Concerning the Pump of Mendeleyev, Kirpitchev, and Schmidt," *Liebigs Annalen*, 165, p 63, G

"Applicability of the Periodic Law to Cerite Metal (Answer to the Work of Rammelsberg)," *J*, 5, p. 135; also *Liebigs Annalen* 168, p. 45, G; also *B*, 6, pp. 558–560

"The Boiling of Mercury in Barometer Tubes," *J*, 5, p. 189

"Preliminary Remarks on the Determination of Height by Means of a New Differential Barometer," *J*, 5, pp. 188, 255–256; 296–301; 6, II, p. 84; 1874

1874

"The Breaking of Glass Tubes Due to Pressure," *J*, 6, pp. 7–8, also *B*, 7, p. 126

"On the Need of the Metric System for Exact Temperature Measurements. A New Oil Thermometer, for Air," *J*, 6, I, pp. 8–9, II, pp. 10–12; also *B*, 7, pp. 126–128

"A General Formula for Gases Including the Formulations of Boyle, Gay-Lussac, and Avogadro," *J*, 6, pp. 208–209; also *B*, 7, pp. 1455–1456

"Remarks on Groshan's Work on the Nature of the Elements," *J*, 6, p. 59; also *B*, 7, p. 128

"Preliminary Note on the Elasticity of Rarefied Air," with Kirpitchev, *Bulletin de l'Académie de Sciences*, 19, p. 466, F; also *B*, 7, p. 486; and *J*, 6, I, pp. 124–125, II, pp. 72–73

"A New Type of Mercury Barometer," *J*, 6, II, p. 84

"Concerning Silvestrom's Research on the Compressibility of Rarefied Air," *J*, 6, I, p. 209; II, pp. 126–131

"A New Specimen of Iron Ore in Orlov Province," *J*, 6, pp. 287–289

"A Mercury Pump without Cocks and Valves," with Th. Kapustin, *J*, 6, I, pp. 175–176; II, p. 120; also *B*, 7, pp. 731–732

"The Use of the Manometer in Measuring Altitude Above Sea Level," *J*, 6, II, p. 106

1875

"A Formula for the Expansion of Mercury," *J*, 7, II, pp. 19, 75–95; also *B*, 8, p. 540

"On the Samples of Spherosiderites in Orlov Province," *J*, 7, pp. 49–51; *B*, 8, p. 262

Elasticity of Gases, Pt. I, 263 pp., 12 figs., St. Petersburg, R
"In Memory of Kirpitchev," *J*, 7, pp. 145–147
"Concerning Air," *Encyclopedia* of Beresin, R
"Proposal for the Establishment of a Commission for the Study of Spiritualist Phenomena," *J*, 7, II, pp. 152–153; 8, II, pp. 1–2, 214–217
"The Determination of the Coefficient of Expansion of Air," with N. Kayander, *J*, 7, p. 316; II, pp. 323–327
Solutions, St. Petersburg, R
"A Differential Thermometer," *J*, 7, I, p. 147; also II, pp. 61–62; also *B*, 8, pp. 539–540
"The Temperature of the Upper Layers of the Earth's Atmosphere," *J*, 7, II, pp. 260–265, 327–331; also *C*, 81, pp. 1094, 1182
"The Identity of Gallium and Eka-aluminium," *J*, 7, pp. 316–317; II, p. 331; also *B*, 8, p. 1680
"Remarks apropos the Discovery of Gallium," *C*, 81, pp. 969–972

1876

On the Leveling of Barometers and Height Measurements, St. Petersburg, 184 pp., R
"The Difference in the Composition of Different Layers of the Atmosphere," *J*, 8, pp. 9–10
Information for Critical Judgment of Spiritualism, St. Petersburg, 382 pp., R
Mond's *Meteorology*, translated into Russian under editorship of D. Mendeleyev
"Compressibility of Gases at Low Pressures," with Boguski and Gemilian, *C*, 8, I, p. 192; II, pp. 286–287; also *B*, 9, p. 1312
"The Effect of Moisture on Barometric Pressure," *J*, 8, II, pp. 5–6
"The Depression of Mercury in Tubes," with K. Gutkovskaya, *J*, 8, II, pp. 212–214
"The Union of the Chemical and Physical Societies," *J*, 8, II, pp. 58, 103
"The Construction of a Meteorological Station," with Lenz and Rykatschev, *J*, 8, II, pp. 220–224
"The Temperature of the Upper Layers of the Atmosphere," polemic with Rykatschev, *J*, 8, II, pp. 19–53, 95–100
"The Coefficients of Expansion of Gases," polemic with Ussov, *J*, 8, II, pp. 3–5

1877

Principles of Chemistry, 3rd ed., R
"On the Corrected Coefficients of Expansion of Gases (Alpha equal to 0.003670)," *J*, 9, pp. 11–12; also *B*, 10, p. 81
"The True Coefficients of Expansion of Gases," with Kayander, *J*, 9, II, pp. 215–216
"The Status of the Petroleum," *J*, 9, pp. 36–37; also in F, *Révue Scientifique*, No. 18, F; also in *B*, 10, pp. 229–230
"Researches on Mariotte's Law," *Nature*, E
"The Kinetic Energy of Gas and Vapor Molecules," *J*, 9, p. 192; also *B*, 10, p. 975
The Petroleum Industry in Pennsylvania and in the Caucasus, 304 pp., R
"Determination of Chrome Content in Chrome Siderites," *B*, 10, p. 414

1878

"Construction of a Balance for Weighing Gases," *B*, 11, p. 1261

1879

"The Periodic Law of the Chemical Elements," *Moniteur Scientifique*, F
"Concerning Gallium," *J*, 11, p. 86
"The Periodic Regularity of the Chemical Elements," *Chemical News*, pp. 40, 41, E

1880

"Standing before Koundzhi's Painting" ("A Night on the Dnieper"; pastoral), *Goloss (The Voice)*, St. Petersburg newspaper, R
"The Resistance of Fluids," *J*, 12, II, p. 117; also *B*, 13, p. 2405
"The Results of a Summer's Journey to the Caucasus for the Study of the Present Development of the Petroleum Industry," *J*, 12, pp. 308–309
The Resistance of Fluids and Flight through the Air, St. Petersburg, R
"Concerning the History of the Periodic Law," *B*, 13, pp. 1796–1804
"A New Method for Distilling Mixed Fluids," *J*, 12, p. 309

1881

"The Distillation of the Baku Petroleum," *J*, 13, pp. 454–456
"The Metals of the Cerite and Gadolinite Groups" (Scandium as Ekaboron and the Periodic System)," *J*, 13, pp. 516–520; also *B*, 14, pp. 2821–2823
Where to Build the Petroleum Works, St. Petersburg, 84 pp., R
The Elasticity of Gases, Imperial Technological Society, 25 pp., R

1882

"Researches on the Distillation of Various Petroleum Samples," *J*, 14, p. 54
"On the Quality of Petroleum Distillation" (Answer to Markovnikov and Ogloblin), *J*, 14, pp. 54–56
Principles of Chemistry, 4th ed., R
"An Apparatus for Demonstrating the Diffusion of Gases," *J*, 14, p. 110
"The Inner Friction of the Petroleum Hydrocarbon and Lubricating Oil," with Andreyev, *J*, 14, p. 199
"A Note on the Heat of Combustion of Hydrocarbon," *J*, 14, pp. 230–238; also *B*, 15, pp. 1555–1559

1883

"The Extraction of a Safe Illuminating Oil from the Baku Petroleum," *J*, 15, XXIII
"Isolation of Pentane from Baku Petroleum," *J*, 15, p. 3
"Use of Newton's Third Law in the Mechanical Formulation of Chemical Substitutions, and Application to the Constitution of Hydrocarbons," *J*, 15, p. 3; also in *B*, 16
"A New Proven Apparatus for the Determination of Vapor Density," *J*, 15, p. 60
"Fractional Distillation of Baku Petroleum and the Investigation of Its Distillates of Lower Boiling Point," *J*, 15, pp. 189–194; also *B*, 16, pp. 1225–1227
"Lamps for Using the Heavy Petroleum Oils," *J*, 15, pp. 270–272
"Reaction between Sublimate and the Fluid Petroleum Hydrocarbons," *J*, 15, p. 570

1884

"The Expansion of Fluids" (Answer to Prof. Avenarius), *J*, 16, II, pp. 475–492
"Again on the Expansion of Fluids," *Annales de chimie et de physique* (6) 2, pp. 271–282
"A Note on Solutions (Their Compressibility)," *J*, 16, p. 93; also *B*, 17, p. 157
"The Dependence between the Densities of Solutions of Salts and the Molecular Weight of the Dissolved Salt," *J*, 16, pp. 184–187; also *B*, 17, pp. 155–157
"The Soda of the Lubimov and Solvay Factory," *J*, 16, pp. 277–279
"The Dependence between the Modulus of Expansion of Fluids and Their Critical Temperatures," *J*, 16, pp. 452–455; also in *B*, 17, pp. 301–302
"The Density of the Normal Hydrate of Sulphuric Acid," *J*, 16, pp. 455–458; also *B*, 17, pp. 302–304
"The Distillation of American Petroleum," *J*, 16, pp. 458–459; also *B*, 17, pp. 312–313
"The Contraction of Solutions on Formation," *J*, 16, pp. 643–644
"The Dependence of the Specific Weight on the Structure and Temperature," *Industrial News*, St. Petersburg, R
The Need of a New Building for the Laboratory of St. Petersburg University, St. Petersburg, R

1885

Letters on Factories, St. Petersburg, R
"Concerning Petroleum Matters," *Industrial News*, R
"Thoughts Concerning a Petroleum Pipeline Baku-Batum," Imperial Russian Technological Society, pp. 200–231

1886

The Extraction of Baku Petroleum in the Year 1886, 139 pp., R
"The Specific Gravity of Solutions of Sulphuric Acid," *J*, 18, pp. 4–7
"Change of Specific Gravity in Chemical Association of Sulphuric Acid with Water," *B*, 19, pp. 379–389; also *J*, 18, pp. 64–65
"Heat as an Index of the Association of Sulphuric Acid and Water," *B*, 19, pp. 400–405
"Regularity under the Atomic Weights of the Elements after Rydberg," *J*, 18, p. 434
"Inapplicability of the Periodic Law for Induction of the Unity of Matter," *J*, 18, pp. 66–67
Lectures on Theoretical Chemistry in 1886–1887 at the Higher Course for Women, St. Petersburg, R

1887

"In Memory of Butelerov," *J*, xxx–xxxii
"A Balloon Ascent at Klin during Solar Eclipse," *Northern News*, R; also *J*, 19, II, p. 336
"Dependence between the Density and the Structure of Sulphuric Acid Solutions," *J*, 19, pp. 242–243
"Specific Gravity of Solutions of Sulphuric Acid," *Zeitschrift für physikalische Chemie*, 1, pp. 273–284, G
"Concerning Alcohol Solutions," *J*, 19, pp. 335–336

Investigation of Aqueous Solutions by Means of Specific Gravity, St. Petersburg, 521 pp., R
"The Work of the British Association in Manchester," *J*, 19, pp. 491–492
"Concerning the Meteorites of Ochansk," *J*, 19, p. 550; 20, p. 513

1888

"A Journey in the Don Basin," *J*, 20, p. 536
Future Strength Reposing on the Shores of the Don. The World Significance of Stone Coal and the Don Basin, Northern News, 144 pp., R
Calculations for the Development of the Stone Coal Industry of the Don Area, R

1889

"The Present Position and Prospects of the Caucasian Petroleum Industry," *Journal of the Society of Chemical Industry*, London, E
Concerning the Growth of Rumors Relative to the Exhaustion of the Baku Petroleum Productivity, Northern News, 12 pp., R
Principles of Chemistry, 5th ed., 780 pp. with 12 portraits, R
"A Note on the Dissociation of Dissolved Substances," *J*, 21, pp. 198–202
"The Reduction of Silicium Dioxide by Magnesium," *J*, 21, p. 90
"The Periodic Law of the Chemical Elements" (Faraday Lecture), *J*, 21, pp. 233–257; also *Journal of the Chemical Society*, 55, pp. 634–656, E; also in appendix of Mendeleyev's *Principles of Chemistry* in English translation, Longmans, Green and Company, New York. (Out of print but available in some libraries.)
An Attempt to Apply to Chemistry One of the Principles of Newton's Natural Philosophy, Northern Urals, 13 pp., R; also see preceding reference
"A Trip to England and Mond's Gas Battery," *J*, 21, p. 451
Two London Lectures, St. Petersburg, 59 pp., R
The Need of a Chemical Laboratory at St. Petersburg University, R

1890

"On the Analogy of the Dissolved Silver of Carey Lea with the Colloidal Constitution of Several Bodies," *J*, 22, pp. 73–74
"Regarding the Discovery of N_3H Family of Acids," *J*, 22, pp. 506–515; also *B*, 23, pp. 3464–3472

1891

The Principles of Chemistry. English translation by G. Kamensky, 2 vol., Longmans, Green and Company, London
"The Change in the Density of Water Due to Heating," *J*, 23, II, pp. 183–219

1892

The Tariff, St. Petersburg, 730 pp., R
Principles of Chemistry, translated by L. Jawein and A. Thillot, St. Petersburg, G
"Crystalline Glycerine of the Krestovnikov Factory," *J*, 24, p. 58

Appendix

1893

The World Exposition in Chicago, R
Survey of Factory Industry and Commerce of Russia, St. Petersburg, R

1894

"The Weight of a Liter of Air," *J*, 26, pp. 50–51, published from *Annals of the Bureau of Weights and Measures*, I, pp. 57–88; also *Proceedings of the Royal Society*, p. 59, E

1895

Principles of Chemistry, 6th ed., R
"On a Theorem in Geometry," *C*, 121, pp. 421–422
"The Weight of a Definite Volume of Water," *Annals of the Bureau of Weights and Measures*, 2, pp. 1–52, R
"The Change in Density of Water between 0 and 40," *ibid.*, 2, pp. 133–143
"Progress in the Production of New Standards of Length and Weight," *ibid.*, 2, pp. 157–185

1896

"On the Weight of a Cubic Decimeter of Water at Its Maximum Density," *Proceedings of the Royal Society*, 59, pp. 143–158
"Smokeless Explosive Powder," *Marine Archives*, 1895–1896, R

1897

The Principles of Chemistry, 2d English ed., London
"Technique with an Exact Balance," *Annals of the Bureau of Weights and Measures*, 3, pp. 3–84; also *J*, 27, pp. 509–513
"Extension of the Article on the Density Change of Water," *ibid.*, 3, pp. 133–135
An Examination of the Conformity among the Fundamental Measures of Russia, France, and Great Britain, F
"The Place of Argon in the Periodic System," *J*, 27, pp. 69–72
"Comparison of the Russian Platinum-Iridium Half-Sagene Length with the English Imperial Standard Yard," *Annals of the Bureau of Weights and Measures*, 3, pp. 93–107, R
Principles of Factory Industry, St. Petersburg, 196 pp., R
"Discussion with Ramsay and Lockyer about Argon and Helium," *J*, 27, p. 508
"Gold from Silver," *Journal of Journals*, pp. 1–11, R

1898

"Experimental Investigations on the Oscillations of Balances," *Proceedings of the Royal Society*, 63, pp. 454–459, E; also *Annals of the Bureau of Weights and Measures*, 4, pp. 33–45, 1898–1899, R
"Concerning Dulong's Formula for Determining the Heat of Combustion of Fluid and Solid Combustibles," *J*, 29, p. 144

1899

Thoughts on the Development of Farm Industry, St. Petersburg, R

The History of Chemistry by E. v. Meyer. Translated from the German into Russian under editorship of Mendeleyev, St. Petersburg, 514 pp.

"How I Found the Periodic System of the Elements," *Revue Générale de Chimie pure et appliquée*, 1, pp. 211, 510, F

Principles of Chemistry, translated into French by Achkinasi, Paris, 1896–1899

1900

Memorandum Regarding Calendar Reform, St. Petersburg, R

Studies of Industry, Library of Technical Knowledge, St. Petersburg, R

"The Chemical and Petroleum Industries," in W. Kovalevsky's *Russia at the End of the Nineteenth Century*, St. Petersburg, R

The Iron Industry of the Urals in the Year 1889, 866 pp., R

"The Paris World Exposition," in newspaper *Russia*

1901

Remarks on the Nature of Peoples of Russia, St. Petersburg, R

1902

"An Attempt toward a Chemical Conception of the Ether," *Prometheus*, Berlin, 1903, G; also in appendix of English translation by Kamensky of Mendeleyev's *Principles of Chemistry*

Tables of Comparison of Russian, Metric, and English Masses, with Foreword, St. Petersburg, R

1903

Principles of Chemistry, 7th ed., St. Petersburg, R

Articles on "Vaseline," "Matter," "Spirit Combustibles," "Periodic Law," etc., in *Encyclopedia-Lexicon of Brockhaus-Effront*, 1891–1894

1904

"Concerning Spiritualist Problems," *New Era*, R

Last Thoughts, St. Petersburg, 1904–1905, 428 pp., R

1905

The Principles of Chemistry, 3d English ed., translated by G. Kamensky, Longmans, Green and Company, London

"Oscillations (balances)," *Annals of the Bureau of Weights and Measures*, 7, pp. 167–169, R

Principles of Chemistry, 8th ed., 816 pp., 1905–1906, St. Petersburg

1906

A Project for a School for Teachers, St. Petersburg, R
Toward Knowledge of Russia, 159 pp., R. (Appeared in five editions.)
The Map of Russia, R

1907 (appeared posthumously)

"Preparations for the Determination of the Absolute Gravitational Attraction in the Bureau of Weights and Measures," *Annals of the Bureau of Weights and Measures*, 8, pp. 1–41
Toward an Increase of Knowledge of Russia, St. Petersburg, 109 pp., R
 A list of 40 additional works may be obtained by writing to Dr. D. Q. Posin, in care of the publishers.

Appendix II

Bibliography

Academy of Sciences of the U.S.S.R., *The Work of the Mendeleyev Centenary Congress*, 2 vols. Mostly in Russian, but also in French, German, and English, giving proceedings of the International 1934 convocation in Moscow and Leningrad.
ARCHANGELSKY, A., *D. I. Mendeleyev, His Scientific and General Work*, F. Feodorov Press, Orlov Province, Russia, 1907. In Russian
BARING, MAURICE, *Landmarks in Russian Literature*, The Macmillan Company, New York, 1912
BEKHTEREV, V. D., and R. WEINBERG, *The Brain of the Chemist D. I. Mendeleyev*, W. Engelmann, Leipzig, 1909
BYRON, GEORGE G., *Poems*, especially those on Greece and "Darkness"
CHELTSOV, I., article on Mendeleyev, *Biographical Dictionary* of St. Petersburg University, vol. 2, pp. 17–21, 1898. In Russian
COOPER, JAMES FENIMORE, *The Pathfinder*, Thomas Nelson & Sons, New York, 1938
DUBROWSKI, K., *The Great Chemist*. In Russian. (Out of print. See New York Public Library.)
GARRET, A. E., *The Periodic Law*, D. Appleton–Century Company, Inc., New York, 1909
HARROW, BENJAMIN, *Eminent Chemists of Our Time*, D. VanNostrand Company, Inc., New York, 1927
HUGO, VICTOR, *The Toilers*, especially "The Combat with the Octopus," Heath and Company, Boston, 1911
JAFFE, BERNARD, *Crucibles*, Simon and Schuster, Inc., New York, 1930
Journals of the Russian Chemical Society (later called "Physico-Chemical Society"), 1869–1909. In Russian
KAPUSTIN-GUBKIN, NADEZHDA I., *Family Chronicle*, First Mendeleyev Congress. Publisher M. Frolov, St. Petersburg, 1908. In Russian. (This is by the younger Nadezhda referred to in this biography.)
KARPOVICH, MICHAEL, *Imperial Russia, 1801–1917*, Henry Holt and Company, Inc., New York, 1932
KUZNETSOV, B. G., *Lomonosov, Lobachevsky, Mendeleyev*, Moscow, 1945. In Russian
LOWRY, T. M., *Historical Introduction to Chemistry*, The Macmillan Company, New York, 1936
MAIKOV, A. N., *Complete Collection of Creations*, St. Petersburg. In Russian

MENDELEYEV, ANNA IVANOVNA (POPOV), *Mendeleyev in Life,* M. & S. Sabashnikov, Moscow, 1928. In Russian. (This is by the Anna of the story.)

MENDELEYEV, D., "An Attempt to Apply to Chemistry One of the Principles of Newton's Natural Philosophy," address presented before the Royal Society of Great Britain on Friday, May 31, 1889. (To be found in several sources, including the appendix of *The Principles of Chemistry.*)

―――, "The Periodic Law of the Chemical Elements," Faraday Lecture before Fellows of the Chemical Society in the Theater of the Royal Society on Tuesday, June 4, 1889. (In the appendix of *The Principles of Chemistry* or *Transactions of the Chemical Society,* 1889, 55, pp. 634–656. The lecture was not delivered in person for reasons made evident in the story.)

―――, "The Present Position and Prospects of the Caucasian Petroleum Industry," a letter to the editor of the *Journal of the Society of Chemical Industry,* August 27 (new style, September 8), 1889.

―――, *The Principles of Chemistry,* 3d English ed., translated from the Russian 7th ed. by George Kamensky, St. Petersburg, Thomas H. Pope, editor, 2 vols., Longmans, Green and Company, New York, 1905. (Out of print but available in libraries.)

―――, *Selected Works.* In Russian. (Out of print. See New York Public Library.)

MIRSKY, (PRINCE), D. S., *Contemporary Russian Literature, 1881–1925,* Alfred A. Knopf, New York

MUIR, PATTISON, *History of Chemical Theories and Laws,* John Wiley & Sons, Inc., New York, 1907, pp. 365–374

OZAROVSKAYA, OLGA E., *D. I. Mendeleyev,* Press "Federatsiya," Moscow, 1929. In Russian

PARES, BERNARD, *A History of Russia,* Alfred A. Knopf, New York, 1926

"Presentation of the Copley Medal of the Royal Society," *Proceedings of the Royal Society,* 1906, 77, p. 117

SLETOV, P. V., *D. I. Mendeleyev,* Zhurnalno-Gazetnoe Obedeeneniye, Moscow, 1933. In Russian

SPOTTISWOOD, WILLIAM, speech in connection with the award of the Davy Medal to D. Mendeleyev and Lothar Meyer on November 30, 1882, *Proceedings of the Royal Society,* 1882, vol. 34, p. 339

STANKEVITCH, V. B., *Great Russian Chemist,* YMCA Press, Ltd.; American Issue, Prague, 1923. In Russian

THORPE, T. E., *Essays in Historical Chemistry,* The Macmillan Company, New York, 1894. (Discussion of the great chemists of the nineteenth century.)

―――, "Scientific Work of Mendeleyev," *Nature,* February 14, 1907, vol. 75, pp. 371–373

TILDEN, W. A., *Famous Chemists. The Men and Their Work,* George Routledge & Sons, Ltd., London

―――, "Mendeleyev Memorial Lecture," *Journal of the Chemical Society,* vol. 95, p. 2

TOLSTOI, (COUNT), LEO, *Death of Ivan Ilytch* and other stories, The Thomas Y. Crowell Company, New York, 1887

TUTCHEV, FEODOR, *Poems,* especially "Silentium," in *Russian Poetry,* edited by Babette Deutsch and Avrahm Yarmolinsky, International Publishers Co., Inc., New York, 1927

VENABLE, F. P., *The Development of the Periodic Law,* Chemical Publishing Company of New York, Inc., New York, 1896

―――, *The Study of the Atom,* Chemical Publishing Company of New York, Inc., New York

VERNE, JULES, *The English at the North Pole,* Warwick House, Salisbury Square, London; Ward, Lock & Co.; 1936

―――, *Michael Strogoff. Courier of the Czar,* A. L. Burt Company, Inc., New York, 1937

VINOGRADOV, A. K., *The Chronicle of the Malevinskys,* Moscow, 1941. In Russian

WALDEN, P., "Dmitri Ivanovitch Mendeleyev," *Berichte der deutschen chemischen Gesellschaft,* 1908, vol. 13, p. 4719. In German

WEEKS, MARY E., "Discovery of the Elements," *Journal of Chemical Education*, 1945, pp. 391-396
WINICOW, W. R., "Some of Mendeleyev's Personal Characteristics," *Journal of Chemical Education*, 1937, pp. 372-375

Encyclopedia References

Annual Register, 1907, pt. 2, p. 112. Obituary
Brockhaus Konversations Lexicon (New Encyclopedic Dictionary), St. Petersburg, 1912, vol. 26, pp. 263-269. In Russian
Encyclopedia Dictionary, vol. 28, pp. 459-462. In Russian
Large Encyclopedia, edited by S. N. Iuzhakova, St. Petersburg, 1909, vol. 13, pp. 36-38. In Russian
Large Soviet Encyclopedia, Moscow, 1938, vol. 38, p. 781. In Russian
New International Yearbook, 1907, p. 486. Obituary
Small Soviet Encyclopedia, Moscow, 1930, vol. 5, pp. 124-125. In Russian

Miscellaneous

Current Literature, "Greatest Chemical Genius in the World," December, 1906, vol. 41, pp. 682-684
Independent, February 21, 1907, vol. 62, p. 454. (Estimate of Mendeleyev's service to chemistry.)
Popular Science, September, 1906, vol. 69, pp. 285-286. (Mendeleyev's contribution to chemistry.)
Review of Reviews, "One of the World's Greatest Chemists," March, 1907, vol. 35, pp. 372-373
Scientific American, May 9, 1907, Supplement, vol. 63. Sketch. October 19, 1907, Supplement, vol. 64. (Work of Mendeleyev.)

"A Night in the Ukraine," a painting by Koundzhi. Mendeleyev wrote on the theory of the evolution of art from "body" art, as in Greek creations to modern landscape art; he used the Koundzhi painting as an illustration of the transition from self-contemplation to a love of nature. The article was written in 1880 for *Goloss (The Voice)*, a Russian newspaper. A copy of the painting is at the Frick Art Reference Library, New York. The original is owned by Tretyakovskaya Galereya, Moscow.

Index

Fictional characters listed in the Index are indicated by the use of italics.

A

Abel, Sir Frederick, 275
Acids, 174, 184, 248, 277
Adams, John Couch, 195–196
Air, composition of, 149, 213
　dust in, 149
　weight of, 138, 293
Akhmatov, Madame, 192
Akhmatov, Sergei, 188, 191–194, 222, 317
Aksakov, A. N., 200
Alaska, 163
Alcohol, 139, 142, 277
Alexander I, Tsar, 29, 58
Alexander II, Tsar, 125, 136, 224, 240
Alexander III, Tsar, 249–253
Alice, Princess, of Edinburgh, 291
Alleghenies, 208, 217–218
Altai Mountains, 20
Aluminium, 122, 138, 187, 234
America, 123, 197, 207–218, 222, 233, 243, 248, 313–314
American Museum of Natural History, 209
Ammonia, 183, 187, 276
Ammonia gas, 245
Ammonia salts, 183
Anderson, William John, 273, 275, 278–279
Andrei the Chemist, 7, 13, 15, 17–18, 24, 26–27, 48, 50, 52–53, 63, 66, 139
Andrews, Thomas, 139, 184, 245
Andreyev, the cultivator, 113–114
Aniline dyes, 245
Antimony, 170
Anton the Furnace Man, 17, 25–26, 46, 296
Aquarius, 195
Aremziansk, 3, 20, 31, 52, 96, 113, 120, 125, 157, 264, 296, 316, 318
　Glass Factory, 4–5, 8, 10, 21, 23, 28, 77–78, 106, 121, 139, 144
　fire at, 13–19, 48, 86, 167
Arfvedson, J. A., 234
Argon, 293, 312
Argyrodite, 248, 298
Armstrong, Professor, 275, 279, 281
Arsenic, 170
Ash, for the soil, 183
Astronomy, 276
Atmosphere, 149, 200, 254, 256–257
Atoms, 136, 139, 167, 169, 173, 178, 184, 246, 276–277, 289, 312
　weights of, 140, 173, 184–185, 248, 274, 306
Avdotya, 17
Avogadro, Count Amadeo, 140
Avogadro's principle, 140

B

Baku, 123, 125, 205, 208, 217–218, 271–272, 284
Balances, oscillations of, 293
Balloon, hydrogen-filled, 256, 259–263, 266–268
Baltic Sea, 22, 85, 93, 255
Baltinsky, Stepan Stepanovitch (see *The Strannik*)
Barium, 170
Barometers, 257, 262–263, 267
Bassargin, Nikolai (Kolya), the Decembrist, 9–11, 14–16, 18–19, 24, 29, 31, 39–43, 50, 52–64, 118–119, 136, 142, 151, 190, 296, 311
Bassargin, Olga Mendeleyev, 9, 14, 16, 31, 38, 40–43, 61, 64, 109, 134, 136, 150–151, 319
Battle of Chernaya, 130
Bauer, P., 183
Bauer Institute, Moscow, 220
Becquerel, Henri Antoine, 303
The Bee, a journal, 224
Beethoven's Fifth Concerto (Emperor), 225–227, 235, 270
Beilstein, F. K., 196
Beistrov, Dr., 272–273
Beketov, Andrei Nikolayevitch, 221, 230, 232, 236–237, 274
Belinsky, Vissarion Grigorivitch, 41–42, 53, 141
The Bell, a journal, 141
Benzene, 284

335

Benzol, 139
BeO (see Beryllium)
Berlikov, 175, 183, 199
Beryllium, 170, 173, 274
Bessemer process, 209
Biarritz, 232–233
Biology, 168, 179
Bismuth, 170
Black Sea, 127, 130
  oil deposits near, 149, 204–205, 217
  pipe line to, 284
Blavadskaya, Helena Petrovna, 200
Blok, Alexander Alexandrovitch, 307
Boblovo Hill, Mendeleyev's estate, 145, 149, 158–159, 163, 176, 182, 198, 223–224, 229, 240–241, 243, 256–257, 264, 268–269, 274, 278–279, 317–318
Boisbaudran, Lecoq de, 201–202, 245, 248, 280, 303
Borax, 24
Borgman, Professor, 200
"Boris Godunov," 30
Boron, 187
Botkin, Sergei Petrovitch, 232
Brakhman, schoolmate of Mendeleyev, 51
Bramwell, Sir Frederick, 275
Brandt, F., zoologist, 102
Brandt, N., chemist, 170
Brauner, Boguslav, 274, 278, 299–300, 303
Bredif, a medium, 200
Breslau, 298
British Chemical Society, 169, 196, 273, 279–281
British Chemical-Technical Society, 275
British Scientific Association, 270
Buhrig, von, Professor, 274
Bulgarin, Faddei Venediktovitch, 30
Bunsen, Robert Wilhelm, 138
Bunsen burner, 138
Butelerov, A. M., 200, 222
Byron, Lord, 246, 298

C

Cadmium, 202
Caesium, 184–185
Calcium, 139, 173, 187, 234
Cambridge University, 291
Cannes, 314
Cannizzaro, Stanislav, 139–140
Carbon, 27, 122, 143, 155, 170, 234
  compounds of, 142
Carbon dioxide, 149, 184
Caspian Sea, 19–20, 80–81, 85, 113, 123, 125, 177, 204, 208, 217, 318

Cathedral of Saint Basil, 86
Catherine the Great, 55, 58
Caucasus, 130, 204, 217–219, 284, 294, 318
Cavendish, Henry, 170
Cerium, 186–187, 274
Challis, James, 195
Charing Cross Hotel, London, 275, 291
Chemical Congress, Karlsruhe, 139, 141
Chemical industry, Russian, 143
Chemistry, 110, 118, 157, 166, 168, 179, 234, 245–246, 276, 306
  applications of, 247
  courses for women in, 209, 222, 272, 311
  inorganic, 140
  organic, 140
  principle objective of, 147
Chess, 226, 228
China, 177, 313
Chistyakov, Pavel Petrovitch, 230
Chizhov, the mathematician, 98
Chlorine, 148–149, 170, 187, 276
  liquid, 148
Chousovaya River, 82
Chromium, 170, 306
Church of the Archangel Michael, 31, 38, 296
Coal, 149, 209, 245, 287, 289, 294, 297, 318
  mining of, 239
  in Siberia, 295
Coal tar, 142
Cobalt, 26, 170
Color, 248
  of burning substances, 27, 139, 148
  of liquids, 148
Comptes Rendus, journal, 199
Continental Hotel (fictitious), New York, 211
Cooper, James Fenimore, 240, 270
Copley Medal, 312
Copper, 18, 122, 138, 140, 148, 170
Copper chloride, 148
Copper-sulphate solution, 148
  electrical current through, 147
Cossa, chemist, 298
Cossacks, 20, 58, 129–130, 219
Crimea, 116, 124–132, 219, 289, 318–319
Crimean War, 129–130, 177
Crookes, physicist, 275, 278
Crystallization, 199
Crystals, 143
  carbon, 183
  hydrated, 277
  structure of, 121, 167
Curie, Marie, 306
Curie, Pierre, 306

Index

D

Dalton, John, 312
Darwin, "James," actually Charles, 212
Davy, Sir Humphrey, 239
Davy Medal, 1882, 239
  1903, 307
Decembrist uprising, 30
Decembrists, 23, 30–31, 40, 136
De Chancourtois, B., 195, 280
Del Rio, Martin Anton, 234
Delyanov, I. D., 168, 286–287, 289
de Ulloa, Antonio, 170
Dewar, Sir James, 276–278
Diamonds, 149
Dmitri of the Don, 57, 85
Dokoutchaev, Professor, 222, 236–237
Domidov Prize, 142
Don, the, 219–220, 228–229
Donetz River, 209, 272, 289, 294–295, 318
Dostoyevski, Feodor, 53, 94, 124, 141, 162, 235
Dostoyevski, Mikhail, 53
Drake, E. L., 208
Dropsy, 104
Dumas, Jean Baptiste André, 140–141
Dust, 149
  cosmic, 149
Dviboron, 194
Dyadon, Count, 151
Dynamic equilibrium, 277

E

Earth, 200, 234, 254
  analysis of, 184
  evolution of, 149, 179
Eb45 (*see* Ekaboron)
Eclipse, total solar, 252, 255–268
Eeshim, 80
Efremova, Anna Logginovna (*see* Popov, Madame)
Eka-aluminum, 187, 194, 201–202, 234, 248, 253, 280
Ekaboron, 187, 194, 233–234, 248, 280
Ekasilicon, 188, 194, 247–248, 253, 280, 298
Electricity, 138, 276
Elements, 148, 157–159, 299, 306, 312
  argon, 306
  atomic weights of, 140, 183–186, 239
  case histories of, 169, 234
  chemical, 170
  letters representing, 166
  number of known, 167–169, 171, 173
  periodic system of, 172–173, 175, 184–187, 239, 280, 293, 303
  chart of, 279
  in 1871, 189
  in 1902, 304
  in 1948, 305
  revised, 1886, 247
  unity of, 123, 157, 167, 169, 173, 183, 195, 233, 246, 273–274
  unknown, 185
  prediction of, 187, 195, 197, 202, 233, 247, 274, 298
  valencies of, 184–185
England, 123, 129, 157, 195, 197, 208, 233, 245, 248, 270, 273, 284
English Chemical Society, 196
Ethide, 248

F

Faraday, Michael, 276
Faraday Lecture, 273, 279
Feodorov, Feodor Aleksandrovitch, 221
Ferafontovna, Praskovya, 83
Filosov, D. A., 315
Flour, bread and starch, 142
Fluorine, 170
Fontov, supervisor of Mendeleyev estate, 153–158, 161
France, science in, 138, 157
Frankland, Professor, 275, 278
Fritzsche, Academician, 120, 143

G

Galileo, 166
Galle, Johann Gottfried, 195–196
Gallium, 201–202, 207, 222, 234, 245, 248, 253, 280
Gases, 138–140, 148, 218, 245, 276
  carbonic acid, 25
  composing air, 149
  densities of, 138, 143
  rare, 312
George, Prince, Duke of York, 291–292
Gerard, New York hotel manager, 211
Gerhardt, Charles Frédéric, 140
Germanium, 248, 253, 280, 298
Germany, 123, 136, 148, 157, 195, 197, 233, 247–248, 281, 298
Germs, 149
Ghersevanov, M. N., 256
Gladstone, Professor, 275
Glass, 143, 164
  annealing of, 26

Glass, blowing of, 25–26, 205
  Bohemian, 24
  formulas for, 24–27
  potash, 24
  (*See also* Aremziansk, Glass Factory)
Glycerine, crystalline, 290
Gogol, Nikolai Vasilivitch, 53, 125
Gold, 170, 185, 287
Goldenberg, a student, 146
Golikov, Madame, 188
Golovin, the lawyer, 237
Gontarov family, 174
Gorchakova, Countess Elena Sergeyevna, 220
Grapes, 127–129, 132, 319
Grigoriev, a political prisoner, 95
Grigoriev, a student, 295
Grigory, Chieftain, 20
Gubkin (husband of Nadezhda Kapustin), 314

H

Heat, 183–184, 276
Heidelberg, 138–139, 141
Helium, 306, 312
Herzen, Alexander, 141
Hoff, van't (*see* van't Hoff)
Hoffman, E., 136
Holland, 248
Huggins, Sir William, 312
Hugo, Victor, 292
Hydrocarbon, 143, 277
Hydrogen, 122, 138–140, 149, 170, 173, 187–188, 234, 248, 262–263, 266, 274, 276–277, 306

I

Ice, 148
  from salt water, 167
Ilyin, Professor, 152
Imperial Free Economical Society, 142
Indium, 186–187, 202
Inostrantzev, Professor, 222, 236–237
Iridium, 184–185
Irkutsk, 5, 263
Iron, 122, 138, 147, 155, 170, 209, 234, 287, 295, 297
  metallic, 149
Iron sulphide, 148
Irtysh, first Siberian newspaper, 21
Irtysh River, 3, 69, 264, 318
Isle of Camarga, 184
Italy, 233, 248, 278, 298

Ivan the Second, 57
Ivan the Terrible, 20, 57, 84, 86

J

Jacobi, assistant to Mendeleyev, 183
Japan, 310
Jefferson Hotel (fictitous), New York, 213, 218
Jerusalem, 6, 125
Journal of the Chemical Society of London, 197
Journal of the Society of Chemical Industry, 284

K

Kalyazinsky District, 267–268
Kama River, 82
Kapustin (husband of Ekaterina Mendeleyev), 158
Kapustin, Anna, 161
Kapustin, Ekaterina Mendeleyev, 105, 109, 158–163, 165, 176, 198, 221, 224–225, 228–229, 301
Kapustin-Gubkin, Nadezhda Yakovlevna, 160, 163, 172–173, 176–182, 197–198, 220–229, 232, 261, 264–265, 268–269, 274, 279, 282–283, 289, 314, 330
Karlsruhe, 139–140
Kash, Sophia Markovna, 134
Katerina the Matchmaker, 7–8, 13–16, 44–50, 52, 63, 65, 150, 296
Kazan, 205
Kazan University, 29–30, 87, 130, 175, 197
Kerosene, 205
Khabarov, a merchant, 293–294
Kirchhoff, Gustav Robert, 138, 148
Klaproth, Martin Heinrich, 170
Klin, 93, 176, 180, 241, 244, 257–258, 264–265, 267–269, 281–282, 317
Klodt, a dancer, 230
Kondratyev, Dr., 273
Korniliev, Maria Dmitrievna, 9, 22
  (*See also* Mendeleyev, Maria)
Korniliev, Vassili, 9, 21, 85–87, 92
Korniliev family, 21, 159–160
Kostenitch, Dr., 308–309, 319
Kotinsky, 175
Kot-Mourlika (*see* Wagner, Nikolai Petrovitch)
Koundzhi, Arkhip Ivanovitch, 230, 238–239
Kourgan, 80
Kouznets, 295

Index 339

Kouznetsov, a dancer, 230
Kovanko, Lieutenant, 257, 259–261, 265
Kramsky, an artist, 230
Krayevitch, professor of physics, 200, 230, 236–237, 257–259, 265
Kreml, the, 84–85
Kronstadt, 228
Krypton, 312
Kyr-Maku volcano, 217

L

Labrador, a vessel, 207
Ladenburg, Albert, 298
Lake Ilmen, 56
Land problems, 143, 253
Latin, 28, 38, 40–41, 51, 59–60, 292
Lavrov, Yefim Khrisanovitch, 258, 264
"Law of Octaves," 169–170
Lead, 170, 285
Leboir, 140–141
Lebrun, 246
LeChaplain, 246
Leibnitz, Gottfried Wilhelm, 290
Lemokh, a sculptor, 230, 291
Lentov, the doctor, 174, 194
Lenz, Emil, Professor, 102
Leshchev, Feozva Nikitichna (*see* Mendeleyev, Madame Feozoa)
Leverrier, Urbain Jean Joseph, 195
Light, 149, 276
  scientific measurement of, 138
Lime, 24, 183
Liquids, 245
  characteristics of, 138
  Mendeleyev's experiments on, 139
Lithium, 170, 173, 184, 187, 234
London, 247, 273, 278, 312
Lozhinsky, a student, 146–147
Luetin, friend of Mendeleyev, 295

M

McAuliffe, J. R., 211–212
Magnesium, 155, 170, 173, 234
Magnitsky, a courtier, 29
Makovsky, an artist, 230
Mamonov, Madame, 224
Manganese, 170, 287, 290
Manganese peroxide, 24
Marfa (wife of *Matvei*), 11–12, 15, 20–21, 35–37, 63, 66
Maroosya (*see* Oblontov, Maroosya)
Mathematics, 28, 132, 179, 290

Matter, atomic and molecular constitution of, 136, 139
  chemical constitution of, 139
Matvei the Night Watchman, 3–4, 7–8, 11–13, 15, 17, 19–20, 24, 35–37, 48, 61–66, 190, 296
Maxwell, Clerk, 276
Medical Council of Interior Affairs, 274
Mediums, 200
Men of December (*see* Decembrists)
Mendel, Gregor Johann, 213
Mendeleyev, Madame Anna, second wife of Mendeleyev, 238–242, 245, 247, 249–251, 253, 256–259, 261, 264–265, 269–276, 278–279, 281–283, 285, 289, 291–292, 297, 300–302, 307–309, 314–317, 319
  (*See also* Popova, Anna Ivanovna)
Mendeleyev, Apollinaria (Polya) (sister of Dmitri), 9, 17, 29, 41, 296
Mendeleyev, Dmitri Ivanovitch (Mitenka; Mitya), 9, 14–15, 18–19, 21–23, 38, 47–48, 60–63
  in America, New York, 210–215, 218
    Pennsylvania, 217–218
  annual haircut, 240–244, 251
  appointed Director of Russian Bureau of Weights and Measures, 290–291
  professor of inorganic chemistry, 165
  awarded Copley Medal, 312
    Davy Medal, 1882, 239
    Domidov Prize, 142
    gold medal on graduation, 119–120
  balloon ascension, 256–263, 266–268
  biographical notes, 313
  in Cannes, 314
  character of, 119
  in the Crimea, 127–132
  death of, 317
  as delegate to Prussian Academy of Science, 298
  description of, 9–10, 97, 167–168, 192, 210, 222, 271, 314
  divorce of, 237
  doctoral thesis of, 143
  early interest in chemistry, 24–26, 118–119, 121–122
  education of, 27–29, 31–34, 39–43, 51–53, 60, 86, 88–89, 91, 94
    financing of, 32–37, 61
    in Latin, 28, 38, 40–41, 51, 59–60, 71, 73, 75, 82, 100–102
    at Pedagogical Institute, 102–103, 108–110, 118–126, 133, 135–136
    examination for, 101–102

Mendeleyev, Dmitri Ivanovitch, education of, in Russian history, 54–58
  elected Foreign Member of Royal Society, 285
  in England, 245–247
    for Copley Medal, 312
    as Faraday Lecturer, 273, 279–281
    for honorary degrees, 291–292
    before Royal Society, 273–278
  and expansion of Russia's trade, 289
  experiments of, 149, 167, 284
    agricultural, 152–161, 176, 182–183
    on ammonia, 183
    on electrical current, 143
    on explosives, 289
    on liquids, 139
    (*See also* Mendeleyev, research of)
  failing eyesight of, 299–308
  Fiftieth Jubilee of, 310
  first love affair, 134–135
  Friday night socials, 229–230
  at the Glass Factory, 24–29
  government missions, to America, 207–218
    to the Caucasus, 204
    to France and Germany, 136–141
    to the Urals, 294
  and higher education for women, 253, 272
  in chemistry, 209, 222, 272, 311
  honorary degrees of, from University of Edinburgh, 245
    from Göttingen, 310
    from Oxford and Cambridge, 291–292
    from St. Petersburg, 310
  hobbies of, 283
  humanitarianism of, 119, 143–145, 176–180, 190–194, 244, 253, 259–260, 271, 290
  illnesses of, 119–129, 171–176, 231–233, 236, 314–315
  and inner freedom, 286
  journey to Moscow, 69–78, 82–86
  as lecturer, 147–150, 167–168, 270, 284, 287–288, 311
  letters to Anna Popova, 226–227, 229, 232, 235, 239–240, 285, 319
  liberal influence of, 312
  made charter member of Russian Chemical Society, 165, 168
  marriages, first, 143, 145, 151
    second, 237
  master's thesis of, 132–133, 136
  in Moscow, 86–92
  and New Religion, 293

Mendeleyev, Dmitri Ivanovitch and newspaper "*Uplift*," 289
  in Odessa, 132
  and public baths, 283–284
  research of, 143, 159, 199–200
    on air, 213
    on coal, 272
    on iron, 294–297
    on oil products, 204, 271
    on soil analysis, 142, 161
    on unity of elements, 123, 167, 169, 171–173, 184–187, 280, 303
    (*See also* Mendeleyev, experiments of)
  resignation from University of St. Petersburg, 286, 298–299
  returning health of, 129–132
  scientific memberships of, 310
  and spiritualism, 200–201
  and spread of scientific information, 299
  and student uprisings, 142, 188, 192–194, 240, 285–286
  translation of foreign technical works, 142
  and Tsar Alexander III, 249–253, 319
  writings of, 135–136, 139, 143, 171, 184–185, 197, 217, 222, 253–254, 284, 289, 302, 311, 320–330
    Knowledge and Art of Russia, 311
    Map of Russia, 313
    Principles of Chemistry, 280, 283, 289, 311–312, 314, 317
      first book, 166
      second book, 167, 184
      second English edition, 293
      seventh edition, 302–303, 306
      third edition, 227
      third English edition, 311
    Toward Knowledge of Russia, 313–315

Mendeleyev, Ekaterina (sister of Dmitri), 105, 109
  (*See also* Kapustin, Ekaterina)
Mendeleyev, Elizabeth (sister of Dmitri), 9, 15, 32, 38, 40–41, 52–53, 61, 64, 70–78, 82–87, 89–93, 96, 99, 103–109, 235, 319
Mendeleyev, Madame Feozva (first wife of Mendeleyev), 150–151, 155–156, 159–165, 171–172, 174, 176, 188, 194, 198–199, 231–232, 235–238, 289, 319
Mendeleyev, Ivan (brother of Dmitri), 109
Mendeleyev, Ivan (son of Dmitri), 245, 247, 274, 309

Index

Mendeleyev, Ivan Pavlovitch (father of Dmitri), 9, 22, 88, 96–97, 296
  death of, 23, 29
  origin of name, 22
Mendeleyev, Liubov (daughter of Mendeleyev), 240, 247, 264, 270, 274, 307, 309, 315
Mendeleyev, Maria (daughter of Mendeleyev), 247, 274, 309
Mendeleyev, Maria (sister of Dmitri), 41, 109
  (*See also* Popov, Maria)
Mendeleyev, Maria Dmitrievna (mother of Dmitri), 9–11, 14–19, 21, 23, 27–29, 32–34, 37–39, 47, 51–61, 63–67, 158–159, 235, 271–272, 296, 315–316, 319
  death of, 107
  education of, 21, 38–39
  illness of, 103–106
  journey to Moscow, 69–78, 82–86
  last blessing of, 109–110
  in Moscow, 86–92
  in St. Petersburg, 93–107
  in Tobolsk, 40–51
Mendeleyev, Olga (daughter of Mendeleyev), 165, 172, 176, 197, 209, 235, 247, 257
Mendeleyev, Olga (sister of Dmitri), 9, 14, 16
  (*See also* Bassargin, Olga)
Mendeleyev, Paul (brother of Dmitri), 9, 38, 40, 109
Mendeleyev, Vassili (son of Mendeleyev), 247, 272–274, 279, 282–283, 309, 319
Mendeleyev, Volodya (son of Mendeleyev), 155–157, 162–163, 172, 174, 176, 186, 197, 209, 224, 247, 257, 259–260, 265, 268, 291, 297
Menshutkin, Nikolai, 168, 175, 184, 196, 201–202, 222, 230, 233, 270
Mercury, 170
Mercury oxide, 148
Metals, 148
Meteorites, 149, 234, 289
Meteors, 234
Metropolitan Museum of Art, New York, 209
Meyer, Lothar, 141, 195, 239
Miloradovitch, Governor-General, 30
Minerals, 125, 270, 295
  for the soil, 155
Molecules, 136, 139–140, 148, 167, 246, 277
Molybdenum, 170
Mond, Ludwig, 275, 278, 284

Moon, corona around, 262
Moscow, 5, 23, 31, 38, 42, 47, 51–52, 57, 60, 63, 65, 73, 77–79, 81–92, 120, 136, 142, 155, 162, 171, 183, 220, 240, 256, 258, 318
  history of, 84–85
Moscow River, 92
Moultanovsky, Dr., 272–273
Mouzhiks, 3, 15, 64, 71–73, 77–79, 81, 83, 152–157, 161, 163–165, 177–180, 241–244, 255, 259–260, 266–268, 296

N

Nadezhda (daughter of *Anton the Furnace Man*), 17, 44–47, 56, 63, 65–69, 80–81, 113–117, 160, 206
  (*See also* Kapustin-Gubkin (another *Nadezhda*)
Naphtha (*see* Petroleum)
Naphtha springs of Russia, Mendeleyev's report on, 149
Napoleon, 13, 58, 86
Natural resources, 74, 89, 125–126, 204, 216–217, 247, 287–288, 313
Natural science, 118
Nature, a magazine, 312
Nazzini, Professor, 278
Neon, 312
Neptune, 196, 201, 248
Nevsky, Alexander, 56
New York, 208, 210–218
Newlands, J. A. R., 169–170, 195, 275, 280
Newton, Isaac, 166–167, 196, 276–277, 290
Nicholas I, Tsar, 9, 13, 29–30, 124, 311
Nicholas II, Tsar, 311
Nickel, 170
Nikita, the barber, 240, 242–244
Nikolayev, a student, 118
Nilson, L. F., 234, 248, 274, 280, 303
Nitrogen, 122, 138–139, 149, 155, 170, 183, 234, 276
Nizhny Novgorod, 5–6, 19, 47, 56–58, 63, 65, 80–81, 113, 117, 205, 293–294
Novocherkassk, 221

O

Oblontov, Ivan Grigorivitch, 4, 13–15, 17, 32–34, 54, 63, 65, 296
Oblontov, Maroosya (wife of *Ivan*), 4, 13, 32–34, 63, 296
Odessa, 132, 150
Odling, Rector of Oxford, 141, 292

342   Mendeleyev

Oil, 89, 125, 143, 149, 204, 287
   in America, 208, 213, 217–218
   in the Caucasus, 204, 217, 284
   heavy, 284
   illuminating, 284
   in Russia, 208, 271, 297, 318
      (*See also* Russia, natural resources)
Oil Creek, Pennsylvania, 208
Oliv, assistant to Mendeleyev, 183
Omsk, 40, 43, 52, 105, 109, 124, 158
Orchards, Crimean, 127
Organic combinations, theory of, 143
Orlov, a student, 51
Orlov, Ivan Ivanovitch, 279
Orlov, Nikolai Alexandrovitch, 301
Orsk, 80
Osmium, 184–185
Ostragradsky, Professor, 102, 118
Ostrovsky, a student, 118
Ourupenskoy Station, 219–220, 228–229
Ovsyannikov, Professor, 222
Oxford University, 292
Oxides, 24, 26–27, 148, 248
Oxygen, 122, 138–139, 148–149, 155, 170, 173, 184–185, 187, 234, 248, 274, 312

P

Paris, 138
Paris Academy of Sciences, 199, 201, 312
Pavel the Gatherer, 14, 25–26, 296
Peasants (*see* Mouzhiks)
Pedagogical Institute, St. Petersburg, 22, 88, 97–99, 101–103, 131, 237
Peel, Rector of Cambridge, 291
Pell, Dr., 274
Pennsylvania, 213
   oil techniques in, 207–208, 217–218
Penza, 88, 96
Periodic law (*see* Elements, periodic system of)
Periodic Table of the elements, 222, 234, 246, 279, 317
   in 1871, 189
   in 1902, 304
   in 1948, 305
   zero group in, 312
      (*See also* Elements)
Perkin, William Henry, 245
Perm, 79
Pertinsky, a student, 51
Pestel, Paul, 30
Petalite, 234
Peter the Great, 58, 84, 93
Petrashevsky, a political rebel, 53

Petroleum, 236, 243–244, 247, 254, 284
   by-products of, 217, 284
Petropavel Fortress, 142
Petrov, friend of Mendeleyev, 118, 123
Petrushevsky, physicist, 199–200
Petterson, chemist, 274, 303
Petti brothers, 200
Philadelphia World's Fair, 207
Phosphorus, 155, 170, 183, 234
Physics, 28, 132, 168, 179, 234, 276, 306
Pirogov, Nikolai Ivanovitch, 131
Pitchblende, 306
Pitov, assistant to Mendeleyev, 183
Pittsburgh, 209
Platinum, 170, 184–185
Plato, 167
Pletnov, Ivan, 96–99, 103
Podolsky, a landowner, 33
Poland, 57
Political rebels, escaping, 43
      (*See also* Decembrists; Student uprisings)
Polkonov, 256
Popov, Ivan Evstafyevitch, 219–221, 231, 234, 237
Popov, Maria Mendeleyev, 162
      (*See also* Mendeleyev, Maria)
Popova, Madame, 219
Popova, Anna Ivanovna, 219–237
      (*See also* Mendeleyev, Madame Anna)
Popova, Maria, 219–221
Posen, a sculptor, 230
Potash, 183
Potassium, 18, 122, 139, 154, 170, 173, 184–185, 234
   burning, 148
Potassium chloride, 24, 154
Potassium salts, 184
Prague, 123, 183, 274, 278, 299
Prakhnovsky, Count, 242
Prakhov, Adrian Viktorovitch, 224, 230
Princeton University, 202
Prussian Academy of Science, 298
Pushkin, Alexander, 30–31, 235

Q

Quartz, 24

R

Rabbits, digestion of, 183
Radiation, 138
   from uranium, 303, 306
Rammelsberg, chemist, 274, 306
Ramsey, William, 245, 278, 298, 312

Index

Regnault, Henri, 138, 140
Rhone River, 184
Richelieu High School, Odessa, 132
Rome, 234–235, 237
Roscoe, Sir Henry Enfield, 306
Rousseau, Jean Jacques, 313
Royal Society of Great Britain, 239, 245, 273, 275, 277–278, 312
Rubashkin, Vladimir Platonovitch, 221, 228–229
Rubidium, 184–185
Ruprecht, botanist, 102
Rus (Men of the Sea), 22
Russell, J. G. R., 208, 210–215, 218, 247, 275, 279
Russia, 13, 18–22, 33–34, 52–53, 78, 84, 88–89, 96, 116, 130, 150, 158, 209, 216–217, 318
   agricultural experiments in, 183
   coal in, 272, 284, 294
   compared with America, 313–314
   Douma, dissolving of, 313
   establishment of, 312
   eclipse of 1887, 255–264
   history of, 54–58, 124–125
   ignorance in, 292
   industrialization of, 288, 313
   iron in, 294–295, 297
   naphtha springs of, 149, 204
   natural resources of, 74, 89, 125, 204, 217, 247, 287–288, 313
   need of education in, 253
   oil in, 204, 218, 247, 254, 272, 284, 294, 313
   public instruction in, 302
   science in, 136, 141–143, 168, 254
   technology in, 253, 313
   tribes of, 205
Russian Bureau of Weights and Measures, 290, 293, 297, 310–311, 313, 315
Russian Chemical Society, 165, 168, 171, 174–176, 183–184, 196, 199–200, 204, 222, 247, 252, 274, 280, 284
Russian Physico-Chemical Society, 284
Russian Physics Society, 199–200, 247
Russian Technological Society, 256
Russo-Japanese War, 311
Rybinsk, 82
Rye, 152, 161
Ryleyev, the poet, 31

S

St. Petersburg, 22, 29, 81, 88, 90, 113, 116, 120, 132, 142, 159, 168, 171, 183, 191, 205, 220, 229–230, 238–239, 257–258, 272–273, 294, 318
   history of, 93
   Medico-Surgical Institute, 93–96
   workers' uprising in, 311
   (*See also* Pedagogical Institute)
St. Petersburg Academy of Art, 220, 224, 231
St. Petersburg Academy of Knowledge, 235
Saltikov, V. D., 267–268
Salts, 167, 276
   permanent, 187
Sand, for glass, 24
Sanglie, Captain, 208
Saratov, 22, 40, 58, 78–79, 83, 88, 96–97, 205
Savitch, Professor, 102
Scaliger, Joseph, 170
Scandium, 233, 248, 280
Scheele, Karl Wilhelm, 234
Schmidt, assistant to Mendeleyev, 183
Schroeder, scientist, 170
Science, 10–11, 33, 42–43, 86–87, 89, 91, 102
   in France and Germany, 136
   function of, 167
   pure, 143, 297
   in Russia, 168
   and truth, 147, 179
   Western, 137
Sea of Japan, 255
Séances, 200
Second Congress of Naturalists, 183
Semochkee (sunflower seeds), 78, 113–114, 129, 210
Seneca Oil Company, 208
Serfs, 9, 20–21, 29–30, 33, 58, 83, 93, 130, 136–137, 253
   freeing of, 141–142
Sevastopol, 129–130, 177
Shishkov, Admiral, 30
Shostenitch, assistant registrar, 191
Siberia, 3, 10, 19–22, 31, 55, 67, 69, 77, 94–97, 136, 141, 145, 150, 158, 162, 209, 217, 295–296, 318
   first printing press in, 21
Silica, 24
Silicon, 234
Silver, 140, 170
Simbirsk, 142, 183
Simferopol, 127, 129–130
   Gymnasium at, 124, 128–129
Simferopol Hospital, 130–131
Simple bodies, atomic volumes of, 184

344 Mendeleyev

Sinegoubova, Alexandra Vladimirovna, 220, 231
Skerletov, Nikolai Pavlovitch, 93, 95
Slavs, 22
Smithsonian Institution, 196
Smolensk, 142, 183
Sodium, 122, 148, 155, 170, 173, 184, 187, 234, 276
Sodium uranate, 306
Soil, 153–154
  analysis of, 183–184
Sokolov, Pavel Maximovitch, 22
Soldat, the horse, 11–12, 15, 62–64, 66, 69–79, 82, 84–87, 89, 91, 93, 102–103, 107, 146, 150, 152, 161, 164–165
Solutions, 271–272
Sound, 276
Sovetov, Professor, 222
Spas Ougol, 267, 269
Spectroscope, 138–139, 148, 201–202, 248, 264
Spectrum analysis, 201
Spiritualism, 200
Spores, 149
Starlight, through spectroscope, 148
Starosta (*see Oblontov, Ivan*)
Steam, 148
Stenka Razin, 58, 205
Stepanov, Stepan (son of *Timofei*), 117, 206–207, 264, 318
Stepanov, Timofei Arkadivitch, 4–6, 11, 13–17, 25–27, 32, 44–45, 50, 52–53, 55–56, 63, 65–67, 69, 80–81, 113–117, 150, 160, 205–206, 264, 296, 318
Strannik, the, 5–6, 13, 15, 17, 19–20, 24, 45–47, 52, 56–58, 63, 65–69, 80–81, 113–117, 206, 296, 318–319
Strannik's story, 67–69, 115, 117, 318
Strecker, A., 136, 196, 280
Stroganov Art School, Moscow, 220
Strontium, 170, 173
Student uprisings, 94–97, 142, 188, 192–194, 240, 271, 285–286, 289
Sugar, 142
Sulphur, 148, 157, 170, 234
Summer salts (*see* Potassium salts)
Sunflower seeds (*see Semochkee*)
Sunlight, and chemical processes, 149
  through spectroscope, 148
Sunshine, 153, 158, 161, 164–166
  crystal, 158, 164–165, 319

T

Tambov, 22, 88, 96

Tar, 284
  (*See also* Coal tar)
Tariff, Russian, 289
Tartars, 9, 20–21, 56–57, 85, 129
Tavda River, 73
Technological Institute, St. Petersburg, 152
Technology, 143, 216, 253
Tellurium, 170, 185, 274
Temperatures, 148–149, 157, 248
  critical, 139, 245, 262–263, 290
  of earth's atmosphere, 200, 213, 254
Thermochemistry, 184
Thermometers, 257, 262
Thomsen, Julius, 184
Thorium, 186
Thorpe, Sir Edward, 275, 298, 302, 312
Times, a journal, 141
Timofei the Glass Blower (*see Stepanov, Timofei*)
Tin, 170
Titanium, 170, 187, 194
Titusville, Pennsylvania, 208
Tobol River, 69, 80
Tobolsk, 3, 9, 21–22, 31, 41, 52, 55, 69, 80, 88, 96, 120, 134, 256, 264, 295–296, 318
  Gymnasium at, 27–29, 32, 38, 40, 59
Tolstoy, Count Leo, 130, 177, 220, 235, 313
Tomsk, 158, 162, 256
Toura River, 74
Tourinsk, 80
Trapp, Dr., 274
Trirogov (husband of Olga Mendeleyev), 291
Tsaritsin, 115
Tuberculosis, 41, 55, 122, 131
Tula, 130
Tumen, 80
Tungsten, 170, 234
Turgenev, Ivan, 125, 163
Turks, 130
Tutchev, Feodor, 246
Tver, 93, 267

U

United States (*see* America)
U.S. Department of Agriculture, 196–197
Universe, 283
  inductive study of, 147, 166
  man in relation to, 167
University College, London, 278
University of Edinburgh, 139, 245
University of Moscow, 23, 31–32, 40, 52, 87–89, 197

Index

University of St. Petersburgh, 96–99, 197, 221, 233, 244, 284–288
  (*See also* Pedagogical Institute)
Ural Mountains, 3, 23, 52, 65, 74, 78, 89, 123, 125, 209, 270, 294–295, 297, 313, 318
Uranium, 171, 173, 185–186, 274, 303, 306
Uranus, 171, 195
Uplift, a newspaper, 289
Usulov, Stepan Andreyevitch, 66, 89, 143–145, 157

V

Valentine, Basil, 170
Vanadium, 234
Vanka the Fool, 7–8, 13, 15, 17–18, 28, 44–45, 47–50, 59–60, 296
Van't Hoff, Jacobus Hendricus, 298–299
Vanya (see *Vanka the Fool*)
Vapors, 139, 234, 245
  density of, 143, 186
Varnikov, a student, 295
Vaseline, 284
Vasilievsky Ostrov, 220
Vassar College, 209
Ventilation, 149
Verne, Jules, 270, 316
Vineyards, Crimean, 127–129
Vishnegradsky, friend of Mendeleyev, 122
Volcanoes, 217
Volga River, 79, 82, 85, 115–116, 177, 205, 267, 318
Volkov, Professor, 230
Volkovo Cemetery, 107, 109, 120, 125, 235, 297, 317
Volodya, flower woman's son, 133–134
Volzov, Dr., 219
Voronezh, 219
Voronov, Mayor of Klin, 258–259
Vorontsov, Dr., 244, 260, 264
Voskresensky, Alexander, 102, 119–120, 122–124, 141, 165
Vreden, assistant to Mendeleyev, 183
Vyatka River, 79, 82

W

Wagner, Nikolai Petrovitch, 200, 222, 230, 307
Wagner, R., 142
Washington, D.C., 196–197
Water, 139, 248, 290, 293
Weinberg, B. P., a student of Mendeleyev, 287
West, American, 209
Wheat, 152–153, 165
Winkler, Clemens, 247–248, 280, 298, 303
Witte, Sergei, 290, 311
World Exposition, Chicago, 290

X

Xenon, 312

Y

Yaloutorovsk, 31, 80
Yanovsky, Professor, 315
Yaroshenko, Maria Pavlovna, 238
Yaroshenko, Nikolai Alexandrovitch, 238, 240
Yasnaya Polyana, 130
Yttrium, 200

Z

Zassorin, the driver, 164, 180–182, 241
Zdekauer, Physician Professor, 121–124, 131
Zimmerman, Clemens, 274, 306
Zinc, 122, 170, 202
Zinc blende, 201–202
Zinin, Professor, 102, 118, 196
Zirconium, 170, 194